Control and Constraint in E-Learning:
Choosing When to Choose

Jon Dron, University of Brighton, UK

IDEA GROUP PUBLISHING

Hershey • London • Melbourne • Singapore

Acquisitions Editor: Kristin Klinger
Development Editor: Kristin Roth
Senior Managing Editor: Jennifer Neidig
Managing Editor: Sara Reed
Assistant Managing Editor: Sharon Berger
Copy Editor: Jillian Kozak
Typesetter: Cindy Consonery
Cover Design: Lisa Tosheff
Printed at: Yurchak Printing Inc.

Published in the United States of America by
        Idea Group Publishing (an imprint of Idea Group Inc.)
        701 E. Chocolate Avenue
        Hershey PA 17033
        Tel: 717-533-8845
        Fax: 717-533-8661
        E-mail: cust@idea-group.com
        Web site: http://www.idea-group.com

and in the United Kingdom by
        Idea Group Publishing (an imprint of Idea Group Inc.)
        3 Henrietta Street
        Covent Garden
        London WC2E 8LU
        Tel: 44 20 7240 0856
        Fax: 44 20 7379 0609
        Web site: http://www.eurospanonline.com

Product or company names used in this book are for identification purposes only. Inclusion of the names of the
products or companies does not indicate a claim of ownership by IGI of the trademark or registered trademark.

Library of Congress Cataloging-in-Publication Data

Dron, Jon, 1961-
  Control and constraint in e-learning : choosing when to choose / Jon Dron.
     p. cm.
  Summary: "This book unifies and synthesizes an assortment of theories about learner control, autonomy,
self-direction, adult learning for educationalists, e-learning practitioners and e-learning developers; it provides a
theoretical approach to building computer systems to support adults learning via the Internet, existing e-learning
environments and how they should be used, and the process of education in general"--Provided by publisher.
  Includes bibliographical references and index.
  ISBN 978-1-59904-390-6 (hardcover) -- ISBN 978-1-59904-392-0 (ebook)
  1. Internet in education. 2. Computer-assisted instruction. 3. Adult learning. I. Title.
  LB1044.87.D76 2007
  371.33'4678--dc22
                                2006033764

British Cataloguing in Publication Data
A Cataloguing in Publication record for this book is available from the British Library.

All work contributed to this book is new, previously-unpublished material. The views expressed in this book are
those of the authors, but not necessarily of the publisher.

Control and Constraint in E-Learning:
Choosing When to Choose

Table of Contents

Section II. E-Learning, Control, and Constraint

SECTION III. DESIGNING BETTER E-LEARNING ENVIRONMENTS

Foreword

I was delighted to receive Jon Dron's invitation to write some words of welcome to his first book. My response to the invitation was affirmative even before I saw the manuscript because of what I knew about the author's previous work. A couple of years ago, one of my doctoral students introduced me to Jon's writings about transactional distance and self-organisation in network-based learning environments. I was very impressed, and concurred with my student's opinion that she had discovered a source of some inspirational scholarship. We initiated a correspondence with Dr. Dron, and one of the consequences was his request that I write this foreword.

I felt it appropriate that I take this on, for I see in this work the sweet beginning of the closing of a circle, the connecting of disparate domains that is long overdue. I refer to the quiet and often overlooked domain of distance education theory, on the one hand, and on the other hand, the ebullient, energetic, indeed, brash, new domain of practice referred to as e-learning. What Dron does in this book is show how the future success of the latter will be more assured as a consequence of better understanding of the former. This theory is not simply about the technology that makes e-learning possible. It is primarily about the relationships of learners to teachers, to each other, and their responsibility to themselves. This is, in other words, an important study of pedagogy in the post-modern context.

Reference to post-modern context compels me to admit that it is more than thirty years since I also was first intrigued by questions regarding the ways in which relationships of learners and teachers are mediated through communications technologies. Especially, I was intrigued by all the anecdotal evidence of learners who managed their own learning, more or less autonomously, either without the help of a teacher, or drawing on teachers through technology, more or less as one might hire a consultant, to help achieve their personal objectives. During a decade as an adult educator, most of that time spent in Africa, I had met people of all educational levels who individually (and also collectively) were self-directing learners (though

I probably did not have a label for that behavior at that time). I remember the old man in Kwale in Kenya who wanted to learn to read and write so he could make a history of his tribe, and the 92-year-old Open University student in England who wanted to graduate before the "honours' stage," so he could get on with writing a history of the primary school he had once been a teacher in. As a student myself, being more of a loner than a mixer, I noted how much more I enjoyed time passed in a library than time spent in the classroom, which seemed to be an environment more suited to grandstanding by either teacher or certain students, or both, than the disciplined effort of study or research. It was not until I met Charles Wedemeyer at the University of Wisconsin, and became his student and colleague that I found a philosophical justification for this "learning alone"—what he called "independent learning." In those days, for those independent learners who needed it, the correspondence course provided the kind of structure and the opportunity for cool dialogue with someone who knew more about the subject, which made the difference between "study" and serendipitous learning.

What I had noted in cases like those referred to above was what Wedemeyer's friend and colleague, Cyril Houle, in his study of the adult learner's "inquiring mind," famously described as the adult's "itch to learn," an idea pursued by his student Alan Tough in a string of empirical studies that unearthed for the first time just how much adults are able to do for themselves when they really want to learn. As it became more obvious that not all learners need or desire the same degree of help from teachers, it became apparent that the research question was how to get the right balance between giving independent learners the expertise that professional teachers acquire over a lifetime (e.g., setting achievable objectives and knowing where to look for resources that will help achieve the objectives relatively efficiently) while, at the same time, not asserting such control that we impede the learner or reduce learners' capacity for self-management, or indeed de-motivate them. Recognizing this as a question took time, and, in my own case, years of analysing and thinking about hundreds of mediated teaching-learning programs. This led to a crude model that conceptualized a continuum of different degrees of autonomy that educational programmes might allow a learner in deciding what would be learned, how it would be learned and what would be evaluated, or conversely, the extent to which control is held by teachers. The hypothesis derived from the model said that the more teacher control was desirable for a particular learning project, the greater the extent of mediated dialogue between teacher and learner and the more highly structured in terms of objectives, learning strategies and evaluation the teaching program would be.

The book you are about to read takes this theory, and others related to it, including particularly work of Saba, Saba and Shearer, T. Anderson, Candy, and Garrison and Baynton, and pulls it into the 21st century. It deals with some of those same issues about learning and teaching—though in a much more refined way—in the context of learning environments using communications technologies that were literally unimaginable thirty years ago. Then, I worked with printed correspondence texts, and this book talks of wikis and blogs. At that time, I could only conceive of dialogue between instructor and learner, mediated through the postal system, and now we can observe the dynamics of virtual groups interacting in global cyberspace. PLATO was the last word in educational computer technology, and now we have multi-user, interactive, multimedia environments and more. What is so impressive, however, is not only how different the technologies are, but also how robust and perennial the learning management challenges that face the thoughtful teacher and administration are, and yet also notable is how much more differentiated, less gross, more specific, these questions have become. That surely is the mark of a maturing field of study, as well as reflecting honorably on the students and researchers who have taken those early, simple conceptualizations and broken them apart to reveal the complex, internal mechanisms and dynamics lying within the distance teaching and learning relationship, particularly in the modern, highly sophisticated, technological environment.

I repeat, "teaching" and "learning," for that is what is commendable about this book. The book is certainly about new technology, but the questions it asks press far beyond how to make technology work within conventional pedagogical structures. The questions are always about how to teach, how to learn, but—more importantly—how to change the ways we think of teaching and learning so as to take advantage of the special attributes of the new technology. It is this focus on pedagogy and change that makes this book stand head and shoulders above many others that deal with so-called "e-learning." The whole idea of "e-learning," so helpful in attracting the attention of the general public to the merits of distance education, does sometimes have the unhelpful effect, because it is associated with technology that is new, of leading to the idea that the issues regarding teaching and learning communicated by technology are themselves new phenomena. This might not be important, except that it frequently results in research questions being posed that disregard the substantial body of existing data, and practices being tested that disregard previous experience, both being a waste of resources.

Because it is soundly based in theory, this book makes no such error and will help correct any such imbalance, as it asks its readers to consider such issues as the changing role of the teacher, the project as a learning strategy, the nature and nurture of self-directed learning, managing dialogues of learners with learners and learners with teachers, changing concepts of learning structures and teaching systems, with each of these issues based on sound theoretical referents. For example, Dron builds on Tough's seminal work as he develops his own innovative idea of the learning trajectory. To disarm those who would have us devalue the role of the teacher, he finds a delightful quotation from Bruner: "Learning something with the aid of an instructor should, if instruction is effective, be less dangerous or risky or painful than learning on one's own." Taking Dewey's idea of the key importance of the learning environment and the transactions that occur among the many forces in that environment, he poses the central theme of his book, how environments should be constructed and used in the Internet age. To do this he draws further, and deeply, from systems theories and the implications of Senge's maxim that "structure influences behaviour." It is indeed the author's sophisticated understanding of educational theory that empowers the author to offer so many stimulating and challenging insights into the impact of new technology on both teaching and learning. Lest my reference to dead (some of them!) theorists gives the impression that I think of this book as backward looking, let me re-emphasize that nothing could be further from the truth. It is neither stuck in past theory, nor marooned in a theory-barren doldrum of new technology. Instead, it draws on the theory to make bold predictions and hypotheses about future applications of new technology. As such, it is a perfect book for its time, a time when for example: "A message on a discussion forum is not just the information that it contains, but contributes materially to the way that the environment is presented to all other participants. *A discussion forum reifies the discussion.*" This "seemingly trivial observation," says Dron, "will prove to be central to understanding the promise of e-learning." That, I believe, is Dron's significant achievement—to link his sound understanding of the theoretical roots with his mastery of new technology—and thus, to project the future of new environments in which learners who are able to exercise autonomy will have control, without denying support when needed to those who need support. This would be significant progress towards a learner-centred pedagogy and a learning society.

As a final comment, I would like to encourage readers to reflect on how they might contribute to the further unraveling and elaboration of the ideas discussed here, through their practice certainly, but also through research. Just as I see the ideas developed in this book as breaking open some of my own primitive ideas, so I hope the variables that constitute Dron's model will in turn be taken and subjected to closer examination, and thus lead to further advances in the evolution of the theory and practice of e-learning specifically and distance education in general.

Michael Grahame Moore

Professor, The Pennsylvania State University, USA

Michael Grahame Moore is a professor of education in the Graduate School at The Pennsylvania State University (USA), where he supervises doctoral research and teaches post-graduate courses in distance education, both in the classroom and on the Web. Widely known in academic circles for developing the theory of distance education, he is the founder (1986) and editor of The American Journal of Distance Education. *More than a hundred publications include* Distance Education: A Systems View *(with G. Kearsley), also published in Chinese, Japanese, and Korean, and* The Handbook of Distance Education *(2nd edition, 2007). With a list of appearances in more than 30 countries and as many U.S. states, he remains in demand, as a conference and workshop presenter. From 1996-1998, he was a visiting scholar with the Department of Human Development at the World Bank, and besides continuing as consultant at the bank, he works for many national and international agencies, including UNESCO, the International Monetary Fund, and the Commonwealth of Learning.*

Preface

Learning Trajectories

Every learner is on a trajectory: an individual path that involves decisions about where to go next, what to learn, and how to learn it. Typically, some of those decisions are made by the learner and some are not. The question of who makes those decisions and how they are constrained is central to understanding how learning can be achieved and, particularly, the role of education in that process.

Decisions to engage in a set of learning activities and the directions that those activities take are determined by choices and constraints. Over time, most learning experiences are the result of many choices by many people: teachers, learners, authors, parents, children, friends, relations, governments, programmers, instructional designers, educational software developers and (potentially) many more, up to and including chance acquaintances on a bus or even the family dog.

Constraints on those choices operate at all levels: from the rules of grammar to the legislative requirements of governments, from the laws of physics to the demands of narrative, from the shape of a classroom to the prior knowledge and demands of the learner, and from the interests of the teacher to the effects of the weather. Some constraints are absolute, while others simply nudge or cajole. The interplay of a potential myriad of choices and constraints determines the level of control that any individual may exert over a learning trajectory.

A central goal of education is that learners should be able to learn autonomously—to be in control of their own learning. However, the process of becoming independent often involves some delegation of control to others. Many methods that people employ to learn, whether online or not, offer too much or too little constraint. Those needing the freedom to choose and explore may be prevented from doing so by a system that is too constraining, often leading to boredom and frustration. Conversely, the last thing that those who are lost or bewildered need is unconstrained freedom to choose. They wish to be *taught*. Apart from some exceptional circumstances (primarily involving one-to-one tuition), most educational systems tend to compromise, inevitably offering too little control to some but too much to others.

This book offers an exploration of the ways that a learning trajectory is determined, and, in particular, how an online learning environment can affect that trajectory. It provides suggestions about how, primarily through technologies that underlie what is vulgarly known as "Web 2.0," networked learning environments should be constructed to give control to learners *if* they need it, *as* they need it, and *when* they need it.

As a guiding principle, the book is based on the belief that an effective educational system should enable the learner to choose whether and when to choose. A learner should be *in* control of the *amount* of control he or she may exercise over his or her learning trajectory. The learner should be able to *take* control or to *delegate* control as needed. This is a stance that is fundamentally opposed to a culture of managerial control and Fordism in education, that abhors the industrialisation of learning. The book will present arguments that support a way of thinking about education that hinges on the needs and wishes of the learner, not as some abstract or generalised entity, not as the subject of another's wishes to offer advice, but as a real individual with real needs in a real context. It will provide explanations and examples of how, in broad terms, this can be achieved efficiently, engagingly and effectively in an e-learning environment.

Who Should Read This?

This book is written with three main audiences in mind: those interested in the theory of e-learning, creators and facilitators of e-learning (e.g., teachers and instructional designers), and developers of e-learning environments (e.g., programmers and computer system designers).

1. **Educators and others interested in educational theory.** The principles espoused here have a wider application to the process of education in general, especially when conducted at a distance, and may offer something to anyone involved in learning and teaching.

2. **Creators/facilitators of e-learning.** The book contains an examination of existing e-learning environments and offers thoughts on how they should be used. Therefore, another audience will be those who wish to use e-learning as part of an educational process, whether through direct teaching or through the design of educational materials and resources.

3.   **Developers of e-learning environments.** This book will provide a theoretically grounded approach to building computer systems to support adult learning, using networked technologies. Therefore, an important audience is the community of developers of e-learning software.

What This Book is About

Understanding the Dynamics of Learning Trajectories

This book is grounded in an attempt to unify and synthesise aspects of an assortment of theories about learner control, autonomy, self-direction, adult learning and so on, into a single theory of *transactional control*. Transactional control is a refinement of an aspect of transactional distance theory (Moore, 1997), presenting a particular systems perspective. This is by no means the only systems perspective that may be employed to this end and it necessarily presents a blinkered view of its subject matter. Indeed, in many ways, it says less than transactional distance theory about the nature of online, distance, or face-to-face education. Its purpose is not to usurp but to augment other theories, most of which retain their place unchallenged. It is just another perspective—another way of knowing. By analogy, it is undoubtedly possible to explain the behaviour of birds by describing the movement of electrons within the birds' brains, but it would not say much about the process of flocking nor of birds' roles in an ecosystem.

Senge (1993) writes of the beer game (a device contrived to demonstrate systems behaviour):

If literally thousands of players, from enormously diverse backgrounds, all generate the same qualitative behaviour patterns, the causes of the behaviour must lie beyond the individuals. The causes of the behaviour must lie in the structure of the game itself.

This book is about the structure of the game of education; it is more about its rules than about how it should be played.

Building and Using Learning Environments

Transactional control theory provides ways of considering some structural aspects of learning transactions. Structure always influences and, sometimes, determines behaviour. A learning environment provides or manifests structure. Consequently, a learning environment will inevitably affect how people learn within it. It is desirable that the environment should offer as much support as possible to the process of learning and should not make the process less effective. Learning environments that are too constraining will be harmful to some learners but, equally, so will those that offer too many choices. The design and use of most existing learning environments does not take this dynamic into account. As a consequence, learners (and, indeed, teachers) may be unduly constrained when they need freedom, or be offered too many choices when they need constraint.

The ideal balance of control will vary from person to person and context to context. Even for an individual learner, the need for control will vary constantly and will change as the learner learns. In a perfect learning environment, the learner would be able to take exactly the control that he or she needs at any point—no more, no less. The conventional way to achieve something approaching this is through dialogue, which may serve the function of, among other things, negotiating control. Dialogue works well but, in the context of control, scales poorly and may not fit in with the timing of learning requirements. To fill the gaps, the structure of the learning environment should therefore be able to adjust, adapt, or otherwise cater to these dynamically changing needs. As the book progresses, some strong recommendations will be made as to how that might be achieved in online systems through a design paradigm derived from and informed by transactional control.

What This Book is Not About

There are plenty of excellent books and treatises that seek to explain the processes by which adults learn, espousing theories or blends of theories that are behaviourist, cognitive, constructivist, andragogist, situational, experimental, experiential, social, developmental…the list is endless. This book is not one of them.

Although it is about the processes of adult learning, transactional control is not about *how* people learn. The theory is not dependent on understanding how learning occurs or even, beyond some aspects that relate directly to control, what are the best ways to help it happen. It is only important *that* someone makes choices about a learning trajectory, and they do so in a particular context with particular constraints. It is mostly left to other theories to provide the rationale for *what* choices are made.

Considering the learning process from the perspective of transactional control is to attempt to model the characteristics of educational transactions in a consistent fashion and to provide a common ground that allows significant aspects of their structures to be compared and analysed. Different structures will lead, inevitably, to different consequences and offer different benefits to different learners. The affordances of different media and modes of online teaching will be examined closely and sometimes matched to the needs of a range of learners. As a result, the book's pedagogic neutrality is far from absolute: pronouncements will be made on the suitability of certain forms of learning environment and certain approaches to teaching and learning that will be appropriate for certain learners.

Some readers may be lulled by the title into thinking that this book is about psychological aspects of control. This is far from the intention, although there will occasionally be passing references to the area. Such concerns are raised only insofar as they affect the dynamics of the system as a whole.

Those in the computer industry may recognise the term "transactional control" as meaning something quite distinct about the behaviour of database management systems. This is nothing at all to do with what this book is about.

Organisation of This Book

The three sections of this book cater to, broadly, and in turn: those interested in the theory of e-learning, creators and facilitators of e-learning, and developers of e-learning environments. However, it is hoped that there will be something for anyone interested in learning throughout the book.

Section I. Control and Learning: A Theoretical Background

The early section of this book is concerned with establishing a theoretical basis for what follows. In particular, it describes a framework for understanding educational systems in terms of choice and constraint. Among other things it will look closely at how choice and constraint may meaningfully be looked at from a wide range of perspectives and at many scales, and at the systemic behaviours that arise through simple interactions of individuals constraining the choices of others.

Chapter I (Introducing Concepts) is concerned with defining the field and clarifying what is meant by key terms such as 'teacher' and 'e-learning' because some of the ways that these terms are used in the book are distinctive and may not have meanings shared by all. Some basic observations are made regarding how structure can influence behaviour. The unique nature of the computer, as (simultaneously) a tool, a medium, and an environment, is outlined and the implications considered.

Chapter II (From Transactional Distance to Transactional Control) lays the groundwork for the theory of transactional control, discussing some of the literature related to control and learning, with a strong emphasis on Michael G. Moore's theory of transactional distance. The chapter includes a working definition of the central concept of transactional control—the theory that underpins much of what follows.

Chapter III (Making Choices: The Need for Teachers) is about the nature of choice and various conceptions of it, why it is a good thing in education and why it may be a bad thing, touching on what freedom means in an educational context. In particular, it shows that control may be reduced both by too many and too few choices.

Chapter IV (All About Constraints) is an examination of constraints and the ways in which they operate to determine a learning trajectory. It considers a range of extrinsic factors and those that are intrinsic to the process, leading to a model that views constraints in terms of context and content.

Chapter V (Scale) is concerned with the central importance of scale in understanding a learning trajectory, and identifying appropriate levels of granularity to consider when looking at learning choices. It is shown that choice and control may operate at many different scales, and that the smaller scale choices tend to be more constrained by the larger than vice versa. This chapter provides the authoritative definition of transactional control.

Chapter VI (Transactional Control in Traditional Institutional Learning) contains examinations of a broad range of typical learning activities from the perspective of transactional control, leading to an identification of the process of analysis that might be followed in attempting to identify the dynamics of control in any series of learning activities.

Section II. E-Learning, Control, and Constraint

The second section of the book concerns the application of the model developed in Part One to some specific, and predominantly, e-learning situations and modes of e-learning. It contains explorations of the dynamics that can occur in such systems. It is observed that the structural aspects of different technologies influence the kind of learning trajectories that might emerge with them. Sometimes, these can be used to the learner's advantage, but, at other times, strategies must be employed to curtail these constraints.

Chapter VII (Electronic Publication) contains discussion of various means of publishing and presenting content on the web and the ways that it might enable control by the learner and the teacher. Amongst other things, it considers approaches to the design of hypertext and the use of learning objects. Suggestions are provided to assist teachers attempting to cater to the need for control and the need for constraint in such a system.

Chapter VIII (Finding Good Stuff) presents a number of popular methods of assisting learners in finding appropriate resources, covering some aspects of resource-based learning, the uses and limitations of search engines, recommender systems, and adaptive hypermedia.

Chapter IX (Asynchronous Communication) is concerned with typical approaches to the use of asynchronous discussion such as Web forums, e-mail, and bulletin boards, examining ways in which control may be distributed among participants. It includes an example of a discussion, which is analysed in detail to explore the levels and ways that control emerges. A number of principles are suggested for both reducing and increasing learner control.

Chapter X (Synchronous Discussion) is about synchronous communication tools such as Internet relay chat, instant messaging, and Web conferencing, in the context of the dynamics of control, observing strengths and weaknesses of different systems to support differing levels of control.

Chapter XI (Integrated Tools and Environments) considers integrated environments, in particular, focussing on learning management systems. It includes an analysis of one of the more popular examples of the genre, thereby attempting to explain generic issues of top-down control in such systems. It gives advice on reducing the pernicious effects of top-down design and includes a discussion of alternative and emerging methods of building integrated learning environments.

Section III. Designing Better E-Learning Environments

The third and final part of the book attempts to extrapolate some lessons from the application of transactional control theory. Notably, this implies that Web 2.0 technologies, especially social software, may have innate advantages when compared with currently popular learning environments. This leads to a set of eight principles for the design and construction of social software for e-learning and a description of some examples of the kind of online learning environment that follows from them. The dangers and weaknesses of social software are explored with a view of identifying the future systems that will support learning and education.

Chapter XII (Social Software and E-Learning) is primarily about the unusual nature of social software systems, the foundation of Web 2.0, whereby the group is a first class object within the system. Considering the group as a distinct actor in the system implies a change to the ways that e-learning has so far been conceptualised. In particular, it offers new opportunities for approaches to building learning environments that, by their nature, allow learners to choose the level of control they have at any point in their learning trajectories by generating structure through dialogue.

Chapter XIII (Design Principles for Social Software in E-Learning) provides eight principles that should be followed when designing social software that lets learners choose. The theoretical underpinnings of these principles include aspects drawn from (particularly) self-organisation in biological systems, city planning, information systems design, and pragmatic requirements for socialisation in an educational environment.

Chapter XIV (Social Software in E-Learning: Beyond Blogs and WIKIs) provides an overview of some instances of learning environments that use the eight principles to a greater or lesser extent. The chapter includes an in-depth discussion of the ways that two learning environments written by the author conform to the principles to achieve self-organisation.

Chapter XV (Problems with Social Software for E-Learning) discusses some of the failings of such learning environments and identifies some large research questions that still remain, particularly those relating to problems of sequencing, the weaknesses of stigmergic dialogue, and the stupidity of mobs.

Chapter XVI (Potential Futures of E-Learning) summarises what has gone before and peers into the future. A variety of speculations are made about potential futures for e-learning, framed in the context of the Edinburgh Scenarios (Cross, 2004). A number of thought experiments are used to envisage some of the potential consequences of building and using software according to the principles outlined in this book.

Summary

This is a book about the dynamics of control in intentional adult learning and the consequences for how online learning environments should be designed and used. It is not a book for those seeking to discover how people learn in general, nor will it be of much use to those wishing to understand psychological aspects of control. It presents a view of educational transactions from a systems perspective, which enables different educational techniques and learning environments to be compared and evaluated in terms of affordances and constraints. Based on this perspective, online teachers and learners will be able to take a more reflective and informed perspective on appropriate choices of methods and tools, while the makers of those tools will gain a better understanding of the effects they may have on behaviour. If that were all that this book achieved, it would be a good result. However, it may be possible to make a larger claim; from first principles, the arguments and examples in this book demonstrate that some ways of building the technologies of learning are better than others. This book does not contain all the answers: far from it. What it may provide is the means to ask the right questions.

References

Cross, J. (2004). The Edinburgh scenarios. Retrieved September 8, 2004, from http://www.internettime.com/lcmt/archives/001121.html

Moore, M. G. (1997). Theory of transactional distance. In D. Keegan (Ed.), *Theoretical principles of distance education* (pp. 22-38). Routledge.

Senge, P. M. (1993). *The fifth discipline: The art and practice of the learning organisation.* Chatham: Century Business.

Acknowledgments

I would like to acknowledge the help of all involved in the production of the book, including all the staff at Idea Group Inc. and the very helpful anonymous reviewers. Special thanks go to Lynley Lapp for her early support and encouragement and Kristin Roth for her patience and helpful answers to endless questions.

Also, thanks to all of the staff and students of the University of Brighton who helped me to put this together.

Very special thanks go to Michael G. Moore for so many things, but in particular for his inspiration and support, and for supplying the foreword to this book.

Many thanks go to my children for putting up with my absorption in this project. Above all, my deepest gratitude and undying love go to my wife, for all of her help and support through the long, stressful and consuming process.

Jon Dron
Brighton, UK
August 2006

Section I

Control and Learning:
A Theoretical Background

Chapter I

Introducing Concepts

Words are our tools, and, as a minimum, we should use clean tools: we should know what we mean and what we do not, and we must forearm ourselves against the traps that language sets us. (Austin, 1979)

Introduction

This chapter is mainly concerned with introducing and defining some of the key terms that will be used throughout the book. In particular, it contains an exploration of conceptions of learning projects, teachers, e-learning and e-learning environments, each of which is defined in a specific way that is a refinement of some popular usage.

A representative list of the kind of technologies that may be found in a typical online learning environment is provided, primarily for those who are familiar with the Internet, but who have not yet explored the potential of e-learning. This also helps to illustrate a few of the many ways that the affordances of an environment can radically shape the behaviour of its inhabitants. The chapter concludes with a brief but important discussion of the distinctive nature of the networked computer as, simultaneously, a tool, a medium, and an environment.

Learning Projects and Learning Trajectories

The central theme of this book is the choices that people (e.g., teachers, learners, authors, administrators, others) make in the pursuit of learning. It is about a process that might broadly be described as *education*, whether it is self-taught, distance taught, traditionally taught, or otherwise. To an extent, learning is the stuff of human existence, or as Vaill (1996) describes it, a "way of being" (one which Vaill believes to be far from innate, especially within organisations and institutional settings). In a sense, to be is to learn. It is almost impossible to live one's life without continually learning, whether it be the big things (how to walk, that hot things burn you, how to relate to others) or the little ones (this door is a bit hard to shut, the bus station is in the next street, the price of this jar of peanut butter is lower than that in the other shop). As Illich (1971) says: "Most learning happens casually, and even most intentional learning is not the result of programmed instruction." It is true in most settings, including in the workplace. Eraut (2004) writes, "Most workplace learning occurs on the job rather than off the job." Dewey (1916) has a similarly general view with regard to the commonplace act of communication: "Not only is social life identical with communication, but all communication (and hence all genuine social life) is educative." This rich view of learning realistically captures the complex reality of learning as a situated experience, deeply interwoven with the tapestry of existence. However, it fails to differentiate acts that are recognised as intended to bring about learning as opposed to those in which learning is either incidental or so deeply embedded in practice that it cannot be extracted from it.

Learning Activities

The fact that people do frequently engage in intentional activities that are meant to result in a change in behaviour, attitude, knowledge, and so on, deserves recognition and examination. If people wish to learn, then it is usually the case that they wish to learn well, or at least efficiently, with as little anxiety and effort as possible. The focus of this book will therefore be on those intentional choices that are meant to bring about learning. These will generally be referred to as *learning activities*. A sequence of learning activities form part of what will be described as a *learning trajectory*. The term is closely akin to what Tough (1979) defines as a learning project:

...regardless of what the person is doing if he is trying to learn, trying to change through that activity, then we call it a learning project. People do learn in other ways. There are lots of activities that lead to learning. But if that is not the person's primary intention then we do not include it in our definition of a learning project.

A more succinct version of the same idea is expressed by Moore (1977) in the context of what he describes as a "learning programme": "a purposeful, deliberate planned activity or series of activities by a learner intended to result in a change in knowledge, behaviour or attitudes."

The use of the term "learning trajectory" implies a direction and a dynamic system involving change as an ongoing process. A programme, a course, or a project may also imply sequence and change, but such terms fail to capture the essential elements of movement and direction and, above all, they imply a beginning and an end. A trajectory does not start or finish. A trajectory represents a series of choices rather than a self-contained activity. It is about the journey, not the destination. The terms "learning project" and "learning programme" will be reserved for referring to the completed outcome or relatively fixed sets of learning activities that a learning trajectory may pass through.

Scale in a Learning Trajectory

A section of a learning trajectory may be very short (e.g., "I would like to know how to spell 'antidisestablishmentarianism'") or very long (e.g., "I would like to become a doctor") and most are somewhere in between. It is a very important characteristic of most learning trajectories that they are often composed of elements (in Moore's terms, "series of activities") that help to lead to a learning goal or goals. Indeed, a trajectory may typically be seen as a composite of many smaller trajectories. The scale that is chosen to view these will prove to be highly significant when modelling educational experiences, but for now it is sufficient to suggest that a change in learning trajectory occurs when a learner or some other (most notably a teacher) makes an active (not necessarily conscious) decision to do something else. This does not, in any way, imply that learning is the result of teaching, nor that the only (or even the most appropriate) way to embark on a learning trajectory is to engage in some formal process of education.

What is a Teacher?

"Learning something with the aid of an instructor should, if instruction is effective, be less dangerous or risky or painful than learning on one's own" (Bruner, 1966). There is plenty of learning without teaching and, equally, plenty of teaching without learning. However, there will be many occasions when it will be necessary to consider a role that is most often defined as a teacher, or variants on the theme such as tutor, facilitator of learning, guide, instructor, and so on. Just as a learner may make intentional choices to learn, a teacher may engage in intentional acts to bring about learning.

Typically, a conventional teacher might be involved in defining goals, designing a programme of work, sharing knowledge, motivating learners, controlling the pacing, selecting methods, facilitating discussions, organising meetings, and evaluating success. Though all are important, none of these functions is a necessary condition of being a teacher. Many could be implemented indirectly, or by someone other than a teacher. The definition used here will be a broader one, to an extent following Moore's (1980) quoting of Henderson:

A machine, a conventional text-book or a programmed text as well as a human being [may] be regarded as a teacher [since] one step removed from the text is the author of the text who generated the particular sequence of descriptions, explanations, interpretations or illustrations exhibited in the text.

This sense of the word "teacher" allows for interaction at one step removed through any kind of medium, including computer-based systems, books, journals and television.

Education can be seen as a combination of intentional learners and intentional teachers coming together into some kind of system in which learning occurs. As Moore (1986) puts it, "In education we have deliberate learning and deliberate teaching, and an educational transaction occurs when learning programs and teaching programs are brought together."

Can Teaching Occur without Learning?

A teacher is one who engages, directly or indirectly, in the act of teaching—a set of behaviours that are intended to bring about learning. This is not an uncontentious assertion and there are those who would not regard an act as teaching unless learning has taken place. For example, Freire (1998) writes, "I do not hesitate to say that there is no valid teaching from which there does not emerge something learned." Henderson's definition suggests that the significant factor is the act of instruction, regardless of whether or not it brings about learning. While it is indisputable that *effective* teaching brings about learning, Henderson's definition is more useful that Freire's on the grounds that, like most activities, it can be done badly. It would be mistaken to suggest that a driver who careers off the road is *not* driving; merely that he or she is driving badly. Perhaps it would be clearer to use the more neutral term of *teaching presence*, defined by Anderson et al. (2003) as the:

...design, facilitation, and direction of cognitive and social processes for the purpose of realizing personally meaningful and educationally worthwhile learning outcomes. Teaching presence begins before the course commences as the teacher, acting as instructional designer, plans and prepares the course of studies, and it continues during the course, as the instructor facilitates the discourse and provides direct instruction when required.

A Broader Definition of Teaching

Anderson's notion of "teaching presence" opens up the possibility that a teacher could be anyone, including (especially) other learners but equally the person sitting next to you on the bus, a comedian on the stage or a particularly smart dog. Almost any activity that is intended to bring about a change in behaviour or outlook may, under the right circumstances, be considered as teaching, although lines may be drawn at brainwashing, torture, and some psychological interventions. Taking it still further, it is clear that the teaching role may often be split across many individuals and resources. For example, many distance learning courses are distinctive due to the large number of people, including instructional designers, subject experts, graphic artists, television crew and others, who are directly involved in course development and whose role cannot be easily separated from that of the teacher. Again, Anderson et al's notion of *teaching presence* captures this potentially distributed function better than the simple word "teacher." However, "teacher" is a convenient shorthand and will continue to be used throughout the book where appropriate.

Teachers as Choice-Makers

A teacher, then, might be defined as one (or more than one) who makes *choices* for or on behalf of a learner, in order to help the learner to learn. Such choices do not need to be conscious or explicit, especially where the teacher is one or more steps removed from the learner. The role of the teacher is not necessarily consciously chosen, but may instead be a product of the learner's perceptions and intentions. If a learner were to choose, say, to learn a particular guitar style by watching a video recording of a master playing, there is no implication that the master intended to teach that person or anyone else. Perhaps more significantly, nor is there any suggestion that the *video-maker* intended for viewers to learn to play the guitar. However, the *choices* that the video-maker made when selecting camera angles and close-ups would most certainly have an impact on the success or otherwise of a learner's attempts to learn as a result. But what if there were no video-maker, if the learner were simply sitting and watching the guitarist, making his or her own decisions about what and how he or she should perceive? Not only is this commonplace but it is perhaps the most pervasive form of human learning, accounting for much of what forms us as infants, children and adults in society. This leads to the notion of self-directed learning.

Self-Directed Learning

So far, the possibility of the teaching role residing in some kind of external entity or group of entities is all that has been considered. It is just as possible that a teaching role may reside in the learner. There is a rich body of literature relating to adult learning that does not involve an explicit teacher role, and a great deal of learning that occurs in many different ways, apparently without the aid of a teacher. For example, learning may occur as problem solving, as a result of creative engagement with the world, perhaps even as a result of simple internal cogitation. For instance, sometimes the simple process of writing creates new knowledge, with no obvious involvement of a teacher. Often, an author may not know what he or she thinks until it is written down, and the very process of writing creates a bridge to another Vygotskian zone of proximal development, allowing knowledge to be extended further. This is not to deny that learning is an inherently social activity, nor does it deny the importance of others (including those explicitly labelled as teachers) in bringing about new learning. It is just that, perhaps to some extent in every educational transaction, there are aspects of the educational process that are free of teachers.

Different Kinds of Self-Direction

Self-direction may be seen as a character trait, a process, a philosophical stance, a political imperative, an integral part of institutional learning, a way of life, and many other things (Boud, 1981; Brockett & Hiemstra, 1991; Candy, 1991; Knowles, 1975; Long, 1990; Rogers, 1969; Tough, 1979; Wedemeyer, 1971). It is related to notions of learner autonomy, self-management, self regulation and more. The area is both rich and complex, with many differing views of what it may mean. The emphasis in this book is on the process rather than the propensity. Although personal autonomy and self-regulation in learning are generally to be desired as goals of the learning process, the significant aspect from the point of view of the arguments presented in this book is that learners may make choices that affect a learning trajectory.

E-Learning Environments

What is E-Learning?

To some extent, e-learning may be seen as a subset of the possible forms of distance learning, which is to say where the teaching behaviours are executed apart from the learning behaviours (Moore, 1983). However, this does not necessarily need to be so, or at least not entirely, evidenced by the popularity of blended learning and the significant uptake of managed learning environments or course management systems in higher education around the world. A more inclusive definition would be that e-learning is learning that takes place through and/or with the aid of Internet- or network-based technologies.

Alternative Definitions of E-Learning

The term "e-learning" arose out of the dot-com boom as one of many such derivations of the word "e-mail" (e-commerce, e-business, e-government and so on), all of which were and are defined by the networked nature of the activity. However, there are many who would disagree with this definition, broadening it to include any form of digitally-mediated educational process, including the use of CD-ROMs, standalone computer-aided learning packages, purpose-built educational hardware such as the toys sold to encourage children to read and much more. Such a definition is common among instructional designers, especially those working in the training industry, and the term is used by many who have a vested interest. This is unsurprising: organisations with a rich history and a catalogue of highly developed learning technologies may perceive marketing benefits if all of their products can gain the "e" label. There are numerous definitions of this ilk: "Education via the Internet, network, or standalone computer.... Content is delivered via the Internet, intranet/extranet, audio or video tape, satellite TV, and CD-ROM" (http://www. learnframe.com/aboutelearning/glossary.asp), or, "learning that has an electronic component in its delivery" (http://www.bbk.ac.uk/ccs/elearn/glossary.htm).

A project team with which the author has been involved makes use of the following very inclusive definition: "E-learning is the use of digitally-delivered services and content to help people learn," (http://www.be-la.co.uk/whatis.htm). Perhaps the most accurate definition is this: "It means many different things to people but is a popular media buzz word and should be avoided," (http://www.plymouth.edu/psc/infotech/ tlc/itcc/Glossary.htm). This view is perhaps a little cynical. Although "e-learning" is an evolving and variously defined term, it is settling down to an agreed usage. A glance through the proceedings of the AACE E-Learn conferences or the ACM *eLearn* Journal will quickly reveal that (while the precise spelling of the word may still be a source of contention) the predominant themes that e-learning researchers and practitioners address relate to networked (mobile or Internet) learning technologies, perhaps blended with other modes of delivery. It is this definition that will therefore be used in this book.

What is an E-Learning Environment?

From a naïve perspective, an e-learning environment consists of the computers and software that are used to provide e-learning. However, this is far too narrow a definition. In a learning ecology (Seely Brown & Duguid, 2000) it is impossible to conceive of the environment as something as limited as a piece of software running on one or more computers. The people who use it to interact with each other, who create it and the content it represents, the infrastructure that supports it, the administrational mechanisms that surround it; all of these people, concepts, structures and things are a part of that environment (Moore, 1993). In particular, it is not possible to conceive of it without thinking in terms of the context of its use, the pedagogies that are employed, and the communities that form within it. Any view that attempts to focus exclusively on one isolated aspect of the system will inevitably fail to capture the essence of the whole. An e-learning environment may therefore better be seen as a habitat or micro-habitat that is connected to, or part of, other systems which form the entire learning ecology.

Structure and Behaviour

The second and third parts of this book will include suggestions as to how e-learning environments should be constructed and used. The underpinning and largely implicit principle on which these suggestions are based is captured by Senge's (1993) maxim that "structure influences behaviour" (p. 40) but which is better summed up by Churchill (1943), who identifies the essentially recursive nature of the principle more poetically: "We shape our dwellings and afterwards our dwellings shape our lives."

From an architectural perspective, dwellings are more than simple physical spaces. They incorporate a range of suppositions, approaches, theories, implicit and explicit behaviours. As Tschumi (1996) says, "Space, movement and event are inevitably part of a minimal definition of architecture" (p. 187). Different e-learning environments provide different affordances to the learner and the educator (Conole & Dyke, 2004) and the choice of facilities in learning environments is crucial in determining what activities may be performed there. Although there are those who have attempted to show that the medium is largely irrelevant (Clark, 1983), most evidence suggests that, at least qualitatively (and probably quantitatively), spaces, be they virtual or physical, have a large effect on the learning experience that is achieved through them. Just as architecture need not be viewed as a purely physical phenomenon, structure in an e-learning environment includes a range of behaviours, activities and design principles as well as the virtual spaces themselves.

The Interface

The interface is the nearest thing to a physical space in an e-learning environment. This refers to far more than the look and feel of the space: the interface also includes the system's behaviours and 'physics' (the potential ways it can operate) and may even extend to its 'psychology,' its ability to interact in a human-like manner (Zhang, 2003). Clearly the interface is not the only factor that matters, and may even be relatively unimportant when compared with pedagogical approaches, learner-teacher interaction and other aspects of an educational experience. However, there can be little doubt that the affordances of any medium must determine what can be achieved through its use and, therefore, that the choice of medium will materially affect the learning that it may help to engender.

This is especially true of e-learning.

At a trivial level, if the learning environment does not provide a means of communication, then learner-teacher interaction is going to be pretty dismal. If the communication tools are inappropriate or weak, then the position will not be much improved. More subtly, the kinds of interactions that are encouraged through different kinds of mediators can lead to a predominance of some kinds of discourse to the detriment of others. For example, threaded discussion forums are notoriously awkward environments for enabling groups to form conclusions, consensus or agreement (Hewitt, 2001).

What Might be Found in an E-Learning Environment?

E-learning as described so far is a blanket term, which covers a range of technologies based on Internet protocols and standards together with associated pedagogies. Within this blanket term lays a huge assortment of potential modes of interaction, presentation and communication. There are numerous affordances for learning, provided by existing mainstream e-learning environments. The following examples account for an important subset of the potential array of technologies available, but are by no means the only ones and should be regarded as illustrative rather than complete. By and large, it is assumed that the reader has a passing familiarity with the technologies described here, but for those who are unfamiliar with the territory, definitions, descriptions, and examples of the technologies referred to here, they can be found in the glossary.

Publishing

From the simple ability to create and save Web pages, to content management systems that store formatted text in a database, to bulk e-mailing systems and e-zines, to weblogs (or blogs), wikis or even the simple "cc" option of virtually all e-mail clients, there is a vast array of tools available that can enable one person or a group of people to publish information to one or more recipients. Such systems can range in content from simple, unformatted text through to complex simulations, animations, movies and three dimensional simulacra of the real world. Most are concerned with a one-to-many model of teaching, some variant on the traditional lecture or book. Some make use of the ability of a computer to employ rules or algorithms to provide an "intelligent" response to the learner, in which the computer acts as a surrogate teacher, making decisions about what to display or do next. Adaptive hypermedia and intelligent tutoring systems are the main examples of this genre, typically providing different paths or content depending on factors such as the learner's expressed preferences, success in automated assessment, time spent dwelling on a page, apparent learning style and so on (Brusilovsky, 2001).

Simulations can range from simple, text-based interactions (for example, to provide feedback on figures entered as part of a business simulation) to full-blown multi-user interactive multimedia environments (for example, the use of SimCity™ in an online environment to explore the complexity of city planning). Such complex environments may be a species of publication in which learners are interacting with a machine, but increasingly they allow three dimensional co-presences with others, allowing interactions in an online virtual reality environment, of which ActiveWorlds™ (http://www.activeworlds.com) is among the oldest and most widely used in education, though rapidly being superseded by Second Life™ (www.secondlife.com).

Some forms of publication (such as blogs) enable a multi-way conversation to develop around the published item, straddling a boundary between publication and dialogue. Others allow users to actually modify and contribute to the publication itself. Wikis are perhaps the most extreme example of this form, allowing everyone and anyone to modify anything on the page. This kind of blurring between the author and the reader is characteristic of what some choose to call "Web 2.0," and it offers a range of opportunities that were difficult or impossible prior to the near-universal availability of networked computers.

Asynchronous Dialogue Systems

Asynchronous discussions are by far the most popular form of communication in courses delivered through e-learning. Whether mediated through a threaded discussion, where each message is shown in relation to those it responds to, or linearly, according to time of posting, or even through e-mail, they offer the promise of, amongst other things: asynchronous (any time), asyntopic (any place) engagement with the learning experience; a vehicle for the creation of learning communities; a potential equaliser that gently moves the teacher towards a supporting, guidance role rather than an all-powerful information disseminator; reasoned discussions characterised by reflective and pertinent contributions by participants; a permanent record of the learning experience that can be referred back to and reflected upon at a later date.

Naturally egalitarian, asynchronous discussion forums encourage learners to participate who might otherwise be unheard in a conventional classroom. This view is a little crude and will be refined in a later chapter, but on the face of it there would seem to be clear benefits to asynchronous discussion forums in e-learning. On the other hand, there are few people, even among the zealots, who would choose to use the current generation of discussion forums in preference to face-to-face learning, all things being equal. Few would argue that an online discussion is actually a better educational experience than talking to someone in the flesh. But all things are not equal. The practical benefits of being able to choose when and where to participate drive the use of such systems far more than the pedagogical benefits.

Synchronous Dialogue Systems

From telephone conversations to text chat or instant messaging, to video conferencing and shared virtual reality environments, there is a vast array of tools that are used to facilitate e-learning that rely upon synchronous presence. Like asynchronous tools, there are many benefits to the learner of conducting e-learning this way, including the ability to choose one's location, the potential to record the conversation to create a historical record and so on. It is significant, however, that most of these technologies play a relatively peripheral role in e-learning. To some extent this may be seen as arising from the nature of the technologies. For example:

- effective video conferencing is typically quite difficult to arrange and involves many non-interoperable standards, fast network connections and appropriate hardware;

- text chat depends upon keyboard skills that relatively few possess and which may disadvantage some disproportionally (Woodfine, Baptista Nunes, & Wright, 2005);

- instant messengers employ diverse and non-interoperable standards;

- the mechanisms for arranging conversations are, with the exception of the telephone, not embedded neatly in the culture; and

- if one wishes to talk to another using the computer, it relies upon that person sitting at the computer at the appropriate time, with the appropriate software.

With the growing popularity of Internet telephony this may change, and there is strong evidence to suggest that a new generation of 'digital students' is evolving for whom technological barriers are coming down (Andone, Boyne, Dron, & Pemberton, 2005). Such learners exist in a fluid, multi-tasking world in which they might be, almost simultaneously, chatting via SMS and/or instant messenger, while browsing the Web, checking e-mails and listening to music. For them, technology is not a barrier. Not only are the technologies and the skills to use them becoming more pervasive, but the processes that enable people to engage are becoming more streamlined and integrated. For example, Web meeting software can provide sophisticated Web-based interfaces giving video, audio and text conferencing abilities, real-time voting, slide presentations, and sophisticated social presence and management facilities, including the ability to arrange meetings automatically through e-mail.

Combinations, Parts and Wholes

Many environments combine several modes of delivery or communication, which will defy categorisation as simple publication or communication tools. Examples might include virtual learning environments, learning management systems, managed learning environments, MUDs, MOOs, Web meeting systems and so on, which incorporate a wide assortment of tools in a more or less integrated virtual space.

Several environments are hard to classify as one thing or another. Wikis and blogs, for instance, combine elements of publication and communication, the proportions of which will vary radically according to context and use.

Many tools only make sense when considered as adjuncts to others. While it may (for example) be possible to run an entire course using nothing but e-mail, discussion forums, blogs, Web meeting software or published content, other e-learning tools are less self-contained. For instance, collaborative tools such as shared whiteboards that allow many users to contribute to a picture or diagram, collaborative mind-mapping tools and shared databases of hyperlinks, offer modes of interaction mediated by networked computer systems that are rich and varied, extending the potential of their traditional counterparts in the real world. However, it would generally be difficult to base an entire sequence of learning transactions on such tools as they are unable, on their own, to perform or to support the full range of functions that might be expected of a teacher.

Assessment Tools

Among the most significant of adjunct tools in a learning environment are those that provide some form of assessment. Automated assessment has a long history in the use of computers in education, both for formative and summative roles. Most learning management systems will provide a fair subset of multiple choice, multiple-multiple choice, missing word, free text, jumbled word order, image hotspots, calculated answers, and so on. These can be used to provide instant feedback to learners as well as statistics to teachers. In many adaptive hypermedia and intelligent tutoring systems, the results can be used to automatically alter the path that the learner may take, whether by preventing progress until success on the test, increasing content available, changing the path through materials, adding annotations or changing the emphasis of parts of the content. The same mechanisms can be used to garner opinions, audience feelings, or votes in a real-time Web meeting environment or an asynchronous system, allowing a tutor to gauge the effectiveness or otherwise of the learning transaction.

Free-text assessment tools that apply AI techniques to analyse submitted texts and provide feedback and grades, which agree with those of human markers, are becoming fairly common (Williams & Dreher, 2005).

Mobile Technologies

Increasingly, mobile telephony and SMS messaging are becoming integrated with the web environment, extending the virtual classroom into every aspect of the learners' lives. Messages can be sent to learners to help organise events, remind them of significant issues, inform them of interesting Web pages, or to integrate more fully with different media. For example, the Tamalle system integrates mobile telephone and digital television to provide translations of words and phrases shown on the TV in real time (Pemberton & Fallahkhair, 2005). Again, it would be hard to learn most things with nothing more than a mobile telephone but, as an adjunct to a more functional environment, mobile technologies are potentially powerful tools.

Diversity in E-Learning Environments

From the foregoing examples, it is clear that different types of learning environments provide different affordances, but even within a particular category of learning environment, there may be huge differences between one instance and the next. For example, discussion forums might provide flexible methods of organising and searching for messages, differentiate messages with a different status, show a photograph of the sender, send an e-mail notification when a message is replied to, indicate the number of times a message has been read, allow people to rate its contents, concatenate messages, display rich media (such as voice or video messages), show who is currently online (presence indicators), and much more. Systems providing all these features offer a very different experience to the end user when compared with those which offer none of these options.

The innate features of the richer environment may do more than simply supply richer functionality and ease of use. Features such as photographs, presence indicators, e-mail notifications, and the like, can make the difference between a close-knit community and one that fails. Even the simplest of features, such as the ability to post messages anonymously, can make a significant difference to the success of a discussion (Creed, 1996). They might be categorised as the same kind of environment, but research into the use of one might not transfer easily to another. The difference between a discussion forum that offers e-mail notifications and one that does not may perhaps be as great as the difference between a classroom with chairs arranged freely and a lecture theatre with chairs facing a stage in tiers. Both environments can be shoehorned into performing substantially the same roles. However, a lecture theatre is great for lectures but poor for small group discussions, which inevitably influences on the kind of activities that are performed there. E-mail notifications are great for sustaining relatively prolonged discussions where the pace is slow as they encourage users to return to the discussion when otherwise they might forget, but they are relatively useless to very active discussions where the quantity of messages might seriously impact the ability of users to operate their e-mail accounts effectively.

Unlike a physical room, a discussion forum may simultaneously appear quite differently to different users. For instance, most discussion forums offer the facility to opt in or out of e-mail notifications. Also, they may potentially be integrated with an indefinitely large number of other parts of the online environment, unconstrained by inconveniently placed walls, fixed floor areas, and the placing of whiteboards. Even more interestingly, simply interacting within a discussion forum will change its physical form. A message on a discussion forum is not just the information that it contains, but contributes materially to the way that the environment is presented to all other participants. *A discussion forum reifies the discussion*. This seemingly trivial observation will prove to be central to understanding the promise of e-learning.

On the Special Nature of Networked Computers

Computers occupy a special space not only in e-learning but in the world at large because, to a greater extent than any other technology, they are both a universal tool and a universal medium, and perhaps also a universal environment. Not only do they provide the means for communication, but they also provide its representation and the tools to enable new ways to communicate. We both interact with them and inhabit them. They are tools for creation and the objects of that creation. In a sense, they are self-reifying.

This is an awesome capability.

E-learning is potentially special because it can take advantage of all of these capabilities and modalities. What becomes of McLuhan's famous edict that the medium is the message when the medium is also the tool through which it is itself constructed and the space in which that construction occurs? The recursive circularity that is implicit in this simple observation will prove to be extremely significant as this book progresses, in particular in parts two and three. For now it should be noted that an e-learning environment will consequently possess an unusual flexibility in its potential to provide control to anyone who wishes to exercise it.

Conclusion

This chapter has defined a number of key terms that will be used throughout this book, laying the ground work for what will follow. In particular there has been an exploration of what is meant in this context by the conventional terms of "teacher," "education," and "e-learning." The chapter has also introduced the term 'learning trajectory' to describe an individual's learning path from one choice to the next, and discussed some of the reasons why this is important. A number of common tools and environments that are used within e-learning have been described, noting that there is an extreme diversity in the kinds of environments that are available and the affordances that they may bring. Even minor differences between them might have significant consequences in relation to the learners' experiences and the choices they might make. The chapter concluded with the observation that computers are not just another tool, nor just another medium, but represent something quite unique in the world of learning—a means of indefinitely extending one's learning environment into a space that is not constrained by the laws of physics, nor (at least potentially) by the limitations of physical media. It can be an environment that constructs itself.

Having laid the groundwork, the remainder of this first part of the book is devoted to an analysis of the nature of control in education.

References

Anderson, M., Ball, M., Boley, H., Greene, S., Howse, N., Lemire, D., et al. (2003). *RACOFI: A rule-applying collaborative filtering system.* Paper presented at the COLA'03, Halifax, Canada.

Andone, D., Boyne, C. W., Dron, J., & Pemberton, L. (2005). *Digital students and their use of e-learning environments.* Paper presented at the IADIS International Conference WWW/Internet 2005, Lisbon, Portugal.

Austin, J. (1979). A plea for excuses. In *Philosophical papers* (3rd ed., pp. 175-204). Oxford: Oxford University Press.

Boud, D. (1981). Toward student responsibility for learning. In D. Boud (Ed.), *Developing student autonomy in learning.* London: Kogan Page.

Brockett, R. G., & Hiemstra, R. (1991). A conceptual framework for understanding self-direction in adult learning. In R. G. Brockett & R. Hiemstra (Eds.), *Self-direction in adult learning: Perspectives on theory, research, and practice.* New York; London: Routledge.

Bruner, J. S. (1966). *Toward a theory of instruction.* Cambridge, MA: The Belknap Press of Harvard University Press.

Brusilovsky, P. (2001). Adaptive hypermedia. *User Modeling and User Adapted Interaction, 11*(Ten Year Anniversary Issue), 87-110.

Candy, P. C. (1991). *Self-direction for lifelong learning: A comprehensive guide to theory and practice.* San Francisco: Jossey Bass.

Churchill, W. (1943). *HC Deb 28 October 1943 c403.*

Clark, R. E. (1983). Reconsidering research on learning from media. *Review of Educational Research, 53*(4), 445-459.

Conole, G., & Dyke, M. (2004). What are the affordances of information and communication technologies? *ALT-J, 12*(2), 113-124.

Creed, T. (1996). Extending the classroom walls electronically. In W. Campbell & K. Smith (Ed.), *New paradigms for college teaching.* Edina, MN: Interaction Book Co.

Dewey, J. (1916). Democracy and education. Retrieved August 27, 2000, from http://www.ilt.columbia.edu/academic/texts/dewey/d_e/

Eraut, M. (2004). Informal learning in the workplace. *Studies in Continuing Education, 26*(2), 247-275.

Freire, P. (1998). *Pedagogy of freedom: Ethics, democracy and civic courage* (P. Clarke, Trans.). MD: Rowman & Littlefield.

Hewitt, J. (2001). Beyond threaded discourse. *International Journal of Educational Telecommunications, 7*(3), 207-221.

Illich, I. (1971). *Deschooling society*. New York: Harper & Row.

Knowles, M. (1975). *Self-directed learning*. Chicago: Follett Publishing.

Long, D. G. (1990). *Learner managed learning*. London: Kogan Page.

Moore, M. G. (1977). *On a theory of independent study*. Hagen, West Germany: Fern Universitat.

Moore, M. G. (1980). Independent study. In R. Boyd & J. Apps (Eds.), *Redefining the discipline of adult education* (pp. 16-31). San Francisco: Jossey-Bass.

Moore, M. G. (1983). On a theory of independent study. In D. Sewart, D. Keegan, & B. Holmberg (Eds.), *Distance education: International perspectives* (pp. 68-94). London; Canberra: Croom Helm.

Moore, M. G. (1986). Self-directed learning and distance education [electronic version]. *Journal of Distance Education, 1*.

Moore, M. G. (1993). Is teaching like flying? A total systems view of distance education. *The American Journal of Distance Education, 7*(1).

Pemberton, L., & Fallahkhair, S. (2005). *Design issues for dual device learning: Interactive television and mobile phone*. Paper presented at the mLearn 2005, Cape Town, South Africa.

Rogers, C. (1969). *Freedom to learn*. Columbus, OH: Merrill.

Seely Brown, J., & Duguid, P. (2000). *The social life of information*. Boston: Harvard Business School Press.

Senge, P. M. (1993). *The fifth discipline: The art and practice of the learning organisation*. Chatham: Century Business.

Tough, A. (1979). *The adults learning projects* (2nd ed.). Toronto: Ontario Institute for Studies in Education.

Tschumi, B. (1996). *Architecture and disjunction*. MIT Press.

Vaill, P. (1996). *Learning as a way of being: Strategies for survival in a world of permanent white water*. San Francisco: Jossey-Bass.

Wedemeyer, C. A. (1971). Independent study. In R. Deighton (Ed.), *Encyclopedia of education* (Vol. IV, pp. 548-557). New York: MacMillan.

Williams, R., & Dreher, H. (2005). *Formative assessment visual feedback in computer graded essays*. Paper presented at the Informing Science and Information Technology Education 2005, Flagstaff, AZ.

Woodfine, B. P., Baptista Nunes, M., & Wright, D. J. (2005). *Constructivist e-learning and dyslexia: Problems of social negotiation in text-based synchronous environments*. Paper presented at the 3rd Int. Conference on Multimedia and Information & Communication Technologies in Education, Cáceres, Spain.

Zhang, A. (2003). *Transactional distance in Web-based college learning environments: Towards measurement and theory construction*. Richmond: Virginia Commonwealth University.

Chapter II

From Transactional Distance to Transactional Control

...there is a psychological and communications space to be crossed, a space of potential misunderstanding between the inputs of instructor and those of the learner. It is this psychological and communications space that is the transactional distance. (Moore, 1997)

Introduction

This chapter lays the theoretical foundations which will eventually lead to a set of recommendations about how e-learning environments should be used and constructed. The theoretical foundation draws heavily from Michael Moore's theory of transactional distance, concentrating on the dynamics that underpin it. The theory also draws upon D.R. Garrison's notions of control and Philip Candy's views on learner self-direction, developing a consolidated model that suggests a logical equivalence between the dynamics of Moore's transactional distance and (particularly) Candy's notions of control. A new name is given to this distilled model: *transactional control*, to distinguish it from the psychological aspects of dialogue that are also implied by transactional distance. The theory of transactional control suggests that a key systemic feature of a learning trajectory is the level and pacing of choice, who makes the choices in the first place, and how those choices constrain further choices and the choices of others.

Transactional Distance

Michael Moore's (1973, 1980, 1997, 1996) theory of transactional distance has been justifiably influential among distance educators as both a descriptive and a generative theory. This view of distance sees the most important differentiating factor between educational transactions not as the physical distance separating learner and teacher but the *transactional* distance, loosely speaking related to the amount of communication between them. Among Moore's great contributions is the realisation that distance is a pedagogical, not a physical phenomenon. The notion that it is transactional, not physical distance that is of most significance when considering any educational transaction, is powerful and useful, allowing educational systems to be classified and characterised based on deeper, underlying, structural features rather than simple physical separation. More significantly, it allows falsifiable predictions to be made about educational systems. Although Moore's theory is long in the tooth in the fast changing world of e-learning, it remains as relevant as ever. Tait (2003) explains, in the context of newer theories of e-learning:

The fact that Moore's theory remains, in my view, the crucial framework of ideas against which such assertions as represented here can be tested gives weight to my initial thesis that there is a deal of continuity in e-learning from second generation distance education that is not acknowledged: perhaps inevitable when a radical interruption by a technology occurs. Now, however, is the time to stand back and reflect on what has changed and what in terms of learning theory remains broadly speaking the same.

Transaction distance is concerned with the relationship between three variables in distance learning: structure and dialogue (concerning the relationship between teacher and learner) and autonomy (an attribute of the learner).

Structure and Dialogue

For Moore, transactional distance is primarily measurable in dimensions bounded by structure and dialogue. Broadly speaking, the greater the structure, the greater the transactional distance. The greater the dialogue, the lesser the transactional distance. This notion is taken a step further by Saba and Shearer (1994) who claim to establish that there is a reciprocal relationship between the two: the greater the structure, the lesser the dialogue and vice versa. Saba and Shearer's research involved the application of system dynamics combined with a form of discourse analysis that attempted to extract from an online (televisual) class those occasions when the teacher was in control and those where the learners were engaged in dialogue. They found that the more the teacher controlled the sequence of events, the less dialogic interaction occurred and vice versa. The reasons for this are intuitively persuasive. If a teacher is completely in control, then there is no opportunity for dialogue at all. If there is a lot of dialogue, then the sequence of events cannot be controlled by a single individual, resulting inevitably in more distributed control of events. In this sense, transactional distance theory, as interpreted by Saba and Shearer, provides an immutable law. Increasing dialogue will decrease structure, while increasing structure will decrease dialogue, whether we like it or not. Knowing this, it is possible to plan educational transactions far more effectively than it would be to naively be assumed that both states are possible (Dron, Seidel, & Litten, 2004). It also makes it easier to explain the dynamics of many educational transactions, especially in a distance-taught environment. Moore's theory resonates with some others: notably, Wenger's (1998) notions of reification and participation explore much of the same ground, though making more of the dynamic relationship between them. There are also some interesting parallels with certain architectural theories, such as Tschumi's (1996) concept of movement and space and the exploration of the role of structure as a determinant of interaction in Hillier's (2003) space syntax theory. The mapping of structure and the dynamic use of that structure is a natural and meaningful way of understanding the world.

Limitations of Moore's Theory of Transactional Distance

Despite its strengths as an explanatory and generative theory, there are some notable problems with transactional distance theory, most of which are related to the fuzziness of its formulation.

The Elusive Nature of Structure, Dialogue, and Autonomy

Moore's concept of structure is distinctive. It would seem from some of his writings that his use of the word only applies to the sequencing of events in an educational transaction, the organisation of resources and strategies to meet pedagogic goals (Moore, 1986). Other notions of structure that are common (e.g., hierarchical organisation of materials, clustering of resources, network models of a subject) are sometimes ignored. Jonassen's (1994) conception of constructivism, for example, explicitly denies that a teacher should supply a sequence, but should instead structure an environment in which constructive learning may be enabled. In a more traditional conception of structure, it may well be argued that its imposition might actually be a prerequisite for effective dialogue. For example, many researchers have noted that free-form discussion is seldom as effective in a learning context as one which is at least moderated to ensure that it remains on track (Garrison & Anderson, 2003; Palloff & Pratt, 1999; Salmon, 2000).

Moore's principle is essentially concerned with a tension between teacher-led sequencing and free-form dialogue. However, Moore is not always clear about the distinction and occasionally seems to treat other forms of structure as relevant. For example, in "Independent Study" (Moore, 1980) he writes:

Structure is the extent to which the objectives, implementation procedures, and evaluation procedures of a teaching programme are prepared, or can be adapted, to meet specific objectives, implementation plans, and evaluation methods of individual students. Structure is a measure of the educational programme's responsiveness to the learner's individual needs.

This authoritative definition says little about structure equating to sequence and a lot about choice and flexibility for the learner. Moore seems to be suggesting here that the degree of choice that a learner has in deciding his or her learning trajectory is most important: the greater the choice available, the lesser the structure. This concept supports his earlier work (Moore, 1973), where he categorised approaches to distance learning according to the degree of individualisation available to the learner, with the key insight that such programmes could be classified by the degree of learner autonomy (the ability and will to make choices) that they provided. Later, Moore (1983) observed, "in independent study the learner chooses when and where to study, at what pace and by what methods" and "the learner chooses what to study." He went on to define learner autonomy as "the extent to which, in the learning-teaching relationship, it is the learner rather than the teacher who determines the goals, the learning procedures and resources, and the evaluation decisions of the learning programme" (ibid.). This led him to suggest a three-dimensional

Figure 2.1. Moore's typology of distance education (Adapted from Moore, 1997)

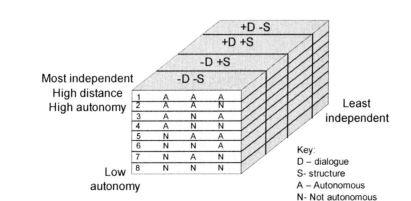

matrix, whose axes are structure, dialogue, and autonomy, which can be used to characterise any educational transaction and the potential engagement of learners within it (Figure 2.1).

Saba and Shearer (1994) have a slightly different interpretation. For them, structure is more related to teacher control of the process while dialogue is closely bound up with and, sometimes, even considered to be virtually synonymous with learner autonomy. In a later paper, Saba (2002) says:

Dialog is the autonomy that the learner needs in order to reach the desired goals. Some students are more autonomous, and need less structure, some require much more structure, and are not comfortable with too much autonomy.

For Saba then, dialogue is less to do with a process of discussion than with the choices that a learner makes. It is interesting that both structure and dialogue therefore are associated (by different authors) with the same concept of choice and control. Moore (1996) has cited Saba approvingly, but Saba's merging of learner autonomy and dialogue is slightly at odds with Moore's interpretation, and springs from his interest in systems behaviour and the linked interactions of the various dimensions. Moore sees autonomous learning as something quite distinct from that which occurs as a result of dialogue or structure. For Moore, autonomous learners are those who can cherry-pick the sources of learning they need, freed from the impositions of structure or the need for dialogue. Autonomous learners are those with maximal ability to choose, with minimal constraint imposed. This dimension is not dependent on the other variables of structure and dialogue, although he does occasionally suggest that there may be a relationship which ties them together (Moore & Kearsley, 1996).

Various Interpretations of Transactional Distance

Moore's theories have been interpreted in many different ways. Lowe (2000) collates a range of interpretations, including this one from Muhammed Betz: "Transactional distance is referring to the quality of the learning transaction with the quality dependent on both participants in the transaction as well as variables of media." For Betz, the claims about structure and dialogue are facets of broader aspects of learning, where the interactions of the participants and the kinds of resources are the significant features, whether or not they are dialogic or structured. A variation on this theme is explored by Zhang (2003), who extends the range of possible interactions to include not only teachers and learners but also the computer interface. Chen (2000), on the other hand, takes a more general perspective on the matter and considers the transactional distance as more to do with how close the student feels to the tutor. While in keeping with Moore at a vague conceptual level, this highly psychological take on the idea allows Chen to consider the ways that rich media can serve to reduce this distance, which seems to bypass the issue of structure versus dialogue almost totally. What began as a concept that related primarily to the nature of interaction between teacher and student thus takes on an entirely different sheen that bears only a passing resemblance to Moore's initial ideas. A variation on this perspective is taken by Stirling (1997), who describes transactional distance poetically as "a physical separation that causes a psychological and communicative chasm—a potential fall-space of misunderstanding between the actors (instructor and learner) in an educative event." Shin (2002) takes this even further and talks about "transactional presence" as a psychological construct that measures the sense of the presence of a tutor in an educational transaction.

It seems that there are two broad themes in interpreting Moore which suggest that the psychological phenomenon of transactional distance is almost entirely distinct from its systemic features relating to control. Stein et al. (2005) echo Stirling's literal interpretation of Moore's view of transactional distance as a "psychological and communications gap." It is important to distinguish these two factors. The psychological gap, which forms the object of many studies, is a quite separate issue from the communications gap, which is a more notably systemic feature of the system. The dynamics observed by Saba and Shearer had more to do with the communications gap, with its implications of negotiated control, than the psychological, with its focus on satisfaction and feelings about the learning experience. Though often mentioned, this dual nature is seldom explored by Moore or others.

Criticisms of Transactional Distance Theory

The dual nature of transactional distance and the ease with which Moore's theory can be reinterpreted and manipulated according to the needs of those fitting it to their own agendas has resulted in some fairly significant criticisms of the model. Garrison (2000), in particular, observes the various ways that fuzziness surrounds many of Moore's formulations:

...the exact nature of the interrelationships among structure, dialog, and autonomy is not clear. There is confusion around whether structure and dialogue are variables, clusters, or dimensions. Unfortunately, Moore has used different terms (i.e., variables, clusters, dimensions) at various times. Understanding transactional distance very much depends upon whether we are discussing a two-by-two matrix, a single continuum, or distinct clusters. This confusion is compounded when we add the concept of autonomy with its definitional problems (psychological or educational autonomy) and its relationship to transactional distance.

The more the concept of transactional distance is examined, the more blurred it becomes and, for some, the inconsistencies and fuzziness lead to inaccurate interpretations that make the theory itself open to doubt (Gorsky & Caspi, 2005). This potentially weakens its power as a meta-model of the educational process. Moore has added tweaks and elaborations over the years, which further muddy the waters and, as Garrison notes, is not always consistent in the way he applies it. For example, the introduction of the concept of learner autonomy as not just a backdrop to transactional distance, but also one of its dimensions, makes the model so susceptible to multiple interpretations that it could become almost useless, despite Saba's attempts to marry them all in a single systemic model. There are also reasons to doubt Saba's conclusion that structure and dialogue cannot both be high (an opinion not always held by Moore), most notably in systems that generate structure through dialogue (Dron, 2004a, 2004b). While such systems may not simultaneously provide high and low transactional distance for any individual learner, they may provide both simultaneously to different learners.

A Closer Look at Saba and Shearer's Model

To help to clarify some of the uncertainties of transactional distance, it is informative to examine Saba and Shearer's (1994) approach more closely. Their experiment was based on an analysis of dialogue and structure in a tele-lesson, but what they were actually testing appears to have been the relative degree of learner control and instructor control, which were then interpreted as structure and dialogue, which in turn were used via a fairly direct formula to generate a measure of transactional distance. As they put it, for their diagram equivalent to that shown in Figure 2.2: "The flow diagram shows direct influence from the level of *instructor control* to the rate of *structure*, and from the level of *learner control* to the rate of *dialogue*."

What is actually portrayed is a dynamic that is thus based on control, not dialogue, structure, or transactional distance, which are just effects of the dynamic, not causes. Indeed, in their model, learner control is directly correlated with dialogue and structure with instructor control. It is possible to remove both structure and dialogue from the equations and the model continues to function in the same way (Figure 2.3). Although such a flow diagram might make system dynamics purists wince, it still produces precisely the same behaviours and results in precisely the same graph.

Despite its usefulness and intuitive charm, Moore's theory resembles a map of the Americas from the days before Columbus visited. Something is there, it is clearly quite big, but no one is quite sure of its shape and there are significant disagreements as to its size and significance. There is a need for a better map if intrepid navigators of the theory do not wish to get shipwrecked on its shores or lost where there be dragons.

Figure 2.2. Transactional distance flow diagram (Adapted from Saba & Shearer, 1994)

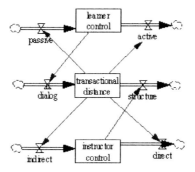

Figure 2.3. Transactional distance flow diagram without structure or dialogue

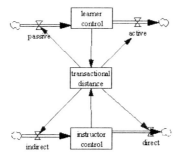

Garrison and Baynton's Model of Control

If Saba and Shearer were actually considering issues of control, it may be worthwhile to explore notions of control further. Garrison and Baynton (1987) offer a slightly different transactional model than that of Moore, which is based on the concept of control, specifically the "opportunity and ability to influence, direct, and determine decisions related to the educational process." This supports the concept of learner control as a process developed by Brockett and Hiemstra (1991) who distinguish self-directed learning (a process orientation) and learner self-direction (a personal, psychological construct). Garrison and Baynton make the important observation that, to be successful, control cannot be possessed by just a student or a teacher, but should be negotiated and shared collaboratively. If control resides too much with one or the other, communication is diminished, and with it, opportunities for the construction of meaning and knowledge are diminished as well. Garrison and Baynton assert that, for a learner to achieve control there is a need for three distinct yet intimately connected prerequisites: power, independence, and support. The learner has to wish to be independent, to have the means to exercise control and to have access to the necessary supporting structures to allow that control to be exercised. Garrison and Baynton's framework is centred heavily on communication as a means of providing a learner with the ability to choose an appropriate educational path. Their theory of control looks at choice and the interaction of choices systemically and is thus close in spirit to the subject of this book, although the intent is quite different.

Candy and Control

In 1991, Philip C. Candy wrote what still is perhaps the definitive work on self-direction in learning, in which he insightfully explored the notions of choice, control, and autonomy in adult learners in great depth and detail. Like Garrison and Baynton, Candy (1991) explores the systemic nature of control and constraint. Candy's work remains a primary source for the vast majority of research in control and self-direction to this day (Dion, 2005; Kaufman, 2003; Koper & Tattersall, 2004; Nokelainen, Miettinen, Kurhila, Floreen, & Tirri, 2004; Rager, 2004; Tattersall et al., 2005). Significantly, he recognises that control can exist on a continuum between the structure provided by the teacher and the control demanded by the learner.

If learner-control is conceived of as a range or continuum (or more likely a series of continuums, for it is possible to exert differing degrees of control over various dimensions), then one end of the range will involve a great deal of learner-control over valued instructional functions. Various instructional strategies could be placed at intervals along this continuum, to imply the differing balance of teacher-control and learner-control. (p. 10)

This resonates very strongly with the earlier interpretation of the findings of Saba and Shearer, suggesting that Candy's notions of control might, in some senses, map directly back to Moore's theory of transactional distance.

Candy usefully distinguishes between self-direction as a goal and self-direction as a process. He refers to these respectively as "autodidaxy" (self-direction as a personal characteristic of the learner, capable of independently managing goals, methods, and resources) and learner-control (loosely, the degree of control that a learner has in determining a learning trajectory within a recognisable educational setting). This is similar Brockett and Hiemstra's (1991) distinction between "self-directed learning" and 'learner self-direction,' where the former is a process orientation and the latter a personal orientation. Exploring the notion further, Candy (1991) observes that neither the process nor the product of autonomous self-direction in learning are fixed, nor are they independent of context:

...autonomy is not simply a personal quality or characteristic, but is a relation involving the interplay of personal and situational variables. Accordingly, any person could vary in the degree of autonomy he or she exhibits from situation to situation. (p. 113)

This paves the way for a systemic view of learning which sees control as a constant and dynamically changing variable, not just because it is a negotiable quantity, but due to the nature of people and their diverse needs as learners.

Candy analyses four distinct dimensions of self-direction:

- Self-direction as a philosophical ideal
- Self-direction as a psychological attribute or educational orientation
- Self-direction as a set of activities outside formal education
- Self-direction as a set of activities within formal education

For Candy, there is a significant distinction to be made between those activities that relate to the management of a learning process (the means) and the kind of self-determination that enables a learner to autonomously select the goals and means in the first place, to become an autodidact. This is an artificial distinction, perhaps a product of historical happenstance, caused by viewing the same phenomenon at different levels of scale. Management of the learning process involves shorter-term goals, while autodidaxy extends this to longer term goals.

Candy identifies a model of self-directed learning which bears a strong resemblance to Garrison and Baynton's model of control, a three dimensional edifice describing differing degrees of competence, rights, and resources. These map interestingly, if not quite exactly, to Garrison and Baynton's *power* (a little akin to *competence*, though Candy's notion is more situated, assuming that the learner is already undertaking a learning activity), *independence* (very similar to Candy's idea of *rights*), and *support* (closely akin to Candy's view of *resources*).

Self direction may be further subdivided into self-control and self-monitoring (Garrison, 2003), as management of learning would, by definition, be impossible without both elements.

Choice, Constraint, and Scale: Introducing Transactional Control

Moore implies that if an educational transaction is highly structured, then the sequence of learning activities is controlled by the teacher. On the other hand, if there is a lot of dialogue, then out of necessity, the teacher is relinquishing control to the students, as they are able to influence the series of events that lead to the learning they desire. What is seen therefore is an exchange of control. This is very much in keeping with Saba's interpretation of transactional distance which adopts the (superficially) strange view of dialogue as a measure of autonomy. The issue of control is also in keeping with Moore's own concept of autonomy as well as his earlier analysis of individualised versus less individualised forms of study. In a complementary fashion, Candy sees dialogue as a significant means of negotiating control within a formal educational setting. The term "transactional distance" has been over-used and defined in too many ways already. "Autonomy" carries shades of meaning that covers too much ground and again comes loaded with a historical context in educational literature. Worse still, these concepts were developed at a time when e-learning was in its infancy and the range of ways that a learner could interact with teacher, content, and above all, each other, was limited. Notions of transactional distance become very fuzzy when considering the possibilities of systems like, for instance, Google or PHOAKS, where learning can come about as a result of indirect interactions with not one or even a group, but rather with millions or even billions of other users (Dron, 2002). Equally, the kind of interactions that are possible through sophisticated adaptive hypermedia systems like AHA! and Interbook (Brusilovsky, 2001) do not lend themselves naturally to easy categorisation in the early instantiations of Moore's or Garrison's views of the world.

Transactional Control

Rather than offering yet another definition of transactional distance or attempting to redefine control theory, self-direction, or autonomy, this shifting pattern of control will be defined here as the level of *transactional control*. Transactional control may be seen as that part of transactional distance that defines its dynamics, the result of the gulf in communication rather than the psychological gulf. Transactional control will look different from the perspective of any individual in a system and is not the same as autonomy, structure, or dialogue, though is intimately related with each of them. In this theory, there are only two significant dimensions: choice and time. Both are affected by a variety of constraints that may come from within an educational system or from outside it and are only meaningful when the scale at which they are viewed is taken into account. It is possible to model this (perhaps

Figure 2.4. Hypothetical view of choices in a series of learning activities

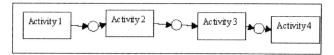

over-simplistically) as a sequence of choices and activities for each individual, as in Figure 2.4. Choices in this case may be made by the teacher, the learner, or a process of negotiation.

This is merely illustrative: there are many other potential agents that might be involved in those choices, such as computer software, books, Web sites, or other learners.

Self-Directed Learning, not Learner Self-Direction

Transactional control is concerned with Brockett and Hiemstra's process orientation, not with personal characteristics of learners. It has far more to do with self-directed learning rather than learner self-direction. While it is important to keep in mind the ultimate goal of enabling learners to become self-directed and to assume personal responsibility for their own learning, this is a peripheral concern to the main inquiry that informs this book.

Benefits of Considering Transactional Control

The significant issue, when considering transactional control, is not whether there is dialogue or structure, but instead who is making the choices about where to go next at any given point in a sequence of learning activities. If the teacher is the chooser, then the transactional control for the learner is lower. If the learner is the chooser (which may be indirect in the sense that he or she is influencing the teacher to go down one path rather than another) then the learner's transactional control is higher. This interpretation makes it possible to model group interactions more effectively than traditional transactional distance theory, based on the principle that a teaching role may be distributed, collective, shifting, or one step removed from an individual. One of the criticisms that might be levelled at Moore's model is that it mainly concerns more traditional views of education where there is a teacher and a group of learners. It says little about occasions where learning may occur in a more egalitarian manner, such as may be found in action learning sets, for example. At any point within a group's interactions, choices may be made by any member of the group, which in turn might reduce the choices available to other group members (or which might on the other hand open up new possibilities and further choices that were previously latent). The teacher is therefore only one of many who are capable of influencing the learning trajectories of other individuals within the group.

Different Aspects of Control

Within the transactional control model, dialogue is only one of the ways that control may be gained by the learner. This becomes much more significant when considering e-learning systems that provide distributed control. It is also significant at an individual level. For example, the learning process that originally led to this book involved neither a teacher (unless the authors of relevant books and papers are treated as representatives of that role) nor a dialogic process, apart from one largely internalised or, on occasion, discussed with interested colleagues or at conferences. Even these exceptions were entirely under the author's control. This remained so until interaction began with the publishers, who took control of the time frame, the number of words, the style, the subject, the structure, even the title of the book. Later still, the feedback from reviewers provided substantial extrinsic control although, even then, it was left to the author to select between different and sometimes conflicting suggestions. Candy (1991) observes that "no instructor taught that proto-human how to shape a stone implement; it was entirely the product of her (or his) own imagination and experimentation" (p. 157). Similarly, Simons (2000) writes:

In many situations, learning is a side-effect of problem solving, working or acting only, and it will appear as experiential or incidental leaning. There is no explicit regulation of learning, nor any conscious attempts of learners to regulate learning as such. They are regulating their actions, problem solving, or working. Learning occurs unconsciously and is regulated by the environment.

Although Moore's notion of autonomy caters for such cases admirably, it sits uncomfortably with a model, like that of Garrison, which puts dialogue at the centre of educational transactions. Because transactional control looks at the world from the perspective of individual learners, but models that world based on the interactions of their choices, it bypasses such complexity.

Transactional control underpins transactional distance. The dynamics of the system that relate dialogue and structure in a reciprocal relationship are, as Saba and Shearer show, actually the dynamics of interconstraining choices.

Transactional control can be seen as a measurement of:

- who makes the choices to engage in specific learning activities;
- the frequency of change between who makes the choices over a period of time; and
- the degree of constraint that is imposed when making those choices.

The level of transactional control that is assigned is highly determined by the scale at which the sequence of activities is viewed.

Similarities with Garrison and Baynton

There are some similarities between this approach and Garrison and Baynton's (1987) analysis of what affects the learner's ability to control the learning experience. They identify independence, power, and support as the key factors determining control in a learning transaction:

- *independence* is the ability of the learner to choose goals and directions;
- *power* is "the ability or capacity to take part in and assume responsibility for the learning process";
- *support* "refers to the resources that the learner can access in order to carry out the learning process."

Though phrased differently and not explicitly mentioning the issue of constraint, it is possible to see how these factors can be mapped to a language of choice and constraint. Support and power are each governed by constraint, while independence clearly maps to the issue of choice, bounded by those constraints. For Garrison and Baynton, this is a stepping stone to the generation of a theory which demands inter-action as a means of establishing learner control. The three factors are "manifested in and determined by the communication process that takes place between teacher and student." Transactional control, too, provides strong theoretical justifications for the use of dialogue as a means of negotiating and distributing control, but the similarity ends there. The concept of transactional control applies equally to all actors within an educational system, not just to the learner but (in particular) to the teacher and a wide assortment of other interested parties and, importantly, covers a range of e-learning systems where dialogue is at best unconventional and may be distributed across many users and resources.

Psychological and Pedagogical Aspects of Control

Transactional control theory does not seek to replace transactional distance theory, which is as much about the psychological gap between learners as it is about the systemic nature of distance learning. The relationship between transactional distance and transactional control is expressed in Figure 2.5, from which it can be more clearly seen that the psychological aspects of transactional distance and autonomy are related to but distinct from the element of control that underpins the dynamic. By concentrating on control it is possible to unify these previously distinct concepts.

Transactional control does not even begin to address the important issues of the learner self-directedness and autonomy as a personal characteristic. How and why people make choices is an issue that can be explored from many different perspectives (Glasser, 2004), most of which will be treated as givens or simply ignored. Psychological theories of how choices are made do not greatly concern this enquiry. They are not significant when looking at the rules of the game, any more than those rules relate to the cognitive aspects of improving learning or the relevance of learning styles.

Choice lies at the heart of many learning theories. For instance, Kolb's (1984) experiential learning theory suggests that learning is the result of and results in adaptive choice. Bateson's (1972) theory of learning takes this further and classifies the kind of choices that may be made. The implications of choice-making are significant and matter a great deal to learners. For instance, Ramsden (1992) writes:

The significance of independence and choice emerges repeatedly in research on student ratings and perceptions of favourable academic environments, at higher and upper secondary education levels. Yet most prevailing systems of learning in higher education adopt mass-production standards; they handle each individual

Figure 2.5. Mapping transactional control and transactional distance

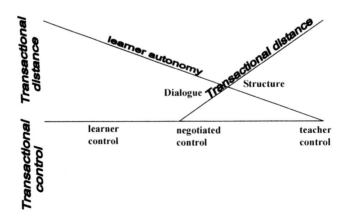

student in the same way, even though we know for certain that they operate in different ways.

Choice forms a major topic of concern for most educational theorists, but usually only as a backdrop or consequence of other things. The ways that people make choices, the how and the why (to a point), are not the main issue here. Although transactional control theory makes some predictions about the kind of educational experience that will result from different patterns of choice and constraint in an individual's learning trajectory, what is significant from the perspective of transactional control is the face *that* choices are made, *when* they are made and *how* they affect and are affected by each other. This does not carry many implications about *what sort* of choices should be made or *how* (beyond the issue of constraints and interdependencies) those choices are made, merely that they *are* made and that somebody makes them some time or times in a learning trajectory. The systemic interactions that are implied by this simple fact have far reaching implications.

Transactional Control and Dialogue

Numerous writers have emphasised the significance of dialogue as a central means of constructing meaning, including Vygotsky (1978), Pask (1976), Wenger (1998), Laurillard (1993), Whitehead (1929), and Dewey (1897; 1938), as well as Moore himself. As Wenger (1998) says, "The first requirement of educational design is to offer opportunities for engagement" (p. 271).

The importance of interaction with others as a central and perhaps the primary means of constructing knowledge is hard to understate. There are many reasons for this, which can be framed in cognitive, behaviourist, or constructivist terms, to name but three of the most significant. Pena-Schaff and Nicholls (2004) sum it up well, telling us: "Dialogue serves as an instrument for thinking because in the process of explaining, clarifying, elaborating, and defending our ideas and thoughts we engage in cognitive processes such as integrating, elaborating, and structuring." Klemm (2002) provides a similarly useful definition:

Conversation is central to exchanging information, making our positions known, and persuading and motivating others. In education, the communication between instructor and student and student-to-student communication contribute to learning in many ways: rehearsal of facts to expedite memorization, exposure to a broad range of information and perspective, deeper understanding, a stimulus for insight and creative thought, and a basis for assessment of learning.

Gordon Pask's conversation theory places this process of communication at the heart of learning. He is also an early proponent of viewing educational systems in their entirety, not divorcing teaching or learning or administration or any other factor from his systems approach. Pask's view of the systemic nature of education considers the individual as a subsystem within a system. Pask's own writings are obtuse, but Rocha (2000) explains Pask's view of the internal system of learning and its relationship to the educational environment thus:

[Pask] developed an extensive theory of conversation that proposed the abandonment of the concept of learning as a one to one mapping of real world to mental categories, for a dynamic, internal, self-organizing process of coming to know, constrained by developmental interaction with an environment and fellow "knowers."

For Pask, learning is truly situated and contextual, an interactive process of construction which incorporates previous knowing with new knowledge in a process of interaction between the learner and other learners, the learner and the teacher, and the learner and the learning resource.

It would seem that conversation and dialogue provide a major cornerstone on which effective education may be based, providing so many benefits that it becomes hard to consider the possibility of education without it, despite evidence to the contrary that this is perhaps even the norm within formal education. Dialogue is one of the primary means of involvement in any community, be it a learning community or otherwise. It gives a sense of identity in relation to those around us, acts as the foundation for relationships of many forms and provides the basis for trust and belongingness.

The Negotiation of Control

To these benefits may be added another. A significant source of the power of dialogue in a learning trajectory is its effectiveness as a means of enabling choice in the service of learning. Boyer (2005) offers a poetic summary of the self-organising exchange of control facilitated by dialogue and an interactive, conversational processes: "The 'dance' of online learning involves interdependence between the roles of faculty and student with the possibility of transferring control of learning tasks to students and student communities."

Boyer's summary is significant in as much as it emphasises different kinds of dialogue, both between two individuals and within a community as a whole. This implies that the community is, in some senses, a distinct entity from the individuals of which it is comprised.

Dialogue provides a mechanism for a learner to enter an unknown learning space with support while maintaining a significant degree of control over the directions that learning will take, to flit between choice and the relinquishment of choice dynamically and constantly. This is the essential lesson that Garrison and Baynton draw in their control theory; it is the essence of Freire's notion of co-intentionality (Freire, 1970) and is implicit in Dewey's (1938) formulation:

Let me speak first of the advantages which reside potentially in the increase of outward freedom. In the first place, without its existence it is practically impossible for a teacher to gain knowledge of the individuals with whom he is concerned. Enforced quiet and acquiescence prevent pupils from disclosing their real natures.

Dialogue provides a mechanism for the exchange of information between learner and learner, learner and teacher, or learner and resource, which can change all parties concerned in the exchange. It will be shown that dialogue occupies an almost unique place in a learning trajectory, due to the interchange of control over choices that it provides. This combination of safety and choice-making is very hard to achieve in any other way.

Conclusion

Moore's theory of transactional distance and related theories, such as Garrison and Baynton's control theory and Candy's model of self-directed learning, are significant and effective approaches to understanding and predicting the behaviour of, in particular, distance learning environments. However, the theories are old, and begin to show weaknesses when examined closely or when applied to newer contexts of e-learning. Transactional control theory will be seen to address some of those weaknesses and will form the theoretical basis for the rest of this book. Transactional control theory does not seek to replace existing theories like transactional distance, but is simply another way of looking at the same phenomena. It is about a purified subset of transactional distance, dispensing with the (undoubtedly important) psychological elements that contribute to its fuzziness. It is a perspective or vantage point that makes it possible to draw the same conclusions about the nature of e-learning as transactional distance theory, but that will also lead to some other predictions that would not be possible in the classical theory.

Transactional control theory, as presented so far, says little. Though it may make it possible to characterise some forms of learning transaction in broad terms, it remains fuzzy and of limited applicability or predictive power. It will be necessary to clarify, elaborate, and refine the theory presented so far, which is the job of the next couple of chapters—looking in detail at issues of choice and scale.

References

Bateson, G. (1972). *Steps to an ecology of mind*. London: Chicago Press.

Boyer, N. (2005). Online learners take the lead in self-direction. *Academic Exchange Quarterly, 9*(4), 244-250.

Brockett, R. G., & Hiemstra, R. (1991). A conceptual framework for understanding self-direction in adult learning. In R. G. Brockett & R. Hiemstra (Eds.), *Self-direction in adult learning: Perspectives on theory, research, and practice.* New York & London: Routledge.

Brusilovsky, P. (2001). Adaptive hypermedia. *User Modeling and User Adapted Interaction, 11*(Ten Year Anniversary Issue), 87-110.

Candy, P. C. (1991). *Self-direction for lifelong learning: A comprehensive guide to theory and practice.* San Francisco: Jossey Bass.

Chen, Y-J. (2000). Transactional distance in World Wide Web learning environments. *Innovations in Education and Teaching International, 38*(2), 327-338.

Dewey, J. (1897). My pedagogic creed. *The School Journal, LIV*(3), 77-80.

Dewey, J. (1938). *Experience and education*. Macmillan Press.

Dion, D-P. (2005). The Lisbon process: A European odyssey. *European Journal of Education, 40*(3), 295-313.

Dron, J. (2002). *Achieving self-organisation in network-based learning environments.* Unpublished doctoral dissertation, University of Brighton.

Dron, J. (2004a). *A loophole in Moore's law of transactional distance.* Paper presented at the ICALT 2004, Joensuu, Finland.

Dron, J. (2004b). *Termites in the schoolhouse: Stigmergy and transactional distance in an e-learning environment.* Paper presented at the Ed-Media 2004, Lugano, Switzerland.

Dron, J., Seidel, C., & Litten, G. (2004). Transactional distance in a blended learning environment. *ALT-J, 12*(2), 163-174.

Freire, P. (1970). *Pedagogy of the oppressed* (M. B. Ramos, Trans.). New York: Continuum.

Garrison, D. R. (2000). Theoretical challenges for distance education in the 21st century: A shift from structural to transactional issues. *International Review of Research in Open and Distance Learning, 1*(1).

Garrison, D. R. (2003). Cognitive presence for effective asynchronous online learning: The role of reflective inquiry, self-direction and metacognition. In J. Bourne & J. C. Moore (Eds.), *Elements of quality online education: Practice and direction* (Vol. 4). Needham, MA: The Sloan Consortium.

Garrison, D. R., & Anderson, T. (2003). *E-Learning in the 21ˢᵗ century: A framework for research and practice*. London: RoutledgeFalmer.

Garrison, D. R., & Baynton, M. (1987). Beyond independence in distance education: The concept of control. *American Journal of Distance Education, 1*(3), 3-15.

Glasser, W. (2004). What is choice theory. Retrieved July 24, 2004, from http://www.wglasser.com/whatisct.htm

Gorsky, P., & Caspi, A. (2005). A critical analysis of transactional distance theory. *The Quarterly Review of Distance Education, 6*(1), 1-11.

Hillier, B. (2003). *The common language of space: A way of looking at the social, economic and environmental functioning of cities on a common basis.* Retrieved May 12, 2003, from http://www.spacesyntax.org/publications/commonlang.html

Jonassen, D. H. (1994). Thinking technology: Toward a constructivist design model. *Educational Technology, 34*(4), 34-37.

Kaufman, D. M. (2003). Applying educational theory in practice. *British Medical Journal,* (326), 213-216.

Klemm, W. R. (2002). Software issues for applying conversation theory for effective collaboration via the Internet.

Kolb, D. A. (1984). *Experiential learning.* Englewood Cliffs, NJ: Prentice Hall.

Koper, R., & Tattersall, C. (2004). New directions for lifelong learning using network technologies. *British Journal of Educational Technology, 35*(6), 689-700.

Laurillard, D. (1993). *Rethinking university teaching: A framework for the effective use of educational technology.* London: Routledge.

Lowe, W. (2000). Transactional distance theory as a foundation for developing innovative and reactive instruction. *Educational Technology & Society [electronic], 3*(1).

Moore, M. G. (1973). Towards a theory of independent learning and teaching. *Journal of Higher Education, 44,* 661-679.

Moore, M. G. (1980). Independent study. In R. Boyd & J. Apps (Eds.), *Redefining the discipline of adult education* (pp. 16-31). San Francisco: Jossey-Bass.

Moore, M. G. (1983). On a theory of independent study. In D. Sewart, D. Keegan, & B. Holmberg (Eds.), *Distance education: International perspectives* (pp. 68-94). London; Canberra: Croom Helm.

Moore, M. G. (1986). Self-directed learning and distance education [Electronic Version]. *Journal of Distance Education, 1.*

Moore, M. G. (1997). Theory of transactional distance. In D. Keegan (Ed.), *Theoretical principles of distance education* (pp. 22-38): Routledge.

Moore, M. G., & Kearsley, G. (1996). *Distance education: A systems view.* Belmont: Wadsworth.

Nokelainen, P., Miettinen, M., Kurhila, J., Floreen, P., & Tirri, H. (2004). *A shared document-based annotation tool to support learner-centered collaborative learning.* Helsinki: Helsinki Institute for Information Technology.

Palloff, R. M., & Pratt, K. (1999). *Building learning communities in cyberspace: Effective strategies for the online classroom.* San Francisco: Jossey-Bass.

Pask, G. (1976). *Conversation theory: Applications in education and epistemology.* Elsevier.

Pena-Shaff, J. B., & Nicholls, C. (2004). Analyzing student interactions and meaning construction in computer bulletin board discussions. *Computers and Education,* (42), 243-265.

Rager, K. B. (2004). A thematic analysis of the self-directed learning experiences of 13 breast cancer patients. *International Journal of Lifelong Education, 23*(1), 95-109.

Ramsden, P. (1992). *Learning and teaching in higher education.* London: Routledge.

Rocha, L. M. (2000). Adaptive recommendation and open-ended symbiosis. *International Journal of Human-Computer Studies.*

Saba, F. (2002, June 5-7, 2002). *Evolution of research in distance education: Challenges of the online distance learning environment.* Paper presented at the Second Conference on Research in Distance and Adult Learning in Asia, The Open University of Hong Kong.

Saba, F., & Shearer, R. L. (1994). Verifying key theoretical concepts in a dynamic model of distance education. *The American Journal of Distance Education, 8*(1), 36-59.

Salmon, G. (2000). *E-moderating: The key to teaching and learning online.* London: Kogan Page.

Shin, N. (2002). Beyond interaction: The relational construct of transactional presence. *Open Learning, 17*(2), 121-136.

Simons, R.-J. (2000). Towards a constructivistic theory of self-directed learning. In G. A. Straka (Ed.), *Conceptions of self-directed learning.* New York: Waxmann.

Stein, D. S., Wanstreet, C. E., Calvin, J., Overtoom, C., & Wheaton, J. E. (2005). Bridging the transactional distance gap in online learning environments. *American Journal of Distance Education, 19*(2), 105-119.

Stirling, D. L. (1997). *Toward a theory of distance education: Transactional distance.* Retrieved July 26, 2004, from http://www.stirlinglaw.com/deborah/stir4.htm

Tait, A. (2003). Reflections on student support in open and distance learning. *The International Review of Research in Open and Distance Learning, 4*(1).

Tattersall, C., Manderveld, J., Van den Berg, B., Van Es, R., Janssen, J., & Koper, R. (2005). Self organising wayfinding support for lifelong learners. *Education and Information Technologies, 10*(1 - 2), 111-123.

Tschumi, B. (1996). *Architecture and disjunction*: MIT Press.

Vygotsky, L. S. (1978). *Mind in society*. London: Harvard University Press.

Wenger, E. (1998). *Communities of practice: Learning, meaning and identity*. New York: Cambridge University Press.

Whitehead, A. N. (1929). *The aims of education and other essays*. New York: The Free Press.

Zhang, A. (2003). *Transactional distance in Web-based college learning environments: Towards measurement and theory construction.* Virginia Commonwealth University, Richmond.

Chapter III

Making Choices:
The Need for Teachers

We do not need competency skills for this life. We need incompetency skills, the skills of being effective beginners. (Vaill, 1996, p. 81)

Introduction

This chapter is concerned with the importance of achieving control of one's own learning, of learning to learn, why it is that teachers are a good thing, why too many choices or choices presented at the wrong time are a bad thing, and beginning to explore some alternative approaches to control, which provide the seed for the approach to learning environment design that forms the third part of the book.

Kinds of Choice

This enquiry is concerned with choices about what to do next to bring about learning. Choices may relate to many aspects of the learning experience. A non-exhaustive list might include:

- choice of subject;
- choice of learning activity/task;
- choice of resources (e.g., books, articles, Web sites, etc.);
- choice of people with whom to engage in learning;
- choice of medium through which to learn;
- choices inherent in or determined by the nature of the subject (for instance, when learning about education, a learner may choose to adopt a stance based on behaviourist, cognitive, or constructivist principles);
- choice of location;
- choice of attitude to take (e.g., sceptical, exploratory, excited, clinical, top down, bottom up);
- choice of method;
- choice of means of evaluation;
- choice of level; and
- choice of time (timeframe, amount of time spent, choice of when to engage).

Each kind of choice implies a different set of skills, predispositions, criteria and purposes, and each will be subject to a different array of constraints that limit those choices. Each choice may be made, to a greater or lesser extent, by the learner and/or some other (typically the teacher). Only some of those choices will have a material effect on a learning trajectory. However, the overall gestalt will be manifest in a learning trajectory over time, which will be unique and distinct for each learner, even though some of the choices will be common and/or shared with other learners.

Why is Choice so Important?

Recognising that this is a dramatic over-simplification of a complex process, within a traditional view of institutional education it is possible to see a continual and perhaps continuous series of changes in the amount/degree of choice available to the learner (Figure 3.1).

In early education, it is usually expected and accepted that learners are not sufficiently schooled to be able to recognise the most appropriate choices to make about their own learning, at least for most of the things that are considered to be educationally important. This is an interesting perspective given that much of what

Figure 3.1. Hypothetical relationship between educational level and choice

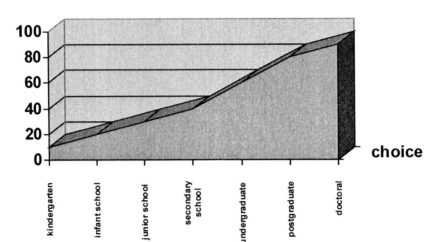

such a child has learnt up until this point has been without any explicit guidance. However, a glance at any kindergarten or early school classroom will reveal that teachers dictate much of the form and content of learning activities. Partly, this is a result of perceptions of children as not knowing the territory, and partly, it is a result of beliefs that they are immature learners, not yet able to achieve that level of meta-cognition about their own learning that is the goal of most adult education courses, at least in higher education. Moore (1986) suggests an alternative that is more learner-driven:

Since children tend to have a self-concept of dependence, it is natural for them to look to adults, including teachers, for reassurance, affection and approval. They are usually willing to follow a teaching program, regardless of its congruence with any learning programs of their own, merely to win the approval and affection of the teacher.

It is probable that some part of a child's self-concept of dependence is a learned behaviour, and there is almost certainly recursive interdependence between adult and child perceptions that reinforces the effect.

At the other end of the scale, much that happens to enable learning at the doctoral and post-doctoral levels (at least, though not universally, in the United Kingdom) is, frequently, almost entirely within the hands of the researcher, with odd bits of guidance and advice being offered on demand by supervisors and peers, especially with regard to learning about the research process itself.

Self-Directed Learning

It is not necessary to look at formal education to find examples of a high degree of autonomy in adult learners. Tough (1979) discovered that the average person (young or old) spends approximately 200 hours each year on some informal learning activity such as learning to sew, learning a new language and so on. Tough's research was limited to a specific culture, and his definition of self-initiated learning is loose. For instance, he incorporated those occasions where the learner actively sought a teacher or evening class, yet excluded 'learning projects' which took less than seven hours. However, Tough's findings help to confirm Illich's (1971) assertion that learning outside an academic institution is the norm, not the exception. This remains the case even when examining higher education in an academic setting. Many lecturers in higher education are teaching subjects that differ radically from what they were taught when they were in the same position as their students. Somehow they reached this state of knowledge, perhaps by being part of a community of practice (Wenger, 1998). Only rarely, perhaps, did this occur through guided educational transactions or institutional learning. A straw poll of 20 colleagues who teach aspects of information systems at the author's own institution revealed that only one had a first degree in a subject related to computing, and nearly half had higher degrees in subject areas other than computing. Although computing is an extremely volatile and youthful area, this is a startling observation. Even of those who had higher degrees in a related discipline, few were teaching anything like the content that they were taught as graduates.

Learning to Learn

A clear goal of education is that learners should become like their teachers and "learn to learn." In other words, they should become capable of making and evaluating their own choices of learning trajectory. In fact, it might be argued that this is perhaps the most important lesson to be taught by any teacher in higher education. Garrison and Baynton (1987) assert: "Developing learner independence and self-directed learning is often cited as the ultimate aim of adult education." This is tempered with the observation that "there is little consensus regarding what this concept means and how independent behaviour is to be attained" (ibid.). Expanding on this slightly and focussing on the process, Moore (1980) states:

The instructor needs to structure his materials and conduct his dialogue in ways that will permit learners to become more autonomous during the course of a programme. This personal growth must be a primary educational goal regardless of the course's subject matter.

Similarly, Boud (1981) writes: "The only realistic goal for higher education is that students should be more autonomous when they leave the course than when they enter" (p. 24). Garrison and Anderson (2003) ask, rhetorically, "Is not the ultimate challenge of the educator to bring students to assume responsibility for their own learning?" For McPherson and Nunes (2004), instruction means "improving the abilities of self-regulation of learning, thinking, intelligence and problem solving." The same authors (p. 51) quote studies suggesting 70% of adult learning is self-directed. Eraut (2004) claims that, in organisations, the majority of learning occurs in the workplace, not in formal training or education. For Knowles (1975), the autonomous setting of goals is a fundamental characteristic of adult learners: "One of the most significant findings from research about adult learning…is that when adults go about learning something naturally (as contrasted with being taught), they are highly self-directing" (p. 129).

The general point that education moves the learner from a position of little autonomy to one of greater autonomy seems largely unequivocal, though this is an over-simplification of a complex process.

Autonomy as a Variable Quantity

The view that autonomy as a distinct characteristic that applies in all circumstances is mistaken. While it is true that mature learners are better able to manage their own learning in some respects, this ability is highly dependent on context. As Candy (1991) rightly observers, "autonomy is not simply a personal quality or characteristic, but is a relation involving the interplay of personal and situational variables. Accordingly, any person could vary in the degree of autonomy he or she exhibits from situation to situation" (p. 113). Indeed, it is highly improbable that anyone could, *without the aid of others*, achieve accomplishment in *all* subjects that they wished to master. However, this represents a naïve view of autonomy and self-direction. A clearer definition of autonomy, that encompasses the ability to choose not to choose—to delegate control to another, is needed.

Autonomy is not necessarily a single and distinct characteristic that applies equally to the entire learning process. Candy (1991) observes, "Learner control is not, as is commonly perceived, a single dimension, but rather a complex entity involving control over multiple aspects such as objective-setting, content, method, sequence, pace and evaluation of learning outcomes" (p. 242). Candy's point is important, but not the whole story. The complexity of control lies not only in what it applies to, but at what scale or level of granularity it is applied. Also, control is not equivalent to the ability to choose, and sometimes (perhaps nearly always) control can entail the delegation of choices to another.

The Centrality of Control

With allowances for issues of context and nuances of control, it seems that the process of education may at least partly be seen as one which enables learners to make increasingly autonomous choices about what they learn next and how they do so. In fact, this can be put more strongly: It *should* be a primary goal of education to move learners from a state of dependence (not knowing what choices to make, having someone make those choices for them) to one of independence (capable of deciding where to go next, what to do, how to do it), at least within a particular field of endeavour. This flexibility of choice also implies that learners should be able to evaluate in any given circumstance whether it is wise to relinquish their freedom of choice and to allow another (whether in person or by proxy, e.g., through a book) to guide them.

Learning to be Controlled

A teacher is one who should, in an ideal world, make the learning process less painful and traumatic as well as faster and more direct than it would otherwise have been (Bruner, 1966). Unfortunately, institutional learning may often have an opposite effect. As Vaill (1996) explains:

If learning is to be a major means of restoring our understanding of the world around us, the learning process itself should not add to our feeling of meaninglessness. Yet that is precisely what the institutional model of learning tends to do as it renders the learner passive and dependent, inundates the learner with great volumes of miscellaneous subject matter presented as absolutely essential knowledge, and then erects a powerful set of extrinsic rewards and punishments to keep the learner's focus on all this jumbled and largely meaningless content. (p. 43)

Vaill is correct, but there is a fine line to be drawn here. If the objective of learning is to enable the learner to make independent choices then choice must be at the centre of all that is done to enable learning, but this does not imply that the learner should always be given absolute freedom to choose. The essential requirement must be that the *ability* to make choices should be enhanced by the educative process. As Dewey (1938) says: "The ideal aim of education is creation of power of self-control. But the mere removal of external control is no guarantee for the production of self-control." Indeed, it would be positively harmful to provide too much choice at the wrong time. Candy (1991) writes, "The unwanted side-effects of inappropriately giving learners control may include anger or loss of confidence by the learner" (pp. 67-68).

Similarly, Hill and Hannafin (2001) tell us: "Learners often express discomfort when the environment is not prescribed, especially when studying ill-defined domains in open learning environments." Dewey's formulation is a linguistic sleight of hand, however, shifting from considering control as a personal characteristic to control as the exercise of some power of the activities performed. Brockett and Heimstra (1991) clarify this common confusion by distinguishing *self-directed learning* (as a process) from *learner self-direction* (as a quality akin to learner autonomy).

The Significance of Choice

Understanding choices and how they affect the process of learning is central to the educational process. It is prior to and generative of the pedagogies and approaches that may be employed. To understand the dynamics of choices is to understand the range and scope of what is possible within an educational transaction—to reveal the perimeter of what can be achieved. Having said that, it will reveal relatively little about what should be within those borders.

The issue is not simply the fact *that* choices are made, but how much choice is available, what kind of constraints restrict choice, and the complex inter-relationships between the choices made by different agents within an educational system. The emphasis here is as much on the intensity of choices and their connections as on the choices themselves. In this sense, the choices made when setting out on a learning trajectory differ from those in other contexts. By looking at the patterns of choices, how their consequences interact or affect other choices, how frequently they are made, how much constraint is involved and so on, a picture can be formed of a sequence of educational transactions. This picture reveals the underlying similarities and differences between many apparently dissimilar activities, making it possible to differentiate between those that may be casually lumped together. Each form of learning activity or method of enabling learning will be seen to have its own distinctive signature which may be compared with those of others. For example, this perspective will help to confirm Laurillard's (1993) perhaps contentious observation that Socratic dialogue is not so far removed from the lecture form as might at first be imagined, because it involves a strong form of teacher control. It will demonstrate that there are some inherent advantages (and disadvantages) in threaded discussion forums because of the inevitable branching of conversations. In particular, it will be seen that there are some affordances of some forms of social software that provide a significantly different pattern of choice than might be available in a traditional face to face or non-electronically mediated system of education.

Is Choice Always Good?

Although the goal of education may be to produce independent, autonomous learners with a full repertoire of choice-making skills (at least within the educational area that they have studied), it is fairly clear that this is not always, or even often, the way to begin. Choice is not equivalent to control. If a learner makes choices without understanding their nature and possible consequences, then he or she is not in control. It is only possible to make wise choices if one has sufficient wisdom to make them in the first place. By definition, learners are seekers of wisdom and therefore do not necessarily have the intellectual tools at their disposal to make well-grounded decisions about their learning. As Moore (1980) writes, "A learner cannot learn effectively if the educational transaction demands more autonomy than he is able to exercise." Knowles (1975) similarly notes: "Many students enter into a new learning situation feeling a deep need for the security of a clear structural plan- an outline, course syllabus, time schedule, and the like. They want teachers who know what they are doing, who are in charge" (p. 37). This is not just a question of subject knowledge.

Choice of Pedagogy

To make effective choices, it is important to know how people learn within that subject area and what it takes for them to move from a position of legitimate peripheral participation to one of expertise and knowledge. Laurillard (1993) makes the obvious, but often missed point, "It is clearly important to base a teaching strategy on an understanding of learning." As well as this, it is necessary to know how students think, for without this "we build on sand."

If autonomy is to be relinquished, choice must be put in the hands of another. The role of the teacher (be it standing in front of a classroom, writing a book or chatting with you in the pub) must consequently include a wide range of functions that *explicitly reduce choice*.

Delegation of Choice

A further incentive to reduce choice is that choices come at a cost and involve effort. Schwartz (2004) claims: "The burden of having every activity be a matter of deliberate and conscious choice would be too much for any of us to bear" (p. 43). Even when a learner may be capable of making choices about the direction of his or her learning, it may frequently be easier and simpler not to do so. This is a crucial theme: in an ideal world, *the learner should be able to choose whether and when to choose.*

The delegation of choices can make life easier in several ways apart from reducing the effort involved. In particular, it can help reduce fear. A new subject or even a new topic within a well-known subject can be scary. Partly, this is fear of the unknown, partly a result of justifiable uncertainty about capabilities, directions, potential pitfalls and so on, that a learner might have to face when exploring this new area. It is one thing to be aware that you wish to climb Everest, another to get there and to do so without a guide would be foolhardy. Left to wander completely freely, learners may drift among the foothills or get lost in dangerous places. Equally disturbingly, even were they to reach the summit they may not realise that they have got there or, worse still, erroneously believe that they have reached it. Garrison and Baynton (1987) observe, "internal feedback alone…may lack accuracy and explicitness." When learning something new, someone who knows the landmarks (and thus guides you away from the irrelevant, the harmful, and the useless) is invaluable. There is perhaps a strange contradiction at work, a corollary to the dilemma posed by Socrates in Plato's Meno (1999):

A man cannot enquire either about that which he knows, or about that which he does not know; for if he knows, he has no need to enquire; and if not, he cannot; for he does not know the very subject about which he is to enquire.

R.D. Laing (1971) expresses not only the fact, but the internal anxiety it causes and, in some sense, the dilemma posed for the teacher:

You may know what I don't know, but not
*   that I don't know it,*
and I can't tell you. So you will have to tell me everything. (p. 56)

Laing's poem raises the interesting issue for the intrepid explorer of Everest, that he or she may not even know that the mountain exists, or might know that it is there, but be unaware of why it might be worth a visit. There is a get-out clause, which is where the role of the teacher comes in. "There is no escape from the paradox of leadership—the requirement that men should be *led* to freedom, that students be taught the autonomous style" (Little, quoted in Boud, 1981).

Learners must come to make independent choices but this is sometimes (perhaps always) only possible through a process that restricts those choices. Boud (1981) writes: "Developing autonomy does not simply involve removing structured teaching; it may require a greater degree of structure than didactic teaching, but of a different kind" (p. 25). The goal of education must be to provide the learner with the means to make his or her own choices about how and what to learn. However, for the learner to reach that point, some of those choices must be made for him or her. It is thus the art of teaching that allows the learner as much control as possible, while making the kinds of choices that will encourage greater autonomy.

Choice Does Not Equal Control

There is a strong sense in which too much choice is bad, even for those who have developed a high level of autonomy within a given context. Schwartz (2004) observes:

...more choice may not always mean more control. Perhaps there comes a point at which opportunities become so numerous that we feel overwhelmed. Instead of feeling in control, we feel unable to cope. Having the opportunity to choose is no blessing if we feel we do not have the wherewithal to choose wisely. (p. 104)

This could be represented on a graph like that shown in Figure 3.2. As the range of choices passes a certain (unspecified) point, then the amount of control diminishes.

Teaching Approaches

Several authors have tried to combine notions of choice and constraint into a single package, attempting to show that one must follow the other. For example, Reigeluth's elaboration theory demands a highly structured, teacher-sequenced set of interactions from the simple to the complex. Reigeluth and Stein (1983) believe that "only a simple-to-complex sequence can allow the learner to make an informed decision about the selection of content" (p. 363). For Reigeluth and Stein, it is the constraints

Figure 3.2. Hypothetical relationship between choice and control

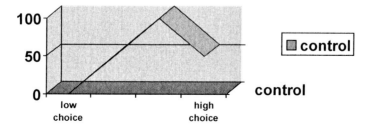

that make choice possible in the first place. A slightly different tack is taken by Allen Tough (1979), who suggests that the role of the teacher should be more like that of a consultant, providing help to autonomous learners: "The distinction between help and control is important, because it helps us to realize that a learner can receive a great deal of help without giving up any of his control or responsibility" (pp. 177-178). From this perspective, structure is provided by the learner, rather than the teacher, at least at a macro level. This is not as clear-cut as Tough suggests, for the kind of help provided by a teacher may often demand that structure will be present in the help given. The underlying theme of much of Garrison's work is that it is only through a transactional process of dialogue which combines both structure from the teacher and a constant refinement through dialogue that learners may reach a state of independence (Garrison & Anderson, 2003; Garrison & Baynton, 1987). Candy (1991) also believes in a kind of structure—one that varies with context and the needs of the learner and is designed to allow the learner to become self-directing.

How Choices May Be Made

The central dilemma at the heart of all education is that, by definition, a learner is unfamiliar with what is to be learned. He or she may not necessarily know the most appropriate path to take. Part of the process of heading into adulthood is to develop strategies and approaches to the process, but in an unfamiliar subject area, these strategies may fail. The author is the proud possessor of a PhD but, when attempting to learn an esoteric form of statistical analysis, floundered terribly, with none of his well-honed learning strategies providing preparation for this alien subject area. Despite entering it with confidence and the delightful anticipation of new discoveries, being armed with a range of Web-based and paper resources, discovering the people who could help and being fully cognisant of the intended goals, he was unable to identify the prerequisite knowledge required, the length of time it would take, and the means to identify successful outcomes in steps along the way. Without the independence, power and support identified by Garrison and Baynton, he was unable to complete the task without, eventually and after much frustration, delegating control to another.

Just as a learner may be unfamiliar with the best way to learn a given subject, a teacher may not know the most effective way to teach a particular learner. Whether or not it is agreed that learning styles are relevant, an unequivocal instance of this would be when the teacher is unaware of the learner's prior knowledge, and therefore runs the risk of boring or confusing the learner. A teacher without at least some tacit understanding of the kind of needs of learners would not be a teacher at all. Where some communication is involved, the educational process is therefore necessarily one of negotiation, although often that negotiation may be internalised or assumed. A teacher may base the sequence of learning activities on the knowledge of learners (real or assumed) and a learner may base what he or she will do next on his or her real or assumed knowledge of the teacher (or teaching presence/teacher role). This dialogic process is, at least ideally, one of constant refinement, of choices influencing other choices. To return to the author's anxiety-ridden attempts to learn statistical analysis, the process of explaining his needs to the teacher involved many questions and answers on both sides, as each explored their conceptions of the other. In any learning situation, although the learner's choices are far from autonomous and the teacher is constrained, the balance between the two ensures that a state resembling that of self-organised criticality may be achieved between them.

Is it Possible for a Learner to make Appropriate Choices without Guidance?

The Case for Guidance

Vygotsky (1978) suggests that learners have a zone of proximal development, outside their current spheres of knowledge, but not so far out that it is entirely disconnected and unattainable. Learning how to ride a motorbike is made easier if one already knows how to ride a push-bike, even simpler if one can also drive a car. If the near but unknown can be glimpsed, then it can be reached with little or no assistance. The problem is that, without a guide, the seeker of knowledge may forever wander around the foothills without ever seeing the mountain. An advantage of a teacher-structured sequence is that the teacher is (hopefully) aware of the bigger picture and of the constraints inherent in the subject matter itself. Without an overview of the ultimate levels of performance expected, a sub-optimal standard may be achieved. Alan Kay (1996) provides a graphic example of this when he describes how, if a piano is placed in a classroom but no examples are given of what might be achieved on it, the most that can be hoped for is children able to play Chopsticks with two fingers.

The Case Against Guidance

Too much guidance can militate against ever becoming an independent learner. Even where guidance is needed, it does not necessarily need to come from a formal teacher role. Wilson and Ryder (1998) recommend, somewhat contentiously, that teachers be dropped altogether:

Rather than being controlled by a teacher or an instructional designer, learners might 'self-organize' into functioning communities with a general goal of support-ing each other in their learning. That is to say, the function of guidance and control becomes distributed among group participants. Specific roles of group members are not assigned but rather emerge from the interaction of the whole.

This is not an absurd position. If learning is seen as a kind of journey, then it may be worthwhile to draw parallels with literal journeys. In a city, a traveller may catch the occasional glimpse of where he or she wishes to go and, even though he or she may not know exactly how to get there, may successfully reach the destination. He or she may do this with less precision than a local inhabitant but, nonetheless, will get there in the end. Now, imagine that two learners address the same problem. Each catches an occasional glimpse of the goal and is aware of his or her local context. Imagine, now, that each learner is able to communicate that context and orientation to the target to the other, say by cellular phone. With their different perspectives, each has a different set of choices and a different set of clues about the best way to reach their common goal. Some of this information will be irrelevant to the other, but some will help to triangulate and strengthen faith in the correct choice of paths to the destination. The greater the number of learners that contribute to this, the more accurate the knowledge of all about the map of the terrain is likely to become, and the clearer the route to the destination. Individuals may make errors and the process of collating information may be hard but, in the end, the resulting combined path might be as good (if not better) than had the route been shown by a local guide. The principle is explored more fully by Feltovich et al. (1996), who talk of *cognitive flexibility* as a means of allowing an individual to think more like a group:

Groups tend to bring different perspectives to a problem-solving situation. Thus, if an individual can begin to think like a group—with multiple perspectives, honoring complexity, this "cognitive flexibility" can help learners develop advantageous skills for thinking about complex subject matter—whether a group is present or not.

This may be more than a simple metaphor. Some networked computer systems exist that actively attempt to mimic this process, achieving effective collaborative learning without necessarily benefiting from the input of a teacher (Ackerman & McDonald, 1996; Dron, Mitchell, Siviter, & Boyne, 2000; Kurhila, Miettinen, Nokelainen, & Tirri, 2002). This kind of system provides a means of representing and generating a "group mind" or collective approach to learning that amplifies the individual choices and intentions of learners, influencing and influenced by the collective meaning generated by the group, not the individuals that form it.

Extending the metaphor of a city further, a great deal of the navigation in cities takes place because of their physical form, which, in turn, is influenced by the way that people navigate. This recursive principle underlies Hillier's (2003) space syntax theory, which demonstrates some surprisingly simple and consistent self-organising patterns within superficially dissimilar and apparently chaotic city spaces. With similarly constructed learning environments, navigation between the major landmarks and through the places of interest could become intuitive—responsive to the group that navigates there and require few maps to get around. Of course, in many ways, this analogy fails to capture the complexity of the problem. In a city, it is reasonable to suppose that all the streets between one's current position and one's destination are going to follow a recognisable and known pattern. The laws of physics are unlikely to change along the way, nor is it likely that the navigator will need to learn a different way of walking. Unlike navigation through a city, learning changes the rules as it is traversed: to learn is to change. One's mental models of reality may well be different by the end of the journey than how they were at the start. The implication of this way of thinking to the design of e-learning environments is potentially profound, perhaps suggesting that, as learners change, so should their learning environments.

Knowing when a Choice is Made

A learning trajectory represents a series of choices which are made by somebody or, more often, involves contributions by more than one agent (person, institution, computer program and so on). While it is possible to look at any historical choice in retrospect and to make a judgement about who or what was most in control at that point, identifying the level of control at any given point on a learning trajectory is harder, and quite a distinct issue. The direction of a learning trajectory is always capable of being changed radically at any moment. In a minimal sense, there are always choices available to learners (if only to stop paying attention) and thus, to some extent, it can be rightly claimed that there is always some latent control available to the learner. Equally, there are accidental, unplanned, or peripheral influences that may make more difference than any planned act of learning. Any learning trajectory is subject to a massive range of extrinsic and intrinsic influences that may change it utterly, from the massive (perhaps a nuclear explosion nearby or the death of a loved one) to the minute (perhaps a chance word, perhaps even misheard, that inspires a total rethink of everything we believe, or jogs a memory to make a connection we had not made before).

Levels of transactional control can be observed in retrospect when looking at any learning trajectory, enabling the identification of choices and who made them, and with what constraints. Unfortunately, this does not provide an infallible means to gaze at a learning situation and to identify current levels of control or to make pronouncements about choices that have not yet been made. On the other hand, in order to make those choices, it is important to be aware of the latent choices in any learning situation. The guiding principle that will be recommended as the book progresses is that, in a perfect educational environment, learners should always, and at every point, be able to choose to choose, whether to make autonomous choices or whether to have those choices made for them. In this sense, the theory makes predictions about effective ways of enabling learning to occur, but it is important to observe that, when an observer is looking at transactional control, the view will often only be accurate when looking backwards, identifying what has occurred, not what is occurring right now or what will occur in the future.

Conclusion

There is a subtle relationship between choice and control, whereby too much choice reduces control as effectively as too little. The fact that learners are, by definition, unable to make effective choices in (at least) some of the processes that might lead to learning provides a rational justification for the existence of teachers, or at least some kind of teaching presence. Under a wide range of circumstances, it is necessary to delegate some choices to others, whether directly or mediated through a book, a computer, or some other medium. In some contexts, at least, it is possible to become more capable of making relevant and effective choices; this is one measure of a mature learner.

The manner, quantity, and form of provision of choices in a learning environment are a fundamental characteristic of its behaviour. Interaction, between people making those choices, the environment and each other, allows the characterisation of a particular environment in a manner that distinguishes it from others.

If the purpose of education is to allow learners to make their own choices, then it is helpful to consider the conditions under which choices are made and how they may be guided. With that in mind, the next chapter is concerned with how choices are constrained.

References

Ackerman, M. S., & McDonald, D. W. (1996). *Answer garden 2: Merging organizational memory with collaborative help.* Paper presented at the ACM Conference on Computer-Supported Cooperative Work '96.

Boud, D. (1981). Toward student responsibility for learning. In D. Boud (Ed.), *Developing student autonomy in learning.* London: Kogan Page.

Brockett, R. G., & Hiemstra, R. (1991). A conceptual framework for understanding self-direction in adult learning. In R. G. Brockett & R. Hiemstra (Eds.), *Self-direction in adult learning: Perspectives on theory, research, and practice.* New York & London: Routledge.

Bruner, J. S. (1966). *Toward a theory of instruction.* Cambridge MA: The Belknap Press of Harvard University Press.

Candy, P. C. (1991). *Self-direction for lifelong learning: A comprehensive guide to theory and practice.* San Francisco: Jossey Bass.

Dewey, J. (1938). *Experience and education*: Macmillan Press.

Dron, J., Mitchell, R., Siviter, P., & Boyne, C. (2000). CoFIND: An experiment in n-dimensional collaborative filtering. *Journal of Network and Computer Applications, (23),* 131-142.

Eraut, M. (2004). Informal learning in the workplace. *Studies in Continuing Education, 26*(2), 247-275.

Feltovich, P. J., Spiro, R.J., Coulson, R.L., & Feltovich, J. (1996). Collaboration within and among minds: Mastering complexity, individually and in groups. In T. Koschmann (Ed.), *CSCL: Theory and practice of an emerging paradigm* (pp. 25-44). Mahwah, NJ: Erlbaum.

Garrison, D. R., & Anderson, T. (2003). *E-learning in the 21st century: A framework for research and practice.* London: RoutledgeFalmer.

Garrison, D. R., & Baynton, M. (1987). Beyond independence in distance education: The concept of control. *American Journal of Distance Education, 1*(3), 3-15.

Hill, J. R., & Hannafin, M. J. (2001). Teaching and learning in digital environments: The resurgence of resource-based learning. *Educational Technology Research and Development, 49*(4), 37-52.

Hillier, B. (2003). *The common language of space: A way of looking at the social, economic and environmental functioning of cities on a common basis.* Retrieved 12/05/03, 2003, from http://www.spacesyntax.org/publications/commonlang.html

Illich, I. (1971). *Deschooling society*. New York: Harper & Row.

Kay, A. (1996). Revealing the elephant: The use and misuse of computers in education. *The Educom Review, 31*(4).

Knowles, M. (1975). *Self-directed learning*. Chicago: Follett Publishing Company.

Kurhila, J., Miettinen, M., Nokelainen, P., & Tirri, H. (2002). *Use of social navigation features in collaborative e-learning*. Paper presented at the E-Learn 2002, Montreal, Canada.

Laing, R. D. (1971). *Knots*. Harmondsworth: Penguin Books.

Laurillard, D. (1993). *Rethinking university teaching: A framework for the effective use of educational technology*. London: Routledge.

McPherson, M., & Nunes, M. B. (2004). *Developing innovation in online learning*. London: RoutledgeFalmer.

Moore, M. G. (1980). Independent study. In R. Boyd & J. Apps (Eds.), *Redefining the discipline of adult education* (pp. 16-31). San Francisco: Jossey-Bass.

Moore, M. G. (1986). Self-directed learning and distance education [electronic version]. *Journal of Distance Education, 1*.

Plato. (1999). *Meno* (B. Jowett, Trans.).

Reigeluth, C. M., & Stein, F. S. (1983). The elaboration theory of instruction. In C. M. Reigeluth (Ed.), *Instructional-design theories and models: An overview of the current status* (pp. 335-379). Hillsdale, NJ: Lawrence Erlbaum Associates.

Schwartz, B. (2004). *The paradox of choice: Why less is more*. New York: HarperCollins.

Tough, A. (1979). *The adults learning projects* (2nd ed.). Toronto: Ontario Institute for Studies in Education.

Vaill, P. (1996). *Learning as a way of being: Strategies for survival in a world of permanent white water*. San Francisco: Jossey-Bass.

Vygotsky, L. S. (1978). *Mind in society*. London: Harvard University Press.

Wenger, E. (1998). *Communities of practice: Learning, meaning and identity*. New York: Cambridge University Press.

Wilson, B., & Ryder, M. (1998). *Dynamic learning communities*. Retrieved 10/8/2001, from http://carbon.cudenver.edu/~mryder/dlc.html

Chapter IV

All About Constraints

The more constraints one imposes, the more one frees one's self. And the arbitrariness of the constraint serves only to obtain precision of execution. (Igor Stravinsky, quoted in Simpson, 1988)

Introduction

This chapter considers the role of constraints in determining the nature of an educational transaction and examines a range of potential sources of constraint. Garrison and Baynton (1987) begin to explore this issue when addressing the concept of "power," loosely speaking, the ability to exert control over a learning transaction. Although they give some interesting examples and relate it to the other important issues of support and independence, they leave it as a fairly fuzzily defined concept. It is easy to underestimate the importance of constraints when examining control in a learning transaction, but impossible to understand control without them. A central outcome of this chapter will be to better understand the nature of constraints that are intrinsic to a system (that arise from the nature of the interactions within it) and those that are extrinsic.

The word "constraint" tends to suggest something negative, but this is not the intended usage here. Constraints often encourage people to seek innovative and creative solutions to problems and, as such, may be positive contributors to effective learning.

What is significant from the point of view of transaction control is that there *are* constraints and that they *do* help to shape the nature of the learning activities that learners engage in. The result may be liberating as much as it may be limiting.

The Limits of Choice and the Role of Constraint

There is no such thing as unconstrained choice. Choices are always made within a context. In fact, with no constraints at all, they would not really be choices: the concept of choice implies that there is a finite range of options to choose from, hence from a constrained set of possibilities. We choose *between* things.

In an educational transaction, there may be constraints imposed by a vast range of things, such as the subject matter, available space and/or time, degree of initial knowledge, personal preference, the weather or even the laws of grammar. For example, the choices that may be made when writing this sentence are not only constrained by the possible range of English words, but also by the laws of grammar and syntax that apply to them. The choice about which word to type next is considerably more constrained than the choice of subject matter or even which sentence will come next. Semantic constraints also mean that it would be highly unlikely that a sentence would be written that is completely unconnected with the subject matter that occurs in the rest of the paragraph. This trivial example is an instance of a more general rule: earlier choices will usually affect later choices. Some choices may constrain further options, while others may open up new avenues of opportunity that were not there before.

In almost all circumstances, the history of choices already made influences the choices that may be made in the present and those that might be made in the future. At the start of this book, the author could have chosen to write about anything of which he had some knowledge. Having decided to write about Moore's theory of transactional distance and its implications for the design of e-learning systems, the range of potential choices were reduced by an exponential factor. Choices may be made from many paths. Once one path is chosen it will usually reduce, but seldom eliminate, the likelihood of jumping across to a different path. Few constraints are absolute.

Choice is often a matter of degree. The fact that this paragraph began on the topic of choices does not prevent it from ending on the subject of cat breeding. The fact that you have read the words up until this point does not imply that you will continue to do so (there, you did!). However, it is far more likely that you will (having got so far) than that you will skip to the next paragraph or put the book down altogether, although it is almost certain that you will do at least one of those things at some point. In fact, the decision to read the next word is hardly a choice at all; it would generally be a far more active choice to skip to the next paragraph than to continue reading this sentence. Once a learner sets out on a trajectory, there is generally a certain amount of momentum that keeps it going in that direction and it takes an act of will and/or a loss of momentum to change. Cat breeding is about selecting traits that you wish to be reproduced in the offspring.

Virtually none of the choices that affect a learning trajectory is totally constrained (a learner can always choose to not learn) but, equally, virtually none is unconstrained. At the very least, we are prisoners of Kant's phenomenal world, limited by our perceptual and conceptual apparatus. There may or may not be a nominal world out there somewhere, but the constraints of being human mean that, of necessity, we are unable to experience it. A teacher in the most traditional (for students) choice-free environment is still constrained by the limits of his or her own knowledge, the requirements of the subject, the nature of the students, the nature of the classroom, the facilities available and so on. At the risk of being repetitive, the meaning of the word "choice" implies that there are not infinite options to choose from, but that certain paths present themselves, which may or may not be selected.

Degrees of Constraint

In all educational transactions, the degrees of choice and constraint are measured in shades of grey, not black and white. The role of a signpost is very different from the role of a fence post, but both provide constraint of some sort. To visualise this more clearly, the trajectory of learning might be modelled as a series of choices made over time, bounded by constraints, as shown in Figure 4.1. Here, within the boundaries of the possible range of choices, any number of choices may be made over a given period, but only within the area bordered by the limits of the range. The closer to the borders of the constraint area, the more constrained the choices may be.

Figure 4.1. Hypothetical chart of choice bounded by constraint

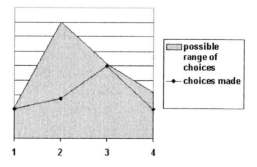

The Necessity of Constraint

Constraints are not only inevitable, but are also, in many ways, a good thing. As the quotation that opens this chapter suggests, constraints may inspire a creative response. Not only are they sometimes a good thing, in general, they are a necessary thing. Ashby (1957, pp. 131-134), for example, describes constraints as being an essential part of any complex system. In hierarchical systems, slower moving parts act as larger constraints than faster moving parts, thus playing a more formidable role in shaping the systems of which they are a part. A similar observation is made by Bateson (1972), who writes:

The principle involved here is general and by no means trivial. It obtains in all homeostatic systems in which a given effect can be brought about by means of a homeostatic circuit, which circuit can, in turn, be modified in its characteristics by some higher system of control. In all such systems (ranging from the house thermostat to systems of government and administration) it is important that the higher system of control lag behind the even sequences in the peripheral homeostatic circuit. (p. 355)

In other words, it is an essential feature of any system in which one part controls another that the more controlling element will be slower and less susceptible to change. *Constraints give shape to a system.*

The Curious Nature of Educational Systems

From the foregoing discussion, it can be seen that constraints may be intrinsic to the learning transaction or extrinsic to it. Intrinsic constraints arise out of the process of the transaction (for instance, the decision to write on a certain subject constrains the potential subject matter in the rest of this book); extrinsic constraints arise from outside it (for instance, the fact that it is impossible to read every relevant paper on the subject means that some important research may have been omitted). There are some constraints that are hard to classify and that sit on the borderline between those arising from the process and those that are extrinsic to the system. For instance, knowledge that is generated as part of an educational process, such as through dialogue or through research, may be seen as somewhat intrinsic, inasmuch as it arises out of the process. On the other hand, it equally has an existence on its own that might be considered extrinsic, changing the boundaries of the external knowledge constraints. Other constraints change as a consequence of learning. Acquired knowledge opens up new vistas and expands the boundaries of constraint.

Systems analysis frequently starts by identifying the boundaries of the system in question. Where the system continues to evolve after it is designed those boundaries may change. The fact that this is not just a feature of an educational transaction but is a defining characteristic of one makes the analysis of an educational system quite distinctive. It is a kind of deferred system, whose shape changes as the system is implemented (Patel, 2003).

Intrinsic Constraints

Intrinsic constraints are consequences of the narrative thrust of what is done to bring about learning. They arise out of the history of transactions within a given learning trajectory, or are generated as a result of the history of the series of micro-transactions within a given transaction. This is most obvious when a dialogue occurs in real-time and is sequential (i.e., only one person is speaking at a time), where there is a continuing exchange of ideas, arguments, concepts, and pleasantries. Each participant in the dialogue influences, and may often determine, the nature of the behaviour of the next. For instance, though there is certainly freedom to choose to do otherwise, the nature of conversation makes an answer the most likely response to a question. Equally, if someone says "hello," then the most likely response is also "hello." If a conversation begins about trees, then it is likely that the conversation will continue either on the same topic or on one that is somehow related. Of course, this is far from universally true or the topic of a conversation would never change.

To a large extent, what comes before acts as an important constraint on what may come after, especially in a focussed context such as that which may be found in most adult education. This is confirmed by Pena-Shaff and Nicholls (2004), who observe of the online discussion forum that formed the object of their study that:

Eighty-nine percent of the messages directly or indirectly addressed the questions or ideas presented in previous messages by agreeing to, elaborating, or debating the ideas presented, showing that students, for the most part, read and constructed their comments based on previous messages.

It is not clear to what extent this behaviour was influenced by the nature of the task itself, which is, of course, an extrinsic constraint, but it accords with the author's experience of such discussions.

In a system that is highly structured, and thus seems determined in its trajectory, the impetus provided by intrinsic constraints still affects the flow of a transaction. The fact that one word has been written immediately constrains the possible range of words that will follow, assuming some adherence to rules of grammar, syntax or semantics. If a teacher has just taught a learner how to critically evaluate a Shakespearian drama, then it is unlikely that the next step will be to evaluate an ABC primer (depending on context). In most successful learning trajectories, there is likely to be some narrative flow where what has gone before, to some extent, determines what comes after.

Extrinsic Constraints

Extrinsic constraints may take many forms and are often more obvious or tangible than those that are intrinsic. Some relate to the laws of physics, such as the amount of time available and the occasions on which a transaction may occur, or the physical space in which learning happens. Others arise from the nature of the subject. For instance, although there may be virtually limitless ways to teach the concept of a balloon, there are probably limited ways to describe one. Further constraints come from the teachers' subject knowledge, their knowledge of how learners learn, and their knowledge of the learners themselves.

There is a subtle interplay between extrinsic and intrinsic constraints at any point and it is not always clear which is predominant in forming the next choice. In the example of Shakespeare versus My First Alphabet related earlier, there is both an intrinsic and an extrinsic set of constraints at work. Extrinsic constraints occur, due to the nature of the subject matter; intrinsic constraints occur because of the logical connections between them and the likely needs of learners within the system.

Constraints are not all equal. They may be broadly split into those that are primary (without which the learning experience would be pointless) and those that are secondary (without which the learning experience would be changed, but not necessarily obliterated).

Subject Matter

There are few learning trajectories where it is not of, at least, some significance what forms the subject matter of the learning project, whether online or not. Often this will impose the most extreme constraints and limitations on how the subject is approached. For instance, there are only a few methods for learning how to spell "antidisestablishmentarianism" that make any sense at all. One might try a process of repetition, one might use the word in a variety of contexts, and one might read it a lot or write it a lot. It may be that the underlying principles for its construction could be learned so that it is assembled from its parts every time it is used. Undoubtedly, there are other approaches but, even so, there are only a finite number of possibilities.

What holds true for trivial tasks also holds true for larger projects, to a greater or lesser degree, despite the combinatorial explosion of potential avenues as a task of greater complexity is approached. Although it may be reasonable to question ways that things are taught in higher education, different disciplines have evolved different methods of teaching that are appropriate to their subjects, not all of which are a result of the intrinsic constraints (the history or the internal dynamics) of the system. If one is teaching graphic design, some medium (e.g., paper, a VDU) will be necessary and it is hard to picture an approach that does not require at least some practical exposure to drawing. Learning a musical instrument implies that the musical instrument itself should be used or at least some close approximation of it. To learn philosophy implies that some philosophical books should be read, or at least that philosophical discussions should occur, probably involving someone who knows a little about the subject. It would be odd (though, bizarrely, far from unheard of) to attempt to teach computer programming without allowing learners some access to a computer. It would be impossible to have learned to swim without having been in the water. To a greater or lesser extent, then, *what* is being taught determines *how* it may be taught.

Subject matter is, for the most part, a primary constraint. Without it, there is nothing to learn.

Context

Educational transactions are not isolated events. Each learner comes forearmed with knowledge (as well as the lack of it), preconceptions, attitudes, personal interests, and other personal constructs that affect the outcomes, often not only for the learner, but for others. Even virtual transactions occur (from a learner's perspective) in a particular time and space. The difference in the learning experience of a learner in reading a book in the middle of a busy railway station when compared with someone reading the same book on a comfortable sofa at home is likely to be very different (though there is no judgement intended here about whether one is better or worse than the other). If this were not so, then there would be no need for architects. Having said that, context is often a state of mind, which is implied or enabled by a space, an influence rather than a determining factor. In a classic experiment, subjects were divided into two groups and asked to perform some mentally taxing tasks while being subjected to loud noises and distractions. The only difference between the two groups was that the second was able to press a switch to turn off the distractions. The second group performed a great deal better than the first but (and here it becomes very interesting) *did not actually press the switch*. The control they knew that they were able to exert was enough to make a difference (Surowiecki, 2004, pp. 212-213). A similar pattern has been observed when providing students with the ability to lock their own work in a wiki-like environment, where otherwise anyone could change anyone else's creations. The simple fact that it could be done made students far happier and more trusting than in an earlier iteration of the system without that facility, despite the fact that none actually made use of it (Dron, 2005).

Temporal sequence and the precise time of delivery may be highly significant. For example, the learning experience of a new parent when reading a book on child-care will be very different indeed from that of someone for whom parenthood is not on the visible horizon. Many authors have commented on the importance of learning needs as a driver for learning and it is clear that, for learning to be optimally effective, it must relate to something that the learner wishes to achieve (Candy, 1991; Illich, 1971; Knowles, 1975; Vaill, 1996; Wenger, 1998). This is true even if that purpose is extrinsic, such as to achieve a qualification, the approval of one's peers, or to pass a test. Although learning for the love of learning is not uncommon, it works far better if there is an actual or perceived need/application for it. This is not just a quantitative but also a qualitative measurement. Where learners perceive a need that is fulfilled by their learning beyond the current application, their approach to learning is different, more focussed and intense (Dron, Mitchell, & Boyne, 2002).

Similarly, some learning needs to be achieved within a particular time frame or it will be of no use. If it took several years to learn the art of nappy-changing, then a learning trajectory that started at the moment a child was born would be of little interest or relevance to new parents.

Temporal and spatial context thus provides a significant source of constraint within a learning trajectory. However, whether it is a primary or secondary constraint depends very much upon that context.

Space

Where learning occurs in a physical space, the nature of that space can have a strong effect on the learning outcomes because of the way that it constrains behaviour. For example, Habbeshaw et al. (1987), write that "the arrangement of furniture in the classroom is probably the single most important factor in determining the success of the tutorial," going on to describe how an elevated, large or separate chair for the teacher will lead to teacher dominance, seating students in rows will discourage conversation, distance and obstructions will reduce communication, use of a board will give privilege to the custodian of information, and so on. To a large extent, this accords with common sense, but the nature of space as a means of liberating or constraining, is not always an obvious or direct relationship.

Space as an Enabler of Learning: The Peckham Experiment

Goodwin (1994) writes of the Peckham experiment, which revolved around "The Centre," a club set up in 1926 to improve community health in disadvantaged areas. Initially, the experimenters set up a swimming bath, a gymnasium, and a theatre, then grouped children by age and allocated times in the facilities for each group. The scheme failed, with few children actually turning up. Success only came when the facilities were made available to the children so that they could turn up individually when they wished. The children did not want to use the facilities in a context of teaching and learning like that found in schools, with instructors in control, but this raised concerns about safety. To prevent drowning, a degree of order was returned by an ad hoc system of chits issued by staff, who would verify that a child was a capable swimmer. A system evolved, through a cycle of action and response, between the staff and the children. This bottom up approach organised itself far more effectively than the designed system imposed from above, through a combination of enlightened staff and an effective process. However, significantly, even then it might not have succeeded were it not for a fortuitous building design. Goodwin (ibid) quotes an account by Sean Creighton (a member of staff at the Centre):

The design of the building was a revelation. That alone was, in my opinion, the master key to the liberation I have referred to. Although primarily designed to facilitate the doctors' observations, the open plan and windows through which the main activities could be viewed, gave members the unique opportunity to move about the building, to watch others enjoying themselves, and to be tempted to join in and have a go themselves.

The Peckham experiment provides compelling evidence that the environment can strongly influence educational outcomes. It is significant that the open plan design of the centre allowed learners to see each other and that this affected their behaviour, a fact that will be returned to later when considering approaches to the design of e-learning environments. As has already been noted, education is an inherently social activity in which the behaviour of others can have a strong influence on one's own behaviour.

Space and the Inhibition of Learning

As much as it can positively influence learning, space can inhibit and constrain. It is probably obvious that much conventional education would be more difficult in, say, total darkness, a very confined space, or in the presence of loud and distracting noises, if only because it would limit the ability to communicate (though it raises some interesting issues regarding the accessibility of education to those with sight or hearing impairment). To a greater or lesser extent, this kind of constraint may operate in many settings. A tiered lecture theatre provides little affordance for class discussions when compared with a circular layout of chairs, small desks will limit the ability of learners to produce large drawings, and poor air conditioning or heating will reduce the ability of learners to concentrate.

Unpleasant surroundings may reduce the potential for creativity and sap the motivation from even the hardiest learner. On the other hand, as with many things, a high level of constraint can inspire creative solutions to what would otherwise not be problems, often leading to innovative ways of learning and teaching. The Peckham Experiment shows how positive features of a space can open up new opportunities but, equally, the negative features can lead to innovation. For example, the tiered nature of lecture theatres has inspired approaches such as pyramiding, which turns out to be a highly effective way of involving a large group in constructing and generating knowledge as well as encouraging participation without much threat, and there can be little doubt that the theatre-like construction of such environments has led to some inspired performances over the centuries, albeit perhaps the minority (Laurillard, 1993).

Virtual spaces can operate in much the same way as physical spaces. Indeed, the control of the system designer is often far greater than in a physical space. Not only does the designer constrain the types of actions that can be performed, he or she may also constrain the process itself through programmatically responding to inhabitants of the space according to set rules.

Depending on context and circumstances, space may be seen as a primary or a secondary constraint. Certain characteristics may be essential for some forms of learning: a space to gather if a learning community is required or a space to perform experiments or activities if that is the need. Other characteristics may be secondary in some contexts. While it may change the character of learning to read if the lighting is dim, it does not make it impossible. If there is no lighting at all, it becomes significantly more difficult.

Power

The relationship between learner and teacher is often one where power is a significant factor. For instance, Berne's (1968) transactional analysis sees a complex range of possible power relationships, characterised by the roles of parent, child and adult, each of which exists in a different relationship of control to the others. Although this book is not especially concerned with issues of psychology, it is interesting to note that people may play a range of roles which place them in positions of dependence, control or independence, depending on the nature of their relationships with other individuals.

Even in the relatively equalising environment of an asynchronous discussion forum, the teacher occupies a special place, as the expert and moderator of proceedings, reinforced by status within the community and years of schooling where the relationship between pupil and teacher is anything but equal. This means that the kinds of constraint that operate in an environment where a teacher is present are determined disproportionately by the tacit or explicit power embodied in the teacher. To a significant extent, then, the potential choices within an environment dominated by a teacher are determined by the nature of the student-teacher relationship. The way this operates may be as restrictive to the teacher as to the learner, demanding the fulfillment of expectations and norms of behaviour.

Other sorts of restrictions based on relationships between individuals may be similarly constraining. For instance, it is not only commonplace but desirable that users of mediated communication systems adhere to some form of etiquette, prescribing what is and is not acceptable behaviour within a community. Face to face relationships may intrude into those online, for better or worse, altering the dynamic of the community and consequently affecting choice. For example, a learning community that discusses work in a pub may well contribute less to discussions when compared with those who only communicate electronically (Dron, Seidel, & Litten, 2004).

Even in the absence of a predefined set of power relationships, constraints imposed by temporal precedence can have a large effect on the behaviour of a group and establish a dynamic hierarchy. For example, it has been demonstrated in meetings that those who speak early on in the proceedings have a disproportionately large influence on the agenda and decisions of the group, and those that speak more are more influential than those who do not, even when they are clearly wrong (Surowiecki, 2004, pp. 186-187).

Cost

While there is a general consensus that one-to-one teaching represents some kind of ideal, it is rarely found in the wild due to its high cost, together with the lack of adequate teaching resources (which is what drives up the cost in the first place). Until recently, computers in universities were a scarce resource, though (in developed nations) they are rapidly becoming an almost ubiquitous accessory owned by nearly every student. Nonetheless, they remain expensive and, for those from poorer backgrounds, often unattainable. In the third world, despite initiatives such as One Laptop Per Child project (http://laptop.org/), the cost of computers puts them out of reach to all but a few. Within the past five years, the author has taught computer-related subjects to students from developing nations who had never touched a computer before, let alone used one. Most universities are constantly balancing the demands of good teaching with an insufficient stream of income. Buildings and classrooms are too small, equipment is expensive to maintain, there are too few teachers, and it is a constant battle to provide a high quality educational experience within a restricted budget. There can be no doubt that economic constraints exert a heavy influence on the ways that subjects can be taught.

Time

Time constraints can operate in several ways, broadly relating to how much time is available, when an educational transaction occurs, and how long it may take to perform.

Amount of Time Available

Within the United Kingdom, the percentage of learners in higher education has risen from less than ten percent of the eligible population in the 1960s to approaching fifty percent in the 2000s. As the population of learners in higher education continues to grow at a rate unmatched by central funding, they become increasingly self-resourcing. In some full-time courses, the majority of students are working in part-time or even full-time jobs. The time left for study is relatively limited. Even were that not the case, constraints on the availability of tutors, and even the number of waking hours in a day, will, at some point, act as a barrier to further learning.

Constraints on when an Activity may Occur

The constraints of time tables and schedules can significantly limit potential interactions in a face-to-face or in a synchronous e-learning environment. This is an inevitable feature of a system where many people with different needs and demands on their time are required to coordinate their activities, especially when (as in much e-learning) activities must be scheduled across time zones.

Some learning activities *must* be performed at particular times. For example, at least part of the process of learning astronomy will need to occur at night—indeed, it must be a *clear* night. Other activities *ought* to be performed at particular times. Assuming that learners are following a traditional sleeping pattern, it is generally the case that it would be better to schedule activities for the day than for the night, but this can vary. For example, the work performed by many distance learners is often constrained to nights and weekends.

Time That an Activity Takes to Perform

Some learning activities operate over a constrained period because of their intrinsic structure. For example, continuing scientific experiments (e.g., those involving the study of the growth of plants) or drama classes (where the date of the performance may determine the schedule of rehearsals). However, there is a certain amount of time that will be required for any activity, which will constrain how it may be performed, whether it is the time required for reading a book, writing a paper, or even holding a discussion.

Temporal constraints may thus be seen as limits affecting the overall amount of time available and the particular period of available time, balanced with the time required to complete an activity.

Personal Traits

There are many aspects of a learner or a teacher that will help to determine the course of a learning trajectory, some of which are intellectual, some emotional, some related to social capacities (Lynch & Dembo, 2004). All of these factors are subject to change and are likely to be changed simply by engaging in a learning activity. While in some ways, they are extrinsic, they are capable of being diminished by the process itself and therefore might be considered, at least to some extent, intrinsic.

Abilities and Capabilities

Although many skills and capabilities including the capacity to learn itself may be learned, people do not all learn at the same rate or with the same innate abilities. Even for the gifted, there is inevitably a gap between current knowledge and that sought to attain, and experience is a significant factor affecting the ability to learn more. Also, whether or not Gardner's notion of multiple intelligences is plausible (Gardner, 1983), gifts are seldom equally distributed. We all have different knowledge and talents that are stronger in one area than another. When these constraints on individuals are combined into a group, it is possible to see two potential outcomes. Either the gifted and experienced will help the weak and inexperienced, or the weak and inexperienced will limit the potential activities of the gifted and experienced.

Emotions and Attitude

Engagement with learning requires motivation and a desire to learn. Any engagement with the world comes with an attitude, and that attitude affects perceptions, interactions, imaginative engagement, and learning. It is significant that, among the key factors sought by the English Higher Education Academy when choosing its National Teaching Fellows, a central characteristic is considered to be the ability to inspire. This is often one of the things that is most often identified when recalling the "best" teachers (though whether or not this should be perceived to be so significant is open to question). There can be little doubt that a lack of interest or a positive antipathy to learning is a major constraint that inevitably limits the success of a learning activity.

Autonomy

While transactional control theory considers autonomy to be a relative and contextually situated trait that fluctuates constantly as a learner moves along a learning trajectory, it is nonetheless true that some learners are, or have become, more autonomous than others, at least within a range of contexts. This is as much a psychological trait as it is a consequence of learning. The need or desire for independence plays a significant role in determining an individual's learning trajectory.

A Model of Constraints

The foregoing paragraphs describe a number of ways in which constraints can operate to influence the trajectory of a learner in pursuit of education. It is unlikely that the taxonomy provided is complete, but some generalisations may be made: it is at least possible to characterise constraints as arising primarily from within the subject itself and externally to it. These two poles of constraint might be labelled as *context* (including the spaces, the resources, other people, learning styles, prior knowledge, the time, and so forth) and *content* (what is to be learned and the narrative drive and history within the learning transaction). Even these poles admit to exceptions, where the two cannot easily be separated. For example, if the process of reflection is important, then the context will, to a large extent, form part of the content.

Accepting that there may be exceptions, a spectrum of constraints might be mapped on two axes, intrinsic-extrinsic and context-content, providing a constraint space, similar to that shown in Figure 4.2.

Within any educational transaction, the overall pattern of constraint will result from the interplay of these different kinds of constraint.

Examples of Patterns of Constraints, Online and Face-to-Face

Of the four axes of constraint, the most fixed in any learning transaction is typically the content. The main decisions about content may be made by the learner (who has the learning need) or the teacher (who may better understand interim steps needed to achieve learning goals). Alternatively, the choice may be made by an external entity such as an examination board, a university, an employer or a school, which may control the curriculum. Whether learning online or not, there may be little difference between the effects of this kind of constraint, although the vast wealth of resources on the Web may provide a greater range of choices as to which resources are used to provide that content.

In a traditional face-to-face educational environment, context is often similarly inflexible. The limitations of time tables (tutor and student) and physical space, combined with assorted systems and processes that accompany the typical implementation of formal teaching or training, often make it more difficult to vary the context than may be desirable.

In principle, context may become far more flexible in an e-learning environment, at least when delivered asynchronously. Learners may often choose the time and place that they engage with the learning activity. Even though they may have limited control over how long it will take, they may have some control over the pacing.

Figure 4.2. Constraint-space

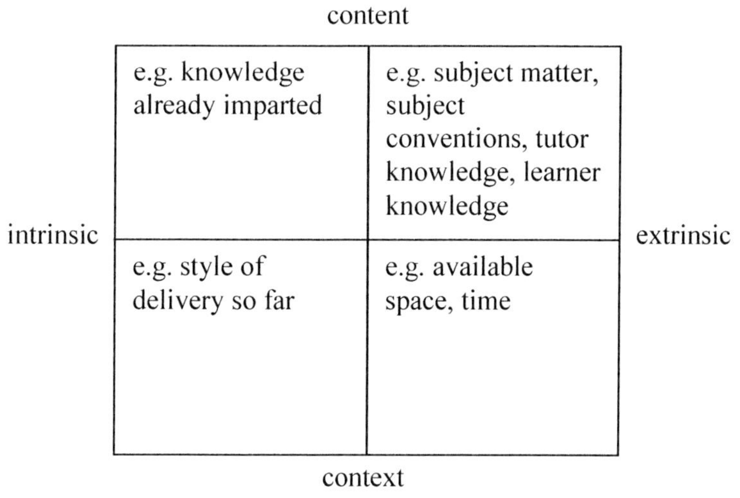

	content	
intrinsic	e.g. knowledge already imparted	e.g. subject matter, subject conventions, tutor knowledge, learner knowledge	extrinsic
	e.g. style of delivery so far	e.g. available space, time	
	context	

The most interesting potential for a virtual environment for learning is that it is itself far more plastic and malleable than physical space—the computer is the medium and tool as well as the environment. Through e-learning, it is therefore possible for the context to actively shift, playing a role in changing both the intrinsic and extrinsic constraints that affect a learning transaction as well as helping to determine appropriate content. A learning environment may adapt to the learner's changing needs and abilities, altering not only the content, but the structure of the environment itself. More interestingly, the environment may be transformed through the interactions of many users, each contributing in ways that will benefit all. A simple example of this may be seen in the development of a wiki such as Wikipedia® (http://www.wikipedia.org), an environment that both shapes (by offering structured knowledge to help learners to learn) and is shaped by its inhabitants. This potential affordance is central to the promise of e-learning and will be returned to in part three, but for now it may be informative to imagine a learner who is trying to learn about cat breeding, first through a traditional class at an institution of higher education, then through Wikipedia.

Learning at a Higher Education Institution

At the traditional university, there are constraints on space and time: the needs of the time table and the availability of teaching staff and the number of students enrolled require a lecture theatre to be booked. This, in turn, constrains (perhaps not too strongly) the kinds of teaching that may be conducted in that space. The teacher's abilities offer further constraints, while the large class size limits the direct knowledge she may have of her students, requiring her to consider a wider range of abilities and interests than would be optimal for any individual in the class, perhaps leading to some being confused and some being bored. The narrative that she devises is, to an extent, self-determining, and to some extent, limited by the subject itself. A high-level overview of the constraint space might look similar to Figure 4.3, where the shaded area represents many constraints on behaviour in all areas.

Learning through Wikipedia®

The learner who decides to use Wikipedia is able to decide when and where to engage with the content. Having some knowledge of the subject, the learner is able to spot a minor error on the page and correct it. Although the information provided is helpful, the learner is puzzled by the term "infrasubspecific" but it is hyperlinked, so he or she goes on to learn abut what it means, thus, extending the content available to him or her. The learner explores a range of cat breeds, but is not entirely happy that he or she knows enough about the subject to start a trade in cat breeding. Luckily, there is a link to the Cat Fanciers Association, where the learner is able to learn more, as well as to make connections with a community of cat fanciers, many of whom are keen to help clarify some of his or her confusions and answer his or her questions. Unlike the real environment, the virtual space is not limited to a particular group at a particular place and time. A high-level overview of the constraint space might look similar to Figure 4.4, where constraints are limited mainly to content. Even then, hyperlinking reduces the intrinsic content constraints because it allows branching at many points. The wealth of resources that may be linked reduces the extrinsic constraints. The malleability of the space makes the context a shifting and adaptable quantity.

Figure 4.3. Hypothetical constraint-space for traditional learning

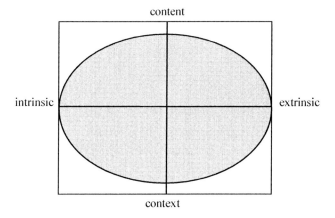

Figure 4.4. Hypothetical constraint-space for wiki-learning

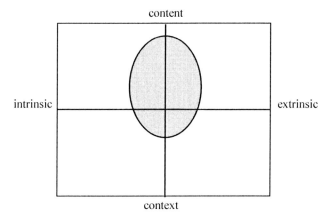

Of course, these examples are only caricatures. The face-to-face classroom would be peopled with other learners who might form a close knit and flexible community, perhaps meeting for drinks after the class. The teacher may well respond and adapt to subtle body language cues from the students, as well as direct questions to offer control to learners. The Wikipedia site may prove to be unreliable, or lacking in important information (though this would be compensated for by the other linked communities). Despite useful signposting, the limited constraints of the wiki approach would also come at a cost, most notably in the responsibility that must be taken by the learner for the choices made, especially bearing in mind the fact that the wiki is organised as an encyclopedia, not as a site intended to help learners.

These examples are merely illustrations of a general principle: online learning can change the nature of constraint in a learning transaction. Finding ways to ensure that the experience is better must wait for a later chapter.

Conclusion

In this chapter, a range of constraints have been discussed and some of the ways that they can broadly or precisely shape learning activities have been examined. Some constraints arise out of and are intrinsic to the process itself, while others are extrinsic limiting factors. These can loosely be categorised as context- or content-related. Educational systems are intended to bring about change. Virtual environments offer the possibility that, as a result, they are themselves changed.

So far, all that has been established is the fact that a learning trajectory *can* be shaped, and that its shape is determined by a wide range of factors. This tells us little about the extent to which it can be shaped; it says nothing of the significant aspects that should be shaped, nor about the effects of doing so. The next chapter addresses this problem and, in so doing, provides the final component of transactional control theory. The chapter is concerned with the central importance of scale and, in particular, begins to show what levels of temporal, physical, and conceptual scale might be appropriate to use when looking at or attempting to influence an educational trajectory.

References

Ashby, W. R. (1957). *An introduction to cybernetics*. London: Chapman & Hall.

Bateson, G. (1972). *Steps to an ecology of mind*. London: Chicago Press.

Berne, E. (1968). *Games people play: The psychology of human relationships.* Harmondsworth: Penguin.

Candy, P. C. (1991). *Self-direction for lifelong learning: A comprehensive guide to theory and practice.* San Francisco: Jossey Bass.

Dron, J. (2005). *A succession of eyes: Building an e-learning city.* Paper presented at the E-Learn 2005, Vancouver, Canada.

Dron, J., Mitchell, R., & Boyne, C. W. (2002). *Evaluating assessment using n-dimensional filtering.* Paper presented at the e-Learn 2002, Montreal, Canada.

Dron, J., Seidel, C., & Litten, G. (2004). Transactional distance in a blended learning environment. *ALT-J, 12*(2), 163-174.

Gardner, H. (1983). *Frames of mind: The theory of multiple intelligences.* New York: Basic Books.

Garrison, D. R., & Baynton, M. (1987). Beyond independence in distance education: The concept of control. *American Journal of Distance Education, 1*(3), 3-15.

Goodwin, B. (1994). *How the leopard changed its spots*: Phoenix Giants.

Habbeshaw, S., Habbeshaw, T., & Gibbs, G. (1987). *53 interesting things to do in your seminars and tutorials.* Bristol: Technical and Educational Services.

Illich, I. (1971). *Deschooling society.* New York: Harper & Row.

Knowles, M. (1975). *Self-directed learning.* Chicago: Follett Publishing Company.

Laurillard, D. (1993). *Rethinking university teaching- a framework for the effective use of educational technology.* London: Routledge.

Lynch, R., & Dembo, M. (2004). The relationship between self-regulation and online learning in a blended learning context [electronic version]. *The International Review of Research in Open and Distance Learning*, 5. Retrieved July 26, 2006 from http://www.irrodl.org/index.php/irrodl/article/view/189/271.

Patel, N. (2003). Deferred system's design: Countering the primacy of reflective IS development with action-based information systems. In N. Patel (Ed.), *Adaptive evolutionary information systems* (pp. 1-29). Hershey, PA: Idea Group Publishing.

Pena-Shaff, J. B., & Nicholls, C. (2004). Analyzing student interactions and meaning construction in computer bulletin board discussions. *Computers and Education*, (42), 243-265.

Simpson, J. B. (Ed.). (1988). *Simpson's contemporary quotations: The most notable quotes since 1950, compiled by James B. Simpson.* Boston: Houghton Mifflin Company.

Surowiecki, J. (2004). *The wisdom of crowds*. London: Little, Brown.

Vaill, P. (1996). *Learning as a way of being: Strategies for survival in a world of permanent white water*. San Francisco: Jossey-Bass.

Wenger, E. (1998). *Communities of practice: Learning, meaning and identity*. New York: Cambridge University Press.

Chapter V

Scale

You certainly can't always look at things from someone else's point of view. For instance, from here, that looks like a bucket of water...but from an ant's point of view, it's a vast ocean, from an elephant's, just a cool drink, and to a fish, of course, it's home. So you see, the way you see things depends a great deal on where you look at them from. (Juster, 1962)

Introduction

Candy (1991) deduces from the literature that there is a qualitative difference between learner-control and autodidaxy. Learner-control is "concerned with the devolution by educators, and acceptance by learners, of responsibility for valued instructional functions within recognisable teaching/learning situations" (p. 127), which is clearly the tradition in which this book lies. Autodidaxy, on the other hand, is concerned with "learning projects that people undertake on their own initiative, without any formal institutional structures or support" (ibid). Autodidacts select the goals, the methods and the resources themselves. For Candy, this makes the two issues quite distinct. This chapter provides an alternative view, suggesting that both lie on the same continuum and that the apparent differences are not matters of kind, but matters of scale.

This chapter is concerned with choosing an appropriate scale for looking at educational transactions and, particularly, the points where learning trajectories may change. It will be seen that perspective makes a great deal of difference to how a transaction or series of transactions is modelled, and that scale operates at a number of levels including the spatial, the temporal, and the conceptual. The intention is to reach a point that will enable the identification of what kind of choices in a learning trajectory are significant and what are not, and at what scales. These crucial finishing touches to the theory of transactional control enable the theory to shed light on teaching and learning practices and, perhaps, to generate new ideas and approaches.

Choice and Scale

Transactional control has been defined as relating to the choices of tasks or activities that are intended to bring about learning. Earlier chapters have shown how such choices are subject to constraint, but which of the myriad of choices that might be considered to affect a learning trajectory are significant has yet to be determined. Some choices are big ("Should I commit to a four-year degree?") and some are small ("Should I read the next word of this sentence?"). If all choices were significant and consciously made, then we would be drowned under a sea of endless possibilities. We would, perhaps, be unable to make any choices at all. Therefore, it is important to discover the appropriate scale at which significant learning choices may be made.

Smaller Choices are Usually More Deterministic

A general feature of the small choices is that they have a tendency to be more deterministic and constrained than the big ones. For example (although other choices are frequently made), in general, little consideration is given to the choice about whether to skip to the next word of a sentence. Slightly more consideration is given to the choice about moving from one sentence to the next, more still for a paragraph, a chapter, a section, volume, a book. Perhaps it would be more accurate to talk of conscious or intentional choices in this respect—it may be that unconscious or habitual choices are made at every scale, but they are not significant efforts to engage in a distinct learning trajectory, nor even, in any meaningful sense, a part of one. Although there is no *a priori* reason why the same degree of autonomy may be exercised at every level of scale, life would quickly become unbearably complex were people to do so. We avoid making too many choices, perhaps because each represents a certain quantum of work and it would be exhausting and emotionally draining to treat every minute movement or even thought as something requiring conscious choice.

Smaller Choices are Usually Easier

Smaller choices are generally easier to make, being more constrained and less emotionally charged. Some interestingly oblique proof of this can be found in a paper by Karampiperis and Sampson (2004); their intention was to investigate the effectiveness of an automated analysis of ontologies and appropriate metadata as a means of sequencing learning objects. The process by which they attempted to evaluate the effectiveness of their approach was to make use of an existing ontology and to compare their automated approach with sequences generated by an expert using the same ontology. The interesting feature of their results is that success was significantly greater when looking at small scale interactions (topics) than at large scale interactions (areas), with those in the middle (units) lying somewhere in between. In other words, choice at a small scale is considerably easier than choice at a large scale, because more constraints operate to limit potential freedom. Small choices are easier than large ones, not just because of their emotional connotations, but because of their innate simplicity.

Consequences are not Necessarily Related to Scale

A hierarchy of scale is not necessarily a hierarchy of importance, nor of consequences. A choice to continue walking when that takes a person into the path of an oncoming vehicle may turn out to have enormous consequences, though the choice was small. Perhaps it would be more accurate to suggest that the choice was easy. Indeed, one means of differentiating the significant from the insignificant choices might be that those points where significant choices are made may be defined as those where making the choice is harder than the choice to continue along the same path.

A Hierarchy of Choice

In an educational context, a hierarchical scale of choices is highly significant. For example, at a structural level, the decision to take a course may be made with relative autonomy (recognising that this is highly context dependent and may not be the case at all). Having made that choice, the decision as to whether or not to attend specific lessons is easier (i.e., more constrained) than the choice about whether to take the course in the first place.

Having decided to attend a lesson, what happens next is very dependent on context. If it is, say, a traditional lecture, the learner may well relinquish any of the choices he or she will make over the next hour or so, apart from whether or not to pay attention. However, even here, there are few shades of black and white to be found. For example, most lecturers will be influenced to some extent by the yawns of their audience (though sadly this is not universally true). A more extreme example of teacher control might be where learners are expected to watch a television programme. Even in this case, there may be occasions where some internalised dialogue is encouraged (Moore & Kearsley, 1996) and, from an individual perspective, different choices may be made by different viewers (for instance whether to agree or disagree with a hypothesis). However, such choices are not usually significant from the point of view of transactional control as they are not directly involved in influencing the *tasks* undertaken in order to learn. Control almost always implies action of some sort. When considering transactional control, the issue is one of control over the *activities* of learners, not their *attitudes* (although teachers should hope that there will be a causal relationship of some sort between the two, probably working both ways).

In a discussion-led tutorial or seminar, the learner may well have more input into the process and will often be expected to at least consider making more choices than a learner in a more passive role. As each participant makes a point or responds to a question or assertion, he or she (at least to some extent) determines the shape of the ensuing discussion, opening up some new options and closing down others. Even for those who do not take an active role, the simple fact that they are able to do so qualitatively affects their attitudes and approaches to the activity.

Density/Frequency of Choices

Depending on the scale that it is looked at, and from whose perspective, there may be a greater or lesser *density* of choices over a given period. In the discussion environment, many choices may be made, by all participants, which may shape the choices of all the others. These will, typically, occur frequently, perhaps with every statement or question any participant may make. In a less interactive system, the range of choice available to any individual may be lower, although, as the case of the television presentation shows, for at least one individual, (the instructor) the choices may be far greater.

Pacing

The number and range of choices available is important, but it is also important to look at *when* those choices are made. Pacing matters. Choice over the rate at which changes in a learning trajectory occur may make all the difference between successful learning and disillusionment. If pacing is too fast or too slow, the learner will be frustrated, bored, stressed, or otherwise disadvantaged. There is little that is more certain to put a learner off a subject than to get too much at once, unless it is getting too little.

The degree of choice over the learning activities is important, but it is also necessary to examine the choices about *when* those choices can be made. For example, an asynchronous discussion forum which takes place over a period of a week or more may present many choices as to when a contribution can be made, whereas a face to face seminar requires choices to be made more or less instantaneously in response to the flow of dialogue. Indeed, it is one of the oft-touted benefits of asynchronous discussion forums that they provide the learner with an opportunity to reflect and consider the responses that are given (Pena-Shaff & Nicholls, 2004), an opportunity to mull. The choice as to whether to engage in a particular area of study may be one that remains latent over a period of years, while the choice to answer a formal exam question usually relates to a period of hours or even minutes. Pacing is also significant as it determines the amount of structure in an educational transaction. Garrison and Baynton (1987) argue that the faster the pacing, the greater the structure. Because of the direct mapping between transactional distance and transactional control, it follows that a major consequence of this will be less control for the learner.

In a traditional educational environment, pacing is often determined by the teacher, who generally decides when and how things may be learned. Disturbingly, tutors will commonly post a fixed set of objectives and a rigid timetable for this, implying that feedback from learners is completely irrelevant to their teaching. This level of control sends strong messages to learners, undermining any autonomy that they may have already developed. However, even in institutional learning, the learner is often given some control over pacing, in which the teacher's role may be to provide the limits of constraint. For example, while the teacher may provide a framework for pacing in the setting of assessments, the framework may be used by learners to control their own pacing within that timeframe. As Garrison and Anderson (2003) put it: "Successful students most often rely on assessment deadlines to both pace and direct their learning efforts." Similarly, although teachers may be in control of the pacing of typical lectures, the spaces between lectures may often be free of such constraint, even if not over the content of learning activities.

Just as scale is important when considering choices of actions to take and the rate at which they occur, so it is significant when choosing when they are to be made.

At What Scale?

Holland (1998) tells us: "To build a dynamic model we have to select a level of detail that is useful, and then we have to capture the laws of change at that level of detail" (p. 45).

The objective of this inquiry is to discover something about educational systems and to find a suitable dynamic model to describe them. It would therefore be useful to be aware of the level of scale that is most appropriate to use when considering the role of choice in educational transactions. Educational systems may be viewed at a wide range of different scales. This is true, not only of choices in learning, but of the nature of learning itself. Looi (2001) describes it thus:

Learning happens at a rich diversity of levels in the learning environment and can be seen from different perspectives. At the individual level, learning happens at the cognitive level. At the group level when the individual learns with peers, interactions take place at the species level as group, peer or social learning interactions. When different species or populations coexist, there is a thriving community. Different communities form a learning ecosystem in which there is interaction within and between each level giving ecosystems complex behaviour.

If scale is so important, it is necessary to identify what scale is most appropriate to use when viewing a learning trajectory. Smaller scale choices are more constrained while, by and large, the reverse is true for bigger choices.

The Fractal Nature of Control

The measurement of transactional control is highly dependent on the degree of detail at which any learning trajectory is viewed. In some senses an educational transaction resembles the fractal coastline of a country, where the greater the level of detail that is chosen to include, the larger the measured size of the coastline will be (Gleick, 1988). At each level of magnification, more and more detail becomes visible.

What looked like a smooth curve at one magnification looks craggy and reticulated at another. In the case of the coastline, it would be possible to increase the scale up to the point of measuring individual atoms or beyond, but this is probably not true of transactional control in education. However, it is certainly possible to measure the interplay of choice and constraint from the largest scale (perhaps an individual's life-choices) to the finest (an individual word or maybe even a letter). This is represented in Figure 5.1, which shows a hypothetical illustration of a segment of a learning trajectory.

Systems in nature as well as man-made environments exhibit a similar characteristic, whereby scale is the main determining factor in how a system is viewed.

The Large and Slow vs. the Small and Fast

Brand (1997) observes that the larger scale, slower changing elements of an ecosystem or a city are more significant in determining a system's character than those

Figure 5.1. A hypothetical learning trajectory from close-up and afar

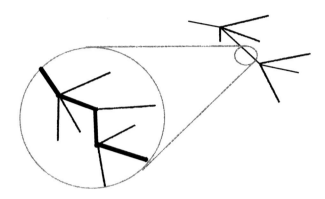

that operate at a smaller, faster scale. For instance, the shape of a street constrains the potential range of forms of the houses on it (and changes less frequently); the shape of the houses constrains the possible configuration of rooms (and changes less frequently); the rooms constrain the faster changing furnishings and decorations, which in turn, constrain the behaviour of the people who inhabit them. The geography of a landscape will determine the kinds of organisms that comprise its inhabitants, while the larger, slower changing of these (trees for example) will usually have a greater effect on the smaller, faster, changing inhabitants (e.g., the insects) which will in turn affect those that live with them or inside them. This is not to suggest that either could exist without the other, merely that the large dictates the scope for the small more than vice versa.

Darwin (1872) explains much of evolution in terms of the generally slow moving continents that drift and separate and reform as a relentless slow structure determining the changes in their faster changing inhabitants. At any scale within a given hierarchy, there will be dependencies which feed up and down the hierarchy, with the fast often (eventually) affecting the slow but with the slow dominating the nature of change. For a microbe, the gut of a fly is a structural feature, a defining control on its possible forms of existence. Jones (1999) observes: "Any zoology text claims that there are more kinds of insects than of anything else; but squash a fly and thousands of microbes unknown to science will be squeezed from its gut." For a redwood tree, the make-up of the land itself and the weather systems arising from the movements of the sun and moon play a more important structural role. For the plants that grow around the redwood and the creatures that feed on them, the redwood dominates the landscape, literally and figuratively.

There are perhaps exceptions that prove the rule, such as the effects of locusts or army ants on an environment although, even here, the individual ant or locust is largely irrelevant. In any complex system, the relationship works both ways to a greater or lesser extent, but in general there is a hierarchy of scale that moves from the slowest changing to the fastest, the largest to the smallest. This underpins one of the key foundations on which the book depends—that structure influences behaviour. A big choice, such as to learn to become a doctor, immediately constrains the possible universe of smaller choices that might be made to achieve that goal. To actively attend a lesson curtails the possible options that might have presented themselves at different lessons. At each level of scale, the constraints imposed by the scales above accumulate, inevitably, making choices easier because there are fewer of them. The effects of the big on the small is a theme that will be returned to repeatedly.

The Large and Small in Institutional Learning

A hierarchy of scale is easily discernible within traditional institutional learning. For instance, the shape of a classroom (slow moving) determines the potential layouts of the desks (faster), which in turn, determines the ways that learners within the classroom may interact (faster still). Similarly, a government may make legislation (large scale), which affects regional authorities (smaller scale), which affect heads of schools (smaller still), which affect teachers in classrooms (smaller), which in turn affect the learner (smallest).

The fact that educational systems and the choices made within them can be observed at many different scales makes meaningful measurement of such systems as difficult as obtaining an accurate measurement of the size of a coastline. If educational choices exhibit similar characteristics then, to some extent, any attempts to measure the relative amounts of choice and constraint within any educational transaction with precision are doomed to failure, or at least would be too costly and time consuming to discover. But is such an accurate measurement necessary or even desirable?

Choosing the Scale

If it is impractical to consider *all* possible choices within a learning trajectory (including the choice of the learning trajectory itself), it is important to consider the scale at which they *should* be viewed. If it is true that the larger, slower changing choices are more significant in shaping a learning trajectory than the small ones, then it is necessary to look first to the larger scale choices.

Really Big Choices

An interesting feature of larger educational/learning choices is that it seems that the biggest ones of all are often taken without the aid of a teacher. Although counsellors exist who will happily take on the mantle of advisor when people seek assistance with career choices, the largest decisions about, say, whether to begin a course of study, are seldom made with the assistance of a teacher, or at least, not with one whose role is to teach what choices to make under these circumstances. This is a peculiar fact. It seems self-evident that such choices are among the most important that an individual will make with regard to their own education, yet they are frequently left in the hands of those who, by definition (or they would not be needing to consider a course of study in the first place) are unfamiliar with the ramifications of their choices. There are three plausible explanations for this:

1. They need help but no one has thought to give it.
2. Help is already being given in the guise of something else.
3. They do not need help as, in this respect, they are sufficiently autonomous learners to make the decisions themselves.

Option 1: Learners Need Help but No One has Thought to Give It

The first of these options is sometimes the case. Career advisors might be considered as specialist career teachers and, indeed, the kinds of personality and aptitude tests, guided reading, personal tutorial (or interview), and so on, that characterise the process, have much in common with aspects of traditional teaching. However, it is often the case that they are dealing with a clearly formed conception that simply needs directing. Thus, although the role may be seen as a kind of teaching, it is a stripped bare variation of this and it is significant that the role is not usually described as 'career teacher' or 'career instructor.' Perhaps the very personal nature of the learning involved means that the concept of an 'advisor,' often seen as an appropriate approach to teaching because of the implication of learner-centeredness that it carries, is actually more appropriate.

Option 2: Help is Already Being Given in the Guise of Something Else

This option may be justified on the grounds that big choices, such as college careers, are often informed by subject knowledge gained at a lower level. This is a persuasive possibility that is clearly true on some occasions. However, when looking at the content of institutional learning, this notion falls flat. There are many paths available to higher learners that do not directly equate to experience at schools and, even where they do, differences in level and approach may mean that what has been learned previously may be a poor predictor of what will be the nature of the subject in higher education.

Option 3: Learners Do Not Need Help – They are Sufficiently Autonomous Learners to Make the Decisions Themselves

It may be that, when making the big choices about learning, learners are sufficiently autonomous to either know what they need or to know how to find the relevant information and help that they require. This seems likely in many cases. A combination of personal interest, recommendations, and approbations by friends, relatives, and acquaintances, family pressures, prior subject knowledge, information about the geographical location of a place of study, knowledge of individuals involved in teaching and research, and so on, may provide sufficient knowledge and understanding to make informed and intelligent autonomous choices. Some may know their preferred career path from early childhood—a fact that will determine their big choices. If this is so, then choice of the large learning direction (a course, an area of study or whatever) is at an inappropriate scale for the current study, falling outside the remit of education per se.

Perhaps Just Chance or Happenstance

There is a fourth option: such choices may occur by chance, by mistake, or by unusually strong external constraints, which have little to do with the need to learn. For example, the choice of a university in the United Kingdom for a student going through clearing is often hurried and hasty. Choices may be (and often are) made based on erroneous information, a desire to be at a particular institution, under duress from parents or peers, wanting to be with friends, or any number of other reasons.

Really Small Choices

At the other end of the scale, things look rather different. For instance, the choice available to either the learner or the teacher about which word to read or use next (still more which letter to use next within a word) is, generally speaking, quite tightly constrained.

A Thought Experiment About Small Choices

Bearing in mind the meaning that I intend to convey in this sentence, the choices I make about which words to use are very limited, and each new word that I add constrains my choices (what word could I put here? 'more?' 'further?' These are the two that immediately spring to mind) further (there, I have made my choice). Combining the constraints of grammar, syntax, semantics, and my own limited vocabulary, it seems to be a pointless exercise to look too closely at the finest details of this passage. Perhaps I will return to these sentences and try to tidy them up or perhaps I will leave them as they are to illustrate my point. The significant choices are to do with the meaning I intend to convey in the sentence, which is, in turn, constrained by the meaning I intend to convey in the paragraph, which in turn, is constrained by the subheading of the section in which it resides, which is, in turn, limited by the subject of the chapter which is, in turn, constrained by the topic of the book. At any one of these points, I could choose to behave differently, but the constraints that lead me in a specific direction make it improbable that I will deviate too far from what is imposed by the element that embeds each choice at a higher level.

The Significance of Smaller Choices

Tiny choices are by no means always insignificant or irrelevant, and small choices do influence and sometimes determine the large. Even individual letters matter: in the author's experience, the meaning of the title of a lesson, "Why some Web pages suck," was significantly altered when one letter 's' was inadvertently changed to an "f," leading to an unexpectedly vivid recall of the issue by all students involved. However, if all things are equal, the very small is not usually worth agonising over when making decisions about what and how to learn. Most significantly, although the examples given might show the matter is of some importance when the teacher is making a choice, it would impose too great a cognitive strain for the learner to have to consciously select which (if any) of the words provided should be chosen and which should be ignored. A notable exception to this might be when the learner is expected to contribute, be it a piece of work, a discussion contribution, or the answer to a multiple choice question. Although this discussion has dwelt on the issue of words, these same principles apply to videos (e.g., minor changes to camera angles), pictures (e.g., details of shading), simulations (e.g., representations of figures), discussions and any other occasion when choices are made. Wherever the small is constrained by the larger, the lowest levels of scale are usually of less significance than the highest when determining the level of transactional control. To some extent, this is implied in the concept of a trajectory—if we were to consciously change direction every second, then it would not really be a direction at all.

Somewhere in Between

If choice of subject is not significant at one end of the scale and choice of word (or small detail of framing in a video, or line in a picture, etc.) is generally of little interest at the other, the aspects of a learning trajectory that offer significant choice to the learner or the teacher must exist somewhere in between.

A defining feature of an intentional change in learning trajectory is that it is the result of a choice. The smallest scale must, by and large, therefore be the conscious choices about an activity that will or might be expected to bring about learning. Thus, selecting a course would certainly be included in this definition, as would switching on the TV to watch an educational broadcast, picking up a book, searching for information on the Internet, subscribing to an academic mailing list, perhaps reading a posting from that mailing list, sitting down and thinking about something really hard, writing an essay, or asking someone for advice.

Clearly, this definition admits to a range of scales and different kinds and level of choice. It would be useful to pin this down further. One way to do this might be to think of each relevant choice point as being a potential bifurcation, or fork in the road. Choices that are *always* available, such as leaving the road or standing still, in some sense cancel out and are of philosophical significance only. The reasons for this are reminiscent of Camus's alleged comment: "Should I kill myself, or have a cup of coffee?" (Schwartz, 2004). Most of the time this is not an issue. The points that are of significance are those where there is a reasonable likelihood that the learner or some other might choose a different path. For example, it would usually be the case that the learner might make an active choice about whether or not to attend a lecture. This may be subject to varying degrees of constraint, such as social pressure or the allocation of marks for attendance or loss of marks for non-attendance in a larger course (and equally, counter-constraints such as illness, attending a wedding, or hating the tutor). Within that lecture, if the lecturer asks a question to which the learner might be able to make an intelligent response, he or she may choose to do so or not, though other factors such as natural shyness or the fact that others might get there first would obviously act as constraints. Within that lecture, it is likely that the lecturer will have made a number of choices of greater or lesser significance along the way as to the form of its presentation.

Hierarchies of Choice in Institutional Learning

A traditional higher education system is conveniently organised in a hierarchic manner. For instance, Graham (2005) identifies blended learning approaches as broadly falling into the categories of activity level, course level, program level, or institutional level and interestingly notes that:

Across all four levels, the nature of the blends is determined by the learner or the designer or instructor. Blending at the institutional and program levels is often left to the discretion of the learner, while designers and instructors are more likely to take a role in prescribing the blend at the course and activity levels.

This is not necessarily a useful or appropriate hierarchy and it may have as much to do with the economics of delivery as the appropriateness of the scale. However, it is a system that has evolved into a state that is recognisable to most individuals and thus provides a convenient measuring stick for looking at issues of scale. Figure 5.2 represents a hypothetical level of learner choice at different levels of the hierarchy within the author's institution, a common enough pattern in United Kingdom universities. It is recognised that different institutions use different terms to mean the same thing (especially in the United States), and often the same terms to mean something different. In particular, the use of the word "course" in the United Kingdom refers to a programme of study that would typically lead to a degree, while the word 'module' refers to what would more commonly be known in the States as a "course." It is also true that the majority of the comments about choices made here are generalisations to which there are (perhaps many) exceptions. The purpose of the taxonomy is to provide a vehicle for discussion rather than to form a definitive set of classifications.

Figure 5.2. Learner choice relative to scale in institutional learning

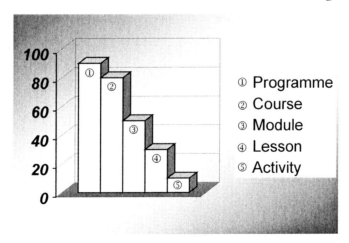

Programme

At the programme level, it is unusual for more than relatively trivial advice to be given. The choice is largely the learner's (subject to entry requirements) and the tutor's role is more a purveyor of goods.

Course

Like a programme, little teaching help is usually given for the learner with the choice of a course. Again, the choice is very much in the hands of the learner, the constraints being the learner's abilities, preferences, and interests, as well as (perhaps) the entry requirements and capacity of the course.

Module

Many courses require that a specific sequence of modules is taken, removing the choice from the learner altogether, while others provide greater flexibility. Most are somewhere in between. Where choices are available to learners, little help is usually given in making those choices. Internal constraints and assessment results may also play a role in limiting choice here. It is interesting to note that, in a recent study undertaken by one of the author's students, when asked if they would prefer to choose modules or not, most undergraduate students preferred not to do so.

Lesson

Having chosen a module, the choice of lesson is nearly always in the hands of the tutor. There are notable exceptions to this, such as research-based or project-based work.

Activity

The degree of control that learners may exercise in determining the activities performed within a lesson depend largely on its nature and the approach of the tutor, who may give more or less control to the learners. However, the range of tasks will typically be highly constrained by the topic of the lesson and the decision to grant control is, generally speaking, in the hands of the tutor.

There are other relevant subdivisions where choice plays a role, such as assessments, learning objectives, and larger chunks or units of a module, which, in almost all cases, provide learners with limited choice.

Bucking the Trend: Giving More Control

At a structural level, a traditional higher education system provides little choice to the learner at the levels at which the learner actively engages and, where it does give choice, provides little assistance in making those choices. It does not have to be that way. For example, the author's institution runs courses such as its MSc by Learning Objectives where virtually every element of the course is chosen by the learner, within the context of a dialogue with the course tutor. Similarly, many PhD programmes are (at least in the United Kingdom) largely determined in a dialogue between learners and their supervision teams, although there is an increasing tendency for these to become more teacher-centric and uniform. However, there is an uneasy tension at the heart of all such initiatives, leading Candy (1991, p. 237) to suggest that providing control to learners over part of the process, while retaining others, cannot allow us to treat them as autonomous. While this point of view has some appeal, it is unnecessarily bleak. By looking at autonomy as a matter of scale, it is possible to accommodate varying degrees of autonomy at different levels. Indeed, it may even be seen as a mark of autonomy that the learner is able to delegate control to others appropriately.

Despite the existence of exceptions, within undergraduate programmes, training courses, many postgraduate programmes and a large number of sub-degree qualifications, choice for the learner only becomes significant when looking at the highest level (which course to take). There is then a large gap in which choice is taken away, which returns only (and relatively rarely) once the scale drops to a specific lesson or chunk, during which a teacher may delegate some control to the learner or, if learners are brave, have it snatched away. At this level the delegation of control typically rests in the hands of the teacher rather than the learner.

Relevant Choices

Choices about what to do next to bring about learning are often made at a wide range of scales, from the very small (e.g., in alternating dialogue) to the very large (e.g., the choice of a programme of study). The important distinguishing factor in identifying an appropriate level of scale is whether that choice is actively being made that will change or influence how a learner will learn, whether or not that choice is made by the learner, the teacher, an automated system or other learners. Such choices have to do with influencing which activities or tasks take place or are performed, not the precise form they will take. This is best illustrated with an example.

A Thought Experiment: Buying Apples 101

Imagine, for instance, that you are an instructional designer or teacher creating a lesson for learners wishing to learn about how to buy apples. You might consider a range of approaches to this, depending on the projected needs and abilities of learners.

Experienced Learners

If the learners are experienced shoppers who have already purchased apples many times before, then it may be more appropriate to choose to engage the group in a discussion of approaches and issues. At that point, you will have made an important decision about the process of learning and to some extent the content, but from then onwards the choices about how learning happens fall into the hands of the discussion participants. If you exert your power and are part of that discussion or choose to demand a certain kind of structure, then you will be one of those making active choices, but those choices will be responsive to the speech acts of the other participants. The conversation may lead in an indefinitely large number of potential directions that may not be predictable at the start. For example, a student may choose to raise the issue of rotten apples, forcing a change of learning trajectory which explores the problems of returning fruit to a shop, the fragility of apples, what is meant by 'rotten' or any number of other issues. While each of these issues bears a relationship to the general area of apple buying, there are many shifts in trajectory that are possible within it as learners construct and co-construct a rich vein of knowledge relating to their needs and interests.

Novice Learners

If the learners are new to the subject of apples, then things are likely to be different. You may choose, for instance, to write a PowerPoint presentation about the subject of apples or, more likely, give them an assortment of apples to handle and perhaps to eat. Similarly, you might choose to create a presentation for the purpose of learning how to make apple purchases, or design some kind of simulation or role playing exercise. You may identify other concerns, such as money handling, market prices, haggling and so on, which require different approaches or pedagogical techniques, each of which will represent a choice along the way. Each instance involves a clear and unequivocal choice about what to do next to learn something. Once you have started creating your simulation, presentation, exercise, discussion structure or whatever you choose to do to address a particular issue, your choices are likely to become far more constrained. If, perhaps, you have chosen to give a presentation about apples, then you may make decisions on content based on your expectations of the learners and knowledge of the subject (Do they need to know about the concept of fruit? Do they want to know about the different ways to eat an apple? Do they need to know about nutritional data?). Of course, as you are a good teacher, you will refine your answers to these questions through explicit or implicit dialogue when the subject is being taught, in which case control will be more negotiated, if only internally.

Each time you make a decision about a subtopic, then you will also make a decision (perhaps not a firm one) about the most effective means of teaching it. It is important to clarify here that any number of decisions may be made and they may not be the right ones. What is significant is the fact *that* a decision has been made about something that will materially impact on a learner. Eventually, there comes a point that is the smallest level of granularity, beyond which you are simply implementing the choice that you have made. For instance, once you have chosen to create a presentation about means of preparing apples, then the implementation will mostly follow from that and will seldom constitute a significant transactional choice in itself. You may decide to use pictures and animations; you may decide to treat the subject linearly or hierarchically, top down, bottom up, whatever. However, each of these decisions is likely to be, in a sense, part of the initial one—how to express the subject. They are not likely to be distinct decisions in their own right that will change the course of a learning trajectory on their own (though of course they might). They are simply a part of that single change in direction. Naturally, any two teachers may disagree about the details of this, and may vary the criteria that they choose to differentiate choices from one event to the next. This is not a science, and interpretation of the choices that are significant in determining a learning trajectory is situated, a product of personal needs, context and understanding of the subject.

The Atomic Unit of Transactional Control

From this example, it can be seen that transactional choices are often a compound or amalgam of other dependant choices, none of which are meaningful on their own. Therefore, it may be tentatively concluded that the smallest significant choice is one which:

- determines a course of action (task, activity, etc.) leading to, or intended to lead to learning;

- may potentially be decomposed into a wide assortment of sub-choices, none of which are sufficient in themselves to identify a learning trajectory.

Then, this,is the atomic level of choice in transactional control theory—the smallest point at which a trajectory changes.

Instructivism, Constructivism, and Transactional Control

Scale helps to explain the disparity observed earlier (Chapter II) between Moore's concept of structure and that of Jonassen's constructivist model. Jonassen (1994) tells us that:

Constructivism believes that learning outcomes are not always predictable and that "instruction" should foster, not control, the processing of the learner. So, the term, "constructivist instruction," is, from a theoretical perspective at least, an oxymoron.

However, even Jonassen's constructivist paradigm sees control being exercised at some scale by a teacher or facilitator, if only in creating suitable conditions for learning. The difference is largely that Jonassen believes the learner should have greater control at a finer scale, not that the teacher should surrender control altogether. Even so, if a learner asks for help or clarification, then a teacher will give it, thus assuming still finer-grained control. An instructivist paradigm focuses on the teacher's control of some of the smaller changes in trajectory, while a constructivist view considers the larger ones and the smaller still. Neither approach is the answer to all learning problems. Constructivism, especially social constructivism, is inherently better aligned with the preferred model of negotiated control, but within a broadly constructivist learning trajectory, it may often be appropriate to delegate control to another and, when viewing it at a finer scale, this may turn out to be the norm rather than the exception.

Conclusion

Issues of scale are central to understanding any learning transaction or sequence of transactions, both temporally and conceptually. Both really large and really small choices seem to fall outside the remit of education, so it is only appropriate to consider those choices that are made continually and (at least potentially) consciously of or in a learning transaction. The important factor seems to be that the description of choices should provide a means of describing the learning trajectory in a meaningful way that distinguishes it from all other learning trajectories, but without such fine granularity that similarities between trajectories are lost in a wealth of detail. This is a difficult challenge as it will vary not only from one learning situation to the next, but also from one learner to the next. A useful heuristic is to consider any choice that is not in itself sufficient to determine a direction on a learning path as subatomic in determining transactional control. All other choices will lead to a change in trajectory, whether large or small. Returning to the point at which this chapter began, it is clear that all such choices, big or small, may either be made by the learner or the teacher (bearing in mind the broad definition of 'teacher' described in chapter one). Thus, it is inconvenient to consider autodidaxy as significantly different from learner control, as Candy (1991) tries to do, as it all depends on the scale that it is viewed at. A learner may control all or any part of a learning trajectory.

The next chapter presents some typical examples of institutional learning with a view of identifying levels of transactional control, leading to some, perhaps surprising, conclusions. This will help to provide a sense of perspective in preparation for parts two and three of the book, which investigate transactional control in e-learning.

References

Brand, S. (1997). How buildings learn. London: Phoenix Illustrated.

Candy, P. C. (1991). Self-direction for lifelong learning: A comprehensive guide to theory and practice. San Francisco: Jossey Bass.

Darwin, C. (1872). The origin of species (6th ed.).

Garrison, D. R., & Anderson, T. (2003). E-learning in the 21st century: A framework for research and practice. London: RoutledgeFalmer.

Garrison, D. R., & Baynton, M. (1987). Beyond independence in distance education: The concept of control. American Journal of Distance Education, 1(3), 3-15.

Gleick, J. (1988). Chaos. London: Heinemann.

Graham, C. R. (2005). Blended learning systems: Definition, current trends and future directions. In C. J. Bonk & C. R. Graham (Eds.), *The handbook of blended learning* (pp. 3-21). San Francisco: Pfeiffer.

Holland, J. H. (1998). *Emergence from chaos to order*. New York: Oxford University Press.

Jonassen, D. H. (1994). Thinking technology: Toward a constructivist design model. *Educational Technology, 34*(4), 34-37.

Jones, S. (1999). *Almost like a whale*. London: Doubleday.

Juster, N. (1962). *The phantom tollbooth*. London: Collins.

Karampiperis, P., & Sampson, D. (2004). *Adaptive instructional planning using ontologies*. Paper presented at the ICALT 2004, Joensuu, Finland.

Looi, C. K. (2001). Enhancing learning ecology on the Internet. *Journal of Computer Assisted Learning, 17*, 13-20.

Moore, M. G., & Kearsley, G. (1996). *Distance education: A systems view*. Belmont: Wadsworth.

Pena-Shaff, J. B., & Nicholls, C. (2004). Analyzing student interactions and meaning construction in computer bulletin board discussions. *Computers and Education, (42)*, 243-265.

Schwartz, B. (2004). *The paradox of choice: Why less is more*. New York: HarperCollins.

Chapter VI

Transactional Control in Traditional Institutional Learning

The dance of learning requires a couple, a partnership, a community, that can move together to transform perspectives and enhance knowledge acquisition. (Boyer, 2005)

Introduction

This chapter presents a range of familiar educational interactions with a view of examining the roles of choice and constraint and their behaviour. This is an attempt to clarify how the concepts presented in previous chapters may be applied in real life. Along the way, there will be some complexities and some unexpected results, but by the end of it, this will lead to clarification of how the interplay of choice and constraint is significant in understanding educational systems. More importantly, this chapter lays the groundwork for the following chapters, which look at similar processes in online learning.

The chapter begins with a high level examination of the general features of transactional control within commonplace forms of institutional learning. Further examples are discussed in greater detail, then a few general principles are abstracted that may be used to examine transactional control in a learning trajectory.

Breaking Down Lessons:
Some Examples

To examine the nature of transactional control within a particular learning trajectory or set of learning trajectories, it is necessary to consider the kinds of constraints and the kinds of scale at which they operate. For any given instance, it is necessary to look at each participant's level of control over his or her learning trajectory from one significant choice to the next, identifying who is controlling that choice, what are the constraining factors, and at what scale they operate. The following examples will take a fairly non-rigorous attitude to this process, in order to see how the concepts apply in an accessible and informal manner. By the end of the chapter, a more rigorous framework will be suggested for viewing any educational transaction.

There are many things that may happen within a traditional lesson in an institutional learning environment, of which, the following is necessarily just a small but representative subset.

Teacher-Led Presentation: Teacher Control

As a general rule, a teacher-led presentation demands few choices from the learner. In a face to face classroom or video conference, this is not always as clear-cut as it may seem, as teachers may be influenced in many small, but significant ways, by the audience. As Wiener (1950) relates:

...there is no task harder for a lecturer than to speak to a dead-pan audience. The purpose of applause in the theater—and it is essential—is to establish in the performer's mind some modicum of two-way communication.

It is also significant that a teacher making use of, say, a poorly written PowerPoint presentation, may be as much a slave to constraint as the students, controlled by his or her pre-prepared slides and the order in which they come. Sensible use of such technologies involves the use of modes of navigation that are not purely linear, but the skills to do this are in relatively short supply.

At a larger scale, a teacher may be bound by lesson plans, course outlines, learning objectives or other constraints that may even have been designed by someone else. However, such constraints (being at a higher level) have a less direct effect on the teacher's choices than those of, at the other extreme, someone else's lecture slides. On the other hand, because they are at a larger scale, they define the constraint landscape in which choices may be made.

Learner-Led Presentation: Joint Control

A learner giving a presentation, as may often be the case in a seminar for instance, may make many choices, albeit within a tightly constraining framework. The subject of the presentation may have been constrained significantly by the teacher and/or the subject matter. Again, the larger scale choices define the perimeters of the range of possibilities for those at a smaller scale. Also, there are likely to be constraints on the timing of and form that the presentation may be allowed to take, with a stronger influence exerted by the presence of evaluation or assessment criteria. The case is interesting because the limitations on other participants' choices are directly defined not only by the teacher, but further, by the learner giving the presentation. In terms of the dynamics, however, a learner-led presentation is much the same for the other learners as one led by a teacher, and offers a similar lack of control to the audience of the presentation.

Classroom Discussions: Negotiated Control

On the face of it, discussion appears to offer the widest range of potential choices to the largest number of learners as control is likely to shift constantly amongst the participants. This negotiated control of a learning trajectory is one of the major benefits of dialogue so strongly affirmed by Garrison and Baynton (1987). However, different discussion forms offer greater or lesser constraint on the individual. Equally, discussions provide a chance to exercise power relationships and may not benefit those who are less assertive or who occupy a less prestigious role within a group.

Discussions can take many forms and, by nature, have a tendency to shift modes constantly as they progress. For example, the following broad categories of utterance may reduce or enhance the control of others:

- **Questions:** questions may be liberating, enhancing control (e.g., "What would you like to do today?") or constraining (e.g., "What is two plus two?").

- **Answers:** answers will, typically, constrain choice: if they are in response to a liberating question, then they will often narrow the subject of discourse; if they are answers relating a matter of fact, depending on whether they are perceived as correct or incorrect, they will channel what happens next.

- **Clarifications:** typically, clarifications are constraining because, almost by definition, they narrow the field of discourse, closing possible avenues that were opened up by the initial uncertainty that they seek to clarify.

- **Interpretations:** interpretations may often be liberating, as they potentially provide a different viewpoint, which in turn, may spark further dialogue, without necessarily losing the context of the original point that was interpreted.

- **Emotive statements/statements of feelings/preferences and so forth:** an emotional reaction is almost always constraining, unless it allows others to freely express feelings that they may have kept to themselves. Emotional responses often demand assent or dissent, and may (for example, in the case of someone expressing frustration or grief) demand that attention is given to the speaker. While this may open up a different trajectory than the one that caused the outburst, it is the outburst itself that caused that change in trajectory and is therefore constraining.

- **Statements or assertions of fact:** assertions are typically constraining because they demand assent or dissent, and often will define the subject that is then under discussion. Especially when spoken by those perceived to have some authority, they may stop conversation in its tracks.

- **Judgements:** to some extent the constraining nature of judgements depends on whether they are intended as summative (in which case, they may close an avenue of enquiry) or challenging (in which case, they may open up new ones). However, in most cases, they are constraining because, whether challenging or summative, they limit the potential responses.

- **Supportive/non-supportive statements:** these are typically constraining. Supportive statements further channel the existing trajectory; non-supportive statements demand a response.

- **Performative utterances:** (e.g., if a teacher proclaims, "This is the end of this discussion,") are almost always constraining, or at least intended to be so.

These examples are purely illustrative and are by no means the only ways that discussions can be classified. In all cases, the actual ways that forms of dialogue can constrain or liberate are hugely dependent on context. However, this short list clearly illustrates the potential for different kinds of conversational act to influence the behaviour of others.

Tutor-Directed Reading: Control at a Distance

Guided reading is a common task, usually set by tutors in advance of seminars, tutorials, lectures, and the like. Choices about the activity are made by the tutor, but learners may often choose when they are going to read it, where they are going to read it, and with what degree of attention. It is notable that students are not always as dedicated as they might be when given such tasks. This raises the significant issue of motivation that affects much education at a distance—where too many of the choices are made by another but where the learning activities are performed apart from the teacher, the learner must be either motivated (intrinsically or extrinsically), duty-driven, or unusually effective at self-management. It presents a curious duality, a pseudo-autonomy, where the learner controls the time and the place, but not the activity itself.

Practical Activity or Exercise: Intrinsic Control

Practical exercises are commonplace in most learning trajectories, helping to complete the Lewin/Kolb cycle of learning (Kolb, 1984). The nature of the task will determine the number of choices that may be made by the learner. If the task is intended to produce a specific outcome (e.g., to measure the rate of change of a chemical reaction), then choice may be highly constrained, whereas a task that admits many potential ways of completion may allow a much wider set of choices.

The results of the activity itself may be a contributor to the level of transactional control. For example, if a learner is performing an experiment, the results of which do not accord with expectations, then it may influence learners to either undertake a further experiment or to refine the conditions of the original. This is an example of intrinsic constraints influencing the course of a learning trajectory. It helps to illustrate how experiential learning is not always entirely autonomous, but may be governed by constraints as great as those found in teacher-led learning.

Assessment: Control of the Past

Assessments (i.e., activities intended to given feedback to the learner on performance) are usually determined by a teacher and often provide among the highest levels of constraint in a traditional, institutional learning setting, guiding huge swathes of activities, acting as strong constraints and extrinsic motivators alike. Garrison and Anderson (2003) quote Dirk as identifying five distinct roles in institutional education:

- Communicate the achievement status for students;
- provide self-evaluation information to the learner;
- student placement for educational paths or programmes (accreditation);
- motivate the learner; and
- evaluate the effectiveness of instructional programmes. (p. 94)

To these five roles might also be added a sixth—the vital role of communicating with potential employers.

The clearest division between types of assessment is between the formative and summative roles, though the fact that the roles are separable does not imply that they are or should be distinct processes. It is safe to suggest the principle that summative assessments should always be formative and formative assessments may sometimes contribute to summative assessment (in evidence-based assessment, for instance).

Feedback is a vital aspect of any learning experience, allowing the learner to assess his or her knowledge in a wider perspective, as well as feeling valued and cared for (Bruner, 1966; Gagne, 1985; Laurillard, 1993). In terms of choice, it allows the learner or teacher to make an informed decision about what to do next, to identify whether the learner is capable of moving to the next zone of proximal development (Vygotsky, 1978). It is a means of closing the feedback loop between learner and teacher, leading to a virtuous circle of control (Pask & Lewis, 1972). At this level of control, it is frequently a deciding factor in taking larger scale decisions about a learning trajectory, but there is no reason that it should not be so for smaller decisions too. It is common for short self-assessment quizzes to be associated with small chunks of learning resources such as learning objects, providing the learner with useful guidance on the state of his or her learning.

Summative assessment often drives the learning experience for learners, both motivating them and shaping the form their studies take to fit the assessment needs (Garrison & Anderson, 2003). Equally, from a formative perspective, it is an important mechanism for the teacher in control of a learning trajectory to identify the needs and capabilities of the learner. Although very much controlled by the teacher, in this way, it provides a kind of meta-dialogue about the learning needs of those being assessed. This is typically an indirect exchange of messages, not like verbal dialogue, but more akin to the footprints of a hunted animal—a means of tracking rather than of conversation. Summative assessments are seldom used by learners to intentionally inform the tutor of their inadequacies. In institutional learning this is often a slow-moving dialogue and, as such, it will often delimit larger changes in learning trajectory, marking the end of one stage of development. Summative assessment has the interesting property of working some of its constraints backwards. Whereas many aspects of control in education act more or less directly, the threat of summative assessment is latent and its effects are largely felt in the past, before it occurs.

Assessment is a useful and probably (in some sense) essential part of any educational experience. Of course, it does not have to be performed by teachers: it may be accomplished by the learners themselves; although in so doing, it will lose some of its effectiveness as a means of communicating success to others.

Evaluation: Control of the Future

The evaluation of the success of a course, module, or teacher is a vital element, which contributes towards the repeatability of traditional institutional learning and the ability of teachers to teach. Evaluations of the learning project provide a wide range of choices to the learner. The reflective process is one that depends entirely upon the learner's perceptions of the learning experience. It is notable, however, that such evaluations commonly occur at the end of the experience, meaning that the only benefit to the learner is usually to reflect upon the process.

From the perspective of the teacher, it is another matter altogether. Evaluations provide useful and meaningful insights into the effectiveness of the teaching which, combined with other factors such as the marks achieved, the prestige of the course, the apparent fun or otherwise had by the learners, the quality of their work (not necessarily at all the same thing as the marks achieved) and so on, allow the teacher to learn from and improve his or her teaching, increasing control.

There are numerous approaches to evaluate any learning activity, including:

Objective data, such as:

- testing (Have the learners achieved expected levels of performance?);
- measurement of effective transfer and performance (Kirkpatrick, 1994) following the learning activity or activities;
- constrained questionnaires;
- measurements of levels of activity and engagement; and
- employability of successful learners.

Subjective data is also commonly used, such as:

- the results of interviews, text responses to questions, course meetings; and
- gut responses by the tutor, a general feel for whether the students are engaged, have "got it" and so on.

A major distinguishing factor that differentiates evaluations from the activities presented so far is the scale at which they work. It is by no means uncommon for the effects of the evaluation to be observed weeks, months, or even a year or more later. In contrast with assessment, the effects of evaluation often work forwards, influencing the future.

One reason that evaluations are often only given at the end of a course is that it is important to know the whole story before giving judgement. To provide an evaluation in the middle of the course might be like judging a detective novel before the denouement: some important information might be gleaned, but it will not be truly meaningful until the whole plot is revealed. Another reason that evaluations are often given at the end of a course is the extra effort involved, both for the evaluator and for the evaluated. There is a fine line between formative evaluation and managerialism (reducing control) and the two are too often entangled in traditional institutions.

Unless managed with great care to ensure anonymity, lack of conferring, and even-handedness, elicited evaluations can provide a much skewed picture of a course and lead to bad decisions about how it may be changed. There are numerous reasons for this, some psychological, others arising out of the nature of the system itself. Psychologically, tutors may often be overly swayed by poor evaluations, even when the majority are favourable and, as a result, may make unwarranted changes. Practically, the fact that all learners are different means that it would not be a common experience for every evaluator to pick the same issues, be they good or bad. In fact, were this the case, there would be good reason to suspect problems with the instrument of evaluation itself. Where multiple and often contradictory viewpoints are expressed, it is difficult for a tutor to decide what to do next and a range of systemic failures (for example, to pay greater heed to more recently or alternatively the first read evaluations) may reduce the control of the tutor and skew the effectiveness of any response.

One way of improving the effectiveness of evaluation is to consider the bottom-line of return on investment—to identify changes in performance leading to increased productivity or profitability. This approach is commonly used to discover the efficacy of training in commercial organisations. For example, Cisco claim that for every dollar spent on e-learning in 2004, they received a $16 return on investment (Kelly & Nanjiani, 2005). This is broadly in accordance with Kirkpatrick's approach to evaluation, which considers transfer (the application of learning in a work context) and results (the improvement in productivity) as essential components of any evaluation (Kirkpatrick, 1994). The danger of such a method, especially in higher education, is that the most useful outcomes of any learning experience may have little to do with the intended outcomes. While Kirkpatrick's approach to evaluation is more holistic than the traditional practices of institutional learning, it is still only focussing on a specific set of desired characteristics and thus can only have limited application.

Group Interaction: Negotiated Control

Group control is a complex issue and tends to be viewable in shades of grey. Even in a lecture, one person yawning may influence others to do the same, which in turn, will (hopefully) influence the lecturer to change the pace or take some other action to counteract apparent boredom. Where groups of learners are expected to interact, the dynamics of the system grow in complexity. Each contributing individual can influence the course of discussion and thereby constrain or liberate the choices of others, including those of the teacher. Imagine the following simple scenario (illustrated in Figure 6.1). A discussion is started by the teacher. Learner 1 responds, thereby limiting the choices of both the teacher and learner 2. Learner 2 responds, thereby limiting the choices of the teacher and learner 1. As the discussion progresses, each contribution from each participant affects the potential range of responses of the other participants. Furthermore, assuming the discussion has a direction, then it develops its own dynamic. Each comment, reply, or assertion potentially reduces the available range of options of the participants. In this idealised discussion, the reduction in choice leads ineluctably to a final conclusion. Of course, few discussions in real life are ever this clear cut, but the general pattern may often apply (at least in an educational setting), whether there are three participants or thirty.

Again, this is a highly simplistic picture. The comments of an individual may constrain the possible responses of another, but it is also common that they may open up new vistas of possibility that other learners had not considered, thereby actually increasing choice by introducing ideas that were not previously available, expanding the range of trajectories that may be traversed. It is hard to generalise, but it is always the case that the choices of each participating individual will influence the range of choices available to others, whether increasing or decreasing the overall potential for the group. As the group increases in size, so the potential for control by an individual typically falls. Like the lecture, the group discussion is only a part of the overall process of learning, representing a point where change occurs. Unlike

Figure 6.1. Hypothetical levels transactional control in a sequence of group interaction

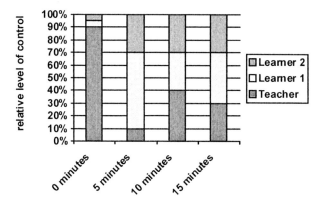

the lecture, what happens next potentially is, at least, partially determined by the outcomes of the tutorial.

Tentative Classifications

Based on these very approximate classifications (all of which admit to exceptions), it can be seen that certain activities enable choices to be made by the learner while others are controlled by the teacher. Broadly they may be classified as shown in Table 1.

Transactional Distance vs. Transactional Control

Of all the examples given here, only dialogue seems to unequivocally support choice on the part of both learner and teacher. Most other activities may (or may not) be sequenced and chosen by the teacher. This lends credence to Moore's (1997) expression of transactional distance as a set of behaviours lying between structure and dialogue, but also demonstrates a weakness in its formulation. Of all the behaviours described, only the teacher-led presentation and assessment give relatively unequivocal control over the learning activity to the teacher. All the other examples given, at least, admit the possibility that learners may make choices that will affect the course of the learning trajectory, yet most are not related in any meaningful way to dialogue. The transactional control model is therefore able to make predictions and descriptions that are not fully distinguished by the transactional distance model as it relates learner autonomy to circumstances that are not significant in terms of structure and dialogue. For the remainder of this book, although Moore will be referred to from time to time, the dominant model used will be that of transactional control.

Table 1. Tentative classifications of traditional educational forms in terms of control

Teacher choice	Either	Both	Learner choice
Teacher-led presentation	Learner-led presentation	Discussion	Evaluation
Assessment	Practical exercise		

An Unexpected Anomaly: Transactional Control in Socratic Dialogue

Socratic dialogue is occasionally touted as an ideal form of teaching: highly learner centred, individualised, and challenging. A naïve view of this process might be that such dialogue represents an exchange between learner and teacher, where the learner participates, if not as an equal, then at least as an active shaper of the discussion (Figure 6.2). From this perspective, there is a constant shifting of choice between learner and teacher, with each choice affecting the available choices of the other. Indeed, this is precisely the kind of relationship that was discovered by Saba and Shearer (1994) in their seminal study of control in a telelesson. However, Saba and Shearer were not looking at a Socratic dialogue and this picture is misleading.

Laurillard (1993) takes a different view, noting that a closer examination of Socratic dialogues reveals a process of bullying and cajoling during which the learner is belittled and diminished by the process. If Laurillard is correct, then the Socratic approach may actually be seen as a process largely dictated and shaped by the teacher, with little learner autonomy and no room to manoeuvre while constantly outflanked by an intellectual superior, intent on changing the learner's conceptions. Take this example from Plato's Meno (1999), tellingly conducted with a slave boy in the presence of his master:

SOCRATES: Mark now the farther development. I shall only ask him, and not teach him, and he shall share the enquiry with me: and do you watch and see if you find me telling or explaining anything to him, instead of eliciting his opinion. Tell me, boy, is not this a square of four feet which I have drawn?

BOY: Yes.

Figure 6.2. Naïve view of transactional control in Socratic dialogue

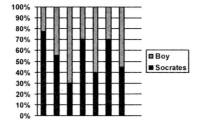

SOCRATES: And now I add another square equal to the former one?

BOY: Yes.

SOCRATES: And a third, which is equal to either of them?

BOY: Yes.

SOCRATES: Suppose that we fill up the vacant corner?

BOY: Very good.

SOCRATES: Here, then, there are four equal spaces?

BOY: Yes.

SOCRATES: And how many times larger is this space than this other?

BOY: Four times.

SOCRATES: But it ought to have been twice only, as you will remember.

BOY: True.

SOCRATES: And does not this line, reaching from corner to corner, bisect each of these spaces?

BOY: Yes.

SOCRATES: And are there not here four equal lines which contain this space?

BOY: There are.

SOCRATES: Look and see how much this space is.

BOY: I do not understand. [*Note: for the first and only time the boy has some small influence on Socrates and exerts an element of choice*]

SOCRATES: Has not each interior line cut off half of the four spaces?

BOY: Yes.

SOCRATES: And how many spaces are there in this section?

BOY: Four.

SOCRATES: And how many in this?

BOY: Two.

SOCRATES: And four is how many times two?

BOY: Twice.

SOCRATES: And this space is of how many feet?

BOY: Of eight feet.

SOCRATES: And from what line do you get this figure?

BOY: From this.

SOCRATES: That is, from the line which extends from corner to corner of the figure of four feet?

BOY: Yes.

SOCRATES: And that is the line which the learned call the diagonal. And if this is the proper name, then you, Meno's slave, are prepared to affirm that the double space is the square of the diagonal?

BOY: Certainly, Socrates.

Clearly the boy has almost no choice at all in the kind of answers that he gives. The experience is almost completely dictated by Socrates and the only thing that the boy can do is give a wrong answer or a right one. Only by giving an unexpectedly wrong answer or expressing bewilderment could the boy have any influence, and even then Socrates still controls the proceedings to ensure that he gives the correct answer. With this less naïve view, considering the power relationship that is implied in the Socratic method and illustrated in the extract from Meno, the picture (Figure 6.3) looks rather different from the previous graph.

In reality, the learner makes choices that are highly constrained by the manoeuvrings of the teacher, who is, in turn, potentially affected by, but not really constrained by how the learner responds, leading the learner ineluctably to a forced conclusion. The single dip in teacher control caused by the boy expressing his lack of understanding is perhaps not as pronounced as illustrated here, as it is certainly possible to inter-pret Socrates' questioning as intentionally leading the boy to a state of confusion at that point. It is possible to charitably look upon Socrates' intention as not being to teach the boy geometry, but to show him a way of thinking and learning. This is an interesting perspective, which emphasises the importance of the process of knowledge acquisition as being on equal terms with the content or product of the

Figure 6.3. More accurate representation of Socratic dialogue

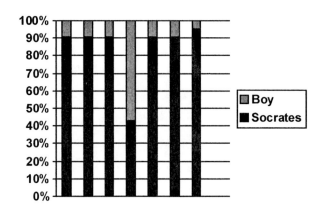

process. Even so, the boy is given no choice at all about how to do this. His learning trajectory is guided solely by Socrates.

A general rule of a discussion where one or more participants take turns (and there are contrary points of view being expressed) is that each is likely to subtract choice from the other. Senge (1993) distinguishes between *discussion* (an adversarial conversation) and *dialogue* (a fruitful exchange of ideas). In a *discussion*, each participant typically *reduces* the choices of the one who follows. A *dialogue* may be liberating, opening new vistas of possibilities for choice through the interchange of ideas. This is seldom the case in a Socratic dialogue, however, which accords more with Senge's definition of *discussion*.

Figure 6.4. Hypothetical naive view of the lecturing process

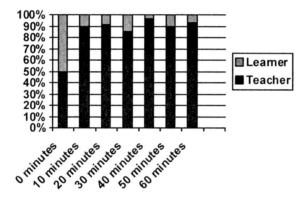

Figure 6.5. Hypothetical view of the lecture from a broader perspective

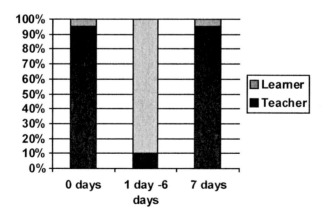

Another Anomaly: Transactional Control in a Traditional Lecture

It has been argued that the traditional lecture is a terrible way to enable learning (Laurillard, 1993). The typically limited degree of interaction of such events, the fact that all are expected to learn the same thing at the same time without regard for their individual needs, current knowledge, or aptitude, often being taught by people with subject knowledge but little understanding of how people learn, militates strongly against their use as a pedagogic form. It is hard to disagree with such arguments, but this has to be considered in a broader context, and the scale chosen is highly significant here. If students spend, say, six hours a week in lecture theatres relinquishing their choice over what they learn next, there *may* still be another thirty hours or more of notional learning time during which they *may* be largely unconstrained in their choices. This will, of course, depend on what tasks may have been set by the lecturers to perform in the interim between lectures. In the author's institution, lectures typically account for less than fifteen percent of the notional time allocated to each taught module, while examinations, tutorials and other time tabled activities account for perhaps another 15%. This leaves a lot of potential time for independent learning, even though in many cases this is used in directed tasks and recommended reading. However, even when activities are rigorously prescribed, the precise trajectory that a learner may take in order to complete those tasks may well differ significantly from one learner to the next. There are many potentially divergent paths that, left to their own devices, they may explore in the ample time that may be available. Compare this to the Socratic dialogue described previously and the balance of choice may conceivably come out in the lecture's favour. Figure 6.4 shows a naïve view of the process over the course of an hour. This view only considers the lecture as an entity somehow dislocated in space and time. It may certainly be true that the lecture is highly constraining for the learner for its duration, but if the process is viewed from a broader perspective and a larger scale, something more like the view shown in Figure 6.5 may be more informative.

It is possible that the learner is able to choose a wide range of learning activities at any point between lectures. The lecture certainly acts as a means of constraint, but in this larger context, it is more in the sense of a sign post than of a fence post. In some ways, it may be possible to view this as closer to distance education than the real thing. Depending on the tasks performed in the intervening gaps between lectures, the level of guidance provided to the learner may be lower than that given in a distance learning programme (Moore & Kearsley, 1996).

Unfortunately, the lecture is only part of a system of constraints that hamper the learning of students in higher education. As always in such complex systems, the reality will seldom be as clear-cut as the graph suggests. Teachers will often set constraining tasks to be completed such as books to be read, exercises to be finished, and essays to be written. Meanwhile, learners are unlikely to spend every available moment in study and will certainly be highly constrained in many other ways: time, space, physical capability and so on, not to mention the need to attend other lectures. The graph shows potential periods of control, but there will be long periods in between when no choice is made. However, it shows that the lecture form is not necessarily as restrictive as some might suggest.

A Suggested Process of Analysis

From the foregoing examples, it can be seen that, from a perspective of transactional control, there are commonalities between different learning activities that appear dissimilar, and dissimilarities between those that are superficially alike. It would be useful to be able to characterise any kind of learning activity in a consistent and reliable manner, so that the dynamics of transactional control may be better understood and, perhaps, behaviour may be modified as a result. The following process provides a step in this direction.

Step 1: Identify the Stakeholders

Identify the stakeholders. Typically, the stakeholders would be learners and teachers, but it would also be significant to look at the wider picture (e.g., the creators of a national curriculum, the writers of textbooks, the leaders of a programme, the head of a school, and so on). The objective is to identify all who may be making choices about the course of a learning trajectory.

Where a large number of stakeholders are involved (for example, in a classroom), identify significant exemplars who should provide a sufficient range of characteristics. This will depend on context and the teacher's understanding of the group. For example, the investigator may choose to select a shy student, a backward student, a gifted student, a disinterested student, and so on.

Identify any hierarchies that may exist, paying particular attention to power relationships.

Step 2: Identify Trajectory Changes

Decide upon the relevant temporal scale, being mindful that the activities and events being observed are part of a wider learning ecology that may be viewed at many scales. It may sometimes be worthwhile to concatenate a number of smaller changes in order to gain a clearer picture of the patterns of control.

Identify the significant changes in learning trajectories: who controls them, what are the intrinsic constraints, and what are the extrinsic constraints. Consider as many relevant constraints as possible, bearing in mind that they may relate to context or content, and be intrinsic or extrinsic to the transaction.

If the situation is complex, draw a graph. Be aware that it may be appropriate to provide more than one graph (or at least the ability to zoom in to further detail), depending on the scale used.

To identify the level of control, consider that there is an overall quantum of control, from the perspective of each individual and for each stretch of learning trajectory, identified as a weighted percentage or proportion:

- **The referential:** Who controls the content/subject (remembering issues of scale)?

- **The structural:** Who controls the method by which learning occurs (the activities, the approach, the pedagogy, and so forth)?

- **The temporal:** Who controls the time and/or pacing at which learning occurs (remembering issues of scale)?

- **The spatial:** Who controls the space (or spaces), both real and virtual, in which learning occurs?

Other factors that may or may not be within the control of one or more stakeholders may be significant, including the cost, the emotional attitude, the capabilities of the learners, the social/personal power hierarchies and so on. Where appropriate, these should be taken into account.

The weightings applied to each kind of control will necessarily vary according to context and scale.

Step 3: Map Transactional Control

For each stakeholder identified earlier, graph perceptions of the level of control they exercised over each choice that led to a change in learning trajectory.

The end result of the process will be a graph and set of lists that can be compared with others. Once a pattern of transactional control has been established, it will be possible to compare a range of learning activities, including those that occur at a distance as well as a variety of e-learning approaches, levelling the playing field.

Design Process

Transactional control is far easier to apply in retrospect than to use as the basis for the design of an educational activity. However, it is worthwhile to reiterate a central recommendation of this book: the ideal position for any learner should be to choose when to choose at any point in a learning trajectory. Sometimes, this will result in allowing others to make the choices; sometimes the choice will be in the hands of the learner. To design a learning activity or set of learning activities that makes this possible requires a different perspective on planning than that which is typically applied to the process of instructional design (although almost any existing instructional design process such as ADDIE, PADDE, Dick and Carey's model, and so forth, can accommodate this perspective).

Conclusion

Modelling learning transactions in terms of control, choice, and constraint can reveal some interesting facets of behaviour that would normally be hidden by other educational theories. It can aid understanding of the systemic effects of many decisions that may be made about what may be suitable for learners. In traditional institutional learning environments, it is mainly through dialogue that learners come to exert control over their own learning but, often even here (as the example of Socrates shows), only some forms of dialogue are helpful. What is also clear is that sometimes learners do not wish to be in control, often with very good reason. To make choices without sufficient guidance is almost certainly worse than having no choice at all when it comes to learning. However, in traditional institutional learning, there is seldom an option. At any given point where choices can be made, the choices are either in the hands of the learner, or the teacher, or other learners. What seems to be impossible, both logically and practically, is that any of these states can exist simultaneously.

Summary of Section I

From a learner's perspective, a learning trajectory may be seen as a series of choices of activity, each one of which may spawn one or more sub-activities which, it is hoped, will lead to a learning goal or which may, in themselves, be valid goals. The degree to which the choices are made by the learner, along with the frequency and intensity of those choices, determines the nature of the learning experience, in terms of transactional control. The ultimate goal of education is to put those choices under the control of the learner but, in order to reach that point; the learner must sacrifice some freedom to make choices until sufficiently well-informed to be able to make them autonomously. A dialogic process is often desirable as, although it involves a sacrifice of some autonomy, it provides a dynamic balance of control.

Although more dependent learners are likely to benefit from delegating control to another, a tightly sequenced set of activities that is outside the learner's control is usually undesirable for more than small chunks of learning, as it is unlikely to fit a learner's needs perfectly. However, it provides the maximum degree of comfort and safety, if only because making choices is a scary and risky affair unless a fairly accurate prediction can be made of the consequences. As a learner is, by definition, unaware of these, a highly structured sequence of activities will suit a less autonomous learner better than one that is less constrained. For most learners, a combination of their own choices together with those made by others is preferred, but this depends largely on the scale at which it is considered.

If choice is a key determinant in shaping an educational experience, but the degree of choice is not a fixed factor, a system that attempts to be all things to all learners is faced with an awkward dilemma—to both constrain and to liberate, to offer limitless choice where wanted, but also to offer limited choice where needed, and to get the right balance at every point where choices are to be made. If it were possible, ethically and economically, for an individual to engage a teacher with a high level of understanding of the learner, the subject, and how to bring the two together, then the problem might go away. However, such a situation is uncommon.

Section II

In the next few chapters, a number of conventional e-learning tools such as Web pages, discussion forums, chat rooms, email, and learning management systems will be examined. Affordances will be critically appraised, and suggestions will be made as to how to maximise the benefits of the various media in terms of choice and constraint. In particular, ways will be sought for maximising the potential of various communication and publication media to cater to the varying degrees of learner control, so that learners may be in a position to choose to choose. It will be observed that no existing systems are entirely perfect and that what is really needed is a change to the environment itself—a change that can most successfully be accomplished through the use of social software and Web 2.0 technologies of the sort examined in part three.

References

Boyer, N. (2005). Online learners take the lead in self-direction. *Academic Exchange Quarterly, 9*(4), 244-250.

Bruner, J. S. (1966). *Toward a theory of instruction*. Cambridge, MA: The Belknap Press of Harvard University Press.

Gagne, R. (1985). *The conditions of learning* (4th ed.). New York: Holt, Rhinehart & Winston.

Garrison, D. R., & Anderson, T. (2003). *E-learning in the 21st century: A framework for research and practice*. London: RoutledgeFalmer.

Garrison, D. R., & Baynton, M. (1987). Beyond independence in distance education: The concept of control. *American Journal of Distance Education, 1*(3), 3-15.

Kelly, T., & Nanjiani, N. (2005). *The business case for e-learning*. Indianapolis, IN: Cisco Press.

Kirkpatrick, D. (1994). *Evaluating training programs: The four levels*. San Francisco: Berrett-Koehler.

Kolb, D. A. (1984). *Experiential learning*. Englewood Cliffs, NJ: Prentice Hall.

Laurillard, D. (1993). *Rethinking university teaching- a framework for the effective use of educational technology*. London: Routledge.

Moore, M. G. (1997). Theory of transactional distance. In D. Keegan (Ed.), *Theoretical principles of distance education* (pp. 22-38): Routledge.

Moore, M. G., & Kearsley, G. (1996). *Distance education: A systems view*. Belmont: Wadsworth.

Pask, G., & Lewis, B. (1972). *Teaching strategies: A systems approach*. Bletchley: OU Press.

Plato. (1999). *Meno* (B. Jowett, Trans.).

Saba, F., & Shearer, R. L. (1994). Verifying key theoretical concepts in a dynamic model of distance education. *The American Journal of Distance Education, 8*(1), 36-59.

Senge, P. M. (1993). *The fifth discipline: The art and practice of the learning organisation*. Chatham: Century Business.

Vygotsky, L. S. (1978). *Mind in society*. London: Harvard University Press.

Wiener, N. (1950). *The human use of human beings*: Discus 67.

Section II
E-Learning, Control, and Constraint

Chapter VII

Electronic Publication

The most hopeful line for the development of our racial intelligence lies rather in the direction of creating a new world organ for the collection, indexing, summarizing and release of knowledge, than in any further tinkering with the highly conservative and resistant university system, local, national and traditional in texture, which already exists. (Wells, 1937)

Introduction

This chapter is primarily about one-way dissemination of content through the World Wide Web. Although such content may potentially be highly *interactive*, this chapter will be more concerned with instances of content where there is little *interaction* between learners and each other or their tutors. The objective will be to discover ways that both choice and constraint can coexist within a published environment, in an attempt to discover appropriate methods of allowing learners to choose whether and when to delegate control of their learning trajectories. As part of this process, the concept of reusable learning objects will be examined and recommendations made for an approach to their development and use.

This chapter, like those that follow, considers published content in isolation. However, the environment of the World Wide Web is never limited to a single form and other technologies that encourage communication are always available. Considering publication as a distinct form necessarily presents an unrealistic and artificial scenario, the purpose of which is to highlight the strengths and weaknesses of this approach. This is not to suggest that it is an approach that would ever be recommended for use on its own, as most technologies will usually be embedded in a larger learning ecology.

Publishing Content

There are many ways of publishing content electronically. Bearing in mind that e-learning was defined earlier as primarily Internet-based, this book will not deal with CD-ROMs, DVDs, and other non-networked media, despite their continuing (though waning) popularity as media for electronic games.

On the Web, the most obvious means of publication is through Web pages. These may be completely static files created with a text editor or specialist editor such as Dreamweaver™, NVU™, or FrontPage®, or provided through a content management system such as Plone™, Mambo™, or Drupal™. However, almost any electronic media may be made available through the Internet, including a wide variety of video, animation, virtual reality (VR), word-processed files, as well as proprietary formats such as PDF and Microsoft® Word. Technologies such as JavaScript, Flash®, and Java™ can provide highly interactive programs with rich functionality. Server-side technologies such as PHP, ASP.net, Java Server Pages, CGI, and Cold Fusion™ may be used to provide a still richer experience, allowing the server to present a unique view to each user of a site, often in conjunction with a database. At this point, there is a danger that the definition may become a little broad: a search engine or portal is such a system, but goes beyond the definition of content publication that will be discussed in this chapter. The focus of this chapter is on the authoring of content intended to bring about learning.

Benefits to the Autonomous Learner

For autonomous learners, browsing Web sites (and, for that matter, reading books and journals) may provide greater freedom of choice than being involved in a face to face dialogue (Collis, 2005; Moore & Kearsley, 1996). Autonomous learners should, by definition, be more inclined to make choices about their own learning, including which learning resources would be most useful at any point, and when they are referenced. However, autonomy is, potentially, a highly variable factor, which changes according to subject, perspective, experience, and so on, at a typically wide range of scales (Candy, 1991). It may be possible to be a very autonomous learner for, say, computer programming, but quite the opposite when approaching quantum theory or the history of design. Even within an area with which a person is comfortable and proficient, there may be aspects that are so far beyond his or her experience and propensities that he or she must relinquish his or her autonomy and choice. For example, a learner may be quite proficient in the use of arrays in programming, but much less so in the use of *associative* arrays. A learner may have learned to learn, but only if he or she avoids straying too far from his or her zone of proximal development. If that person is one of a group of learners, their needs for autonomy will be equally, but differently variable. This presents particular difficulties when publishing resources that are to be used by more than one person. As Moore (1986) says:

The teacher who prepares a teaching program aimed at only one particular learner is able to tailor, organize, or structure the program to meet the learner's specific needs and interests in a way that is quite impossible if the program is prepared for a million viewers, listeners, or readers.

Unfortunately, content that is published on the Web faces this very dilemma: how can it cater to the needs of all learners or even a sizeable subset of them?

Matching Learner Needs Using Dialogue

A key objective for any teacher is to find an approach that adapts to the learner's needs as and when they are expressed. Within a conventional learning environment, whether at a distance, mediated through the Internet or face-to-face, this is usually accomplished through various forms of dialogue, either direct, implicit, or mediated through something like (for example) assessment or a learning styles inventory. A constant process of feedback can allow a teacher to cater to any learner's needs with greater or lesser degrees of accuracy. Sadly, it is often the case that such decisions are made once (at the start) and not reconsidered until at least the next time the learning event is redesigned. This is not too surprising. It is highly labour-intensive and, with some exceptions, prone to error. It is too easy to misinterpret an individual's needs; individuals are not always good at expressing those needs and evaluations can be skewed by extraneous factors. Evaluation is only going to be optimally effective when dealing with a single learner, as each learner has different needs.

A kind of dialogue takes place even where there is no actual interaction between tutor and learner. Michael Moore (1997) puts it like this:

It is worth noting though that, ..., a form of dialogue between teacher and learner occurs even in programmes that have no interaction, such as when the learner is studying through printed self-study materials, or by audiotapes or videotapes. Even in these media there is a form of learner-instructor dialogue because the learner does have an internal or silent interaction with the person who in some distant place and time organized a set of ideas or information for transmission for what might be thought of as a virtual dialogue with, an unknown distant reader, viewer, or listener.

This perspective is perhaps a little optimistic. In particular, this dialogue lacks the key element of the potential for learner control over significant choices that affect a learning trajectory.

An increasing range of "static" resources are becoming dynamic through online annotation tools; wikis, blogs, and annotation systems such as Annotea (http://www. annotea.org/) or ANN (Ip & Canale, 2003) immediately spring to mind, but the principle might also be applied to simpler variations such as group annotation tools in word processors used in conjunction with email.

Limitations of Published Content

There are two main limitations of static media (e.g., Web pages, word-processed documents, most PowerPoint® presentations, movies, Flash movies, and so forth) in the context of choice and control. The first and most obvious of these is the lack of choice that they are able to provide at a micro-level of scale. It is a rare book that provides the means to let the learner ask for clarification of a particular point, or to have it explained differently, although certain Web-based systems do allow something like that to occur. Even where something along those lines is provided, it will necessarily be somewhat limited in scope as it would be indescribably difficult to cater for all possible needs and, even if it were possible, the level of confusion that such a broad range of choices might engender would make it a pointless exercise.

The second and largely distinct major issue lies in choice of the resource in the first place. The skills needed to identify useful books, magazine articles, and Web sites are not trivial for newcomers to a field, but by definition are less troublesome for autonomous learners in a field. This issue will be discussed more fully in the next chapter.

There are further issues that make a resource-based approach to learning potentially constraining. In particular, where such resources are studied at a distance (the norm even in traditional institutional learning), the commitment and motivation needed are usually entirely down to the learner. While this is an ideal situation where the learner has clearly defined needs and goals, it may cause difficulties where the learner needs to enter areas that are dull, frightening, or where the need for discovery is not immediately apparent.

A related problem is that, while the learner may have significant control over the time and space in which learning occurs, he or she may have little control over the activities performed. The learner may have autonomy in management of the pragmatic issues of learning, but not the pedagogic or academic. This, in turn, leads to a potential conflict of messages: the learner is expected to be autonomous in selecting time and place, but not in the activities performed. Autonomy, as a learner, is distinct from autonomy, as an organiser of time.

Linear Media

In the first place, choice of resources may favour autonomous learners, but once a simple, linear publication medium, such as a PDF file or movie is in use, it rarely provides a dialogue or a means of escape from its linear form, beyond stopping reading or viewing it. Having said that, it is relatively easy to provide multiple versions of resources for different learner needs, along with suitable metadata or annotation, to help find those that are appropriate. Similarly, within a given resource or group of resources, it is not too difficult to provide annotations indicating possible paths and recommendations as to which parts are worth visiting for which purposes. Virtual environments make it relatively easy to gather and collate a varied set of resources (or pointers/hyperlinks to them) and with sufficient care, attention, and time, a range of activities can be provided that will give most learners a customised and targeted learning experience.

Internal Dialogues

It is also true that learners do not need to concentrate all their attention at any point: they may be inspired to consider new perspectives by the presentation, they may actively interpret content (implying choice), and there may well be an internal didactic conversation going on which is far less constraining than may at first be apparent.

In an online environment where the typical linear presentation takes the form of an HTML document, a PowerPoint presentation, a PDF file, a Word document, a Flash movie, a podcast, a streaming movie, and so on, the roles of the learners in making choices about their learning trajectories are often several steps removed and occupy the tutor's imagination rather than the actual choices of the learners. This is far from ideal. The choices available to the learner may be no greater than and, due to less intuitive navigation (search mechanisms notwithstanding), sometimes even less than those available to readers of books.

In a linear, printed text such as this one, there are relatively limited opportunities to provide options, though there are tricks that can help. For example, by providing meaningful subheadings throughout the text at points where decisions might be made, the sighted reader can easily scan through and decide whether or not to read that section. In effect, subheadings provide a larger scale view of the text. This technique is generally less effective when used for electronic media, as the limitations of current screens mean that designers cannot usually assume that learners will be able to see more than a small amount of a lengthy page.

At a slightly finer-grained scale, textual signposts that help to explain the structure of the text, such as "I am about to explain that..." or "This section is about..." can help the learner to make informed choices. Similarly, visual signposts such as figures, tables, and images can help to draw attention to significant issues. Digital media often allow the use of multimedia elements such as animations, movies, simulations, and sounds, each of which (if used with care) can provide strong indicators of significant choices that may be made.

Stopping Points, Thinking Breaks

While choice of learning activity may be constrained, choice of interpretation will vary from person to person and subject to subject. It is therefore useful to design an internal dialogic process, which involves at least some choice of interpretation for the learner. Although this is unlikely to lead to a different learning trajectory, it does at least open up greater potential for the learner to decide to do something else apart from reading or interacting with the current resource.

Embedded exercises, especially those with relatively unconstrained answers, may help learners to actively interpret and construct knowledge from an otherwise static and constraining resource.

It is always worth remembering that the act of presentation (be it textual, audio, video or whatever) is an imaginative process for both the creator *and* the viewer. As a rule, no two learners will interpret and understand the same text in exactly the same way. The sorts of learning choices that may be made at a micro level, within even the most rigid of programmed text, may depend significantly on imaginative involvement. If it is accepted that knowledge is in some sense constructed and integrated into an existing framework of understanding, it is certain that every learner's internal representation of the knowledge gleaned from a learning trajectory will differ in some respects from that of every other learner. By explicitly providing opportunities for learners to choose how to engage with a topic, choices may be made at the learner's discretion. If this is scary, then they can always choose to simply go with the flow instead.

The Role of Evaluation

For linear media, learner choice often only comes into play after the event, in the form of evaluations (however these are given) that then allow the tutor to make changes to the next iteration of the presentation. In an e-learning environment, sometimes feedback may come indirectly, such as in the form of reduced numbers of learners taking the course, diminishing numbers, and dropouts over a period of time or, in the case of commercial training, reduced sales. If resources are presented on the Web, server log analysis can and should help to determine their relative popularity.

Non-Linear Branching

Where the media allow linking and branching, the potential for learner control becomes far more significant. It is not only possible, but actually encouraged by the nature of the Web, to provide links from anywhere to anywhere. Processing may be applied on the client (through JavaScript and the like) and/or on the server (through PHP, ASP.net, JSP, CGI and so on), which can provide a highly configurable, personalised path to be generated through a body of material. Similarly, Flash movies allow the embedding of buttons and links, as well as the use of the ActionScript language to provide such functionality. Even without programming, the ability to link any arbitrary content to any other provides a great deal of potential to allow learners to take different paths—to choose their directions through a body of material. To what extent this is used to provide learners with choice depends on the creator. It is by no means uncommon to find examples of texts on the Web that provide a very linear path from one page to the next. While the rest of the Web is never more than a click away, the chance that learners may deviate from a teacher-controlled path assumes a level of autonomy on the part of the learner that may be unwarranted. As has already been observed, there would be no need for education if learners possessed the necessary autonomy in the first place.

Signposts, not Fenceposts

If autonomous or semi-dependent learners are to be given choice, then it is essential that they are not constrained to follow a single trajectory without the opportunity to take another if they wish. This is true for both linear media and hypertext. Conversely, dependent learners should not be set adrift and may benefit from tight constraints, especially where the motivation to attend to the current task (if not the overall venture) is lacking. When creating published resources, it is therefore important to provide clear signposts that point the way, but it should always be optional whether or not the learners actually follow them. Alternative routes may always be taken. Figure 7.1 shows a simple example of this approach, which gives the learner various options as well as links to more detailed explanations and tutorials to assist with the tasks.

Scale Again

In general, screen limitations notwithstanding, it is much easier to provide choice and control to learners in electronic environments than through printed materials. It is in the nature of hypertext systems like the World Wide Web that such paths are very easy to create. Unfortunately, it is not so easy to decide when they should be provided, nor is it cost-free in terms of labour and time. This is especially true where consideration is given of the kind of scales that might be applied. For example, for some learners it might be enough to limit the choices to the large things such as, "What subject shall I learn about next?" For others, the choices may need to be more fine grained, such as "I didn't understand that bit, could you give me some more information?" or "I would like to do an exercise to ensure that I have understood that." Providing learners with a clear indication of which choices will lead to a change in learning trajectory and to what extent the trajectory will change is therefore important, whether through text annotation or navigational cues such as text size, font, or position.

Figure 7.1. Use of options and navigation to further resources

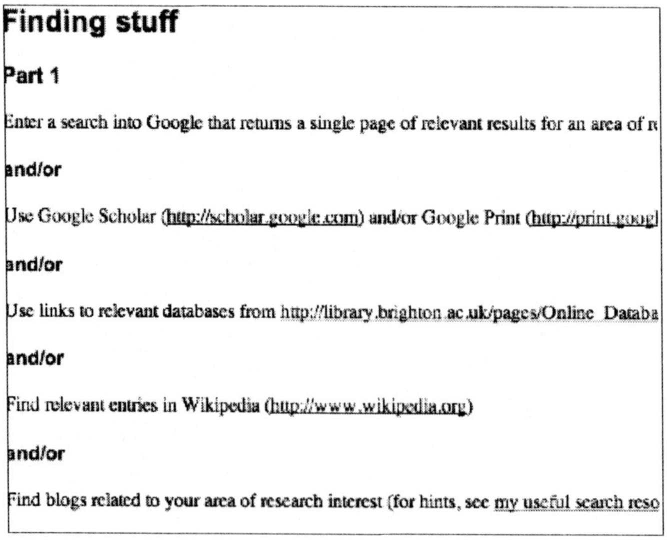

Finding stuff

Part 1

Enter a search into Google that returns a single page of relevant results for an area of re

and/or

Use Google Scholar (http://scholar.google.com) and/or Google Print (http://print.googl

and/or

Use links to relevant databases from http://library.brighton.ac.uk/pages/Online_Databa

and/or

Find relevant entries in Wikipedia (http://www.wikipedia.org)

and/or

Find blogs related to your area of research interest (for hints, see my useful search reso

An Essential Corollary: Multiple Navigation Paths

Linear sequences are often frowned upon in an online learning environment. Jonathan Darby of the UKeU had a fine maxim of "no *next* button" that was drummed into all developers of the site. This is perhaps a little extreme, as Jonathan would be the first to agree, and is itself a signpost rather than a fencepost—a recommended path but not a strict demand. For learners seeking a controlled experience, a *next* button may be a good thing. The essential rule is to provide signposts, allowing multiple paths to the same thing to be taken, some structured and others less so. A combination of hierarchical, Web, and linear structures, combined with an appropriate means of getting back on track (e.g., bread crumbs, links to well known areas such as the home page, site maps, and so on) and, ideally, an intelligent search mechanism will provide maximum choice, but at the same time, may cater to more dependent learners, as long as the options do not become overwhelming. Figure 7.2 shows a typical example of multiple navigation paths, offering both a constrained path (bottom right) and menu options (left) to navigate elsewhere that also indicate the current context.

Figure 7.2. Two forms of navigation

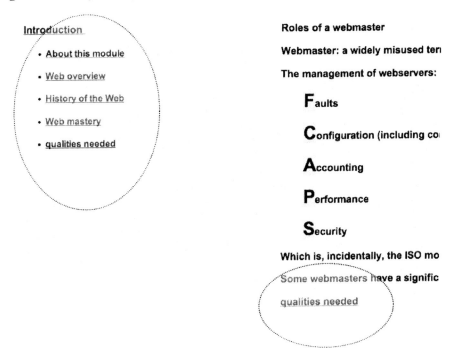

Annotation

Other tricks to help guide learners may be useful, such as using popup windows to display related concepts, without leaving the main pages, or further information on mouse-overs. For example, where a hyperlink is embedded in a piece of text, authors may provide a **title** attribute so that learners have a better idea of where the link leads. On occasions, it may also be appropriate to provide graphical indicators such as icons to help learners make the choice. For example, many wikis automatically create a small icon to indicate that a link leads to an external site, but there is no reason why the principle cannot be extended to provide icons that indicate, say, a more in-depth explanation, a definition, a person and so on (Figure 7.3).

Diversity

A single navigational metaphor of any kind (linear, hierarchical, network, and so forth) should be avoided if at all possible—the key rule should be to cater to diversity and different approaches to discovering and using materials. Of course, a maximally linked hypertext of undifferentiated links would be virtually useless to learners seeking constraint, as much as a single linear narrative would be unsuitable for those requiring freedom. As is so often the case, it all comes down to a question of scale. Choices should be provided that will help to determine a trajectory, not simply because it is possible to provide them.

The issue of scale is significant here for another reason: ideally, choices should be provided at a range of scales so that learners can submit to another's choices at both high and low granularity. To do this successfully, it is important to understand what might constitute a change in trajectory. At a large scale this is simple, though it becomes progressively harder as the granularity becomes finer.

Giving Choices Based on Learning Styles

There are literally dozens of theories that attempt to categorise and define types of learners and which then go on to make pronouncements on the best way of teaching learners with a particular style (Gardner, 1983; Kolb, 1984; Pask & Lewis, 1972). Unfortunately, while learning styles provide a useful explanation of differences between learners and to help to reflect upon what is done to enable that process (Felder & Spurlin, 2005), there is little evidence that this can be used to generate a more effective method of learning. Indeed, it is possible that teaching *against* a perceived learning style may have benefits when compared with teaching *to* that style.

Whether or not it is agreed that learning styles are useful in generating educational activities, a key benefit of a well-considered learning style theory is that it caters to all possible learning needs. This enables teachers to make useful decisions about alternative paths.

Cater to All of Them

Whatever an individual's preferred flavour of generalisation about how groups of learners may be differentiated, transactional control theory suggests one simple rule: cater to all of them. For instance, (without prejudice against other theories) the author happens to have a personal preference for Pask's (1976) simple division of learners into those who prefer a top down approach (holists) and those who prefer a bottom up approach (serialists). Bearing this in mind, materials should be structured in a manner that caters to both groups of users, with detailed step-by-step as well as general-to-specific structuring of activities and resources, each clearly labelled as such. To a large extent, this will be catered to by following the guidelines for multiple navigation mechanisms given above. It should also be a priority to consider the conceptual mapping of the subject so as to discover the appropriate level of scale at which choice should be offered.

A similar consideration may be given for any preferred model of learning style. In all instances where assumptions are made that different approaches will suit different learners (whether these assumptions are true or not), logic dictates that multiple pathways should be provided that suit all of them. A downside of this is that, by increasing the range of choices, the needs of learners for whom choice is not welcome will not be met. In providing such pathways, it is therefore important to clearly separate them and provide a meta-level of description that assists learners in selecting the right path for them. A clear signpost should indicate what a learner should expect if a particular path is followed. Once a path is taken, it should be more difficult (but never impossible) to move across to the alternative path(s).

Perhaps the most significant downside of such an approach is the enormous amount of extra effort required of the instructional designer, amplified by the possibility that at least one of the alternative paths is likely to be a foreign approach for the author. If it is assumed that there *are* such things as preferred learning styles and that something should be done about it, then it is presumably the case that this is true of teachers as well as students. One approach is to make use of the wealth of resources that may already be available on the Internet. Because the Internet provides communities as well as resources, the burden of discovery may be offloaded onto a group of learners and/or teachers. This can be hard to manage effectively, but tools (discussed in part three) are available that may ease the burden considerably.

Engines for Education

An exemplary use of the techniques described here may be found in Schank's (2004) Engines for Education hyperbook, a Web site that attempts to consider all possible learning needs in advance and provides choices for learners at every stage. It is very easy to either give too much choice (leaving the learner insecure and bewildered) or too little (leaving the learner insufficient control to take the best course of action for his or her needs). Engines for Education attempts to overcome this through the use of varied methods of navigation and signposts to well-known areas, combined with a well-informed approach to pedagogy that systematically considers learners' needs. The result is an extremely effective learning resource that gives a great deal of control through nothing but passive browsing through simple HTML pages. However, it is a significant resourcing issue that fourteen people are cited as contributors to the hyberbook.

Providing Layers of Metadata

As Engines for Education shows, wherever choices are provided, it is important to ensure that the learners are given appropriate information that allows them to choose effectively. One obvious way to do this is through text descriptions, abstracts, summaries, and so on. If learning styles are considered, then it is also worth adding to the description some indication of the expected audience and learning needs. However, where density of choices is high, this kind of annotation can destroy narrative flow and could potentially overwhelm the content itself. There are many different ways that information of this nature can be signalled, however. For instance, use of different colours, shades, fonts, and so on, can distinguish text intended for one group from that intended for another. Icons and images can be used to provide relatively unobtrusive signals as to the purpose of a particular piece of content. Electronic sources also allow the use of sound, which may provide a useful alternative for those for whom visual cues are not helpful. A simple example of a site using some of these cues is given in Figure 7.3. In this case, the cues help learners to select appropriate Web sites to assist in a task to reflect on teaching approaches.

For teachers, adding formatting metadata is a relatively low-threshold means of helping learners to make choices and can be an effective way of reflecting on changes in learning trajectory that may not be considered when writing notes or designing learning resources.

Figure 7.3. Use of various simple cues to assist learner choice

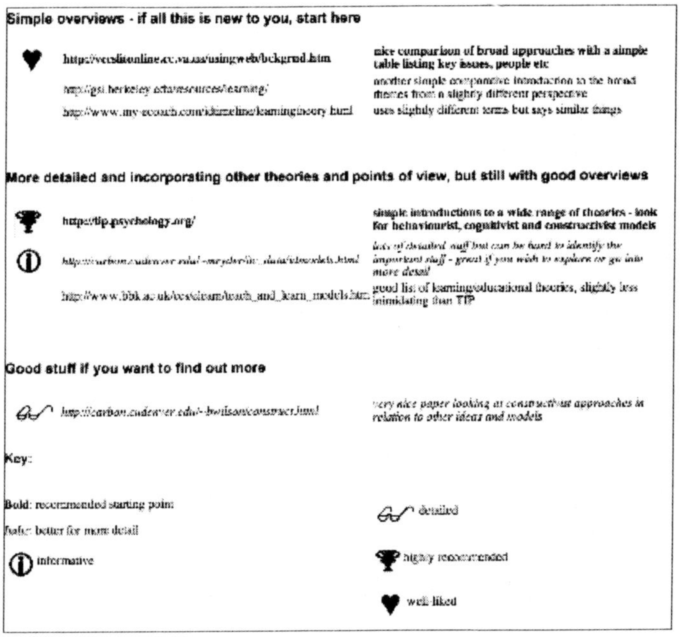

Granularity, Learning Objects, and Choice

It is all very well suggesting that multiple navigation techniques, signposts, and meta-data should be used to provide learners with greater control if and when they need it, but deciding upon the correct number and range of choices is still essential.

Selecting the appropriate level of granularity is a wicked problem that has taxed the learning objects community for some time, and several competing solutions have been proposed (McGreal, 2004; Polsani, 2003; Wiley, 2001). Because trans-actional distance requires an appropriate scale to be identified, it may have some useful applications in deciding an appropriate level of granularity for dealing with learning objects.

Background to Reusable Learning Objects

The notion of reusable learning objects (RLOs) was first proposed by Wayne Hodgkins in 1994 (although Stephen Downes may have invented the concept earlier and it is possible to trace the idea back to at least as far as the early 70s and Ivan Illich). To some extent, inspired by the computer science discipline of object-oriented analysis and design, the concept is broadly that small chunks of annotated learning materials may be created, reassembled, stored, searched for, and shared from object stores, typically on the Internet, similar to Lego bricks (David Wiley prefers the analogy of atoms and molecules), and incorporated seamlessly into any number of potential learning environments and contexts.

Although the use of RLOs is typically associated with an instructivist, knowledge transmission model of education, there is no inherent constraint that means they must be used that way, and a range of techniques have been developed to incorporate them into a constructivist model of teaching (Dalsgaard, 2005; Mason, Pegler, & Weller, 2005).

What is an RLO?

A central issue that remains unresolved by the RLO community is identifying precisely what is meant by the term "learning object." Definitions vary from the relatively precise: "the smallest independent structural experience that contains an objective, a learning activity and an assessment," or, "Learning Objects are … smaller units of learning, typically ranging from 2 minutes to 15 minutes," to the vague and all-inclusive:

Examples of learning objects include multimedia content, instructional content, instructional software and software tools that are referenced during technology supported learning. In a wider sense, learning objects could include learning objectives, persons, organizations, or events. (Polsani, 2003)

This lack of clarity is unsurprising and relates to a failure to identify the relevant scale for looking at decisions about learning trajectories. If the points at which significant choices should be made cannot be identified, then any learning objects that are created may be too small or large, or perhaps choices will be relatively unconstrained but not really useful. Worse still, it may be necessary to make a choice at a point that does not lie at a neat demarcation between two learning objects. This will certainly happen if the objects are too large, as choices will be too constrained within them.

Tying learning objects to a single learning objective is a popular approach (Downes, 2001), but the logic is circular. An objective could equally be "to be an effective architect" or "to learn the correct use of the term *antidisestablishmentarianism*" so they offer no help with determining granularity and learning outcomes are conceptually fuzzy and of dubious merit in the first place (Hussey & Smith, 2002).

Polsani (2003) rightly claims that current determinations of granularity, based on time or size, are irrelevant or useless, but replaces this with "concept or idea" as an alternative. He writes:

The rule to be applied is: how many ideas about a topic can stand alone and can be reused in different contexts? If a LO consists of more than one idea, one of these should be the main idea and the others should be derived from it or be dependent on it. If we take the concept or idea for determining the size of the LO, we free it from subjective considerations such as time and an individual's instructional choices and chosen methodologies.

Polsani relates this to Wittgenstein's language games, where words become meaningful only in the context of their use. If learning objects are seen as functionally similar to words, they only become meaningful in combination with each other. Unfortunately, this is an extremely fuzzy notion that relies upon a clear conception of what is meant by an "idea" in any given context. This sentence is an expression of an idea, but would make a very poor learning object. Worse still, it could be decomposed into a number of subsidiary ideas, depending on how an individual might wish to re-use it. For instance, it could mean that "sentences may represent ideas" or "learning objects are not ideas" or any number of alternative interpretations. Learning objects are intended to be reusable, but if even a small sentence can be interpreted in numerous ways, then it is up to the author to identify metadata that summarise that idea. Worse still, the meaning of an idea may have no relationship with the appropriate means of teaching it or learning it. Learning is as much as anything about making connections, so isolated ideas may be less than useful. This leads to the popularly expressed definition of a learning object as something to which metadata have been attached, describing it as a learning object. Such a definition is circular, assuming that the creators of such metadata already know that the thing that they are marking up is a learning object. It seems that any method of identifying such things is doomed to this kind of circularity or is otherwise meaningless. This leads McGreal to half-seriously suggest that "the assortment of what can be considered to be a LO ranges from anything and everything, through anything digital, to only objects that have an ostensible learning purpose, to those that support learning only in a particular or specific context" (McGreal, 2004).

Critique of RLOs in the Context of Object-Oriented Design

The concept of RLOs borrows much from the computer science notion of an object. However, it loses much of the point of the concept that makes it so powerful in the construction of computer software for several reasons:

1. There is no concept of inheritance (so that one object can be easily based on another), nor real interoperability (beyond the ability to co-exist in a framework) in the idea.

2. Ignoring the possibility that the objects themselves may be active, as far as any other objects are concerned, they are passive lumps of stuff that have certain properties. Objects in computer programming have methods (behaviours that you can ask them to perform), which make them do things. It is possible for one class of object to inherit the properties and methods of another, overriding some if necessary, without destroying the original class on which the object is based. This achieves real levels of reuse. Methods and properties can be overridden by descendents of the original object. In some languages, it is possible to have multiple inheritance, where one object gains its properties and methods from another. Associated with this are frameworks such as the model-view-controller pattern that provide standardised effective means of construction.

3. Objects are active and talk to each other by passing messages. RLOs are passive chunks of data and metadata.

4. Objects hide their inner workings and encapsulate data so that it is only necessary to know what to say to them and what they can say back in order to work with them. None of this makes any sense in the world of RLOs and, as such, they are fundamentally poor when it comes to reusability.

A lot of work has gone into defining RLOs and it certainly makes sense, from a project management perspective, to break down the task of instructional design into controllable chunks. It is also a potentially useful means of reusing work done by an individual or a small team, though it is hard to see how it differs from a more conventional library approach apart from in the explicit need for self-containedness that the method implies.

For learning objects to fulfill the promise that many believe they hold, two distinct issues must be addressed. The first issue is that of granularity, for without that, there is no foundation at all for the concept. The second is the practical problem of how reusability may best be achieved. Transactional control theory has at least partial answers to both concerns.

Using Transactional Control to Define the Granularity of an RLO

Transactional control offers another alternative means of defining the granularity of a learning object: *a learning object should be sufficient to encapsulate a learning need that may be expressed as a choice in a learning trajectory.* Anything that would constitute a change in learning trajectory might be a candidate as a learning object. This allows many potential scales, from the huge ("I wish to become a doctor") to the very small ("I want to learn how to spell 'antidisestablishmentarianism'"). It would be hard, though not impossible, to justify the categorisation of a complete course of study leading to a doctorate as a reusable learning object (Downes, 2001; McGreal, 2004), but it admits the possibility that RLOs may be composed of other RLOs, which in turn, may be composed of others down to a very fine granularity. This is very much in keeping with the computer science origins of the concept and quite effectively expresses the complex variety of different needs that RLOs may address. It also neatly distinguishes RLOs from the more general concept of learning resources (which might include RLOs but would also include pictures, diagrams, charts, and so on).

There are still some major issues related to reusability that must be resolved, notably with regard to the problems of constructing meaningfully connected events for the learner, and there is still the issue of the logic of the learning narrative itself to be addressed. RLOs that present approximately the right choices will frequently clash in style, overlap in content, vary in quality and format, and fail to fit together in many ways.

The question that instructional designers should ask themselves is therefore a simple one: "At any given point, am I making a *choice* about a learner's learning trajectory and is that choice sufficient to constitute a change in direction?" In other words, the smallest learning object should be one that embodies an atomic transactional choice. Once these decisions have been embodied, then it opens up a rich vein of potential ways of enabling or disabling choices. For instance, following from the example given in Chapter IV of teaching a learner to buy apples: if the learner already knows what a fruit is, then there is no need to present that information or, in keeping with the principle of providing both choice and constraint, that choice should have reduced emphasis. If a learner wishes to know about how to eat an apple, then multiple paths may be provided (including providing apples to be eaten, showing how to prepare them, drawing concept maps of the area, and so forth), which result from different choices at the same selection point.

With such an approach, it is inevitable that some objects will be larger (often much larger) than others and most objects will contain others. As the number of contexts in which individual objects are used rises, the number and depth of metadata attached to them will grow accordingly, making it easier to find uses for them in still further contexts. Such an approach requires contextual metadata such as that found in the IMS-LD standard (http://www.imsglobal.org/learningdesign/index. html, accessed June 18th, 2006), a standard that may be used to specify a learning trajectory in some detail.

Transactional Control as a Basis for Inheritance and Re-Use

The application of a transactional control model to RLOs also opens up an intriguing possibility for inheritance. If an atomic choice defines the smallest possible learning object, then other choices alongside it (e.g., of the structure of the resource, the media to use, the pedagogy to employ) may, in some ways, be contingent and potentially malleable.

If a transactional choice is considered as akin to a fork in the road, then other aspects, such as the number of means of transport, the rate of travel, or what the learner decides to look at along the way, are all potentially variable. It is thus possible to imagine the RLO equivalent of base classes in object-oriented programming, determining the direction but not the means of travel. As a principle, this can only be taken so far, as a learning trajectory is always at least partly determined by internal constraints: if the trajectory so far has determined that only a certain kind of choice may be made, then (say) the style of delivery cannot arbitrarily be altered. The choice may well have been determined, at least in part, by earlier decisions.

Conclusion

This chapter has addressed a range of issues relating to the provision of published content. For most published content, once it has been selected, the learner may choose to succumb to the control of the teacher, or to stop reading or otherwise interacting with the content. Important though that choice is, it is common to virtually all learning activities and, as such, may be ignored from the perspective of transactional control.

Of all the issues raised, the most important is that if learners are to be able to choose to choose, they must be provided with choices. However, this in itself is insufficient. To be in control, learners must understand the reasons that different paths may be selected—what benefits they might gain by following one trajectory rather than another. The process of signposting is therefore more than just indicating options. Somehow, these options must be described in a manner that allows learners to select them for a reason.

The use of learning objects presents some potentially useful approaches to combining resources in a flexible manner and transactional control concepts may help to decide how these may best be combined.

An ideal system would allow the learner to shift continually between high and low transactional control as the need demands, but without the large overhead that most traditional approaches to instructional design seem to require. The most natural solution to providing such control would seem to be to take advantage of the vast resources of the Internet. Somewhere in this enormous stuff swamp, there probably exist suitable pages, sites, or people that address almost any learning needs. The next chapter considers the problems that arise when using conventional tools to find, select, and coherently assemble them.

References

Candy, P. C. (1991). *Self-direction for lifelong learning: A comprehensive guide to theory and practice*. San Francisco: Jossey Bass.

Collis, B. (2005). Putting blended learning to work. In C. J. Bonk & C. R. Graham (Eds.), *The handbook of blended learning: Global perspectives, local designs* (pp. 461-473). San Francisco: Pfeiffer.

Dalsgaard, C. (2005). *Learning frameworks as an alternative to repositories*. Paper presented at the ICL 2005, Villach, Austria.

Downes, S. (2001). Learning objects: Resources for distance education worldwide. *International Review of Research in Open and Distance Learning, 2*(1).

Felder, R. M., & Spurlin, J. (2005). Applications, reliability and validity of the index of learning styles. *International Journal of Engineering Education, 21*(1), 103-112.

Gardner, H. (1983). *Frames of mind: The theory of multiple intelligences*. New York: Basic Books.

Hussey, T., & Smith, P. (2002). The trouble with learning outcomes. *Active Learning in Higher Education, 3*(3), 220-233.

Ip, A., & Canale, R. (2003). *Supporting collaborative learning activities with SCORM*. Paper presented at the Educause 2003, Adelaide, Australia.

Kolb, D. A. (1984). *Experiential learning*. Englewood Cliffs, NJ: Prentice Hall.

Mason, R., Pegler, C., & Weller, M. (2005). A learning object success story. *Journal of Asynchronous Learning Networks, 9*(1), 97-105.

McGreal, R. (2004). Learning objects: a practical definition. *International Journal of Instructional Technology and Distance Learning, 1*(9), 21-32.

Moore, M. G. (1986). Self-directed learning and distance education [electronic version]. *Journal of Distance Education, 1*.

Moore, M. G. (1997). Theory of transactional distance. In D. Keegan (Ed.), *Theoretical principles of distance education* (pp. 22-38). Routledge.

Moore, M. G., & Kearsley, G. (1996). *Distance education: A systems view*. Belmont: Wadsworth.

Pask, G. (1976). *Conversation theory: Applications in education and epistemology*: Elsevier.

Pask, G., & Lewis, B. (1972). *Teaching strategies: A systems approach*. Bletchley: OU Press.

Polsani, P. (2003). Use and abuse of reusable learning objects. *Journal of Digital Information, 3*(4).

Schank, R. (2004). Engines for education. Retrieved September 22, 2004, from http://www.engines4ed.org/hyperbook/index.html

Wells, H. G. (1937). World brain: The idea of a permanent world encyclopaedia. Retrieved January 3, 2006, from http://sherlock.berkeley.edu/wells/world_brain.html

Wiley, D. A. (2001). Connecting learning objects to instructional design theory: A definition, a metaphor, and a taxonomy. In *The Instructional Use of Learning Objects*.

Chapter VIII

Finding Good Stuff

First, what's there is stuff: partly information, partly pure nonsense—and it's not always easy to distinguish the two. Second, it's not a superhighway, it's a swamp, albeit a swamp with many remarkable hillocks of well-organized, first-rate data and information. (Crawford, 1999)

Introduction

This chapter focuses on the issue raised in Chapter VII: finding good and appropriate learning resources on the Internet and the issues of control that arise. In the process, there will be discussion of the kinds of criteria that might be used to identify useful and appropriate learning resources and the barriers to such discoveries. In the context of transactional control, the ability to choose will be seen as a complex amalgam of sufficient and targeted information about the content, combined with knowledge of context and the pedagogical process. To illustrate potential approaches to enabling learners to choose to choose in this context, some examples will be given of the ways that recommender systems and adaptive hypermedia may affect learner control.

Resource-Based Learning

Resource-based learning (RBL) has a long history as an educational technique. It provides a means of achieving both subject literacy and information literacy (the ability to use literature to discover new knowledge) at the same time. Learners are provided with or told to seek a wide range of resources and materials, typically with a teacher-specified goal in mind or within a specified subject area. The teacher in a traditional resource-based learning scenario becomes a facilitator, helping learners to achieve their goals, but not directing their activities unless asked to do so. The emphasis is usually on diversity: learners are encouraged to seek information by any means possible, whether by asking people, using tools, reading books, watching videos, or the like. However, traditional approaches still involve a significant degree of control. The teacher acts as a filter, an editor mediating between the tangled complexity of the real world and the (by definition) simpler understanding of the learner. This is really little more than a variation on the traditional lecture format, of which McKenzie (1997) writes:

Good lecturers do tons of extra reading and research into the topic before us. They save us the trouble of doing our own exploration, having "turned down the corners" on the best pages. They synthesize, summarize and report the "best parts." Knowing their audience, they are able to translate what might otherwise seem foreign, confusing, boring, or overly abstract into a half hour of explanation and illumination. They act somewhat as tour guides.

The need to understand, not only the topic but also the needs of learners, is what makes a teacher a seemingly vital part of this method of learning. The huge wealth and diversity of learning resources that is available on the Internet makes an RBL approach appear very attractive as a means of providing guided learning.

WebQuests and Related Approaches

A very popular teacher-controlled means of using the mass of resources on the Internet is the WebQuest, a term and process invented by Bernie Dodge and Tom March in around 1995. The principle of the WebQuest is simple: teachers seek useful resources and provide annotated links to Web resources and a set of associated tasks related to them. Various systems have been developed to simplify this process, notably Walden's Paths (Furuta, 2000) and the adaptation of weblogs to the purpose (Downes, 2004). In themselves, these provide little that is radically new from a learner perspective and are little more than extensions of the traditional classroom and reading list, albeit ones that are far more flexible, cheap, and controllable from the perspective of the teacher as well as being, perhaps, more entertaining from a learner perspective. However, with careful annotation, it is possible to provide more than one route through the same or related resources, thus in principle, enabling greater or lesser control as the learner sees fit. As ever, the key is sign posting rather than dictating the path that must be taken, to suggest a sensible path but always to provide alternatives. In a perfect world, such systems should be combined with mechanisms that encourage discussion; Stephen Downes's own use of weblogs is a good instance of this. The WebQuest and related approaches provide a great deal of control for the teacher, but relatively little for the learner. However, it does provide the learner with a trustworthy guide.

RBL without the Teacher

In Web-based learning, the controlling role of the teacher is far from dead, not least in the smaller scale activity of creating worthwhile resources in the first place. The help provided by tutors (whether real or virtual) can vary from providing the highly structured format of the WebQuest or some forms of adaptive hypermedia (discussed below) to a completely freeform approach where the main assistance given is in helping to learn to search, and perhaps in helping to evaluate the results. However, it is possible that the traditional role of the teacher as the controller of learning may be distributed and diluted still further.

Even without the aid of a single teacher, the Internet is full of learning resources that can help a learner. It may safely be assumed that at least some of these are effective and reliable means of, or resources for, learning. If so, then in principle, it seems possible that all that might be required to provide a useful education is to advise learners to seek resources that will help them to learn, without specifying which should be used. This is not completely crazy, as it is the nature of the Web that it provides some guidance, albeit of a diffuse kind. Brown and Duguid (1995) have observed that all documents are in some sense related, whether on the Internet or not:

From turned down pages, to notes on a dust jacket, to academic essays, to fan zines, to direct quotations and indirect allusions, to stories lifted for future retelling without attribution, we are always commenting on texts, which continually intertwine in a process grandly known as "intertextuality." Documents are not, then, independent. Like biological organisms, every document is always related to some other.

The nature of the Web reifies these connections and multiplies them, but not in an arbitrary way. The Web has a "small world" topology (Adamic, 1999; Buchanan, 2002). Giles (1999) reports on research at the University of Notre Dame, which suggested that, of the billion or so pages available on the Web in 1999, the average distance between two randomly selected pages was in the region of nineteen clicks apart. There is at least a certain amount of self-organisation occurring on the Web that can help guide learners in some kind of direction, if only by keeping them within a particular cluster. Academic (1999) reports on a strongly connected group of sites relating to the pro-life and pro-choice communities by examining cross-links within them, and is thus able to conclude that the community of pro-lifers is more tightly knit and better organised than that of the pro-choicers. Lempel and Moran (2000, pp. 387-409) also investigate and confirm the same range of clusters, which exhibit what they describe as the TKC (tightly knit community) effect. Simply through the independent linking of pages, the Web in its "raw" state, might provide at least the beginnings of the organisation required to structure knowledge. Unfortunately, this does not imply a suitable pedagogic structure will emerge, that matches the needs of the learners.

To make the process easier, perhaps a flesh and blood teacher might offer support and advice where necessary, but even this seems in excess to a learner's needs, given that such guidance exists among the myriad of resources already available on the Internet. Indeed, Hill and Hannafin (2001) identify this as being a distinguishing feature that differentiates the Internet variant of RBL from its traditional forebear, interestingly framing it as an issue of control. Of traditional RBL approaches, they write:

Textbooks, for example, were adopted based on their congruence with established curriculum objectives ... tending to reinforce desired learning outcomes but limiting the availability of resources to pursue related interests or examine concepts from different perspectives.

The issue of control in resource-based learning is, as always, related to scale. While learners may have freedom to select resources at will, once selected, the path may become more constrained. To follow a guided path, even to read a book, a learner must, to some extent, relinquish choice and to allow the writer to control the trajectory. This does not mean that the learner should be passive in the process and, indeed, it is hoped that adult learners might approach the task critically, questioningly, and maybe even sceptically. However, it is important to distinguish between resources that are being studied (novels, research papers, and so on) and resources that are being used to provide guidance and instruction. In the former case, a sceptical attitude might be more encouraged than in the latter case: where the role of the resource is to be directive, control may be considered to reside in the hands of the author. If a learner is to relinquish his or her control, then it implies that she or he must trust whatever means is being used to enable learning to do the job effectively. In e-learning, the relative absence of tacit cues that are found in face to face environments makes this potentially difficult to achieve.

Trust

Prior to the spread of the World Wide Web, a wide range of mechanisms were and still are available to help identify trustworthiness in a learning resource. The publication process involves editors, readers, peer review, and critics in a complex set of inter-related ratings that help to ensure that a given resource is reliable, effective and useful. The affordance granted by the Web to allow anyone with a mind to do so, the ability to publish their efforts has made it increasingly difficult (but by no means impossible) to identify reliable sources.

Criteria for Finding Good Stuff

Finding stuff on the Web is easy, and for most topics which might interest us, it is also not too difficult to find stuff that is relevant to our fields of interest. However, without the sort of guidance provided in WebQuest-style lists of sites, it is very difficult for learners to ascertain the suitability or reliability of those sites, nor to know where to surf to next once one resource is "consumed." As Hill and Hannafin (2001) explain: "Although tools and search engines that are provided typically (and in most cases only generally) help to locate potential resources, they do not help an individual to determine their meaning or relevance."

This puts learners, especially those lacking autonomy in a given subject, at a significant disadvantage. Even when suitable resources have been selected by well-qualified expert information professionals (such as those provided at LII.org, the Librarians Internet Index, for example), there can still be a bewildering choice for the uninitiated learner. If the range of options is too small, then there may be nothing to fit a learner's needs. If it is too large, then the effort of seeking suitable resources may be too great. Worse still, if the wrong choices are made, then it may make a negative impact on learning, leaving learners confused, bewildered, or scared to try again.

Knowing who to Trust

To make effective use of external resources to provide a combination of choice and constraint to learners, it is vital to provide the means to identify the worthwhile from the less worthwhile.

Learners rely on a wide range of cues to identify relevant and valid resources that combine sufficient quality of information with the capacity to help them to learn. Factors that are relevant include, for instance, the source site, the recommendations of others, knowledge of the author, knowledge of the publisher, and relevant citations. In traditional media, implicit trust is placed in the expertise of others (delegating control) to assure the reliability of books, journal articles, and so on.

For resources on the Web, where "alien devil worship" and "sex with animals" occupy equal ground with reliable information and learning resources, it is necessary to develop strategies that make it possible to distinguish the useful from the useless, the good from the bad, and the true from the false.

It is possible to apply similar criteria to those used to identify the value of traditional sources, including the implicit and explicit recommendations of others, recognised authors, publishers, and so on. Further cues may be available such as identifiably reliable hosting organisations (universities, governments, professional bodies, for example) and recognised subject gateways such as BUBL (http://bubl.ac.uk/), EEVL (http://www.eevl.ac.uk/), OMNI (http://omni.ac.uk/) or SOSIG (http://www.sosig. ac.uk/). However, this is only part of the problem.

The list of potential quality criteria may be indefinitely large: for example, for the DESIRE project, Hofman and Worsfield (1996) devised the following list of criteria for choosing appropriate information sources on the Web:

- validity;
- authority and reputation of source;
- substantiveness;
- accuracy;
- comprehensiveness;
- uniqueness;
- composition and organisation;
- currency, and adequacy of maintenance.

Valovic (1994) uses a simpler set of criteria:

- Time value of information: information half-life;
- scope of information: how many people it affects;
- authenticity of source: how verifiable is this;

- dissemination value: if information has been widely disseminated, it may be less useful to an individual or organisation, at least in a business context.

A similar, though not identical approach is taken by the Virtual Chase site for law researchers (2006), which lists:

- Scope of coverage;
- authority;
- objectivity;
- accuracy; and
- timeliness.

The criteria employed in these examples are representative of numerous similar schemas, and may all be useful in determining reliability of a source of information. However, the fact that they differ in many significant aspects illustrates part of the problem that arises when attempting to identify what it is about a resource that is of most value—its usefulness in a given context.

Context Sensitivity

The virtues that are sought in a site or page will vary according to circumstances and needs. Any given set of criteria may not necessarily capture those qualities or virtues of a resource that could make it useful to learners in their specific learning contexts. It is clear that education is more than just the transfer of information from one head to another, so further criteria are needed in order to clarify the benefits of resources in helping learners to achieve knowledge. One approach is to allow the quality criteria to be defined in relation to the context. For example, the author's CoFIND system allows groups of learners to define the criteria that they find most valuable for themselves (Dron, Mitchell, & Boyne, 2003; Dron, Mitchell, Siviter, & Boyne, 2000). This principle, a form of tagging, also underlies a wide range of link sharing sites like deli.cio.us™ or Furl™ or the Flickräimage sharing site, which rely on folk taxonomies, or "folksonomies." Folksonomies are formed of categorisations created by their users (Mathes, 2004; Shirky, 2004). The potential value of such systems is that they allow people to benefit from the collective knowledge and preferences of many others, and to allow them to find others with similar interests, expressed through the similar metadata that they use.

The genre of Internet-based systems that makes use of collective knowledge with perhaps the longest pedigree is that of the collaborative filter, or recommender system.

Collaborative Filters and Recommender Systems

A traditional solution to the problem of high overheads in teaching and learning is to distribute the teaching role, for instance, through recommended books and journals. These behave in some senses as teachers, one step removed. Cost, copyright, and availability may often act as potential constraints on these traditional forms.

The growth of the Internet means that a promising solution is to make use of the wide range of learning resources that are made freely available through Web-based channels. A resource-based learning approach that follows from this reduces the effort required from the point of view of the individual teacher and increases the potential range of choices from the point of view of the learner. However, a significant remaining difficulty for the teacher lies in discovering appropriate, useful, and reliable resources in the first place and then, even when they are found, integrating them into a meaningful learning experience. Without a teacher, the learner is in a worse position.

Recommendations of those we Know

Relying upon recommendations of people who are known and trusted is a time-honoured way of reducing the complexity of finding useful resources, but is (probably) a non-optimal solution. Individuals and small groups are necessarily blinkered in their view of the world. Worse, once the route of reducing choice by accepting the recommendations of individuals has been started down, these individuals become disproportionately influential within the group as a whole. If y believes that x provides good recommendations, and z believes that y provides good recommendations, then z believes that x provides good recommendations. Unfortunately, this relationship is seldom explicit, so x sways the opinions of many others who cannot or will not form such opinions independently. Even if x is consistent in making good decisions, such decisions are based on a necessary limited perspective of the whole docuverse. The effect is an inevitable result of scale in this system, and reduces the problem-solving capacity of the group as a whole.

Googling

A simple search on Google™ for "ethernet tutorial" reveals about 4,120,000 potential results (July 18, 2006), any one of which may be useful to a learner. The problem is becoming more acute every day. When the same search was attempted in July 2004, a mere 1,120,000 results were discovered. In August 2000, the number returned was a paltry 39,700. Even then, many of those results were still potentially useful at the point that Google stopped delivering pages, some 700 or so sites into the search. Allowing for the fact that some of these would have been duplicates, out of date, and so on, discovering what would be *most* useful out of such a plethora of potential sources is nearly impossible and it is usual to rely on Google's PageRank™ algorithms (Brin & Page, 2000) to provide implicit recommendations. This approach is often surprisingly effective. PageRank is a system of Latent Human Annotation, a process that may be observed in a range of Web applications (Fowler, Fowler, & Williams, 1996; Kleinberg, 1998; Lempel & Moran, 2000). The Google system is based on the notion of hubs and authorities, providing a weighting for each Web site based on the back links pointing to it. Each of the sites providing those back links is given a similar weighting, with more authoritative sources getting a higher weighting. The assumption behind it is that links to sites suggest implicit approval on the part of the one providing the links. The result is to provide resources that are more likely to be relevant and trustworthy than those returned by a simple content search alone.

The Matthew Principle

Regrettably, Google's algorithm has a potentially major flaw, which has only come to light as it has gained market dominance. As Google is by far the most popular means of finding resources on the Internet, whatever links it places on the first page are far more likely to be followed than any others. If users like the sites that they find there, they are more likely to place links to those sites on their own pages, therefore increasing the page's rank. This is a variant of the Matthew principle, whereby the rich get rich and the poor get poorer (Surowiecki, 2004). The Matthew principle gets its name from the Bible: "For whosoever hath, to him shall be given, and he shall have more abundance: but whosoever hath not, from him shall be taken away even that he hath" (Matthew, 13:12).

It is a positive feedback loop that rewards the richer and punishes the poorer. If Google reduces the range of possible answers to the problem, the solution that is found may not always be the best available, even though that solution may well be somewhere within the list of pages returned. The effect is ameliorated by the fact that the system is constantly fed with new pages, each competing to be on the first page of Google results. While it is certainly true that equally worthy or perhaps even worthier pages than those that are found may be lost further down the list, evolutionary pressures mean that a page that is *far* fitter will usually rise to the top, supplanting its former rival. Unfortunately, "fit" in this sense is simply a measure of popularity within a particular ecological niche defined by the keywords used in the search. Different learners have different needs and popularity is only one measure of utility on a single dimension. For instance, pages listed on the "Web Pages that Suck" site (www.webpagesthatsuck.com) may achieve surprisingly high rankings. The benefits of appealing to human authorities are linked to the fact that humans know what humans need and can adapt their recommendations to the individual. An algorithm like Page Rank is only capable of aggregating averages.

Recommender Systems

Google is a kind of recommender system, albeit at a coarse and general level. A wide range of technologies that may be grouped in the category of collaborative filters or recommender systems has been developed to allow the combined opinions (explicit or implicit) of a group to identify valuable resources. Such systems provide seals of approval—a sense of trust and assurance that others have in some way vouched for the resources that they recommend. The earliest recommender system was (perhaps) Tapestry, created at Xerox PARC (Goldberg, Nichols, Oki, & Terry, 1992). Since then, they have become pervasive mainstream technologies underlying numerous community and ecommerce sites. The Google search engine is perhaps the most successful of these, but related technologies lie behind many other hugely successful Web sites, including IMDB™'s movie ratings (www.imdb.com), recommendations provided by Amazon™ (www.amazon.com), eBay™'s feedback and star ratings (www.ebay.com), or the kudos points of SlashDot™ (http://Slashdot.org). Collaborative filters vary in sophistication and means of operation. The simplest rely on explicit ratings provided by users and simply aggregate them. Others use implicit data, such as number of clicks, time spent dwelling on a page, and so on, but follow much the same principle. More complex automated collaborative filters identify similarities between users, typically employing algorithms that match patterns of recommendations, whether implicit, explicit, or both. An interesting variation on the theme is the citation index, which uses the implicit metadata of citations in papers to assess the reliability of a given academic paper. A number of Web-based systems attempt this, including Google Scholar (http://scholar.google.com), Citeseer (http://citeseer.ist.psu.edu/), and CiteULike (http://www.citeulike.org/). CiteULike presents a particularly interesting example as it relies on individuals uploading references for their own use then showing the most popular, as well as clustering results for the most popular subject areas and showing the most popular by sign posting them with larger fonts.

Recommender Systems in Education

Chislenko (1997) suggested that collaborative filtering might be used in the service of education to help learners identify suitable resources from which to learn, a process that is applied by, amongst others Dron et al. (Dron, Mitchell, Boyne, & Siviter, 2000; Dron, Mitchell, & Boyne, 2003; Dron, Mitchell, Siviter, & Boyne, 2000), Recker et al. (2000), Anderson et al. (2003), Alamán and Cobos (1998) and Terveen et al. (1997). Such systems are intended to assist learners to find resources that are appropriate to their learning needs. Some take a simple and naïve approach, basing their recommendations on implicit or explicit metadata embodying preferences. For instance, PHOAKS mines Usenet newsgroups for references to Web sites, making use of the categories supplied in the Usenet news hierarchy itself to identify relevant subject matter (Terveen, Hill, Amento, McDonald, & Creter, 1997). Thus, sites mentioned in a newsgroup about the songs of Bob Dylan will be assumed to be recommendations of those sites. Other systems attempt to relate recommendations to learner needs, within some underlying pedagogical framework (Recker, Walker, & Wiley, 2000).

Weaknesses of Recommender Systems for Education

There are potential dangers to such approaches. Most notably, automated collaborative filters that match similar users with one another have proven to be highly successful when recommending items where tastes, preferences, and recommendations are likely to remain fairly stable: books, films, music, trustworthy sellers, interesting writers of messages, and so on. However, learning is by nature a transformative process—a process of becoming—and a learner's early preferences and needs for basic arithmetic resources may not usefully predict his or her current needs for learning how to solve quadratic equations, let alone medieval poetry. To make things worse, collaborative filters that base their recommendations on simpler measures of overall popularity suffer from the Matthew principle. It is not only conceivable but common that fine resources might be overlooked or mediocre resources gain undue prominence. This is a weakness with many traditional forms of recommendation, including the citation index. A simple solution to this problem is to make use of such systems within a relatively constrained setting, such as within a traditional class or subject group, where a certain amount of parity between learners and their needs can be assumed. This is only a partial solution: the corollary of this is that learners will often be more influenced by the opinions of friends and acquaintances than of strangers, all other things being equal. Should the originators of recommendations be known, this might lead to a greater amplification of the Matthew principle.

Recommender Systems and Trust

Collaborative filters provide a potential means for learners to have some trust in the validity or reliability of a resource, acting a little like the explicit recommendations of reviewers in conventional and Web-based media. One important feature of trust is that a relationship, either real or by proxy, needs to be established between tutor and learner. Carlson (1989) describes one of Knowles's key insights as being that "instructors had to care about learners' interests rather than what they believed ought to interest learners." This is a feature that is apparently lacking in a collaborative filtering system which, despite the fact that it gains its structure from human sources, returns those results in an impersonal, non-attributed fashion. The trust that develops is between human and machine, a far less personal relationship than between human and human, which requires a greater commitment on the part of the learner. As Korba et al. (2005) suggest of software agents: "If the agent is empowered to take significant actions on behalf of the user, this will obviously be seen as a riskier situation that will require higher levels of trust than situations where an agent merely provides information or advice" (p. 104).

If recommendations of resources are too impersonal, an alternative approach is to apply the recommendations, not to electronic resources, but to people. For instance, Pitco's Ask-an-Expert (www.askanexpert.com) makes use of ratings of the individuals themselves to identify useful people who might enable learning. A similar approach is taken by Google Answers (http://answers.google.com/answers/), which acts as a kind of marketplace for seekers and providers of knowledge to meet, with answers provided in exchange for cash. Another related system is Amazon's Mechanical Turk (http://www.mturk.com/mturk/welcome). Described as "artificial artificial intelligence," those seeking a processing task best performed by a human submit one or more HITs (human intelligence tasks) and a price they are willing to pay (typically a cent or two for a small piece of research such as finding a specific item in a set of photographs). Anyone can accept a HIT. If it is successfully performed, the HIT requestor pays the price. The system relies on large numbers of people willing to perform tasks. With incredible prescience, Illich (1971) suggested such an array of methods and even named it the "learning Web," nearly 20 years before the World Wide Web was invented. In his scheme, there were four approaches to allow students access to ways of learning: reference services to learning objects (using the term "learning object" much as it is used today), skill exchanges, peer-matching, and reference services to educators at large. This is a principle that may go back significantly further still. Legend has it that the robes worn by university lecturers had voluminous, pocket-like sleeves for the purpose of collecting money from grateful recipients of wisdom, a practice which itself may have been derived from the religious origins of academia, wherein money might have been offered for a good sermon. Whether this is true or not, money for answers remains an underpinning principle whenever someone turns to experts for knowledge, be they insurance brokers, travel agents, plumbers, or lawyers.

However successful such means of bringing learners and the means to learn might be, the development of a relationship between learner and teacher typically requires a more direct form of communication than simple recommendation. As three of the four methods suggested by Illich imply, people are central to enabling learning. The communication such as that found via email, on a bulletin board, or in a chat room, as well as in real life, is crucial to successful learning. A dialogue process will enable more reliable and relevant recommendations to be made as it implies negotiated control of the learning experience, allowing learners to choose to choose with greater success and assurance. The downside of such approaches is the cost: individual advice is expensive. There are some alternatives. For example, the Answer Garden (Ackerman & McDonald, 1996) enables a collaborative knowledge base to develop as a result of peer advice or, where this is insufficient, advice from an expert. Taking a slightly different tack, Nickles et al. (2005) provide a means of presenting heterogeneous viewpoints and perspectives, granting greater control to the learner over which to accept.

Recommender Systems and Control

Collaborative filters possess some interesting characteristics, from the perspective of learner control. In providing lists of recommendations, collaborative filters may be seen as constraining, acting in some ways like teachers in traditional educational systems. However, it is notable that, though the lists are weighted, it is always a *list* that is returned, hardly ever a single item. Even Google's "I'm feeling lucky" option that takes the searcher straight to the top list item is presented at the same time as a list, emphasising, but not dictating, the selection. Recommender systems recommend, not dictate, allowing a significant degree of control for learners to choose more appropriate paths. What is especially interesting about them is that the recommendations come, not from a single individual, but from the collective behaviour of many individuals, potentially including the person seeking a recommendation.

Shared Annotations

Although collaborative filters may be helpful in guiding learners to useful resources, there is a limit to the richness of the metadata they may use. More detailed evaluations require a richer vocabulary, and the ability to annotate arbitrary resources. The annotations in books have long been an influence on others who later read them, a fact that is noted by Seely Brown and Duguid (2000) who recall that:

Flann O'Brien imagined a book handling service for the culturally insecure. For a fee, book handlers would crease the spines of your books, turn down pages, mark passages, put intelligent comments in the margins, or, for a slightly greater sum, insert tickets from operas or classic plays as bookmarks. (pp. 187-188)

Shared annotations bring life to an otherwise dead document and offer potentially rich information about its value. There are many Web-based annotation systems available from the venerable CritLink (Lee, 2002), to D3E's document-centric discussions (Buckingham-Shum, Motta, & Domingue, 1999) to Educo's social navigation (Kurhila, Miettinen, Nokelainen, & Tirri, 2002) to the fully integrated authenticated standards-based architecture of the Annotea project (Kahan, Koivunen, Prud'Hommeaux, & R., 2001).

Blogs

Annotation systems, which allow the creation of links between different resources, are particularly valuable, as they allow learners to exercise choice in their conceptualisation of a subject without significantly disrupting the narrative flow of the original. The system of trackbacks employed by blog servers is a particularly successful and flexible instance of this kind of tool. When used collaboratively they can bring multiple perspectives and, depending on your perspective, provide document-centered dialogue or dialogue-centered documents.

Annotation is central to the community of blogging, allowing published resources to gather comments and communities around them. Blogs have proved to be very useful in a range of educational contexts, allowing students to reflect and discuss, as well as to receive feedback from their peers and their teachers (Bryant, 2006; Downes, 2004; Dron, 2003). The author's students have experienced considerable delight when people from around the world have commented on their blogs, adding to their motivation and increasing their trust in the validity of their work.

Wikis

Perhaps the most extreme use of annotation can be found in wikis, where the process of annotation and document creation merges into a single seamless collaborative Web site creation environment and social space. In this extreme form, all learners have potentially absolute control over the learning resources and can manipulate the embedded dialogue at will. This is not a good thing for all learners, where the loss of control can reduce trust as well as militate against a sense of ownership, reducing motivation (Dron, 2005). Where such concerns are an issue, it is wise to limit access to the wiki for a particular and cohesive group, and to use software that tracks which user made which change, making learners accountable to others for their modifications. Although wikis may scare some learners, for others, they can be very liberating and can lead to some surprising and very learner-centered, empowering outcomes. For instance, after providing a wiki as an almost casual auxiliary to more teacher-centered teaching resources, a group of the author's own masters' students began to use it to discuss the course, their difficulties, and even to provide a more reliable timetable, after discovering weaknesses in the official version, all without the intercession of any formal teaching presence.

Adaptive Hypermedia and Intelligent Tutoring Systems

Another way of enabling learners to be guided towards resources that are customised for their needs is to employ artificial intelligence to guide them through the learning process. This has spawned two somewhat overlapping approaches to be developed, the first of which is the intelligent tutoring system.

Intelligent Tutoring Systems

Intelligent tutoring systems attempt to mimic some or all of the behaviours of real tutors and have a history stretching back over 30 years. Indeed, some suggest that the concept may be traced back as far as 1926, when Sidney L. Pressey wrote of a teaching machine that gave instant feedback on test results (Petrina, 2004). However, only with the advent of computers was it possible to mimic a wider range of tutor behaviours, leading to a mushroom in intelligent tutoring system (ITS) growth from the 1970s onwards (Hartley & Sleeman, 1973). The principle behind the ITS is that each learner receives content that is adapted to his or her needs. Such needs are established by maintaining some kind of user model. This may be based on explicitly provided information about learning styles, content preference, and so on. More often, it is based on implicitly garnered information, usually through tests or by observing the ways that learners use resources (e.g., the amount of time spent dwelling on a particular resource). The typical ITS is now a sophisticated and powerful piece of software, often incorporating agent-based approaches whereby software agents act on behalf of the learner, the teacher, the content, and the system itself to cooperate in the production of a rich and personalised learning experience (Chen & Wasson, 2005). Similarly, basic ITS functionality has found its way into mainstream learning environments such as Blackboard®. However successful or otherwise the ITS has been, few such systems are concerned with the provision of appropriate content and still fewer with granting control to the learner. The primary role for the tutor, as conceived by the designers of such systems, is as a controller. As a means of allowing learners to choose to choose, they can therefore mainly be seen as a stepping-stone or one of several technologies that may be employed to achieve that goal.

Adaptive Hypermedia

Growing out of ITS research, adaptive hypermedia (AH) systems are becoming popular as a means of tailoring hypertext learning resources to the needs of learners (Brusilovsky, 2001). Hypertext provides the benefits of rich navigation, multiple navigation paths, and varied media, lending itself naturally to the needs of learners to choose to choose. With the phenomenal growth of the biggest hypertext of all, the World Wide Web, the application of technologies that can help to shape the chaotic stuff swamp into something more helpful may be seen as a boon to learners and educators.

Like the traditional ITS, AH environments almost invariably involve a combination of a resource-base with a mechanism for user modelling that allows different users to see different views of the system, based on implicitly or explicitly expressed needs. This can be as simple as branching to different points according to the results of an objective test or as complex as a system that varies the content of a page based on a combination of text results, user preferences, learning style inventory, and so on. Most AH and ITS systems work on a closed corpus of tightly constrained and controllable resources, though some are designed to work with an open corpus of arbitrary resources available on the Internet (Brusilovsky, Chavan, & Farzan, 2004; Dron, Mitchell, Siviter, & Boyne, 2000). Some, such as AHA! (de Bra & Ruiter, 2003) are conceived of as intelligent tutoring systems and offer relatively little or no choice to the learners, adapting navigation and presentation of content to suit their perceived needs, while others such as Interbook (Brusilovsky, Schwarz, & Weber, 1996) employ a more freeform textbook analogy, and are more inclined towards providing navigational support, emphasising, de-emphasising or annotating items that are considered to be more or less useful in a given setting. A further variation provides adaptive annotation, allowing more or less detailed explanations of the content, for example.

Adaptive Hypermedia as an ITS

Systems that make firm choices on behalf of the learner may be a poor tool for an independent learner, unless the adaptive system has such a good model of the learner that it makes the same choices the learner or a perfect teacher would make, given sufficient information. Although some excellent progress has been made in this area within highly constrained settings, this is a long way from happening. In the meantime, anything that reduces choice will be of considerably less value to an autonomous learner for whom choice-making is an ideal state. Given the underlying principle of allowing learners to choose to choose, anything that takes away that ability without the permission of the learner will be counter-productive. Highly prescriptive adaptive hypermedia systems are beneficial to more dependent, less autonomous learners, but do not provide the choice that may be needed in a learning environment. However, some such systems allow manual adaptations to be made to the user model, restoring a significant degree of control. Such adaptations are akin to the dialogic process that goes on between learner and teacher that allows the teacher to adapt his or her teaching to the needs of learners. Interestingly, this implies that the user model is, in some sense, at least, from the learner perspective, the teacher, or at least, the "interface" presented by the teacher. Thus, there is a curious blending of teacher and learner that is reified through this process.

Adaptive Hypermedia as an Unconstrained Guide

While explicit user-model adaptability provides a useful element of learner control, adaptive hypermedia systems using social navigation techniques that advise and recommend, rather than prescribe, are the preferred model for allowing learners to choose to choose. Like collaborative filters and recommender systems, they might be extremely useful in providing sign posts, rather than blocking the roads. They make intelligent choices of potential trajectories, rather than the simple hyperlinks provided in static resources, hence providing a real set of alternatives that cater to both autonomous and less autonomous learners alike. For example, the "What do I do now?" button of the DOROTHIE system provides choice for less autonomous learners without constraining those who already know the answer (Hill & Hannafin, 2001). Such an approach can be seen as a form of scaffolding—supporting the weak, but not constraining the strong.

Adapting to the Need for Control

In building or selecting an adaptive hypermedia system, it would be worthwhile to make sure that one level of adaptation is to identify the learner's need for constraint and apply greater or lesser constraint accordingly. Unfortunately, such systems are rare (if they exist at all) and the adaptations that such systems provide tend to relate to measures of success, learning style or explicit preference, rather than measures of autonomy and control. Having said that, there are several systems that allow learners to both view and change the ways that the systems adapt, giving substantial control to the learner. A significant figure in this field is Judy Kay, whose seminal article on learner control (Kay, 2001) distilled a trend towards greater user control over adaptive systems that continues to grow. Her concept of a "scrutable adaptive system" (Kay, 2006; Kay & Kummerfeld, 2006) enables the learner to both view and change not only the user model, but also other models embedded in the system, notably the teacher model. To what extent this is useful depends, to a large extent, upon the interface provided. Too much information and the learner's confusion is increased because of the extra choice available. Too little information and control is reduced. However, this move to scrutability is an important step forward for adaptive hypermedia that offers great potential for learner-selected levels of control. Adaptive hypermedia systems that allow manual control over the user model provide an intriguing blend which blurs the distinction between learner and teacher, making it unclear where the boundary of the user model and the teacher's control begins and ends. Taking this notion one step further, collaborative filters and adaptive hypermedia systems that work on an open corpus using social navigation are particularly interesting, as they can combine the collective behaviour of many rather than relying on teacher-generated rules and structures. This kind of system provides the underpinnings of many forms of social software.

Conclusion

The previous chapter contained what may be boiled down to two essential features of a learning resource that can allow learners to choose to choose:

- Provide signposts, not fence posts: show the way, don't force learners to take it.

- Provide alternative paths: there is no point to having a signpost if there is only one direction to go.

The same rules apply to ways of helping learners to find good resources in the first place. By following a general rule of providing signposts rather than rigid constraints, it is possible to cater to the needs of both dependent and independent learners, and allow them to flit between modes as and when they need to. However, achieving this in conventional e-learning environments requires a lot of work. Even creating a constrained WebQuest requires a large input of effort before and/or during delivery of a learning project, both in providing multiple paths and in creating or discovering the resources that they lead to. The use of collaborative filters and the like suggests some potential ways that this task can be made less onerous, as do shared annotation systems. Adaptive hypermedia environments potentially allow great flexibility in customising the presentation of resources, especially when combined with a controllable user model.

Delivery of Web content is but one aspect of e-learning, an important foundation, but by no means the most interesting nor, perhaps, even the most prevalent source of learning-related Internet traffic. The Internet is primarily a network of people, connected through social technologies such as email, discussion forums, chat rooms, instant messaging systems, IP telephony, blogs, wikis, and much more. With this thought in mind, it is necessary to consider the affordances, constraints, and potential benefits of what remains the most popular form of communication (be it through email, bulletin boards, newsgroups, or blog comments), the asynchronous discussion, which forms the subject of the next chapter.

References

Ackerman, M. S., & McDonald, D. W. (1996). *Answer garden 2: Merging organizational memory with collaborative help.* Paper presented at the ACM Conference on Computer-Supported Cooperative Work '96.

Adamic, L. (1999). *The small world web.* Paper presented at the Third European Conference on Research and Advanced Technology for Digital Libraries, France.

Alamán, X., & Cobos, R. (1998). *KnowCat: An experiment on collaborative learning.* Paper presented at the Conference Name|. Retrieved Access Date|. from URL|.

Anderson, M., Ball, M., Boley, H., Greene, S., Howse, N., Lemire, D., et al. (2003). *RACOFI: A Rule-Applying Collaborative Filtering System.* Paper presented at the COLA'03, Halifax, Canada.

Ballard Spahr Andrews & Ingersol LLP. (2006). Criteria for quality in information: Ballard Spahr Andrews & Ingersoll, LLP.

Brin, S., & Page, L. (2000). The anatomy of a large-scale hypertextual Web search engine. Retrieved from http://www-db.stanford.edu/pub/papers/google.pdf

Brusilovsky, P. (2001). Adaptive hypermedia. *User Modeling and User Adapted Interaction, 11*(Ten Year Anniversary Issue), 87-110.

Brusilovsky, P., Chavan, G., & Farzan, R. (2004). *Social adaptive navigation support for open corpus electronic textbooks.* Paper presented at the AH 2004, Eindhoven.

Brusilovsky, P., Schwarz, E., & Weber, G. (1996). *A tool for developing hypermedia-based ITS on WWW.* Paper presented at the Third International Conference on Intelligent Tutoring Systems, Montreal, Canada.

Bryant, T. (2006). Social software in academia. *Educause Quarterly, 2006*(2), 61-64.

Buchanan, M. (2002). *Small world.* London: Wiedenfeld & Nicholson.

Buckingham-Shum, S., Motta, E., & Domingue, J. (1999). *Modelling and visualizing perspectives in Internet digital libraries.* Paper presented at the Third Annual Conference on Research and Advanced Technology for Digital Libraries, Paris, France.

Carlson, R. (1989). Malcolm Knowles: Apostle of andragogy. *Vitae Scholasticae, 8*(1).

Chen, W., & Wasson, B. (2005). Intelligent agents supporting distributed collaborative learning. In F. O. Lin (Ed.), *Designing distributed learning environments with intelligent software agents* (pp. 33-66). Hershey, PA: Information Science Publishing.

Chislenko, A. (1997). *Collaborative information filtering and semantic transports.* Retrieved November 19, 1999, from http://www.lucifer.com/~sasha/articles/ACF.html

Crawford, W. (1999). The card catalog and other digital controversies. *American Libraries, 30*(1), 52-52.

de Bra, P., & Ruiter, J.-P. (2003). *AHA! Adaptive Hypermedia for All.* Paper presented at the WebNet 2001, Orlando, FL.

Downes, S. (2004). Educational blogging. *Educause Review, 39*(5), 14-26.

Dron, J. (2003). *The blog and the borg: A collective approach to e-learning.* Paper presented at the E-Learn 2003, Phoenix, AZ.

Dron, J. (2005). *A succession of eyes: Building an e-learning city.* Paper presented at the E-Learn 2005, Vancouver, Canada.

Dron, J., Mitchell, R., Boyne, C., & Siviter, P. (2000). *CoFIND: Steps towards a self-organising learning environment.* Paper presented at the WebNet 2000, San Antonio, TX.

Dron, J., Mitchell, R., & Boyne, C. W. (2003). Evolving learning in the stuff swamp. In N. Patel (Ed.), *Adaptive evolutionary information systems* (pp. 211 - 228). Hershey, PA: Idea Group.

Dron, J., Mitchell, R., Siviter, P., & Boyne, C. (2000). CoFIND: An experiment in n-dimensional collaborative filtering. *Journal of Network and Computer Applications* (23), 131-142.

Fowler, R. H., Fowler, W. A. L., & Williams, J. L. (1996). *3D visualization of WWW semantic content for browsing and query formulation.* Paper presented at the WebNet 96, San Francisco.

Furuta, R. (2000). *Evolution of the Walden's paths authoring tool.* Paper presented at the WebNet 2000, San Antonio, TX.

Giles, J. (1999). Why the world is your neighbourhood thanks to 19 clicks of separation. *The Guardian.*

Goldberg, D., Nichols, D., Oki, B. M., & Terry, D. (1992). Using collaborative filtering to weave an information tapestry. *Communications of the ACM, 35*(2), 61-70.

Hartley, J., & Sleeman, D. (1973). Towards more intelligent teaching systems. *International Journal of Man-Machine Studies, 2,* 215-236.

Hill, J. R., & Hannafin, M. J. (2001). Teaching and learning in digital environments: The resurgence of resource-based learning. *Educational Technology Research and Development, 49*(4), 37-52.

Hofman, P., & Worsfield, E. (1996). Specification for resource description methods Part 2: Selection criteria for quality controlled information gateways. Retrieved August 1, 2001, from http://www.ukoln.ac.uk/metadata/DESIRE/quality/report.rtf

Illich, I. (1971). *Deschooling society.* New York: Harper & Row.

Kahan, J., Koivunen, M.-R., Prud'Hommeaux, E., & R., S. R. (2001). *Annotea: An open RDF infrastructure for shared Web annotations annotea: An open RDF infrastructure for shared Web annotations.* Paper presented at the WWW10, Hong Kong.

Kay, J. (2001). Learner control. *User Modeling and User-Adapted Interaction, 11*(1 - 2), 111-127.

Kay, J. (2006). *Scrutable adaptation: Because we can and must.* Paper presented at the AH 2006, Dublin, Ireland.

Kay, J., & Kummerfeld, B. (2006). *Scrutability, user control and privacy for distributed personalization.* Paper presented at the CHI 2006 Workshop on Privacy-Enhanced Personalization, Montreal, Canada.

Kleinberg, J. M. (1998). *Authoritative sources in a hyperlinked environment.* Paper presented at the 9th ACM-SIAM Symposium on Discrete Algorithms.

Korba, L., Yee, G., Xu, Y., Song, R., Patrick, A. S., & El-Khatib, K. (2005). Privacy and trust in agent-supported distributed learning. In F. O. Lin (Ed.), *Designing distributed learning environments with intelligent software agents* (pp. 67-114). Hershey, PA: Information Science Publishing.

Kurhila, J., Miettinen, M., Nokelainen, P., & Tirri, H. (2002). *Use of social naviga-tion features in collaborative e-learning*. Paper presented at the E-Learn 2002, Montreal, Canada.

Lee, K.-p. (2002). *CritLink: Advanced hyperlinks enable public annotation on the Web*. Paper presented at the CSCW 2002, New Orleans, LA.

Lempel, R., & Moran, S. (2000, May 15-19 2000). *The Stochastic Approach for Link-Structure Analysis (SALSA) and the TKC effect*. Paper presented at the 9th International World Wide Web Conference, Amsterdam, The Netherlands.

Mathes, A. (2004). *Folksonomies: Cooperative classification and communication through shared metadata*. Retrieved January 8, 2005, from http://www.adam-mathes.com/academic/computer-mediated-communication/folksonomies.html

McKenzie, J. (1997). In defense of textbooks, lectures and other aging technologies. *FromNowOn.Org, 6*(8).

Nickles, M., Cobos, R., Weiss, G., & Froehner, T. (2005). *Multi-source knowledge bases and ontologies with multiple individual and social viewpoints* Paper presented at the The 2005 IEEE/WIC/ACM International Conference on Web Intelligence, Compiègne, France.

Petrina, S. (2004). Sidney Pressey and the automation of education, 1924-1934. *Technology and Culture, 45*(2), 305-330.

Recker, M. M., Walker, A., & Wiley, D. A. (2000). *An interface for collaborative filtering of educational resources*. Paper presented at the 2000 International Conference on Artificial Intelligence, Las Vegas, NV.

Seely Brown, J., & Duguid, P. (1995). *The social life of documents*. Retrieved August 21, 2001, from http://www.parc.xerox.com/ops/members/brown/pa-pers/sociallife.html

Seely Brown, J., & Duguid, P. (2000). *The social life of information*. Boston: Har-vard Business School Press.

Shirky, C. (2004). *Folksonomy*. Retrieved January 9, 2005, from http://www.corante.com/many/archives/2004/08/25/folksonomy.php

Surowiecki, J. (2004). *The wisdom of crowds*. London: Little, Brown.

Terveen, L., Hill, W., Amento, B., McDonald, D., & Creter, J. (1997). PHOAKS: A system for sharing recommendations. *Communications of the ACM, 40*(3), 59-62.

Valovic, T. (1994). Quality of information: Part 2. *Telecommunications Maga-zine*.

Chapter IX

Asynchronous Communication

A single fibre does not make a thread, nor a single tree a forest.

Ancient Chinese proverb

Introduction

This chapter is about the nature of control in asynchronous online communication. Although primarily looking at Web-based forums, by extension, many of the issues raised here apply to other forms of asynchronous group communication, including the use of email, proprietary systems like Lotus® Notes® or FirstClass®, as well as mailing lists, newsgroups, and the like. The range of asynchronous communication technologies is immense, therefore, not all types and varieties will be covered here. Other forms of asynchronous communication that provide the underpinnings of the hideously-misnamed "Web 2.0," such as blogs and wikis, will be discussed later.

The chapter starts with a general discussion of some of the fundamental issues of control in asynchronous discussions, presents a detailed analysis of an example forum, then goes on to identify approaches to creating, moderating, and using discussion forums that enable a combination of high and low transactional control.

Transactional Control in an Online Discussion Forum

Discussion forums on the Web tend to take one of two main forms. Messages are either presented linearly, in order of posting, or threaded, with each message shown in the context of its replies and what it replies to. Many, perhaps the majority, provide options for users to select which mode they prefer.

The Apparent Parallelism of Threads

Unlike linear dialogues where participants take turns, threaded discussions are, by nature, parallel. Each message posted may constrain or increase the choices for those who reply to it, but, as new threads branch and grow, the effect on overall choice within the system is additive. The learner may equally choose to respond to any of the preceding messages as well as those that are newly added. In principle then, it would seem that dialogues mediated through threaded forums provide a lot of learner choice in an exponentially increasing fashion as a discussion progresses. Consequently, threaded discussions might make poor vehicles for less autonomous learners, not to mention those with insufficient time to follow every thread. However, this is an over-simplistic view and several factors militate against this.

Linearity in Parallel Threads

Tutor control can often inhibit choice, and this is potentially a very good thing, adding structure to the branching chaos and catering better to the needs of the nervous. An online discussion forum may or may not be tightly controlled by a tutor. Certainly, those that follow the precepts of, say, Salmon (2000) or Paloff and Pratt (1999), will enable discussions that allow learners to construct and explore a body of knowledge or ideas with the teacher in a supporting, guiding role rather than the determiner of choice and sequence. Even this role involves elements of structure. Salmon's (2000) five stage model suggests a process of letting go (a move from structure to dialogue in Moore's terms, a move from teacher control to negotiated control in the language of transactional control). Online tutors reward, emphasise, de-emphasise, summarise, and perform numerous tasks to maintain a discussion's momentum.

Constraints on Discussion

For every group of self-sustaining learners, there is at least one other group that is set questions by the tutor that they answer in a highly predetermined fashion. Even where the tutor has relinquished much of the control, learners themselves may act as constraints on each other. Each question, idea, or problem posed, limits the choices of those who follow and, as Surowiecki (2004) observes, early contributions will often play a disproportionately large role in shaping what follows. While there may be no a priori reason why each learner may choose to take any direction in a discussion, it has already been observed that it is the nature of dialogue that the contributions of one will often limit the range of responses of another. If this were not so, then it would be a set of independent statements, not a discussion. The simple fact of threading or connection implies, in some ways, a diminution of choice, as messages are typically characterised as "replies" to the previous message in the thread. If, rather than looking at the system as a whole, the perspective of an individual learner is considered, it may well appear that choice is more constrained than in the example of the lecture given earlier. For instance, students participating in an online course led by the author have, on occasions, observed that failure to participate in a week-long discussion at the beginning of the week may leave them at a disadvantage when they attempt to catch up later in the week. They frequently find that the potential contributions they can make have been constrained by those who got there first (Dron, Seidel, & Litten, 2004). To a large extent, this is dependent upon the kind of discussion and the skill of the moderator, but even when handled with sensitivity and attention to detail, it is all too easy (and often actually desirable) for a discussion to become tightly focussed and constraining. Although there may be benefits in peripheral participation or "lurking" (Preece, 2000), if the learner has arrived late to a discussion, then it is no longer the choice of the learner to act this way.

Mixed Evidence for Parallelism

For all the constraints that provoke linearity, the parallelism of threaded forums is real. Pena-Shaff and Nicholls (2004) observe: "For the most part, the online discussions did not follow the string of alternations found in most face-to-face group discussions, but instead created complicated webs or threads of interactions." However, they also point out that "with some exceptions, messages responding to a discussion a week after its initiation got no reply," which suggests that, despite the potential of threads to allow an ever-growing range of choices, for most students the temporal sequence will, to a significant extent, determine the thrust of the discussion and choice may be more limited than it seems. This is confirmed by Hewitt (2003), who discovered that conference (i.e., forum) users have an overwhelming tendency to focus on recently posted messages to the exclusion of older threads. The internal constraints of the matter under discussion seem to have a large effect on how it can continue. This is counter-balanced by Pena-Schaff and Nicholls's (2004) observation that "messages posted at the beginning of a discussion got more replies than those posted more toward the end." Although they do not discuss the reasons for this, it is tempting to suggest that these messages were the subject of continued responses rather than an indication of flagging interest towards the end (which Pena-Schaff and Nicholls do not observe). It may also be an instance of the early contributors dominating the discussion. Alternatively, the effect may be due to variations in tutor style, the architecture of the system, or the context of use. It is risky to consider a discussion forum as an isolated entity without consideration of the learning ecology of which it is a part.

Patterns of Use for Dependent and Independent Learners

During the course of any discussion, choice will commonly become more limited as the discussion starts to reach a focus. A consequence of this is that a less autonomous learner might be expected to contribute later in a synchronous discussion than one who is more independent as a learner, as choice will be more constrained at this point. More independent learners might be expected to contribute more consistently throughout the process, especially in a threaded discussion where options remain open throughout the process. In a study of online discussion using a threaded bulletin board, Pena-Shaff and Nicholls (2004) observe: "Some students participated regularly during the semester, posting several messages during the same week, while others began to participate more actively toward the end of the semester." Although they do not explicitly describe the learners who typically posted later, they observe that: "In general, graduate students participated more frequently and evenly than undergraduates did." Assuming that graduate students are more independent learners (following the pattern described in Figure 2.1), this supports the predictions of transactional control theory. The continuing posting of messages implies that they are constantly exerting their ability to choose, indicating greater autonomy, whereas more dependent learners wait until constraints appear to guide them. The constraints include those of content (matters already discussed or demanding answers) and style. The example behaviour of others helps to determine what is acceptable or normal in the particular context.

A threaded asynchronous discussion may be more suitable for independent learners as the spread of branches in the discussion tree increases choice. The results reported by Pena-Shaff and Nicholls that graduate students are more inclined to post evenly and frequently throughout an asynchronous threaded discussion provides clear confirmation that the threaded discussion environment (at a minimum) does not act in a manner that is antagonistic to their learning, at least when compared with less autonomous learners.

Difficulties Modelling Transactional Control in Asynchronous Forums

Modelling an online discussion in terms of choice and constraint is far more complex than when looking at a synchronous real-time learning event, partly due to the potential for simultaneous discussion and partly due to issues of pacing, whereby discussions may typically progress at the rate of two or three messages per person per week, which may be posted at any point. Hwang and Wang (2004) sum it up well:

The invisibility of the on-line learning process makes it difficult to assess learner performance in a Web-based learning environment. Some measurements, such as "the frequency of accessing on-line materials" and "the frequency of learning management system (LMS) login," have been proposed as diagnostic tools for instructors to understand students' on-line learning behaviour, but these measurements provide little insight into pedagogical meaning.

Hwang and Wang have developed a model using learning time intensity, burst evaluating equations, and state denotation approaches, which attempts to address some of this complexity. By looking at learning time distribution as a function of inter-arrival time and online time, they mapped the behaviour of a group of students over a twelve week course. Combining the factors led them to the quaint term of "diligence state," which is, loosely, a measurement of the frequency and intensity of bursts of online activity over a specified time period. Each student's diligence state was mapped into clusters depending on whether he or she engaged with the learning management system early, towards the middle, or late in the course (or some combination of the three). Although they had good reason for identifying three phases within the context of the tasks presented to the students, Hwang and Wang's results are highly dependent on the scale at which they chose to cluster. Had they chosen a finer scale, a more complex pattern would perhaps have emerged. It is interesting to note that their most significant conclusion is that students who spend a consistently long time interacting with each other and the resources tend to get better results. In other words, those who work hard tend to do well. This is a hardly earth-shattering result and fails to consider the significance of what the students were doing during the inter-arrival time. However, it illustrates the wickedness of the problem well.

An Example of a
Discussion Forum in Detail

To help provide a context for this chapter, an extract of a discussion conducted during a postgraduate online course on reflective uses of communication technologies follows. This will help to illustrate how messages can act as constraints or liberators to those that follow. There is nothing particularly remarkable about the discussion. Although a less messy example might have been used, the very ordinariness of the exchange helps to illustrate the complexities of control and the contextually situated difficulties of providing an effective analysis of its subtle dimensions.

The Context

The discussion involved seven students and the tutor (the author). Only two of the students were native English speakers and all were novices in the context of online discussion forums. The framework for this discussion was based on a similar course run by a colleague of the author, designed as an introduction to use of discussion forums for online learning. The time frame for completion of the discussion was left deliberately loose, with an outer limit for all related discussions (this was just a small part of one of five stages running in overlapping segments) of around three months. The segment shown took place over a couple of months, including an intervening vacation of around three weeks.

It should be noted that students were also posting to other threads at the same time (or in the intervening period between messages), so this is far from a complete record of the transactions that were taking place on the forums, let alone face to face or via e-mail. However, it is sufficient to serve to demonstrate some of the issues surrounding choice and control in such an environment.

Note that the linear representation provided here makes it slightly difficult to identify the parallel threads of the conversation. All messages are shown with their original spelling and punctuation intact. Only the names have been anonymised.

The discussion starts with a message posted by the tutor:

Author: Jon Dron

Post a message in response to this. In the message write about your current observations/thoughts on the differences between conferencing (what we are doing now) and exchanging emails. It is common to find that some really like it and others much prefer email. Why do you think this is?

Read others' observations and see if you agree

At this stage, the tutor has given a limited range of choices to the students as to how they will engage with this task. Knowing that none of the students are very familiar with this mode of interaction (despite some earlier and concurrent exercises and practice sessions), the questions are designed to allow them to provide constrained answers, while attempting to encourage some interaction, thus driving the discussion forwards without his control.

Who is in control? Unequivocally, the tutor. As long as the students choose to participate, the activity, and consequently, the learning trajectory is strongly under the tutor's control.

After some time, the first student responds:

Author: STUDENT1

I think in conferencing, the invitation is opened to everyone in general. Thus,it is based more on individual's choices whether to participate or not.it depends on the existing knowledge and the interests.As in the e-mail the subject is interpellated, thus the subject is always in the position of concsious that someone awaits for the reply. Thus, the responsibility is given and has yet to be fulfilled.The topic, furthermore, is stg that relevant and familiar to both parties.Thus,interaction flows easily.

The first student bravely leaps in and, without prompting, immediately raises issues of choice and responsibility. The discussion opens up with students still able to respond to the original message or to follow this track. Note, however, that STUDENT1 is now more constrained than before, as she has already answered the question and is therefore likely to wait for responses or further questions before participating again. This is a social constraint rather than an absolute constraint, and there are occasions where posters of messages may respond to their own messages or add further replies. However, the act of participation apparently serves to reduce choice.

Who is in control? This is still very much in accordance with the tutor's intentions, so the tutor is clearly still very much in control. It remains to be seen whether STUDENT1's contribution will allow her to dictate the process. She has established her opinions and interests and, if others respond, will therefore be dictating the learning trajectory to some extent.

STUDENT2 adds her own response to the tutor's question:

Author: STUDENT2

Conferencing is good in a way but I think you lose the sense of human interaction. You have to think more about what you want to say and respond more frequently.

STUDENT2 gives a very firm response, which apparently reduces the range of choices in this thread. Although not overtly phrased that way, this represents a challenge, which others can only agree or disagree with (or perhaps ignore or fail to understand). Of course, this constraint only relates to the current message. As previous messages are still available, the overall range of choices available to most other participants has increased. However, as in the case of the previous message, the poster's own choices are constrained.

Who is in control? Again, the tutor remains the dominant participant, but the two students have opened up the field somewhat, especially at a micro-scale.

This is the only unanswered message now available to STUDENT1, who takes the opening:

Author: STUDENT1

yes i agree, STUDENT2. And you have to be careful of what you wanna say coz your message is an object of the public gaze.

Clearly keen to participate, STUDENT1 takes one of the two main options available to her and agrees with STUDENT2.

Who is in control? The tutor maintains the dominant role as the theme is still very much as intended, but STUDENT1 has followed a path set by STUDENT2, who therefore has a certain amount of control.

At this point, choice for others appears to remain fairly constant, but all is not as it seems:

Author: STUDENT2

Sorry don't understand what you mean......

There is an unexpected twist. Again, STUDENT2 is dominating the choices, this time in the more traditional way of implicitly asking a question. Although STUDENT1 is free to answer any of the other remaining questions, there is an imperative to answer this one.

Who is in control? This is harder to judge. Is this a change in learning trajectory? Perhaps. If so, the tutor's control is slipping. From a broader perspective, the larger scale trajectory remains the same, but the smaller scale fluctuations in trajectory are now more controlled by the learners. But who controls this trajectory? Is it STUDENT1 (who unintentionally prompted the message) or STUDENT2 (who now demands a response)?

Author: STUDENT1

ooh... i'm just adding some points to yr statements earlier on...remember when u say that we have to think carefully of what to write..

STUDENT1 is sensitive to the possible misconstrual of her earlier message. Bearing that in mind, she has little choice but to clarify her previous point.

Who is in control? Though constrained by STUDENT2, STUDENT1 takes the opportunity to reiterate her initial point, thereby increasing the chances that someone else may pick it up.

Author: STUDENT3

I think Iam confused—I always thought of this as using a discussion board rather than conferencing—but I could not define that..

I do not like this much..whatever its name is. It only works whilst the threads are short. Once they get beyond a certain length you lose track of who contributed which message. It is rather tempting to picak and choose as well. This disturbs dialogue as when you post something you cannot be sure it will be read or understood.

Student 3 has clearly been exercising her power to observe on the sidelines and now steps in with a strongly stated point of view that invites reaction, thereby constraining choices for others—it is likely that they will react. Also, notice that she has placed a strong constraint on the tutor by voicing her confusion about his choice of terminology.

Who is in control? Again, at a broad scale, the tutor controls the trajectory, but at the small scale, STUDENT3 has grasped the reins firmly. However, it is important to remember that this is an additive process and most existing choices remain; the other messages have not gone away. In this sense, the student is actually opening out the discussion, perhaps by encouraging others to reflect on their own feelings towards the medium.

But what actually happens?

Author: STUDENT4

Well I think that this is something new, at least for me. I find it interesting. Conferencing give us the possibility not only to read and answer our own messages but also we can read and comment the messages of the others and so interact with the others, something that with the email we can not have because this service is more personal and it is a one-to-one situation, that is inetraction principally between only two people. In the email we, ourselves, have the possibility to forward the meaning to the others if we want, whereas in conferencing everyone can see everything. In this way, with conferencing we can not avoid the fact that our messages will be read and comment by a lot of people, whereas with the email the choice is in our hands.

So, the existence and the use of both services fulfill both our needs, personal and interactive between a lot of people. In this case we need them both!

STUDENT4 responds to STUDENT3, establishing that STUDENT3 controls the current trajectory. STUDENT4 provides a long message with several opportunities for comment embedded in it, opening up new possibilities for discussion. Although it is constraining in some ways, when considered with the other messages that are available to the students, it increases the overall amount of choice available.

Who is in control? This is becoming an increasingly complex issue. The tutor continues to control the larger scale trajectory, but STUDENT3 clearly controls this smaller branch. The number of options that are opened up by STUDENT4 present an interesting situation. While liberating others, any trajectory that follows one of the issues raised will be, to some extent, the result of the choices of STUDENT4. On the other hand, the message echoes some of the earlier concerns raised by other students. Thus, there is a kind of ripple effect, where each student is contributing some control to the overall group trajectory. The fact that the discussion is spreading, without the loss of previous messages, means that repeating themes become amplified, but at the same time, choice increases to a point that it may start to inhibit further participation.

At this point, the tutor perceives a danger that there are too many choices, and attempts to regain control by responding to STUDENT3's message:

Author: Jon Dron

Yes, those are very interesting problems. It is certainly true that this can get confusing very quickly. Anyone got any ideas about how the interface to this system could be improved to reduce that complexity? Incidentally, don't forget to click the "Show options" tab to the top right of the discussion listing, which amongst other things allows you to view many messages at once (albeit in date order, not in the order of the threads).

I also like the idea that this can become a fragmented experience. Again, anyone got any thoughts on this? Is it necessarily bad? Are there ways of overcoming it?

p.s. the use of the word "conferencing" was used by the originator of this modulette, who comes from an OU background where this term is more commonly used.

Again, the tutor attempts to constrain the range of choices available, by prompting with guiding questions. Notice that the direction in which he is pushing the discussion is determined, in a large part, by the comments of STUDENT3 to whom he is responding and, to a significant extent, by the messages posted by the others.

Who is in control? (at least) The pacing is now jointly controlled by STUDENT3 and, to a significant extent, influenced by the ripples of the other students' contributions. However, the tutor's interjection thinly disguises an agenda to explore the nature of threaded discussion and the ways in which it shapes interactions. While following from the students' comments, the issues that are emphasised are those that the tutor sees as significant. This is an almost duplicitous use of dialogue, not dissimilar in style to that of Socrates observed earlier, where the tutor is awaiting key phrases and concepts then pouncing on them to shape the discussion.

In parallel, the tutor also responds to the slightly uncomfortable earlier exchange between STUDENT1 and STUDENT2:

Author: Jon Dron

This is an interesting exchange. It raises the question of interpretation and how this form of communication affects how we negotiate meaning. I detected a slight discomfort here as the meaning was refined. STUDENT1 or STUDENT2, how did this feel? As observers, how did the rest of you feel about it? Is there any significance to the fact that this exchange has been conducted over a prolonged period and has archival permanence?

Again, the tutor is taking the dialogue between the students and using it for his own purposes. Aware of the potential issues that are being raised and keen to encourage reflection on the process, the tutor attempts to open up the discussion, but in so doing, is also constraining the possible range of replies. This imposition of structure is intended to make the process more manageable for students finding it hard to make their own choices about key issues.

Who is in control? Unlike the earlier exchange, this intervention was not planned in advance. The course of this learning event has been largely determined by the behaviour of STUDENT1 and STUDENT2 who therefore seem to be exerting a (probably unintended) control over the learning trajectory. This presents an interesting example of intrinsic constraints shaping the overall trajectory of all participants.

In parallel, the tutor responds to STUDENT1:

Author: Jon Dron

It's nice that you are feeling positive about this kind of interaction. Let's hope it stays that way! It is good to recognise the different uses to which these modes of communication can be put.

My suspicion is that you will feel less well-disposed towards it after a little while. Is anyone beginning to feel the strain already?

Once more, the tutor attempts to introduce more control through a guiding question. However, there are now several opportunities available to the students for response. The tutor acts as a guide, but thereby provides multiple channels for the students to select. This parallelism is significantly different from the kinds of interactions that typically occur in a traditional linear group discussion. There are new options for simultaneous discussion and dialogue.

Author: STUDENT3

Well i keep clicking on peoples names and getting the option to email them rather than the message I intended to read. I am too hasty and slapdash

This message is difficult to categorise; the student is a little afraid of the technology and, rather than commenting on the poor interface, is self-deprecating. This invites some affirmation or sympathy, providing a subtle constraint to the tutor and perhaps her colleagues. As one of the recipients of an e-mail generated this way, the tutor had already replied with a personal, reassuring e-mail to this student explaining how the system worked. In retrospect, it would perhaps have been more helpful to give this positive affirmation publicly.

Author: STUDENT5

I agree with STUDENT4 when she says that conferencing gives us the possibility of more interaction with others compare to the mail where interaction is more personal but i also think that it does not give a sense of unity, I feel lonely. The fact that we do not communicate at the same time make me feel strange, as i do not know when people are going to read my messages, or even who is going to read my messages. Reading the meassages without being able to view them all togheter as on a chat board, make the discourses fragmented, while I would like to have more simultaneously interaction. A strange feeling occured to me while I was reading the discussion between people I felt like an invador I felt like i was interferring in something that was not directed to me. Even the fact that we can read the date when the discussion was held make it more fragmented and far away from our daily living. What do you think?

The discussion starts to develop into a conversation of feelings about the experience. Student 5 makes some perceptive comments and ends with a question, demanding a response. This may be a learned behaviour gleaned from the tutor's relentless questioning, demonstrating another factor relating to control. As the students explore this new medium, they begin to develop strategies and styles that are influenced both by the tutor and by each other. They are learning not only the content and connections between knowledge, but also the approach to its discovery.

Who is in control? STUDENT5 is responding to STUDENT4 directly, so STUDENT4 may be seen as the controller at the micro scale. The tutor's agenda still defines the limits and perhaps has started to intrude into the style of posting. However, there appear to be themes developing that are drawing on strands scattered throughout the dialogue. To an extent, the control is becoming distributed through the group, the ripples overlapping and creating complex patterns (and novel insights).

The tutor responds:

Author: Jon Dron

I like the concept of invading the conversations of others- the separation of the public and the private is not always as explicit as in other forms of conversation. Or is this all public? And, if so, how does it change how we communicate? Is there anything like it in traditional discourse?

Again, the tutor provides constraint, but in doing so, is very much controlled by the theme begun by STUDENT5, who therefore gains partial control. It should be observed that, while leading, these questions are intended to open up further avenues for discussion and to provide the learners with (constrained) choices.

Author: STUDENT3

Subject: Re: Stage 1 Activity 4 - Conferencing vs. email

I agree that it does make you aware of visibility to the whole group and lifespan of your message. Will what you write sit here forever- how scary is that? What is being said might actually have the intention of being temporary—like a spoken conversation. The form adds weight which people have to get used to—and we do not always feel comfortable about it.

STUDENT3 expresses an anxiety and continues the thread started nearly two weeks earlier without reducing the choices for others. Indeed, by emphasising her reaction to the perpetuity of discussions, she opens up more options for those that follow.

Who is in control? This thread remains controlled to some extent by the poster of the original message. From this point onwards, it is significant to observe that the ripples of control have become tightly intermingled and it is increasingly hard to eliminate any individual when considering the overall dynamic of control.

Author: STUDENT6

Subject: Re: Stage 1 Activity 4 - Conferencing vs. email

I m not so satisfied with what we do now. I really prefer the way e-mails work.I agree with STUDENT5 when she says that she felt lonely with this particular procedure. Though, i like to see others thoughts and observations in a different period of time. For me e-mail is a more interactive way of communication among each other because it is more personal.By the use of e-mail others cannot invade in my thoughts,except from the recepient.

STUDENT6 is a relative latecomer to the proceedings and has to relate his message to previous participants' comments. The message is quite constrained and there is clearly a certain amount of effort involved in coming up with something distinctive. This is not yet an independent learner in this context and he has adopted a perfectly sensible strategy of watching and learning before contributing. This has a number of benefits, not least that there are now multiple paths that might be followed by responding to different messages. However, the fact that much has already been said limits what he feels able to comment on.

The tutor follows up quickly, in an attempt to encourage the student to participate further:

Author: Jon Dron

Interesting observations!

The difference between public and private communication is well worth exploring. How does communication with the anonymous crowd differ from being in class (if at all)? Is it a kind of fear? Does this form of communication mean that we lose the real or imagined feedback of face to face (and to some extent email) interactions and hence lose control?

Personal reflection: in some senses I think this form of communication gives more control - you choose when to browse and to respond, whereas email seems more pressing because it comes to you and demands a response within some (undefined?) period.

I'm intrigued by this concept of the forum being a lonely space. Has anyone come across any references to this anywhere?

The tutor once again imposes constraint with questions. He also exercises the power relationship by adding his own reflections about the nature of the discussion. This is brought on by an awareness that what he perceives to be a major issue has yet to be discussed.

He attempts to encourage students to tie in their immediate experience with academic knowledge, again shaping not just the content, but the way that other participants are expected to think about the process. The bait is not taken as the students become more autonomous and the discussion starts to draw to a close.

Who is in control? The tutor is attempting to shape the conversation, albeit providing a range of potential paths, but in this case fails to do so. His control through the overall structure and previous messages continues to be felt, but now the discussion is developing its own dynamic, increasingly controlled by the students.

Author: STUDENT7

Well, i find e-mailing very practical not only for one-to- one communication but also when i have to send the same message to many persons. You can do it easily with little effort. That's great! You have not to write or call to everyone for the same reason. But I agree with x and with most of you that e-mail is more personal while conferencing fulfills our need for interaction. It is a new way of interaction and i find it interesting. Of course, it is not like face to face interaction and cannot replace communication in real life. Also, it is visable for all over time and you have to think a little before you write so i don't feel very comfortable about it. Communication may be fragmenent as well, but i think that it gives you a sense of freedom-the opportunity to participate in a disscussion when yoy feel the need and have time-even if you are far away (for example, "m in Greece this moment).

STUDENT7 arrives almost a month after the first participants and is forced into a position of fitting his message into the framework established by earlier participants. This student experienced more difficulties than most in coming to grips with the course, and it is entirely appropriate that he contributes later in the proceedings. At this stage, many of the main points have been made and therefore, choice is more constrained. On the other hand, because a range of issues have been addressed, there are plenty of examples of dialogue to follow, reducing the potential for embarrassment. This is clearly a good thing, as he is able to add a new strand to the conversation by introducing the notion of distance, thus increasing choice for others. It is a feature of threaded dialogue that the unexpected is always possible and topics can diverge. Dialogue can always open outwards, with participants introducing new ideas at will.

Author: STUDENT2

Conferencing I think is when a group of people can talk at the same time. Share ideas and use communication tools to access information together..Where as e mail is more remote. That is what I think others may disagree

STUDENT2 encourages disagreement, attempting to constrain the discussion a little. She simultaneously follows another thread:

Author: STUDENT2

Also the beauty of conferencing allows you to be in a protected environment and there is more of a sense of participation. It also helps because we have met we know the other recipients..where as with the sending of emails we don't know who we are sending to. Asynchronous communication is currently perhaps the most popular technology being used in online learning, and there are numerous packages and tools available.

Asynchronus communication outways further than synchronous communication. It can only advance and improve better.

STUDENT2 attempts to pull some threads together. On the face of it, the message neither constrains nor liberates, but in summarising the discussion, the student is potentially driving the discussion to other things.

Who is in control? Does this provide greater or lesser freedom for others? To an extent, it constrains by removing some topics from the potential range that may be discussed, but in another sense, it liberates by leaving the field open for whatever other learners choose to come next.

Author: STUDENT1

Yes,at first when i wrote it, i never thought that the other party will perceive it differently.That's the difficulty when interacting online because we really have to be careful of ambiguous meanings.We might hurt others unintentionally.

STUDENT1 responds to the tutor's questions from over three weeks prior. Again, the message does not put any special constraints on those that follow. In this sense, it follows Senge's (1993) definition of "dialogue," as opposed to "discussion."

Author: STUDENT1

Subject: Re: Stage 1 Activity 4 - Conferencing vs. email

Personal reflection: I think conferencing really creates the fear of interacting with a stranger because sometimes people might comprehend the meanings differently from what your intent is.As in e-mail, you really know the person and you can say anything within the shared context with that person without ever hurting the other party's feelings.

STUDENT1 moves towards a conclusion, with a relatively neutral message that may invite response (or not). Note, in passing, that there has been a significant time-lag between the posting of this message and the last, although the student has been online frequently in between.

Author: STUDENT3

Subject: Re: Stage 1 Activity 4 - Conferencing vs. email

I am more aware of what i am saying in any written form of comunication- including e mail. Sometimes I think that email is more stark, or to the point. Humour can be difficult to manage without body language and it can be easy to take offence where none is intended. Perhaps it is because we have to write our response and can't sort out meaning quickly. In the conference situation we have defined tasks, does that make it simpler?

STUDENT3 is also moving to a conclusion. The summary is built upon the knowledge that has been constructed throughout the discussion and draws it gently to a close, despite the leading question at the end of the message.

Author: STUDENT1

So again we are back to private vs public communication.It's simple to express our thoughts in either e-mail or conference coz we direct our thought to the responses expected of us. The difference is our responses in a conference is exposed to the public gaze, that makes it a little scary coz each individual might interpret it differently, the unknown after-effect that is scary.

The dialogue continues by confirming what came previously. Again, choice is becoming more constrained and the discussion is becoming more focused. The learners are reaching a shared conclusion. Note the fact that the student emphasises the "scariness" of the medium and relates it to uncertainty. The need for some form of constraint is well identified.

Author: STUDENT5

I agree with STUDENT3 when she questionnes the lack of bodylanguage that virtual and non face to face communications implays, it is interesting especially when i consider italian language and the importance that body language has in our culture, so many thoughts can be expressed with just one body sign. How can we reduce this gap of electronic communication?

STUDENT5 attempts to gain control of the conversation with a leading question, but is constrained by STUDENT3's comments.

Author: Jon Dron

Interesting that this may vary more in one culture than another. We have a very wide range of cultures represented in this group, it would be worth exploring this. Can anyone offer a different cultural perspective?

The tutor (perhaps unnecessarily given the blossoming dialogue) introduces a further constraint in a vain attempt to guide the conversation onwards:

Author: Jon Dron

Do you think it would be worse or better if we had not already spent time together f2f?

STUDENT4 responds:

Author: STUDENT4

First of all, Happy New Year to all!I agree with STUDENT5 when she says that there is a gap in the electronic communication. When we send an e-mail or we are conferencing it is difficult to express ourselves exactly with the way we want to or we feel, because the others do not see us in order to understand what we want to say by combining the words with the body language. In this way, we are obliged to think before we write something for the others to understand, in order to avoid missunderstanding.

Student 4 is constrained by student 5, but leaves others with a relatively neutral choice.

Author: STUDENT6

When we have to interact with anonynous crowd we are more careful about what we are going to say when we interact.On the other hand when we are in a class,even we do not know the others our facial expressions and our body language can help the others to understand easier what we want to say and what we want to communicate.

Student 6 follows the thread, again, quite constrained by previous messages, without particularly adding to or subtracting from the control of others.

Who is in control? By this point it is very hard to distinguish the control of one student from the next. The overall shape of the discussion is still very much determined by the tutor, but the ripples of control that now permeate the discussion emanate from all the participants, not just one. It is interesting to note STUDENT1's continuing contributions throughout play a key role in directing those ripples. Whether this was a result of being first or being an enthusiast is hard to say for certain.

The ultimate control rests with the tutor, who now exercises it unambiguously:

Author: Jon Dron

Subject: OK, let's finish this one now!

You're welcome to continue to contribute here, but it's probably time to move on if you haven't done so already. We should be aiming to start stage 3 about now.

Don't forget to write your blogs! If you're stuck for ideas, it wouldn't be bad to look through the discussions in stage one and two to see if there is anything of interest that you agree of disagree with, or would like to reflect on further.

The tutor abruptly ends the dialogue (though simultaneously started further dialogues in other discussion forums), exerting almost complete control over the proceedings. The option is left open to students to continue with this discussion, but in the almost certain knowledge that nothing will happen. Controlled by the tutor, the community will move away from this discussion, leaving no one around to respond, even if the odd individual were to decide to make a contribution.

This serves as a strong reminder that the tutor has control over the bigger picture and is the shaper of the landscape. Although the students have tussled for control throughout and have contributed towards an overall gestalt of group control, they have only done so within the rigid limits defined by the tutor, who now draws the last perimeter, fully parcelling the learning landscape.

Lessons Learned From the Discussion Forum

The example provided here is a very short excerpt from a much larger and richer set of dialogues, several of which were operating simultaneously. Many (but by no means all) of the students were meeting each other face to face as the dialogue progressed, so there are a great many hidden factors that may have been at work here. However, from the transcript, it is possible to draw some tentative conclusions:

- It is far from simple to analyse even a simple excerpt such as this in terms of choice and constraint. This is partly because the medium hides some of the tacit cues about constraint that are available in synchronous linear dialogue, partly because constraints are embedded in social nuances and understandings, partly because choices are seldom clear-cut, and partly because the issue of scale is significant even at this level.

- Despite the threaded discourse, the discussion is temporally bound and messages have a tendency to follow a sequence. The conversation has a clear beginning, middle, and end. Partly, the tutor dictates this, but also, there is an internal dynamic to the conversation that leads to increasingly firm conclusions towards the end from the students.

- Control becomes increasingly distributed as the discussion progresses, due in part to the co-constructed knowledge of the students, but also to the nature of the discussion forum, with its dual role of communication and reification of that communication. There is a cumulative rippling of control that eventually largely overwhelms the individual contributions. These ripples suggest (almost) emergent control—a direction that is not exclusively dictated by one individual but by the group as a whole.

Dialogue is an effective way of negotiating control, but is subject to the proviso that poorly managed dialogue may be as constraining or as excessively liberating as any other transactional form. The closer that threaded dialogue is examined, the harder it is to identify levels of choice within it. A dialogue that works can be liberating and allow the learner to establish precisely the amount of choice involved in the transaction. A discussion forum can equally inhibit choice so that there is only one possible outcome. Of course, this may be exactly what the learner requires at that point. Therefore, it is useful to separately consider the meta-dialogue that must take place to identify learning needs, which may then lead to a more or less constraining dialogue to actively attempt to bring about learning. As dialogues progress, it is desirable that these modes become intertwined. This supports models such as that of Kolb (1984) or Pask (1976), which emphasise the iterative nature of a learning dialogue. In this context, Kolb's reflective and abstract conceptualisation phases may be seen as being underpinned by choice and constraint respectively. Similarly, Pask's teachback alternates between choice and constraint in a positive feedback loop.

Dialogue, Choice, and Constraint

Even where the issues addressed are clear-cut matters of fact or skill acquisition, learning generally works better when done with others. Although there may be some concerns about the degree of online presence observed in a discussion forum, and this can vary greatly, such environments clearly provide something akin to a learning community. However, there are potential weaknesses and pitfalls associated with online approaches to discussion that make it hard to maintain both high levels of choice and high levels of constraint for all participants. It is important to discover where those issues lie and how to manage online communication in a manner that makes the most of the environment, catering to those needing control and those needing to be controlled.

Distributed Dense Choices

A threaded discussion distributes control among all the active participants so that the system as a whole potentially represents a highly choice-intensive environment. From an individual's perspective, choices are not quite as prevalent as in the system overall, as they are constrained by others within the system, the history of their own contributions, and by the nature of the online system being used. However, the fact that the density of potential choices typically increases as time goes by, combined with the negotiation of meaning and elaboration of needs of all participants, means that, to some extent, a threaded dialogue both constrains and liberates. This is an interesting dynamic.

Moderator Direction

In a threaded dialogue, where the moderator is constantly summarising and weaving threads and subject matter (Salmon, 2000), the discussion has an easily discernible structure and a clear direction. Such a discussion is well-suited to the needs of learners who require more constraint in the choices available to them. The more free-wheeling and unmoderated the discussion, the less structure it provides. Indeed, the hierarchical nature of a threaded discussion actually militates against the development of structure as well as denies a number of benefits of face to face discussion (Dron, Mitchell, & Siviter, 1998; Peters, 2000). Beyond a certain point, the ever increasing number of parallel choices available make it ever more difficult for a learner to maintain control of his or her learning trajectory, no matter how autonomous he or she may be.

General Recommendations for Transactional Control in Threaded Dialogue

As much as it is necessary to provide a variety of choices and constraints in static resources, achieving a balance of choice and constraint in a threaded discussion is primarily a problem of maintaining sufficient diversity at the same time as preventing too many parallel threads.

Parcellate the Landscape

Providing a highly moderated route employing constraining questions as much as possible as well as a less-moderated route is one simple approach that can achieve some success, as long as some restraint is applied to the less moderate route to prevent it from running out of control. A "café" area is one popular way of providing unconstrained discussion that can run alongside the main moderated forums (McPherson & Nunes, 2004), although by its nature, it is less likely to be used for the purposes of intentional learning. Having said that, spontaneous discussions frequently break out in such forums that are unequivocally related to the learning on a course or module. They are particularly valuable spaces for discussions about the process—a topic that often gets lost in more focussed, subject-specific discourse.

Cultivate Different Threads

Being aware of the ways that choice and constraint are operating within a particular discussion is half of the battle. With care, some threads can be cultivated that are highly directed, while others can be encouraged to move in more free-form directions, with open-ended questions and multiple branches to encourage a diversity of discussion. If this approach is taken, it is important to clearly signal the intention in advance, so that students are armed with sufficient information to make informed choices about where and how they contribute. This signalling may be explicit (e.g., "This discussion will be monitored and controlled closely by the tutor, who will ensure that it stays on track and reaches a sound conclusion") or implicitly, through open or directed questions. The tutor may let go gently over time, in accordance with the precepts of Salmon's five stage model (Salmon, 2000).

Use Flexible Technologies

If possible, technologies that provide multiple mechanisms for ordering messages should be used. Most email, forum, and newsgroup software provide some kind of facility for this, if only to offer a choice of view by thread or by date. Many will also allow views based on sender, subject, whether read or unread, flagged, noted as important/urgent and so on, helping to provide a richer range of structures that, if well used, can give a lot of control to the learner over how the discussion is presented. If the environment provides limited choice, then great care needs to be taken to ensure that the discussion fits the medium. Linear, date-based ordering is potentially more constraining, while threads offer a lot of choice, with the corollary that they also provide a potential for a lot of confusion. This is an odd dynamic: by providing two views the structure of a threaded discussion forum can offer both high choice and high constraint at the same time, albeit not simultaneously for an individual learner. Therefore, at first glance , such an environment is a highly adaptable system that might suit the control needs of many different learners. However, the benefits of this are a little mixed. The problem with such systems is that the structures that constrain or liberate are fixed and will always structure messages in the same ways, which may be largely incompatible with each other. If some learners are responding to messages in the thread and others are following a linear sequence, both are likely to be confused (especially those caught in a linear mode). Although this problem is somewhat offset by the aforementioned tendency to linearity and sequence that appears to be common in threaded dialogue, there seems little that can be done about this problem apart from encouraging learners to use *both* structures as and when they feel it is appropriate.

Limit the Number of Messages

Control over the dynamics of choice can be exerted, to a degree, by limiting the number of messages available. Some systems allow the moderator to control the length of time that messages are available, often with the option to send the older ones to an archive of some sort, thereby maintaining focus on the matter at hand, without losing the reified discussion that led to it. The fewer the messages, the greater the constraint. As always, constraint is most suitable for dependent learners, so this technique is especially suited to the introduction of new topics, as long as the archive is available to those needing to backtrack.

Use Student Moderators

To create greater diversity usually requires the posting of more messages. Unfortunately, the nature of the power relationship that is typical in a learner-teacher relationship may mean that, rather than being liberated, the dependent learner will be overwhelmed by too many messages. At the same time, the independent learner, if influenced by the power relationship, may feel that it is important to respond to more than one message rather than to make the choice. In the example given earlier, STUDENT1 displayed this characteristic. The route out of this dilemma is ideally to encourage postings from fellow students and to persuade them to become moderators. This can provide a range of benefits, not only related to control. Evans (1983) notes that peer to peer interaction is significantly higher in peer-led groups than in those led by a tutor, although the lack of tutor-imposed structure means that there is a "danger" that some ground will not be covered. Based on an analysis of student interactions in tutor-led versus student-led groups, Evans (1983) says:

I can state that even if the students end up knowing *less (which is by no means proven) most of them* understand *more because what they know has been integrated and made meaningful. Their preparation is more diligent; they are far less likely to come to a student-group unprepared than they are to a tutor-led group. In a word they are more* motivated.

This affirmation of constructivism provides support for the importance of conversation and teachback (Pask, 1976) in the pursuit of deep learning. This results in a deep learning approach with more personal involvement with the learning task.

If peer tutoring is not possible, then diversity can, to some extent, be managed by parcellation, creating different forums for different purposes. This gives the potential for a lot of choice, but by limiting interactions to smaller areas, it is less intimidating for more dependent learners. In effect, it is adding a further layer of structure, which may allow paths to be more easily determined.

Use Guiding Questions

If greater structure is required, then the moderator can exert a significant amount of control by asking leading questions, with an expectation of clear, unequivocal answers. Though not exactly challenging, this can provide a reassuring level of control to learners feeling lost. Like much of teaching, it is a means of helping to establish trust, encouraging learners to have some faith that the teacher is guiding their progress.

Observe and Respond to the Learners' Need for Control

Of course, if the level of discourse remains guided for too long, it will frustrate those learners who are gaining confidence and independence. Therefore, it is important that the moderator establishes mechanisms to identify the level of confidence. Often this is clear from observing the content of the dialogue itself or through tacit clues, such as changes in levels of activity.

Layer the Discourse

Also, it is often useful to establish a further layer of discourse. As observed earlier, this may arise naturally in the forums or the "café" area, but it can be useful to establish a separate discussion for the purpose. For instance, meta-forums may be created to discuss the process itself. Although such forums rarely attract more than a few participants (and then predominantly those who are already in control of their own learning), they can be a useful source of feedback and can be of benefit to "lurking" learners, whose own learning processes are less advanced.

Tutor Time Constraints

As with most methods of exploiting existing infrastructures to offer variable control, the biggest problem with discussion forums is the extra work that is entailed by having to maintain a structured and an unstructured discussion at the same time. It is not uncommon for moderators of online forums to spend double or more of the time that they might spend on broadly equivalent face to face sessions (Palloff & Pratt, 1999), and strategies that cater to different degrees of autonomy can only make matters worse. Not only that, there are potential dangers (as well as some benefits) to both autonomous and less autonomous learners if they are able to share learning spaces. Both problems can be offset somewhat by encouraging learners to play the role of moderator and to parcellate discussions wherever possible, with a view to developing small ecosystems of threads, each of which has its own distinctive dynamic. It needs to be carefully managed, as a proliferation of threads, forums, and related dialogues will leave the dependent learner (and for that matter everyone else) with a cacophony of choices that may prove intimidating.

Conclusion

Asynchronous discussion forums are an extremely popular mode of enabling e-learning and a significant amount of time has been spent examining the details of how they limit or expand choice and control for both learners and tutors. As ever, the emphasis of the recommendations made here relate to the need to provide learners with choice over whether they make their own choices or are guided by those of others. In any dialogue, there is bound to be a degree of negotiated control, but there are many degrees of control that may be exerted and many facets of control that may be relevant. The reification of dialogue within a discussion forum causes ripples of control spreading outwards and affecting the whole group's behaviour, sometimes far removed from the posting of the initial message. These ripples can affect content, style, and themes, generating a collaboratively constructed learning trajectory for the whole group.

The structure of a threaded discussion has a significant effect on the way that the discussion is likely to develop, a factor that can be both confusing and liberating, allowing parallel developments and increased control. These effects can be controlled through a number of strategies, including parcellating discussions, providing a meta-commentary (in particular, through summarising), sensitive moderation, clear directions, and sensitive use of student-led discussions. It is notable that these approaches are commonly recommended by authors in the field (Palloff & Pratt, 1999; Salmon, 2000; Simpson, 2002).

Although asynchronous discussion is by far the most popular of pure communication technologies used in online education (at least in institutional settings), a significant amount of dialogue occurs synchronously, through technologies such as IRC, instant messaging, and conferencing tools. The next chapter explores the nature of control and constraint in these settings.

References

Dron, J., Mitchell, R., & Siviter, P. (1998). From answer garden to answer jungle. *Education and Training, 40*(8).

Dron, J., Seidel, C., & Litten, G. (2004). Transactional distance in a blended learning environment. *ALT-J, 12*(2), 163-174.

Evans, C. (1983). Studies in French literature. In G. Collier (Ed.), *The management of peer-group learning-syndicate methods in higher education*. Guildford: Society of Research into Higher Education.

Hewitt, J. (2003). How habitual online practices affect the development of asynchronous discussion threads. *Journal of Educational Computing Research, 28*(1), 31-45.

Hwang, W.-Y., & Wang, C.-Y. (2004). A study of learning time patterns in asynchronous learning environments. *Journal of Computer Assisted Learning, 20,* 292-304.

Kolb, D. A. (1984). *Experiential learning.* Englewood Cliffs, NJ: Prentice Hall.

McPherson, M., & Nunes, M. B. (2004). *Developing innovation in online learning.* London: RoutledgeFalmer.

Palloff, R. M., & Pratt, K. (1999). *Building learning communities in cyberspace: Effective strategies for the online classroom.* San Francisco: Jossey-Bass.

Pask, G. (1976). *Conversation theory: Applications in education and epistemology.* Elsevier.

Pena-Shaff, J. B., & Nicholls, C. (2004). Analyzing student interactions and meaning construction in computer bulletin board discussions. *Computers and Education, (42),* 243-265.

Peters, O. (2000). The transformation of the university into an institution of independent learning. In T. Evans & D. Nation (Eds.), *Reflections on creating educational technologies* (pp. 10-23). London: Kogan Page.

Preece, J. (2000). *Online communities: Designing usability, supporting sociability.* Chichester, UK: Wiley.

Salmon, G. (2000). *E-moderating: The key to teaching and learning online.* London: Kogan Page.

Senge, P. M. (1993). *The fifth discipline- the art and practice of the learning organisation.* Chatham: Century Business.

Simpson, O. (2002). *Supporting students in online, open and distance learning* (2nd ed.). London: Kogan Page.

Surowiecki, J. (2004). *The wisdom of crowds.* London: Little, Brown.

Chapter X

Synchronous Discussion

imbred: im a he

Bronco: delivrance

LadeezMan: lol

Pashmina: STOP IT

Host_Chris2: it should be "inbred"

imbred: actually it should be "imbored" but I missed out the o

Bronco: oh

Pashmina: r u bored imbored

imbred: yes

connection to server has been terminated ...

(Dowling, 2004)

Introduction

In this chapter, the dynamics of control will be explored, as they apply to an assortment of real-time (or synchronous) communication systems. A particular emphasis of the chapter will be on text-based real-time chat systems such as instant messengers and Internet relay chat (IRC) as such tools are by far the most dominant in current learning environments. It will be suggested that, for many purposes, most real-time text chat systems make a poor tool for learning. This is for a variety of reasons, some technical, some pedagogical, but at least partly due to the limited control over choice and constraint that they provide. As long as this is recognised, then it is still possible to use them fruitfully in many circumstances and, when combined with other tools, they make powerful educational tools. The chapter will continue with an overview of some other synchronous tools for education such as video and audio conferencing. Such systems will be seen to be of relatively limited use when used on their own, exhibiting many of the same weaknesses as synchronous text chat. However, in combination (particularly through Web meeting systems), they might provide greater ability for learners to choose to choose their learning trajectories than many face-to-face learning environments.

Synchronous Text Chat

There are many synchronous text chat systems available from instant messaging systems (IM) like AIM™, MSN® Messenger, and Google™ Talk, to Internet relay chat (IRC), to MUDs (multi-user dungeons) and MOOs (MUD – object-oriented), to facilities provided by proprietary Web conferencing systems like LiveMeeting™ (www.microsoft.com/office/rtc/livemeeting/default.mspx) and Webex™ (www.webex.com). All allow some form of almost (seldom exactly) real-time communication through typed text. Some provide other communication mechanisms, such as avatars, with more or less fine-grained control over the information conveyed by them. For others, text chat is simply an alternative channel to the main communication medium (typically video conferencing and/or audio chat).

Time Constraints

The most immediately obvious constraints on any synchronous dialogue, whether through text or otherwise, are that:

1. all participants must be present at the same time; and
2. there is a distinct and absolute start and end to the conversation.

This, in turn, affects the nature of the discussion. During the early phases of a synchronous dialogue, some time is typically spent getting acquainted, seeing who is here, dealing with minor technical hitches, and so on. The discussion that occurs is then moulded towards the finish by the knowledge that the end *is* nigh. A somewhat similar dynamic may occur within an asynchronous discussion, but the desperate intensity of a real time conversation tends to amplify the effect.

Copyright © 2007, Idea Group Inc. Copying or distributing in print or electronic forms without written permission of Idea Group Inc. is prohibited.

Quasi-Linearity

Beyond the limited time frame in which a synchronous chat will run, the next most obvious constraint on choice in a synchronous online dialogue is its linearity. This means that there is inevitably a coherent temporal flow that shapes dialogue. When the medium is text, the actual flow is seldom quite linear, due to the overlap of messages and the bizarre effects of near-simultaneous postings without the protocols that inhibit such events in face-to-face conversation. This quasi-linearity is somewhat reduced in some systems that provide an indication that another participant is currently typing a message, but when more than two or three people are involved in a conversation, this can be unwieldy and may provide a more stilted conversation even when it works.

To a large extent, the quasi-linear sequence of the discussion dictates the kind of structure that is possible. When used within a classroom context and without the structure provided by threading, dialogue in a chat system has a tendency to self-constraint, although a cursory examination of the excerpts of a chat below demonstrates that this may be a slight over-generalisation. Replies to one message will often be interspersed with new topics, replies to other messages, and a confusing melange of simultaneous discussions intertwined and sometimes overlapping each other. That said, the fact that there is nearly always a linear direction to dialogue means that each message provides a stronger constraint on those that follow than in a threaded discussion.

Pacing

Synchronous chat is an environment of constraint, which typically exists as a stream of terse, abbreviated exchanges, then evaporates as fast as it began. Its transitory nature is belied by the fact that it usually dissipates leaving an exact record of its progress as it passes, but somehow this never quite captures the breathless immediacy and urgency of actually being involved with the chat. Chat is performance—a flash of fireworks—perhaps a sprinting event. The sense of involvement and presence that results is not really captured by the words of the session when viewed at leisure, though perhaps this is due to the way they are compressed and reified into a single narrative. The pacing of the chat is a major structural feature, but it is relegated to small annotations of a few events in its reified form.

Pacing has a significant effect on the control that may be exercised by a learner: control decreases as speed increases (Garrison & Baynton, 1987). The simple fact that synchronous chat demands that everyone is available at the same time reduces the amount of control available to the learner. Also, the limitations on how long a chat session may last means that, in a teacher led session, there is simply not enough time to allow for learners, wishing to take things more slowly, to control events to their liking.

Democratisation and its Inverse

In most linear chat systems, there is a strong democratising effect that means the teacher/moderator tends to simply become part of the blend, although some systems (such as the Blackboard® example shown below) provide cues such as colour coding to distinguish the messages of moderators. Other factors, such as the ability to exclude users and to delete messages, may often establish a stronger power relationship than is at first apparent.

The linear format of most online real-time chat systems means that control typically alternates between the more prolific posters, constraining those who are more dependent or less confident with the technologies. This effect may be catastrophic for those with various disabilities such as dyslexia or sight impairment, who may be excluded to a very large extent from the quick-fire chat (Woodfine, Baptista Nunes, & Wright, 2005). Currently, among the best solutions to such difficulties is for the tutor or moderator to actively constrain participants by demanding slower responses. For those who are not limited by such extrinsic constraints, the dominance of the few may be a good thing, allowing independent learners to provide something like structure for the less autonomous. However, this is entirely dependent upon context. For subjects where knowledge of the subject matter is more important than the ability to converse, it may potentially leave the control in the hands of less able learners.

Is "Presence" Really Presence?

One of the first things any moderator of a synchronous online dialogue learns is to give advice to participants that they should not answer the phone, make coffee, or otherwise become distracted during the discussion. This is true, whether it is text-based or not. The lack of physical cues or any real sense of the context of other learners can make it hard to manage. To attempt to exercise control is simple, but monitoring its effectiveness is not. One of the peculiar features of online communication is the fact that the participants are occupying (at least) two spaces: one virtual and the other physical. It is all too easy for these worlds to collide, to the detriment of both. Time should be spent discovering the physical context of the participants, both as a means of monitoring its potential intrusion and to help to amplify a sense of virtual presence.

Potential Benefits

Synchronous text chat plays a relatively small role in most e-learning. Threaded asynchronous discussions are by far the more common communication tool, especially if it is remembered that e-mail is an instance of the genre. There are good reasons for this: in particular, the amount of time they give learners to reflect, the flexibility of time and place that means all students get a chance to participate, and their archival nature. However, there are sometimes good reasons for wishing to use real-time chat, such as IRC or instant messaging (IM) systems, especially where time is limited or where there is a need for instant feedback. Most notably:

- they can be an effective means of negotiating control in a timely and responsive fashion;

- students often enjoy synchronous chat sessions far more than the more sluggish asynchronous dialogues—for example, Graham observes the importance of being able to bond, to be spontaneous when meeting in real time (Graham, 2005); and

- synchronous chats can be useful motivational tools, sign posts along a larger learning trajectory in much the same fashion as traditional lectures (with all the constraint that this implies).

Example of a Text Chat Session

To illustrate some of the issues, there follows a series of excerpts from a chat session conducted with the same group, whose use of asynchronous discussion was studied in the previous chapter.

The first issue that is worth observing is that only four of the original seven students were present here, plus one other participating asynchronously via e-mail due to technical constraints. The constraint of having to be present at the same time completely excluded the remaining two members of the group.

The system used was the rather limited and unreliable virtual classroom component of the Blackboard system. The purpose of the discussion was supposed to be to explore and reflect upon the potential of the medium in juxtaposition with the earlier asynchronous dialogue.

The discussion's beginning is typical of such online meetings, as the learners gather in the virtual space. At this point, a lot of the dialogue involves constraining questions to which potential answers are limited:

Jon Dron > Hi STUDENT1- first one here!

STUDENT1> hi jon nice to see you virtually of course

STUDENT2 has entered. [04:52:55 PM]

STUDENT2 > hi!

Jon Dron > Hi STUDENT2! Glad you can join us

STUDENT2 > i m glad too

STUDENT1> Hi .TUDENT2

STUDENT1> sorry STUDENT2

Jon Dron > Feel free to chat among yourselves till the others arrive - we'll spend a while getting used to chatting this way anyway

STUDENT3 has entered. [04:55:15 PM]

STUDENT1> ok so what are you doing STUDENT2?

STUDENT3 > Hello to all

Jon Dron > Hi STUDENT3, good to "see" you

STUDENT2 > i m fine .I really have a very intense week!

STUDENT3 > so and I

STUDENT1> I know me too but i'll soon be on holiday ;-)

STUDENT1> hi STUDENT3

STUDENT2 > hi STUDENT3.How are you and where are you?

STUDENT3 > home

STUDENT2 > home here or in Greece?

STUDENT3 > here

STUDENT1> STUDENT3 have you finished all the module?

STUDENT3 > you?

STUDENT3 > almost

STUDENT2 > i m here. i ll stay till the 8 of July

STUDENT1> Great i have had a really tuf week just studying but lucky me I'm going to italy in two days

Jon Dron > I've just received apologies from STUDENT5 - she's unlikely to make it, but she'll read teh transcript later

STUDENT3 > you are going to vote STUDENT2?

STUDENT2 > to vote for what?

STUDENT1> do you have elections again?

STUDENT3 > euro elections

STUDENT4 has entered. [04:59:06 PM]

STUDENT2 > no!i have to?

STUDENT4 > Hello!!!!!!

STUDENT4 > how are you all!

STUDENT1> so maybe i should vote as well in italy, have no idea haven't been very political active in the last period

STUDENT1> bad girl

STUDENT1> ciao bella STUDENT4

STUDENT4 > ciao!

STUDENT1> Ti mando un bacio

STUDENT4 > i am home and i can see yu all!

Even the introductory pleasantries are confused and overlapping, and it is not always clear to whom particular messages are addressed. Herring (1999) describes the dynamics of such chat sessions as "a chaotic cocktail party in which every conversation is taking place, equally loudly, in the presence of every guest," an analogy that seems very appropriate here. Interesting, too, is the fact that the tutor is establishing his position of control by explicitly suggesting to students that they should chat among themselves, highlighting that this is not the usual nor the expected state of affairs. The battle for control has begun.

As the discussion gets underway, some issues are explored, but as brief impressions rather than as in-depth analysis. The dialogue excerpt continues with the tail-end of a previous discussion overlapping slightly with a prompting question from the tutor. The quasi-linearity of the dialogue makes this not only commonplace but a natural feature of the environment:

Jon Dron > I'd like us to start with a couple of reflections about the asynchronous modulette. I though it was a fascinating process but when I left you to your own devices there were clearly a few problems maintaining momentum. What were your thoughts on this?

STUDENT2 > stats??what it means

STUDENT3 > sorry starts

STUDENT4 > Well what I have otice is that in the beginning we were all participating ery often

STUDENT1> I felt i didin't always know how and when to interact with others

people thoughts

STUDENT4 > but as the time was passing we had a little regression

STUDENT2 > yes...but then we were not so interactive

STUDENT1> it was hard to read through all the threads

STUDENT3 > At the beginning I had problems with the login and I was busy

with the assignements

STUDENT1> And even the fact that many days had passed since last

interaction made it all loose sense

STUDENT4 > and also I personnaly did not want to start a new thread and speak about a subject of my interset because everybody can not be interseted t it

STUDENT2 > yes i agree

The situation is tightly constrained as a result of the tutor's specific question. The learners are free to answer how they wish, but the form of the activity is entirely controlled by the tutor. This accords with Cox et al.'s (2004) analysis of a synchronous discussion, in which they observed tutor contributions outnumbering student contributions by a factor of more than three to one, suggesting that the tutor "was able to dominate and control almost all exchanges." However, it is also interesting to see how the students themselves begin to constrain each other's responses and start to dictate the direction of the discussion, albeit within the area defined by the tutor.

The discussion continues for some time under tutor control (with occasional asides and interjections along the way) and reaches its conclusion with a confused attempt to organise a meeting, rounding off the structure of the session. Notice in passing the difficulty experienced in attempting to get consensus over a meeting date. Partly this can be seen as a structural constraint of the chat environment, which only allows linear progression, causing confusion when a group interaction is required:

STUDENT1> ok so which day are we meeting?

Jon Dron > How many people cannot make the 11th (please include "11th" in your reply)?

STUDENT3 > me

STUDENT5 > i guess it's just me

STUDENT5 > yet maybe i could depending on the time

Jon Dron > OK, that's 2 of you who can't make the 11th. 16th is bad because of lectures - does that module run all week? If not, when does it finish?

STUDENT3 > because i have and the CBM 02 presentation on 16th

STUDENT1> what about the 18?

STUDENT4 > the module is from the 14th until the 16th

STUDENT3 > sorry 17th

STUDENT2 > 18 is ok for me

STUDENT1> we have the ma day the 17

Jon Dron > The 18th is possible - anyone have any problems with that?

STUDENT2 > can we all do it on 18?

STUDENT5 > gotta go,pls email me

Jon Dron > bye STUDENT5!

STUDENT3 > yes 18th

STUDENT2 > cfiao STUDENT5

STUDENT1> bye STUDENT5

STUDENT4 > bye STUDENT5

STUDENT5 > bye........

STUDENT3 > bye

STUDENT5 has left. [06:09:41 PM]

STUDENT1> 4

STUDENT2 > no STUDENT1

STUDENT4 > 9th?

STUDENT1> sorry didn't want to type 4

STUDENT1> what 9?

STUDENT4 > for the presentation

STUDENT3 > no way

STUDENT4 > of June

STUDENT2 > it is too early i think

STUDENT1> STUDENT3 can you the 18?

STUDENT2 > what is wrong with 18

STUDENT4 > it is ok the 18 then \

STUDENT3 > yes

Jon Dron > OK, I think we are reaching consensus: let's provisionally go for the 18th

STUDENT1> great have a good evening i'm living kiss to everybody
STUDENT2 > ok. see you to,morrow i suppose3

STUDENT2 > at 4?

STUDENT4 > yes see you tommorow

Jon Dron > I suggest 18th, 2pm, room to be announced. Put it in your diaries!

STUDENT1> confirmed for me at four, ciao STUDENT2

STUDENT2 > yes of course

STUDENT4 > and with me confirmed

STUDENT2 > ciao to everyone

STUDENT2 has left. [06:12:18 PM]

STUDENT3 > bye to all

STUDENT4 > bye

STUDENT4 > have a nice evening!

STUDENT3 has left. [06:12:38 PM]

STUDENT1> ciao belli e baci a tutti

Jon Dron > Thanks everyone for coming along - it's been fun. Keep those blogs going, stay in touch. I'll be posting stuff tonight on studentcentral, so don't forget to check tomorrow. Bye all!

STUDENT4 > ciao bella

STUDENT4 > an bacetti!

STUDENT1> abcini e bacioni

STUDENT4 > thank you Jon - it has been really fun

STUDENT1> see you

STUDENT1has left. [06:13:33 PM]

STUDENT4 > see you

STUDENT4 has left. [06:13:44 PM]
Jon Dron has left. [06:16:23 PM]

This extract demonstrates clearly how text chats can be very poor tools for group consensus at least partly because, although each message goes to potentially many participants, there is no mechanism for simultaneous feedback. This is related to the problem of quasi-linearity, whereby the time-lag between typing a message and when it is displayed can lead to a complex entanglement of overlapping messages, what Herring (1999) calls "disruptive turn adjacency." There are some approaches that can assist, such as context support (Mcalister, Ravenscroft, & Scanlon, 2004), threaded chat or graphical/cartoon chat that allows simultaneous messages to appear in context, but in this raw form, the chat format has a highly distinctive and constraining dynamic of control that differs radically from any conventional educational setting. Whether this is a strength or a weakness depends very much on the uses to which it is put.

It is also worth noting in this last example that the tutor's attempts to constrain the kinds of replies, by asking the students to specify to what date they are agreeing, have a limited effect. Perhaps, the requirement was misunderstood, or perhaps the furious pace of the chat meant that it was lost. Although chat does give the opportunity to negotiate meaning in a more timely fashion than the asynchronous forum, it is also a cause of that need for negotiation of meaning.

Each of these brief extracts illustrates how synchronous discussions, at least in this common list format, can be a constant battlefield for control, with each participant exerting constraint on the next. To some extent, there are similar ripple effects to those seen in an asynchronous environment, but the rapid and staccato exchanges make it harder to build a consensual frame of knowledge. The tutor's style and the context of use are major factors in shaping any discussion, but even when the tutor attempts to provide as little control as possible, the dynamics of this kind of environment provide limited affordances for a more consensual style.

Some Approaches to Managing Synchronous Chats

Only Use them where they are Useful

Chat systems are an ideal form for applying a Socratic approach although, as discussed previously, this is a highly constraining and, for the learner, control-free form of teaching. For less independent learners, it may therefore be quite useful, but does not allow the learner to choose to choose.

Most linear chat systems do not lend themselves well to unconstrained teaching and, for them to be effective, it is often necessary to interject and apply restraint. On the other hand, when a teacher is not attempting to direct in any way, learners often find synchronous chat a useful way of coordinating projects and group work. The linear nature of the dialogue is actually helpful in coordinating and negotiating control, as long as there are not too many participants and all are technically able and technologically literate.

Establish Firm Ground Rules

Given the lack of cues as to physical presence and the ease with which anyone can be distracted, it is important to establish a set of clear ground rules. Participants should be advised to make their environment as free from distraction as possible: to take the phone off the hook, to make coffee in advance, to avoid chatting, or listening to the radio and so on. Without the full attention of its participants, a text chat can leave no one in control.

Control the Controllers

Graham observes that an issue with synchronous dialogue is that it is often hard to ensure equal participation (Graham, 2005). If enabling choice rather than applying constraint is considered to be important, then it is the role of a moderator to restrain some members so as to ensure choice for others, for instance, by actively encouraging reticent learners to contribute or gently dissuading dominant learners from excessive activity to the detriment of others. As is often the case, applying constraint in one area frees up choices in others. The moderator's role is to distribute choice as effectively as possible, within a given learning situation.

Parcellate

To provide learners with greater control, one key to success lies in cultivating diversity, segmenting chats into clearly defined "rooms," some of which are highly moderated and some of which are freer form. Most chat software contains functionality of this nature. A fringe benefit of this is that, if such environments are viewed from an ecological perspective, parcellating the population encourages speciation and rapid evolution (Calvin, 1997). However, in accordance with this evolutionary principle, it is also necessary that the groups that develop in this way must, at some point, be brought together, or at least there should be some constrained movement between them. Coordinating such gatherings can, however, be difficult.

Give Training

The speed of a chat session means that any who cannot type with sufficient speed are at a disadvantage, and most chat systems are not as reliable a means of communication as e-mail or the Web. Therefore, it is worthwhile (as, to an extent, with any mediated communication) to ensure that everyone is technically able to use the system before using it in anger. Exactly how this training occurs will, of course, depend on the autonomy of the learners in this context. For some, it will be enough to let them play with the chat program; for others, a more constrained approach may be needed. Deciding which approach to use is not easy but, as ever, the rule should be to provide alternative approaches if possible. If not, then a practice session will quickly reveal those who are having more difficulty, although it may not immediately reveal whether the causes are social or technical. If possible, it is best to conduct a session in a controlled, face-to-face environment prior to attempting a real class online. This allows the tutor to use a variety of non-textual cues to help identify the kinds of difficulties that learners are experiencing. If all the negotiation of learning needs occurs online, it is significantly harder to identify problems. Chat is a poor substitute for face-to-face meetings when there is a need for rich communication.

Other Synchronous Systems

While a simple text chat may have its uses, it seems to have few benefits in the context of giving learners the means to choose to choose, actually reducing some of the benefits of negotiated control inherent in any dialogue, due to its abbreviated and impoverished dialogic cues. Hence, it is useful to consider some other approaches to synchronous discussion, which may offer different benefits, in particular, drawing attention to the kinds of things that happen when they are used in combination.

Instant Messaging

Instant messaging (IM) tools are distinct from the kind of chat system discussed previously inasmuch as they usually leave small applets running in the background, while learners perform other tasks on the computer. While the mode of interaction is broadly the same as that found in IRC and similar systems (and they can often be used in exactly the same way), this small extra feature has potentially large consequences. In particular, IM offers a means of maintaining constant contact over a prolonged period, providing an almost continuous awareness of others. This may be especially valuable as a means of reducing the sense of isolation felt by distance learners and, for such learners, can provide a useful means of getting instant solutions to problems that might otherwise be obstacles to effective learning. In the context of control, IM can be a useful means of augmenting the sluggish dialogue of asynchronous forums by giving learners some control over not just *whether* they control a trajectory, but also when.

Students Using IM to Help Each Other

The author leads a distance-taught programme in which students make extensive use of IM to help each other solve difficulties with assignments. As computing students, they are often asked to perform programming tasks. Programming can be a particularly fiendish subject for numerous reasons, among the most prominent of which is the fact that it is possible to spend literally days tracking down a problem that may be caused by a single character in the wrong place. Although debugging is an essential aspect of being a programmer, there are other skills that must be developed, and a small error can act as a large obstacle to achieving a successful learning outcome. This is a simple illustration of the larger point that teachers often need to reduce choice. Another pair of eyes may often easily spot these small errors and it is one of the roles of a teacher to help to overcome them. Unfortunately, asynchronous tools such as discussion forums and e-mail seldom lead to timely responses to such problems and distance learners, often busy, working individuals with deadlines to meet, rarely have the time to wait for a reply. IRC and its kin are only useful if an arranged chat coincides with a specific need. IM provides a simple and effective solution, giving learners a great deal of potential control over their learning trajectories. Students on the author's programme play tutor roles for each other (in other words, taking control of the learning trajectory, but in response to the controlling influence of others' pleas for help), which can be a very valuable process for both the helper and the helped, providing learning through teach back (Pask, 1976).

Issues with IM

IM is great for collaborative problem solving, for allowing learners to delegate control to another at any time, but sometimes, the problems go beyond the learners' zones of proximal development. Consequently, if tutors are available by the same means, this can be a great boon to learners. Unfortunately, the extra load that this places on tutors can make this kind of permanent connectedness impractical, unmanageable, and very expensive. Constant interruptions caused by IM can make any other work, especially where concentration is needed, untenable and have other counter-productive effects on both tutor and student (Hewlett-Packard, 2005; Knight, 2005).

Richer Tools

Text chat is far from the only means by which real-time online learning may be facilitated. Other possibilities include:

- collaborative whiteboards and drawing programs;
- shared applications;
- video conferencing;
- audio conferencing (whether through phone or VoIP);
- real-time quizzes, questionnaires and polls;
- 3D VR environments;
- collaborative mind-mapping software;
- real-time slide presentations; and
- collaborative Web-browsing.

Many of these forms of software offer affordances that improve upon the constraining nature of text chat. For example, audio and video provide multiple channels of communication: tone or voice, expressions, background noise, environmental context, and so on, can provide a richer experience for the learner. However, as Downes (2002) puts it, "We read a lot faster than we listen or watch." Although audio and video streams can contain a lot more information than text chat, the time it takes to listen or watch is fixed and out of the control of any but the current speaker. Even then, the medium is innately constrained by the ability to comprehend speech or to speak beyond a certain density of words per minute. By contrast, it is possible to read Web pages or catch up with a thread of a discussion in a fraction of the time, especially as it is possible to choose to ignore paragraphs or even whole pages that are of lesser interest (which must consequently be suitably sign posted to make that process easier).

Video conferencing is a particularly deceptive medium that promises more than it gives, at least in its current affordable forms. For instance, Gladwell (2001) describes William Condon's analysis of a four and a half second segment of film in the 1960s, where he noted a remarkable synchronisation of micromovements between conversants, measured in tiny fractions of seconds. Given that video across the Internet often takes longer than that to be transmitted, the chances of even high definition, high speed video conferencing coming close to face-to-face conversation are slim indeed. Add to that issues like the difficulty of looking into a person's eyes (it is unnatural to look at a camera when talking to someone) and the simple fact that one has not made the effort to go to a place (and cannot leave with the person one conversed with afterwards), not to mention the loss of cues such as scent and peripheral vision, and it is clear that the experience is a long way from matching that of a face-to-face meeting. Even if it were, it suffers from all the temporal constraints that beset an audio discussion.

Web Meeting Systems

For all their inherent weaknesses in the context of choice and control, text chat, video, and audio are often combined with each other and with other forms, at which point their potential value rises exponentially. For instance, when linked to a presentation using Web meeting software like HorizonLive™ (http://www.horizonwimba.com/), LiveMeeting™ (www.microsoft.com/office/rtc/livemeeting/default.mspx), Webex. com™ (http://www.webex.com), or Centra® (http://www.centra.com), text chat can enliven an otherwise static and highly constrained medium to an enormous extent, providing depth, enriching and extending the potential of the medium, even beyond what is usually possible in a live presentation.

Multiple Channels, Parallel Conversations

Web meeting systems typically provide real-time presentations, audio, video, and text conferencing, shared whiteboards and real-time polls. This opens up opportunities for control that can exceed face-to-face equivalents, in some respects. The pacing is more controllable than in a live event, as chat can often take place whilst the presentation is going on, in stark juxtaposition to a traditional live presentation that would normally have to stop if questions were asked. Indeed, it is common for attendees to chat with each other, which would be intrusive and rude in a traditional face-to-face meeting or lecture. Similarly, Web meetings are often presented by two or more tutors, one of whom presents while the other fields questions and provides support—a process that is often facilitated by management features in the software. Even when conducted single-handedly, the tutor is able to collect questions and feedback without breaking the flow, allowing control over the whole process, but control that is led, to some extent, by the learners and their messages. Again, the affordances provided by simultaneity affect the dynamics of control. Learner control is greatly enhanced by the fact that such presentations may often be recorded. With the ability to replay the session (at different speeds and with associated slide or text presentations), the amount of control that this gives to the learner is comparatively great, yet there is also a great deal of structure available to those who require it.

Chen et al. (2004) usefully distinguish a range of distinct modes for using Web meeting software, in particular, noting that it can be used in a structured, formal way, with pre-prepared slides and lesson plans, but can also be used for more tutorial-like, collaborative processes. In the latter mode, learner control can be significantly greater than in a face-to-face setting, due to the ability to interact in different ways simultaneously. It is possible for more than one person to be "talking" (whether through audio/video or text chat) at the same time without necessarily disrupting the flow, it is easy to form break-out groups; it is possible to get group consensus through polling tools, and so on.

Scheduling

Most Web meeting systems simplify the typically tricky process of ensuring all participants are available at the same time, providing facilities to automatically mail users with passwords and instructions for joining a session. However, especially when participants are geographically widely dispersed, scheduling becomes a major issue. Finding a suitable time for participants in America, Europe, and Asia, for example, is extremely difficult, but even under ideal circumstances, the benefits provided by other forms of e-learning of being any *time*, any place are significantly curtailed. Scheduling becomes a significant constraint that reduces control for all but the organiser of the meeting (Downes, 2002). This constraint is slightly compensated for by the ability to replay recorded presentations, but these lose the immediacy and negotiation of control that are such strong features of the live sessions.

Other Uses and Issues with Combined Synchronous Media

When embedded in a rich environment of the sort found in MUDs and MOOs, especially given the natural capacity of such environments to provide parcellation and to combine media of many sorts, as well as transient fast and persistent slow communication, chat enters a different dimension of control. It can be used to enable negotiation of meaning for those seeking it, without impacting on the constraints for those seeking a more structured experience.

Synchronous communication can also be very useful when combined with remote-control or application sharing software to help to explore issues with computer-based resources, especially where some demonstration is needed. Systems such as Microsoft's NetMeeting™ combine chat, application sharing, whiteboarding, video and audio conferencing, and file sharing to allow a great deal of potential flexibility in the approach to synchronous conferencing. However, in common with many similar tools, this software is limited to use on a single operating system.

Complexity, Technical and Otherwise

The success of more sophisticated forms of synchronous conferencing is hampered by its relative complexity. Even relatively simple, pervasive and easy-to-use tools, such as IM and IRC chat, employ many competing standards, most of which are not easily interoperable, and may be blocked by firewalls. Thankfully, the thrust by Google into this area with a strong emphasis on open standards (the XMPP protocol used by Jabber) may change this landscape soon. Even without this, the large players in this field (Google and AOL®, Yahoo®, and Microsoft) are beginning to enable some interoperability between their IM systems, though whether this will extend to VoIP protocols used for voice messaging remains to be seen. In the meantime, it is notable that, even using the simple system that underpinned the example chat presented in this chapter, one student was unable to participate due to firewall constraints.

MUDs and MOOs involve a very steep learning curve and are not easy for the uninitiated to use, although some now offer relatively straightforward Web interfaces. VR environments such as ActiveWorlds™ or Second Life® are proprietary and often require subscriptions. The majority of Web meeting systems are very expensive, requiring substantial investments in both the software itself and the infrastructure to support it, or employing a subscription model that prices many cash-strapped learners and educational establishments out of the market, even in the developed world. The justification for this appears to be that their target markets are commercial and their unique selling point is that, expensive though they are, they are a lot cheaper than paying for geographically dispersed learners to travel to a single location. There is hope on the horizon with the advent of free systems such as Dokeos® (www.dokeos.com) and ePresence™ (http://epresence.tv/index.htm). However, again, such systems are not usually interoperable and many rely upon complex software that is limited to a subset of operating systems, may have difficulty traversing firewalls, or that uses Java applets or Flash, both of which depend on proper client set-up and which are, consequently, notoriously difficult to reliably deploy to diverse users and machines. The growth of Web 2.0, and, in particular, the rapid growth of the technologies of AJAX (Asynchronous JavaScript and XML) offer a great deal of hope for potential growth in this area, allowing standards-based, firewall-resistant tools to be developed using nothing more than a simple, unadulterated Web browser (Garrett, 2005).

Conclusion

The synchronous chat room is perhaps the closest equivalent to conventional face-to-face teaching in online text-based environments. In such environments, the process of dialogue acts as a continuing constraint on the behaviour of the participants, tutor, and learner alike. This can make them very useful tools as part of an e-learning ecosystem, but on their own, they limit the ability of learners to choose to choose. Video-conferencing, multi-user virtual reality, audio conferencing, some online gaming environments, and MUDs and MOOs, provide closer approximations of a face-to-face setting. Such systems add context and more semblances of reality and, in some ways, provide a greater range of control than their face-to-face equivalents, primarily due to the possibility of interacting in more than one mode simultaneously. An assortment of issues that relate less to the tools themselves and more to the limitations of the technology currently inhibit their effectiveness. Web meeting systems possess the capacity to give teachers and learners significantly greater control, but tend to cost a lot and lack interoperability. It is likely that the years to come will see prices fall and technologies become more interoperable, which may lead to great richness in the range of learner and tutor control such technologies provide.

As the concluding sections of this chapter began to hint at, combinations of tools can change the rules, offering affordances and constraints that are different from the sums of their parts. The next chapter is mainly concerned with the most ubiquitous of such amalgams—the learning management system.

References

Calvin, W. H. (1997). The six essentials? Minimal requirements for the Darwinian bootstrapping of quality. *Journal of Memetics, 1.*

Chen, N.-S., Kinshuk, Ko, H.-C., & Lin, T. (2004). *Synchronous learning model over the Internet.* Paper presented at the ICALT 2004, Joensuu, Finland.

Cox, G., Carr, T., & Hall, M. (2004). Evaluating the use of synchronous communication in two blended courses. *Journal of Computer Assisted Learning, 20*(3), 183-193.

Dowling, T. (2004, Friday February 6, 2004). Chat room. *The Guardian.*

Downes, S. (2002). Synchronous learning on the Web. Retrieved December 29th, 2005, from http://www.downes.ca/cgi-bin/page.cgi?db=post&q=crdate=101 1640827&format=full

Garrett, J. J. (2005). Ajax: A new approach to Web applications. Retrieved January 2, 2006, from http://www.adaptivepath.com/publications/essays/archives/000385.php

Garrison, D. R., & Baynton, M. (1987). Beyond independence in distance education: The concept of control. *American Journal of Distance Education, 1*(3), 3-15.

Gladwell, M. (2001). *The tipping point: How little things can make a big difference.* London: Abacus.

Graham, C. R. (2005). Blended learning systems: Definition, current trends and future directions. In C. J. Bonk & C. R. Graham (Eds.), *The handbook of blended learning* (pp. 3-21). San Francisco: Pfeiffer.

Herring, S. (1999). Interactional coherence in CMC. *Journal of Computer Mediated Communication, 4*(4).

Hewlett-Packard. (2005). Abuse of technology can reduce UK workers' intelligence. Retrieved January 2, 2006, from http://h41131.www4.hp.com/uk/en/pr/UKen22042005142004.html

Knight, W. (2005). Info-mania dents IQ more than marijuana [electronic version]. *New Scientist.* Retrieved April 22, 2005 from http://www.newscientist.com/article.ns?id=dn7298.

Mcalister, S., Ravenscroft, A., & Scanlon, E. (2004). Combining interaction and context design to support collaborative argumentation using a tool for synchronous CMC. *Journal of Computer Assisted Learning, 20*(3), 194-204.

Pask, G. (1976). *Conversation theory- applications in education and epistemology*: Elsevier.

Woodfine, B. P., Baptista Nunes, M., & Wright, D. J. (2005). *Constructivist e-learning and dyslexia: Problems of social negotiation in text-based synchronous environments.* Paper presented at the Third International Conference on Multimedia and Information & Communication Technologies in Education, Cáceres, Spain.

Chapter XI

Integrated Tools
and Environments

One Ring to rule them all, One Ring to find them,
One Ring to bring them all and in the darkness bind them.

(Tolkien, 2002)

Introduction

So far, this book has focused mainly on tools that embody a particular kind of identifiable functionality. However, such single-function tools represent only facets of what are usually described as e-learning environments, not so much the environments themselves as what is found there.

By and large, e-learning environments are composed of a package of tools and functionalities including publishing, synchronous communication, asynchronous communication, assessment, learner management, and many other features. While the lessons learned from examining such tools in isolation may be applied when they are used as part of such an environment, the potential gains from combining them can be great. Conversely, there may be hidden dangers, especially those that relate to control.

This chapter is an investigation of learning environments that provide rich and varied functionality. Their strengths and their weaknesses as a means of enabling learners to choose to choose will be explored. The centrepiece of the chapter will be an analysis of a particular learning management system, in the context of enabling learners to choose to choose, and the levels of institutional, administrator, and system-designer control that it entails. In the process, the benefits and perils of centralised versus decentralised control will be examined, as will the potentially unwanted effects of structure on behaviour. This analysis is provided by way of example and is a critique of the genre rather than a critique of the specific tool. The chapter goes on to describe a number of alternative models that offer hope to those seeking an alternative to centralised control.

Integrated Tools and Environments

There are many purpose-built virtual or managed learning environments, course management systems, learning management systems and so on, not to mention a vast array of similar software (e.g., MUDs and MOOs, portal servers, knowledge management systems, content management systems), which can be pulled into the service of online learning. Indeed, they represent among the oldest classes of computer-based learning: the first MUDs appeared in the late 1970s, but the PLATO system made its first appearance nearly two decades earlier, developing into a system with both communication and content presentation that was built as early as 1973 (Woolley, 1994).

Nowadays, these environments are nearly all Web-based and typically contain an assortment of other tools, including content management and creation, discussion forums, chat, assessment systems, user management, announcements, scheduling, wikis, blogs, monitoring, polling, and often much more. The smorgasbords of opportunities that are enabled by such tools should, at least in principle, make it easy to pick and choose the modes of delivery and interaction that best suit learners in different situations.

A wide range of terms are used to describe these integrated online environments used to support learning. In the United Kingdom, the term virtual learning environment (VLE) is commonly used to describe a system that incorporates a range of tools to deliver a learning experience. A subset of the VLE is the MLE or managed learning environment, which is a VLE that provides tools to manage learners (rather than learning). For instance, they may provide user management, tracking, and statistical analysis of behaviour and test results. In the United States and elsewhere, it is more common to use the term "learning management system" (LMS) for such environments, although this terminology varies somewhat in its application and a further classification of course management system (CMS) is sometimes used to distinguish those intended for use in academia. For the majority of this chapter, "learning management system" will be used as a catch-all term for a wide range of products. Examples include commercial products such as Blackboard®, WebCT® (now merged with Blackboard), Granada LearnWise™, Lotus® Learning Space®, and ANGEL™, and open source products such as Moodle™, Bodington™, Dokeos™, Sakai™, and Claroline™. In addition to around three hundred or so open source and commercial products of this nature, there is an indefinite number of home-built in-house systems that have been developed to provide more tailored solutions.

Control and the LMS

From the perspective of control, the learning management system is interesting inasmuch as it may be considered at a different scale than the technologies that have been looked at so far, framing and encompassing them. Consequently, it may be seen as the larger, slower moving structure that determines (to some extent) the boundaries and constraints that influence the rest. By incorporating other species of technology, it provides a larger ecosystem in which they can compete and/or coexist, some feeding on and connecting with others, some displacing others.

From a naïve perspective, the cornucopia of choice provided by the LMS offers the promise that, rather than dictating the mode of delivery, the software can liberate, allowing the learner or teacher to choose the methods and technologies that are most appropriate in a given situation. Indeed, there is a fairly widely held perception that most of the popular learning management systems are pedagogically neutral or, at least, nearly so (Laanpere, Poldoja, & Kikkas, 2004). However, this idyllic perception is somewhat at odds with the reality. Friesen (2004) asserts that it is not possible for a system to be both pedagogically neutral and pedagogically relevant at the same time. While there may be exceptions, the fact that structure influences behaviour makes it likely that some pedagogical suppositions will be embedded (at least implicitly) in most systems used for e-learning.

The LMS as a Controller

The following discussion revolves around the effects on control of Blackboard—a popular centralised LMS. Blackboard has evolved from quite humble beginnings, prior to the company's formation in 1997, as a quick and dirty home-built solution to an e-learning problem, to its current pole position. At the time of writing, Blackboard was by far the most popular LMS in adult education in the United Kingdom, followed by WebCT, together accounting for perhaps 80% of the United Kingdom's higher education LMS market (Jenkins, Browne, & Walker, 2005) and maybe the majority of the United State's market (Blackboard Inc., 2005). There are signs that this position is under threat from Moodle, an open source system with similar functionality. Some estimates even suggest that Moodle may have usurped Blackboard's pole position in higher education, with a market share of 54% (Rosen, 2006). Be that as it may, Blackboard remains a prominent system in higher education worldwide.

The comments that follow relate to a particular implementation of Blackboard in a specific institution and it is not improbable that by the time this book is published some of the problems may have been solved, especially in the light of the company's recent (at the time of writing, 2006) acquisition of WebCT, its biggest competitor, and the recent release of version seven of its software. Like many of its competitors (including Moodle), Blackboard is a behemoth, an e-learning juggernaut that is constantly absorbing, devouring, and digesting new technologies and ideas as it goes. This passage is intended to illustrate a range of issues of control and some ways that they can arise, not to offer a definitive criticism of a particular product. That said, the central issues are common to many such systems and, if the analysis is correct, will remain so.

Because most learning management systems have evolved out of pragmatic needs and observations of interesting practices in e-learning, most (if not all) embody a particular world view or pedagogy, assumptions about their intended uses, biases that determine what is available, and how easy it is to manipulate (Dunn, 2003). Blackboard is no exception. Its pedagogic roots are firmly embedded in traditional American college soil, with a predominantly instructor-led pedagogical model. Indeed, the standard organisational unit within the system is the "course," a name that the system will not allow to be changed or diversified to reflect the hierarchy of course and module commonly found in United Kingdom universities. This is not just a minor irritation, as to cater to it requires a subtle but significant institutional move, an alignment with the software rather than vice versa. Once into the system and inside one of its course areas, the assumption of teacher control is revealed at every turn. For example:

- The default entry point for every course is the announcements page, emphasising the tutor's total control over the learning space, as announcements may only be made by a teacher (or one with a role of authority within the system). This default can easily be changed to a more flexible area such as a discussion forum, but the system is mainly used by those who have neither the technical knowledge nor the enthusiasm to delve into the system's inner workings, so most of the time, it is left with its default settings. Structure influences behaviour. A survey carried out at the author's own institution revealed that 99.15% of well over 7,000 individual Blackboard courses were using the default setting (Dron, 2006). Of the remaining 0.85%, around half were the direct responsibility of the author. A poll of 33 computer-literate tutors, all of whom had at least two years of experience using Blackboard, revealed that nearly 80% did not even realise that there was an option to change the default. Over half of those said that they would consider making changes to the entry points for their modules in future.

- A calendar is provided, but purely as a means of disseminating time table information. Students may add events for their own individual benefit, though why they should do so remains a mystery, as the tool is a poor example of the genre with no means of connecting with any other tool.

- A large amount of emphasis is placed on content creation and management, with sophisticated tools and procedures to support the teacher. Although Blackboard's WYSIWYG editor is primitive and platform specific, clearly a large amount of effort has gone into providing a system that supports the teacher as a controller, with timed release, identification of viewing, and other features that would significantly contribute to the teacher's control, but which offer nothing more than a Web page to the learner.

- A varied assortment of communication tools are provided, including a discussion forum, chat room, virtual classroom, e-mail integration, and group spaces. However, these tools each assume teacher control of all things. The teacher is the only one who can moderate a discussion; the teacher decides who can join in the virtual classroom, and when and where they can contribute. Oddly, the teacher is the only one able to see how many times a message in a forum has been viewed. Group areas make it possible for a teacher to decide to give students a limited range of group working tools. None of what goes on in these areas can be hidden from the teacher.

- The potential for collaborative or student-led assessment is virtually non-existent, and assessment is tied up intimately with the highly sophisticated and powerful management system.

- The highly sophisticated and powerful management system emphasises the position of control that a teacher possesses in the system, treating learners as a set of numbers and graphs that measure their performance. Worse, assuming that teachers follow the ethical path and tell learners that they can monitor what they are doing, there is a danger of suggesting that the learners are not trusted to manage their own learning. This is a poor lesson to impart. In so doing, the system reinforces any feelings of inadequacy as self-directed learners that they may already suffer.

- Blackboard has great strengths in its interoperability with other management systems such as those that maintain student records and registrations on modules. This aspect is clearly linked to institutional control, not that of the learner or even of the teacher, although some benefits may filter down to the teacher in the form of accurate class lists and so on.

- Although instructors are in control of what goes into their course areas, how and when they are used, and monitoring what goes on there, they are unable to delegate that control to their students at anything but the coarsest of levels (i.e., giving access to all). There are limited degrees of control: with some very minor variations of role, it is all or nothing. Again, the software author is in control.

- Blackboard's interface is unusually rigid for an LMS, at least for teachers, tying menus to a fixed and frame-based side bar. This is not only inflexible but also reduces accessibility to learners with various disabilities. While it is, in principle, possible to custom-build navigation into content pages, it is impossible to escape from the imposed interface without reducing functionality to unacceptable levels. If tutors wished to provide greater constraint, the menu system would prevent it. On the other hand, if they wished to provide a more liberating interface, the menu system would prevent it. Control is not in the hands of the teachers or the learners, but instead resides with the system programmers and designers.

- The way that Blackboard has implemented its security can make it difficult to provide free guest access to parts of a site, unless such access is the default system-wide. If guest access is turned off, learning resources that were once available freely on the Web will disappear behind password-protected spaces, reducing freedom to share of content and ideas. Blackboard provides limited control to the teacher over what is visible and what is not. This often puts control into the hands of administrators, who have to make decisions that upset the fewest number of people. Because many teachers still cling on to the belief that their content is of value in itself, or are too ashamed to show what they have done, the easiest route for the administrator is to block access to everyone who is not registered with the institution. Again, it does not have to be that way, but structure influences behaviour and the easiest route is the one that is likely to be taken.

- Because of its hierarchical security model, it is difficult or impossible to create a federation of Blackboard servers (depending on the choices made by system administrators when installing the system). For example, users who have signed on in one college cannot transparently make use of resources on a different Blackboard server, even if its licensing conditions allowed it. Therefore, it is not easy to distribute control of the system.

- The security model also means that the administrator must make some decisions about content and structure. In a large institution, this results in a lot of unnecessary information, announcements, and news to be displayed to everyone, whether it is relevant or not, as well as a standardised look and feel that may suit some, but will actively deter others. Learners feel devalued as they are lumped with everyone else, the information is distracting and often means they may miss messages of genuine importance, and (most importantly) they have no control over it.

It is possible, of course, to make everyone into a teacher or one of the near equivalents. However, there is little control over the granularity of control given; it is pretty much all or nothing. This can be overwhelming and disconcerting for students who wish for some control, but not too much. It also raises difficult issues regarding the privacy of others.

Because of all the weaknesses of the basic system, a wide range of plug-ins known as Building Blocks are available from third-party suppliers, which can fill some of the holes. However, they are required to fit into the inflexible framework that Blackboard provides and more collaborative and learner-controlled tools, such as wikis and blogs, do not sit comfortably alongside the constraining influences of Blackboard's own system. To make matters worse, Blackboard Inc. zealously guards its APIs (application programming interfaces) and charges significant amounts to those who wish to use them.

Proprietary Lock-In

If all of these problems were to eventually lead a teacher to abandon Blackboard altogether, this is made extremely difficult. Despite some adherence to IMS and SCORM standards, it is virtually impossible to export content from Blackboard intact into another system without loss of potentially important information, not because there are any insuperable technical obstacles nor because other systems lack the functionality, but through the massive inertia caused by investments in training, development, and marketing, within the institution. Because Blackboard Inc.'s target market is large institutions, which have made a big financial commitment as well as the time, the training, and the emotional, social, and personal commitments of its users, shifting to a different system may be almost unthinkable.

Systemic Pressures: A Brief Case Study of Centralised Control

Blackboard is a sophisticated and large piece of software, requiring a significant amount of support if it is to be technically effective and reliable. Consequently, it is the focus of strategic initiatives at the author's institution, attracting large amounts of funding and a centralised pooling of resources. A cottage industry approach that was popular in the mid to late nineties has given way to a more industrial, perhaps even Fordist approach—"you can have any learning management system you like, as long as it's black (-board)." To some extent this is the result of economic necessity.

In the author's institution, throughout the nineties, a wide range of intranet-based systems, home-built VLEs, and customised groupware solutions were developed by different schools and faculties, each separately managed, with different, but often overlapping functionality. As staff left or funding dried up, many of these systems were set adrift, unsupported, and often unsupportable, without the technical knowledge of those who were no longer there. Many of the systems were unreliable, leading to student dissatisfaction and impacting badly on learning. Often springing from research initiatives, they were frequently quirky and inconsistent, with interfaces that ranged from the inspired to the abysmal (sometimes both). Few integrated with central management systems, leading to the maintenance of duplicate user databases with their inevitable inconsistencies and disparities. At best, users had to remember several passwords; at worst, they were denied access or caused a large administrative burden on support staff. Few were scaleable to meet the demands of an institution with over 30,000 users. Most lacked some important areas of functionality. If e-learning were to be used effectively, it was essential that a more sustainable and managed approach should be used.

Becoming More Centralised

As a consequence of weaknesses in home-brewed VLEs and a range of pressures from government and other institutions (again, the large influencing the small), the author's institution invested heavily in the infrastructure, support staff, software, and support contracts to maintain a Blackboard-based central LMS. Heavily promoted and well-supported, its role embedded in institutional strategy, the system quickly engulfed most of the smaller initiatives and was taken up by a startling large percentage of tutors around the university. Any stragglers were sucked in, primarily as a result of bottom-up demand from students, who were pleased to have an easy means of accessing course notes and time tables, despite the extra cost incurred for printing them. Once they had experienced the LMS in one context, they demanded it for all of their modules and courses.

The learning technology evangelists, the author among them, were at first pleased with this result, but gradually the problems with this top-down/demand-led approach became clear. As observed previously, the environment itself provided subtle constraints on the kinds of uses to which it was put. At the same time, the personalised view of a student's study areas became engulfed in a range of features and facilities in which they had no interest.

Switching from a Home-Brew to a Commercial LMS

For example, the author runs a blended but largely distance-delivered course for diverse students who are geographically dispersed. The course had previously been delivered through a home-built server that was highly evolved for the needs of the students, who had contributed extensively to its ongoing design and development. The funding had dried up, so the server had succumbed to the forces described earlier and was no longer sustainable: it became unreliable, and new development work was sporadic at best.

The transfer to the Blackboard system was a process that involved a great deal of restructuring and creative use of its restrictive course model. The students shared online teaching, but attended face to face events at different institutions. This led to a natural hierarchy, embodied in the original system, but a situation that Blackboard was unable to cope with, forcing the course team to create separate course areas to cater to local needs rather than integrating them in their natural hierarchies. This meant that previously integrated functions now moved into different areas, some of which ossified and were little used as a result. What had been a vibrant community of passers-through became a community of passers-by. Though pleased with the system's greater reliability, students were constantly irritated by advertisements on the Blackboard system for on-campus events and generalised announcements that assumed a traditional mode of study—office hours for paper hand-ins, library times, building-work announcements, and so on. Collaborative activities were curtailed due to restrictive security permissions, and the evolution of new technologies came to a halt as the administrators of the system were (quite rightly) reluctant to experiment with untried and potentially unstable components on a system designed to support over 30,000 users.

The Influence of the Large Scale on the Small Scale

Meanwhile, the conflicting demands of different needs and contexts were often resolved through centralised initiatives, for instance, providing standardised items in every course area, a corporate look and feel, and so on. Gradually, the large, slower moving, controlling influence of the institution, itself being shaped by the learning environment's constraints, began to shape and mould the smaller, faster moving courses, the even smaller modules, and eventually the lessons themselves. Demands for consistency, as much from students as from administrators, led to uniformity. Most modules used the same menu items, had the same look and feel, and were distinguishable mainly by their content, not their style or mode of delivery. The isolated pockets of tailored, crafted e-learning spaces (some better crafted than others) succumbed to the industrial approach, which moulded their potential forms, stamping a pattern that was, hopefully, suitable for the majority and, definitely, of higher quality overall, but which stifled innovation and diversity.

Of particular note is the fact that many of the decisions were not made by tutors engaged in dialogue with students. Although a collaborative process led to many of the features of the system, this was largely collaboration between administrators and tutors, and perhaps the occasional token student. The learners themselves played a small part in negotiating control within the environment and the greatest control was supplied by administrators. No matter how well-meaning and enlightened these administrators might be (and they were both), the constraints that they exerted on the system inevitably shaped the processes that went on within it to a large extent.

Saving Graces

The foregoing discussion paints a bleak picture, which fails to observe the many good things that have come from the use of an LMS, such as the renewed focus on how to teach, not what to teach, the increased sense of collegial unity, the inventive and creative ways that the system has been used by many teachers, the improvements in administrative systems that used to be papered over by informal processes, and so on. It has been introduced, in an exemplary way, with numerous workshops, research seminars, and public events designed by the university's centre for learning and teaching, not to inflict it upon the institution, but to allow any staff to collaborate in its ongoing development.

The institution has been blessed with intelligent, enlightened, and skilled e-learning support staff, who have constantly struggled to provide less restrictive tools, for example, adding building blocks for wikis and blogs, interactive help systems and content that enthuses and inspires, as well as wisely seeing Blackboard as just one (large) component of a longer term strategy to use numerous tools to embed e-learning in the institutional ethos. All of these actions are commendable examples of best practice, when faced with the constraints of an LMS. However, the bleaker side of the initiative shows that the effects of an institutional drive to employ an LMS can cut deep and run counter to the good intentions of those who create such policies. If it is true that learning environments strongly influence pedagogy, then the result of a large campaign to achieve high uptake may have had unintended consequences.

Within a conventional face-to-face teaching environment, the (similarly draconian) constraints that are mostly lived with relative equality have arisen out of a rich combination of factors, many of which are related to the necessity of bringing people together in a single physical space. Time tabling of classroom space, availability of resources, organisational, and administrative functions are hugely influenced by the laws of physics and the consequences of living in a three dimensional environment. While it is natural to transfer similar ways of working into virtual spaces, it is unnecessary and possibly harmful, especially where it unthinkingly transfers the same constraints.

Surely, there must be a better way. Well, yes, there is.

Open Sources, Open Architectures, Open Frameworks

To pick mercilessly on Blackboard (although it is an easy target) is perhaps unfair. To a greater or lesser extent, the vast majority of learning management systems exhibit similar and often worse foibles. Some may offer even less control to teacher and/or the learner and many lack the sustainability and scalability of the Blackboard system.

Most of the criticisms levelled at Blackboard or others like it could apply across the board, especially the systemic problems that result from control exercised at an institutional level. Clegg et al. (2003) claim: "A critical issue for lecturers in Higher Education is who has control over curricula and teaching methodology. Traditionally these have been in the control of the individual scholar so choices to innovate using any media have been hers/his." They go on to observe that the LMS can be a vehicle for managerialism that takes away control from the teacher. At the bottom of the hierarchy, the learner is in a still worse position. Although there may be technical solutions to most of these issues, the problem is not, fundamentally, to do with the technology itself. It is caused by the monolithic approach to design and management that it engenders. This can be uncomfortable and may sit uneasily with those for whom such an approach is anathema.

Given the improbability that a given system will fit the needs of all institutions, teachers, and learners, it is hardly surprising that this youthful field continues to spawn countless numbers of new environments, most of which are fairly hard to differentiate in functional terms, but which differ considerably in design and implementation. However, the creation of new variants on the same theme does not address the inherent inflexibility of the monolithic approach. Just as the PC usurped the mainframe as the preferred computing platform, so a more distributed and controllable approach is needed to usurp the dinosaur LMS (and just as the mainframe never died, nor will the LMS). A number of distinct solutions have been developed to address this problem, including open source, open architecture, and open framework approaches.

Open Source

The open source movement has achieved great success in a wide range of areas from embedded systems, to operating systems, applications and, above all, servers. Often mistakenly confused with free software, open source is concerned with the availability of source code for modification rather than how much it costs—free as in speech, not free as in beer. Having said that, the interesting initiatives in this area all use licences such as the GPL, BSD™, Apache™, or Mozilla™ licences that virtually guarantee that at least the software (if not the considerably more expensive support and infrastructure to support it) is free as in beer. Open source software is typically developed by communities of developers who contribute their time for a range of motives. Some are paid (e.g., academics), some do it for the glory or prestige, and others do it for the lucrative support contracts that may ensue. Much open source software is well-funded and sustainable. From the perspective of control, open source software offers opportunities for software to be customised and adapted to suit a wide range of needs and, at least, when successful, tends to spawn a wide range of add-ins, customisations, and distributions to address a wide diversity of uses and contexts. Driven by forces that do not rely on the need to maximise profits, such environments occupy ecological niches that the larger environments cannot penetrate (Raymond, 2000).

There is a wide range of open source learning management systems available, many of which are extremely popular and supported by a rich and vibrant community. The pre-eminent example at the time of writing is Moodle, but there are at least thirty worthy competitors that offer similar sophistication.

Open source is an approach, not a technology, so it requires programmers with relevant skills to implement changes. This makes it very far from free to implement successfully within an institutional context, and the cost may be similar to or greater than that of the commercial equivalents.

Perhaps the greatest strength of the open source approach is that it provides the potential for diversity and the ability to customise an environment to a given set of needs. Unfortunately, the cost of implementing such customisations means that, for the large part, this kind of environment is often funded and maintained using the same centralised model that beset the Blackboard example discussed earlier. In such circumstances, the main benefit will be that it is no longer the slow-moving, controlling structure that influences the institution, but is instead controlled by the institution and its needs. This is potentially better than the inflexible monolithic approach, but it does not encourage diversity or pockets of innovation to any great extent.

There are many small departmental initiatives in most institutions in which an open source LMS is installed to support specific needs. This allows the more adventurous online tutor to set up and experiment with a variety of different environments at relatively low cost. However, this kind of initiative comes with all the disadvantages of poorly supported systems described earlier, albeit with improved stability and, sometimes, better interoperability.

Open Architecture: OKI

The Open Knowledge Initiative (OKI) was initiated by Massachusetts Institute of Technology in 2001. It's mission was to provide "an architecture that precisely specifies how the components of a learning technology environment communicate with each other and with other campus systems" (Eduworks Corporation, 2002). Although there is no requirement for implementations to be free, many of the applications written to the OKI architecture are released as open source. The flagship product is Sakai™ (http://www.sakaiproject.org/), a rich learning environment which provides a good match for the likes of Blackboard or Moodle, as well as many of their weaknesses. However, OKI does not end at that point. If users are dissatisfied with some aspect of it or wish to use components that it does not possess, it is possible to use those provided by a wide range of other tools, including CHEF (http://www.chefproject.org/index.htm), Coursework (http://coursework.stanford.edu/), and many others. This extensibility and flexibility answers many of the concerns voiced about the LMS monoliths. However, control still tends to reside in the technocrats and managers who decide which components should or should not be employed. On the bright side, adaptations can be implemented more easily and fluidly than through the simple open source model. As a consequence, an OKI system is, potentially, a faster changing and more adaptive environment.

Unfortunately, OKI itself is complex and largely reliant on the use of Java™ which, though freely available on almost any platform and is cheap or free, was, until recently, a proprietary programming language controlled by Sun™. More importantly, it is complex to implement, demands a relatively high specification of server, and requires a particular blend of good programming skills, limiting its uptake. The Harmoni project makes it possible to integrate the more popular and user-friendly PHP language, but for some, this is too little and too late, and still fails to provide the flexible integration between systems that many see as necessary. OKI is also resolutely server-based, with integration between different systems possible though tightly constrained. It is therefore not very surprising that the same survey that gave a 54% market share to Moodle™ put Sakai at a mere 0.67%.

Open Framework: ELF

The e-learning framework (ELF, www.elframework.org) is an initiative initially funded by the United Kingdom's Joint Information Systems Committee (JISC), which attempts to address a similar problem area to OKI. However, rather than relying on a specific technology, it specifies the ways that applications can talk to each other through a set of standards known collectively as Web services. Web services standards are used in a vast range of applications, both on the Web and off it, and are supported by a vast percentage of relevant companies, including the biggest of them all, such as Microsoft™ (for whom it is central to their .net initiative), IBM™, and Sun™. The intention of ELF is "not to provide a blueprint for an open-source solution, but rather to facilitate the integration of commercial, home-grown, and open source components and applications within institutions and regional federations, by agreeing common service definitions, data models, and protocols" (JISC, 2004). The standards cover a wide range of functionality including chat, whiteboarding, messenging, audio/video conferencing, authentication, authorisation, digital rights management, search, workflow, presence, e-mail management, content management, logging, annotation, user preferences, calendaring, scheduling, and more. As long as applications are written to make use of the ELF framework, they will be able to interoperate, exchanging information about learners, content, their roles, their context, their communication, and so on. Significantly, ELF services can be distributed among many systems. Should it prove to be successful, ELF answers many of the problems that have beset OKI, allowing the flexible interoperation and reconfiguration of applications of any size and complexity, from the biggest to the smallest, without constraining developers to use any particular language or platform. This, in turn, means that those who wish to use it in teaching can pick the parts that they believe will offer the right blend of choice and control, adapting the environment to their needs, achieving diversity and assisting the formation of parcellated ecological niches.

If ELF is simply used to create more monoliths then it will be a pity. To support ELF and related technologies, it is important that control is shifted from the centre. Although there will remain a need for technical experts to install and maintain components, this should be at the level of service provision, not the construction or an entire learning environment. Those involved in the technical support of the implementation should be close to those who need the implementation (teachers and learners), so the components provided are more in accordance with teacher and learner needs. The time, effort, and skill needed for such support is considerably less than that involved in managing the software and hardware of a conventional centralised system, but (until such time as effective and simple authoring tools become available) still greater than most teachers would be willing to expend.

It is currently (2006) in relatively premature stages of development and it remains to be seen whether ELF will be successful, but the signs are good and the technologies are promising. Developers of both OKI and ELF standards are working closely together on interoperability, further improving the chances of success.

General Issues of Control with Learning Management Systems and Stop-Gap Solutions

Until technologies such as ELF reach maturity, most educators and learners must grapple with the traditional LMS if they wish to make use of e-learning. Whether they provide flexibility and control or not, there are some aspects of integrated virtual learning environments that are common to virtually all. The combination of potential interactions and modes of delivery and hierarchical management leads to a range of problems for control in an LMS. The dangers lie mainly in the sheer wealth of choices that may be available to online teachers and learners. All of the suggestions made earlier in this book regarding the use of individual components remain relevant, but it is potentially much harder to use them together than separately. It is too easy to confuse students with multiple paths, but equally it is too easy to constrain them. Because the LMS is a complete and integrated environment, the control of the tutor may reach far further and have greater impact.

Giving and Taking Choices

For dependent learners and teachers alike, the range of choices afforded by an LMS may be confusing and disorientating, especially as most of these kinds of system impose a rather inflexible structure to the environment to enable navigation between components, often to the detriment of the components themselves. However, if they were to constrain and control the range of technologies available for any learning trajectory, they may inhibit those who require greater choice.

As always, the simplest solution to the problem is to provide a multitude of approaches and modes of interaction, with a clearly defined linear path for dependent learners, augmented with choices wherever possible for those who prefer a less constrained form of interaction with each other, the learning resources, and the teacher. This does not mean that every tool should be provided to the learner—far from it. In fact, it is often worthwhile to explicitly reduce the range of choices of tools provided so as to increase control. For example, rather than offering the complete gamut of available tools, one or two carefully chosen subsystems (e.g., blogs and discussion boards) may be used. The key to providing for diverse needs is in how those tools are used. Rather than allowing oneself to be governed by the intentions of the programmers, designers, and administrators of the system, it is better to consider the learning needs and then select tools that can offer assistance to assorted learners. A wiki, for instance, can provide all of the benefits of a published site with great potential flexibility and learner control.

Unfortunately, integrated systems can sometimes get in the way of this and many are technically impoverished when it comes down to the details. Even with a well-designed system, it is far from simple to provide learners with sufficient control when they need it, while at the same time, reducing control for others. Navigational tools that are built into the system will often override even the best laid plans for constraint. The example described earlier of distance students being overwhelmed with information that was surplus to their needs shows how easy it is for top-down control to marry uncomfortably with local needs. In such an event, explicit guidance should be provided to learners as to what can be ignored, and as much use as possible made of cues such as large fonts, colours, and graphics to draw attention to this guidance.

Overcoming too Little Skill

The ease with which relatively professional looking learning environments can be created encourages wide and enthusiastic uptake by less experienced staff (rather less so by staff that are aware of the issues of e-learning and have experienced better, specialised tools). This can often lead to systems that are too constraining or that offer insufficient guidance. It is significant that, of the wide range of functionality offered, nearly 100% of United Kingdom higher education users make use of an LMS for presenting course material (Jenkins, Browne, & Walker, 2005), which offers the least point of resistance and the highest return within a conventional institutional setting, appealing to tutors and students alike.

Effective use of an LMS requires significant training in its technical operation and learning of how to use it effectively in order to provide the optimum level of control for learners. Somewhat paradoxically, to be able to provide control, it is usually necessary to be able to take control, a process that requires mastery of the medium. Time spent learning to use the tools is an essential investment if they are to be used to afford learners the ability to choose to choose.

Letting Go: Making Learners into Teachers

If the system allows it and issues of privacy can be resolved, there is much to be said for giving learners complete control by granting them the role of teacher or some near equivalent. While the overall shape of the system will still constrain, learners may at least be lifted from the bottom rung of the ecological hierarchy. Giving control to learners does not mean that they have to take it, but the mere fact that the option is there can help to instil a sense of autonomy and, where learners are already sufficiently autonomous, can allow them to actively shape and guide the learning experience. For the less autonomous, it is necessary to provide guidance and training if this is to be successful. In the author's experience, when students are simply given the rights to make changes, very few will take advantage of the opportunity, mainly through fear of unknown consequences or of appearing foolish.

Breaking Out

If the tools provided by the LMS are too limited or constraining, and components to extend the system are unavailable or too expensive, a last resort may be to leave the environment altogether. One of the few distinct benefits of Blackboard's use of frames is that other sites may often be presented as though they were part of the same system, but even where this is not the case; links can usually be provided to other sites and pages from within an LMS. There are many weaknesses to such a method and it should be used with care. Notably, if the site needs to identify an individual (say, for a discussion forum), a further login will usually be required, which will reduce usability and increase confusion. Combined with almost inevitable differences in interaction design, this could leave learners feeling frustrated and ill at ease.

Somebody needs to maintain the other site and, if the resources for this are not available, this can lead to problems of reliability and consistency. It is always possible to use large commercial services, but experience suggests that these may change the functionality and terms of service on a whim. When this happens in the middle of a large learning trajectory, the effects can be devastating.

Learners may also be confused when presented with many systems that provide overlapping or redundant functionality (Anderson, 2006), reducing control.

Conclusion

A large part of this chapter has been occupied with a discussion of the weaknesses of centralised, general purpose, learning environments. Learning environments, especially those that may form a significant part of the context for a wide range of activities, influence behaviour. They are the large, slow moving elements of the virtual environment, significantly affecting the potential forms that the smaller, faster moving parts of the ecosystem may take. The more roles that are taken on by the environment, the more it will affect behaviour.

A monolithic solution will often shape the behaviour of its users in ways that may be considered undesirable in many circumstances, controlling the range of activities that are performed in unexpected ways, leading to systemic failings that are to the detriment of the control of learners and teachers alike. To avoid being drawn along the easiest path that such environments present requires effort and an act of will.

Recent developments such as ELF and OKI offer opportunities for greater flexibility and consideration of the needs of learners for control, but it is sobering that the monoliths still account for a massive proportion of LMS use and, with the merging of Blackboard and WebCT (will the new environment be called "BlackCT?"), the alternatives may have to struggle to survive.

Summary of Section II

This concludes the examination of a fair subset of what are currently the most popular systems to support e-learning. A few principles are clear. The structure, affordances, and constraints of an e-learning environment can be seen to influence behaviour in many ways, sometimes enabling and sometimes constraining choice. If learners are to be given the ability to choose to choose, dialogue appears to be an effective means to an end, but it is easy for the structural aspects of a technology to influence and perhaps overwhelm the intentions of tutors. On the other hand, too little guidance is as bad as too much. Worst of all is guidance in the wrong direction. Sign posts, in various forms, are always preferable to fence posts, giving guidance to those that need it, but allowing other paths to be taken. The effort involved in bending an intransigent environment to achieve this can be great, involving a constant struggle with the larger, slower moving parts of the system.

About Section III

Section III of this book moves beyond the mainstream and explores a very different kind of approach, in which the environment not only shapes the behaviour of its users, but is shaped by it. This approach may spark ideas and enthusiasm for ways of building learning environments that are antithetical to ways of the monolithic dinosaurs that currently infest our educational institutions.

References

Anderson, T. (2006). *Social software applications in formal online education.* Paper presented at the 6th IEEE International Conference on Advanced Learning Technologies, Kerkrade, The Netherlands.

Blackboard Inc. (2005). Company overview. Retrieved December 30, 2005, from http://www.blackboard.com/company/

Clegg, S., Hudson, A., & Steel, J. (2003). The emperor's new clothes: Globalisation and e-learning in higher education. *British Journal of Sociology of Education, 24*(1), 39-53.

Dron, J. (2006). *Any color you like, as long as it's Blackboard®.* Paper presented at the E-Learn 2006, Hawaii.

Dunn, S. (2003). Return to SENDA? Implementing accessibility for disabled students in virtual learning environments in UK further and higher education. Retrieved December 29, 2005, from http://www.saradunn.net/VLEreport/index.html

Eduworks Corporation. (2002). *What is the Open Knowledge Initiative(TM)?* Massachusetts Institute of Technology.

Friesen, N. (2004). Three objections to learning objects. In R. McGreal (Ed.), *Online education using learning objects* (pp. 59-70). London: Routledge.

Jenkins, M., Browne, T., & Walker, R. (2005). *VLE surveys: A longitudinal perspective between March 2001, March 2003 and March 2005 for higher education in the United Kingdom.* Oxford: Universities and Colleges Information Systems Association.

JISC. (2004). *The E-Learning Framework (ELF): Summary.* Joint Information Systems Committee.

Laanpere, M., Poldoja, H., & Kikkas, K. (2004). *The second thoughts about pedagogical neutrality of LMS.* Paper presented at the 4th IEEE International Conference on Advanced Learning Technologies, Joensuu, Finland.

Raymond, E. (2000). *The cathedral and the bazaar.* Retrieved January 7, 2006, from http://www.catb.org/~esr/writings/cathedral-bazaar/cathedral-bazaar/

Rosen, Z. (2006). Higher-ed LMS market penetration: Moodle vs. Blackboard+WebCT vs. Sakai. Retrieved July 19th, 2006, from http://www.zacker.org/higher-ed-lms-market-penetration-moodle-vs-blackboard-vs-sakai

Tolkien, J. R. R. (2002). *The lord of the rings.* London: HarperCollins.

Woolley, D. R. (1994). PLATO: The emergence of online community. Retrieved January 7, 2006, from http://www.thinkofit.com/plato/dwplato.htm#plato

Section III
Designing Better
E-Learning
Environments

Chapter XII

Social Software and E-Learning

And I know not if, save in this, such gift be allowed to man

That out of three sounds he frame, not a fourth sound, but a star.

From Abt Vogler, Robert Browning

Introduction

This chapter is about ways that technologies that underpin what some have (misleadingly) called "Web 2.0" can be used in e-learning. It describes an approach to the design of e-learning environments that takes, as its basis, the concept of transactional control and extrapolates cost-effective and useful ways of achieving a balance of choice and constraint that favours the learner.

The chapter delves a little into the principles that underpin social software, providing some examples from the periphery and outside the educational field. Social software moves beyond notions of individuals working together as a group, instead treating the group as a distinct entity with an active part to play in the overall dynamics of the system. A significant contribution that this chapter makes is that current thinking in learning technology theory fails to consider this aspect, ignoring important modes of interaction between the many and the one, the many and the content of e-learning, the many and the many, and the many and the any. The chapter ends with suggestions for useful broad approaches to the design of e-learning environments, concluding that there are two main avenues that might fruitfully be taken: to generate dialogue through structure, or structure through dialogue. Each of these routes has the potential to allow learners to choose to choose at any point along their educational trajectories.

The central thesis can be expressed easily. Moore's (1997) theory of transactional distance shows that there is a continuum between structure and dialogue, and that learners need varying amounts of each. Consequently, to cater to as many needs as possible, e-learning environments should generate structure through dialogue. If it were possible to build such a system, it might simultaneously provide both high and low transactional distance within the same environment, though not (it should be emphasised) simultaneously for the same learner.

Because of the mapping between transactional distance and transactional control, this can be expressed even more simply and perhaps more powerfully: learning environments should both control and be controlled by their inhabitants. This is a very literal spin on Churchill's (1943) recursive claim that "we shape our dwellings and afterwards our dwellings shape our lives."

The Current Generation

The detailed dynamics of several types of educational transaction, in terms of transactional control, have been found to be complex and elusive phenomena. The rich complexity and range of human interactions in an educational system can both liberate and constrain, sometimes both at the same time. The exercise of choice or constraint at inappropriate points in a learning trajectory can have a deleterious effect on learning and it often arises without apparent awareness on the part of the participants. To take advantage of the potential benefits of appropriate control in the service of learning, there are perhaps two main paths available to teachers and facilitators of learning:

1.   Through reflective and theoretically well-informed action, to shape educational processes to fit the needs of each learner, guessing or negotiating when and where they will need control. This is hard, expensive and prone to error.

2.   To provide a mechanism to make *both* choice and constraint available to the learner at any significant point where control may be exercised. This too is hard, but offers many benefits to both the learner and the teacher.

In previous chapters, a number of systems and environments for education have been examined to discover to what extent they allow learners to have some control over the level of control they exercise over their learning trajectories. Every instance of an e-learning tool or environment discussed so far has some potential to be used this way, but generally only by bending it into an unnatural shape and employing active strategies that allow it to happen. It is also fair to say that most of the ways presented so far for enabling high and low transactional control require a significantly greater input of time and money from tutors, learners, or both, than the more traditional approaches to mass education. Part of the reason for this is that the learning environments themselves have a fixed structure and set of functions. It does not have to be this way.

Deferred Systems

A deferred system is one in which its purpose, structure, and use only emerges after the initial design (Patel, 2003). A classic example might be the spreadsheet, a tool which can become many other tools depending on the needs of its users. The term does not apply to simple publication or content creation tools where the emphasis is on the finished product; a word-processor or a Web authoring tool would not fit this category as the software continues to have only one purpose (complexities of macro languages notwithstanding).

What makes a deferred system worthy of the name is the fact that the actual system itself, crucially including the processes that it embodies, develops after the initial design. To an extent, some forms of virtual learning environment, such as MOOs, fit this category, but most learning management systems are little more than publication, communication, and management tools bound together in a predetermined framework. This means that, at one end of the scale, they rely on the choices of teachers (and systems designers) to determine their use, while, at the other, they attempt to be neutral communication tools. The dynamic space that lies in between typically remains largely untouched.

There is a particularly valuable range of deferred systems that step outside the mold and exhibit emergent structure, developing through use to become something else. Such tools are embodiments of social ecologies, spaces in which not only people interact with and change each other but also, as a consequence, change the structural elements of the systems that they inhabit. This is a fundamental characteristic of many of the technologies that drive Web 2.0. The potential malleability of such environments will be seen to be their most promising and exciting features that might differentiate e-learning from virtually all previous forms of education. In particular, they allow for the unfolding of an emergent structure to the learning environment.

The systems looked at so far are environments that are designed by individuals or groups of individuals. However, the fact that a computer system can interact with its users to be a determinant of its own structure can make it more like an ecosystem than a built environment. It can develop structural features determined not by an architect, but by the myriad interactions of itself and its users. This facility springs from the nature of networked computer systems that can simultaneously be tools, media, and inhabited environments. The dominant tools/environments that display these characteristic most vividly are instances of what has come to be known as "social software."

Social Software

Clay Shirky has provided a number of definitions of social software, most recently (2003) settling for "software that supports group interaction." However, in an earlier and more profound definition, he has described it as software that "treats groups as first-class objects in the system" (Allen, 2004). The group is something distinct from the individuals that form it, and this is what makes social software environments into deferred systems. Shirky (2003) says of them: "Groups are a run-time effect. You cannot specify in advance what the group will do, and so you can't substantiate in software everything you expect to have happen."

Traditional forms of computer-mediated communication have been concerned primarily with one-to-one and one-to-many communication, which focus on the individual act of communication. Social software acts as a different kind of mediator, allowing many (as a unified entity) to communicate with many (as individuals). Take, for example, the del.icio.us™ link sharing system. At first glance, the most obvious motivation for an individual to contribute to del.icio.us is that it provides a simple and effective means of storing one's bookmarks so that they are accessible from anywhere, categorised using metadata known as "tags." This is a personal activity which could be (and historically has been) performed in complete isolation from other users. Then, the del.icio.us system is able to concatenate the categorisations of many users into a "tag cloud" and to present a consolidated view or "folksonomy" (Mathes, 2004; Shirky, 2004). More popular tags receive greater visual emphasis so that it is possible to see trends and behaviours, not of the individual, but of the group as a whole. It is also possible to identify others with similar interests, defined by the tags that they use. Most of the time, nobody designs these groups: they emerge out of many individual and independent decisions. However, there is nothing to stop them from being used intentionally, for example, to enable a group of researchers to collaborate on a specific (tagged) project. Many automated collaborative filters, which apply pattern matching to identify similar users, work in a related but slightly different way, by enabling many-to-one communication. Each individual sees a view of the group that is adapted to his or her own needs, not the results of the recommendation of the whole group.

Beyond the crudest of approaches (votes, mob behaviour, and so on), the kind of communication enabled by social software would be impossible without the aid of networked computers. The combination of processing power and a malleable interface, combined with willing participant users, creates something that is comfortably familiar, yet is quite new in the world of social systems. Through bottom-up processes, it provides organisation of not just social groupings and interactions but of an environment, capturing small local interactions and extrapolating or emphasising hidden connections and patterns.

History and Background

Social software arises out of a long history of computer mediated communication. Allen (2004) provides us with a history that starts at the advent of digital computing with Bush's hypothetical Memex (Bush, 1950), then straddles a number of false-starts and wilderness years before the emergence of electronic information exchange systems in the 1970s. These evolved into the groupware and Computer Supported Cooperative/Collaborative Work systems of the 1980s, on to the resurgence of groupware and Web-based collaboration systems in the 1990s. Early systems to support group working were often involved with the automation of work-related group processes and were primarily oriented to the purely virtual world of collaborative computer use. When Clay Shirky began to use the term in the early 2000s, he was seeking something which encompassed *both* online and off-line interactions, to help describe systems like Friendster™, which describes itself as "an online community that connects people through networks of friends for dating or making new friends" (www.friendster.com). Friendster relies on its users establishing networks of existing friends, thereby creating a web of trust which may be used to discover new friends via old connections (Boyd, 2004). This is a commercial variant on the theme of the more distributed Friend-Of-A-Friend standard, which can be used to mine connections between people (http://www.foaf-project.org/). Other similar tools include FriendsReunited™ (www.friendsreunited.co.uk), Classmates™ (http://www.classmates.com), MeetUp™ (www.meetup.com), Orkut™ (http://www.orkut.com), and many others. This straddling of real and virtual communities is seen by Mejias (2005a) as a key benefit to the use of social software in education, stating that "social software can positively impact pedagogy by inculcating a desire to reconnect to the world as a whole, not just the social parts that exist online." However, Mejias has a rather broader notion of social software than most, and lists the following:

- multiplayer gaming environments: multi-user dungeons (MUDs), massively-multiplayer online games (MMOGs), and so forth;

- discourse facilitation systems: synchronous: instant messaging (IM), chat; or asynchronous: e-mail, bulletin boards, discussion boards, moderated commenting systems (e.g., Slashdot, Plastic, K5);

- content management systems: blogs, wikis, document management (e.g., Plone), Web annotation utilities;

- product development systems: especially for Open Source software (e.g., Sourceforge);

- peer-to-peer (P2P) file sharing systems (e.g., Napster, Gnutella, BitTorrent);

- selling/purchasing management systems (e.g., eBay);

- learning management systems (LMSs) (e.g., Blackboard, WebCT, Moodle);

- relationship management systems (e.g.; Friendster, Orkut);

- syndication systems: list-servs, RSS aggregators; and

- distributed classification systems (e.g., Flickr, del.icio.us).

While many of these systems have social elements, a definition such as this that includes Blackboard® and IM systems is too inclusive to be meaningful or distinct from any other definition of communication technologies. It is very hard to see how the group is a first class entity in an environment such as Blackboard, with its top-down hierarchies of control, or IM, which is essentially a means of one-to-many or one-to-one communication. A more useful definition (which will be used here) is that one of the most distinctive features of social software is that control and structure can arise through a process of communication, not as a result of design, but as an emergent feature of group interaction.

The Value of a Network

It is significant that successful social software environments have many members, not only because that is the definition of their success. Metcalfe's Law states that the value of a network is approximately equal to the square of the number of users of the system (Kelly, 1998). This is nowhere more evident than in social software, which relies on large numbers of users to create an adequate number of connections in order for it to be valuable. Although it does not have to be Internet-wide, nor even a small subset of it, social software is generally only particularly useful when there are many people using it. FriendsReunited, which brings old classmates and workmates together, would be of little use if were only used by two people. Greater numbers can lead to chaos and unusability in many earlier forms of mediated communication. For many forms of social software, the opposite is true.

Examples of Social Software

There are many examples of social software that are used in a range of contexts from play to work to education. Most collaborative filters could be viewed as a kind of social software, as could most systems that employ social navigation (a means of using the navigation of others to help guide the current user, discussed in a later chapter). To some extent, the blogosphere may be seen as a huge piece of distributed social software, most notably due to the combination of RSS feeds, blogrolls, track-backs and tags, which combine to create emergent clusters of interrelated activity and interest. This fact is capitalised upon by Technorati™ (www.technorati.com), which harvests such information to assist seekers of relevant blogging communities. Similarly, wikis (Web pages edited by an arbitrarily large number of people) are the work of many and, especially when large, appear to exhibit an emergent form and content that is not controlled by any single individual or group.

A very popular use of social software is to support social networking: some pre-eminent examples include MySpace™ (www.myspace.com), Friendster, and FriendsReunited.

A significant amount of social software is concerned with distilling the wisdom of the crowd to provide recommendations of things to see and news that is interesting: Digg™ (www.digg.com) and SlashDot™ (www.slashdot.org) are good examples of this genre.

Another popular use of social software is to share media and resources: Flickr™ (www.flickr.com) and YouTube™ (www.youtube.com) are perhaps the most notable examples, and are among the most popular sites on the Web. Their use of tagging resembles that of del.icio.us.

Because many systems make use of similar approaches to tagging, it is increasingly common to find sites that combine information from many others in the form of mashups, several hundred of which are listed at Mashup Feed (www.mashupfeed.com). Examples include VirtualPlaces (http://apps.nikhilk.net/VirtualPlaces/), which combines numerous RSS feeds and displays them on a map and DiggDot (http://dig-gdot.us/), which combines feeds from SlashDot, Digg and del.icio.us.

Social software has experienced a massive growth over the past five years or so and the bottom-up principles that it embodies are increasingly appearing in mainstream and commercial systems. For instance, it is now possible to use the Ning™ site and its technologies (http://ning.com) to create your own social software system, often with minimal or no programming experience. Ning hosts a vast array of social software systems which include systems that allow collective interactions to (for example):

- Capture and correlate star sightings;
- Track DVDs;
- Establish whether you are handsome or not;
- Choose beer;
- Identify good hiking trails in the Bay Area (and people to share them with);
- Share stories;
- Share restaurant reviews;
- Share photographs;
- Find others interested in bulldogs; and
- Create reviews and ratings of bead stores.

Many of Ning's sites are mashups, which combine information from many sites. This merely scratches the surface of the Ning community of social software environments, but illustrates the range of interests and the growth of uses to which it is being applied. Social software is a huge growth area.

Social Software in Institutional Learning

An important use of social software is to help people to explore, communicate, and construct knowledge—to learn. Communities of interest that form around bulldogs or hiking in the Bay Area are not dealing with topics usually addressed in higher education, but slowly this kind of tool is being drawn in to the educational arena. Anderson, for example, uses Furl for social book marking, and a tool called Me2U that is broadly social in nature, providing profiles, blogs, and so on (Anderson, 2006a, 2006b). He was inspired by a blog posting by Mejias (2005b), who has made significant use of blogs, wikis, and del.icio.us to run a course on social software. The author, too, has made extensive use of blogs, wikis, and other social software in his teaching, gaining benefits from the fact that the group (as well as and distinct from the individuals of which it is comprised) becomes its own teacher (Dron, 2003, 2006). Other examples abound (Barker, 2005; Godwin-Jones, 2003; Klamma et al., 2006; Lin, Liu, Kakusho, Yueh, & Murakami, 2006; Weller, Pegler, & Mason, 2005; Williams & Jacobs, 2004). In almost all cases, current writings provide experience reports or speculations on potential uses of the technologies as means of enabling the kinds of open, student-led learning of which many teachers would subscribe. It is intuitively obvious that social software has a natural place in education and many are leaping onto the bandwagon. However, few are considering the profound implications of using software where the emergent will of the group plays a prominent part in deciding the structure of the environment and path that learners will take through it.

Group Minds

Social software is less to do with machine intelligence and more to do with augmenting social capacities (Coates, 2002), of combining human intelligences. In this sense, it provides the best of both of the worlds of computers and of people. It deploys the social, creative, intelligent behaviour of humans and the processing power and connectivity of machines, without trying to make either behave like the other. Many of the uses to which Ning is being put may be seen as a process of collaborative knowledge construction, of people teaching other people, albeit often for relatively low level tasks like identifying useful retailers or discovering like-minded communities of interest. Significantly, it is possible to engage with the site at any level from a passive browser to an active creator, and almost every active creator is also a passive browser. Such sites may therefore be seen as both controlling and controllable, a process that is under learner control or to which control may be delegated. Social software is created by the people who inhabit its spaces, arising out of human needs and interactions. If this capacity were to be applied to educational uses, there might be a great deal to be gained.

A New Framework for Mediated Communication in Education

Garrison and Anderson (2003) provide a framework for considering the forms of interaction that e-learning enables (Figure 12.1), which is itself a similar model to Laurillard's conversational framework (Laurillard, 1993) and which also echoes Michael Moore's work in the area (Moore & Kearsley, 1996). In Garrison and Anderson's framework, there are three main classes of actor, the teacher, the learner and the content, instances of each of which may interact with the instances of the others or other instances of itself. This is a useful and apparently comprehensive framework (although it may be speculated that context might also be considered as a relevant factor) but, apart from content-content interaction, there is little in it that distinguishes e-learning from any other form. In the light of Shirky's observations about social software, it is clear that there is another major class of interactions for each of the critical actors, the class of those that occur with the entire group, or some emergent properties of it.

Tool, Medium, and Environment

The capacity of e-learning environments to be both tool and medium, to be capable of being the determinants of their own structural change, allows for the possibility of considering a much richer variety of interactions than those between simple components. If the group is an identifiable emergent phenomenon that is in some sense reified, then it becomes a distinct entity in its own right, composed of, yet distinct from, its parts. Therefore, to a significant extent, it may be possible to consider the individual interactions as capable of forming, in a very concrete sense, something greater than the sum of its parts—an ecosystem or perhaps a kind of gestalt—like the relationship between notes and melody described by the Gestalt theorist Wertheimer (1938):

What I really have, what I hear of each individual note, what I experience at each place in the melody is a part which is itself determined by the character of the whole. What is given me by the melody does not arise (through the agency of any

Figure 12.1. Garrison and Anderson's model (Based on Garrison & Anderson, 2003)

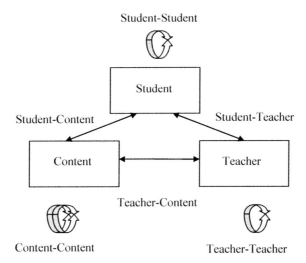

auxiliary factor) as a secondary process from the sum of the pieces as such. Instead, what takes place in each single part already depends upon what the whole is. The flesh and blood of a tone depends from the start upon its role in the melody: a b as leading tone to c is something radically different from the b as tonic. It belongs to the flesh and blood of the things given in experience [Gegebenheiten], how, in what role, in what function they are in their whole.

In a gestalt, the combination is very different from the individual components of which it is comprised. This is notably true of social software. By themselves, tags are simply convenient classifications for individuals. When combined with those of others, they are a reflection of the group mind: an expression of opinion that emerges from no single individual and, more importantly, a means of guiding individuals to matters of great interest. If this perspective is overlaid onto Garrison and Anderson's diagram, it leads to something much messier, but with many more possibilities (Figure 12.2).

Interacting with the Group

From this perspective, it can be seen that e-learning that incorporates features of social software could have far greater potential than it has so far been credited with, introducing a whole new category of potential interactions, which are qualitatively different from those of traditional systems. In particular, what it implies is something akin to a "dependent system" in the world of economics. In such systems, the actors behave in a way that is determined by the way that the actors behave or, more accurately, how they perceive that all the other actors will behave. This circularity leads to some exotic and often unpredictable behaviour for social software, its form emerging from the ways that it is used, which in turn determines its form.

New Classes of Interaction in Social Software

There are four new classes of interaction represented in the diagram that do not fit with Garrison and Anderson's model of e-learning: group-content, group-group, learner-group, and teacher-group.

Group-Content Interaction

For the whole to interact with content might initially seem a peculiar notion, but it is a crucial element of recommender systems, including Google and del.icio.us. This effect can occur both indirectly and directly. Indirectly, creators of content

Figure 12.2. Extending Garrison and Anderson's model to encompass social soft-ware

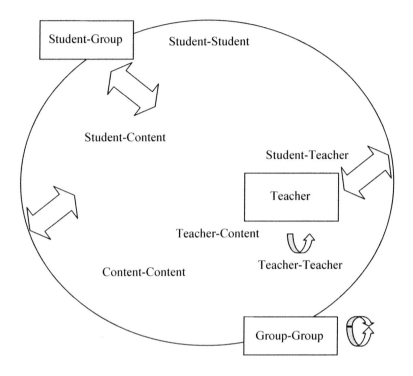

may be influenced by the opinions and categorisations that emerge from a system like del.icio.us, or the implicit ratings of Google, encouraging them to change it as a result. Directly, the changing font sizes of tags within del.icio.us, topics and qualities in CoFIND (www.cofind.net), tags in Ning, clusters in Flickr, and tags in the Technorati blog-finding site may be seen as modifications of content that are an immediate consequence of the influence of the many.

Group-Group Interaction

The second and perhaps the strangest new class of interaction is that of the group with the group. To some extent, this may be seen as almost contradictory: if it is the whole, then it contains everything that is significant to the system. However, it should be remembered that this is about classes of actors, not the actors themselves. It is perfectly conceivable that a given whole might have some interaction with another, and indeed the beginnings of such interactions can already be seen in the form of mashups, albeit seldom in an educational setting. For example, many tools exist that match tags used in different forms of social software, creating new mashups of emergent structure—indeed, another whole. RSS feed aggregators that combine blog entries and other information published using RSS are a common application of this principle. This is a hierarchical relationship: this group might interact with the next, which might interact with other groups, and so on. The general principle, that the ability to consider a system at a range of scales is a significant part of what can make it dynamically stable, is central to building a complex system. It also suggests many opportunities for a federated learning environment that is no longer constrained by institutional or organisational structures and habits, a combination of systems each of which is a whole in its own right.

Learner-Group Interaction

Because the learner is part of the group that generates the form of social software, there is a recursive relationship between the two that can lead to a very fluid level of control. In some senses, from the perspective of transactional control, the learner is both the controlled and the controller.

Teacher-Group Interaction

The role of the teacher in social software systems is potentially less significant than in conventional e-learning environments. This is despite the fact that, in an institutional environment, use of such software may be initiated at a larger scale by the teacher and that he or she may determine goals and outcomes, shaping the ecology in which it resides. A consequence, for example, might be that the teacher's own notes may be less significant to learners than other sources (Dron, Mitchell, Boyne, & Siviter, 2000). If notes are provided in the form of a wiki, students may change them, or comment and seek clarification. The resulting amalgam results in a significant loss of control for the teacher.

Although the teacher may have a reduced role in creating the form that a social software system may take, the embodiment of the group that social software entails can tell the teacher a great deal about the group, their preferences, their interests, their needs, their weaknesses, and their strengths.

Approaches to Online
Learning Environment Design

The optimal degree of learner control at any point will exist somewhere between the two extremes, complete autonomy and total control by another. The difficult task for a both teacher and learner is to decide exactly where that point is. A perfect educational system would be one that offers the learner the means to choose at any point what level of control he or she may exercise.

But how?

It has already been observed, at a systems level, that transactional distance maps directly to transactional control—where dialogue is high, learner control is high; where structure is high, teacher control is high. The inverse relationship between structure and dialogue opens up an interesting possibility, in terms of providing the flexibility to cater to both at once, without too much effort. In order to build e-learning environments which inherently provide maximal choice and constraint, there are two potentially valuable approaches to the design of software that will allow learners the option to choose or not to choose which direction they take next:

1.   To generate dialogue through structure; and
2.   To generate structure through dialogue.

These may not be the only ways. For example, a sufficiently intelligent AI could probably learn or be programmed to identify and adapt to a learner's need for control. However, the flexibility and adaptability of a system that is primarily composed of humans is likely to offer more benefits in the foreseeable future, not only in utilising collective intelligence, but also in closing the psychological gap of transactional distance.

It should be noted that the use of the word "dialogue" here is looser than its traditional definition, and admits all the possibilities of Garrison and Anderson's (2003) model, as well as the additions to it that might arise emergently. Perhaps a better word would be "interaction," which is more neutral in its connotations. The first option, dialogue through structure, is useful, but not especially exciting and will be dealt with summarily in the next section.

Dialogue Through Structure

Using the structure of an environment to encourage dialogue can be relatively straightforward in technological terms. To a significant extent, the thread structure of a threaded forum, for all of its potential shortcomings, makes a kind of sense of complex dialogues and simplifies the interface for its users. This is borne out to some extent by Ravid and Rafaeli (2004), who demonstrate that threaded discussions typically exhibit a small-world network structure, showing emergent patterns of behaviour that enable them to self-organise into a stable structure fit for their purpose. The rippling of control observed in Chapter IX might be seen as one manifestation of this sort of self-organisation. An alternative approach is to use a linear structure, which resembles that of a synchronous chat environment, or some combination of the two such as that found at Slashdot, where topics are subdivided at a top level, but the actual discussion is represented in linear form. Many systems allow the users to decide for themselves. For example, the Usenet News facility, built into many mail clients, allows a variety of methods of organisation including threaded, by name, by date, by subject, by poster, and so on.

Document-Centred Communication

The D3E system, which underpins a number of sites both educational and otherwise, most notably the journal of Interactive Media and Education (JIME, http://www-jime. open.ac.uk), provides a good example of the interplay of structure and dialogue in an educational environment. D3E presents a relatively fixed document (structure) around which dialogue is centred (Buckingham-Shum, Motta, & Domingue, 1999). Documents are typically split into multiple sections that are presented in sequence. Each section spawns a threaded dialogue around it. The tyranny of the threaded structure is significantly softened by the use of further metadata, which provides a richer picture of the shape of a discussion, applying principles of computer supported collaborative argumentation (CSCA) to indicate the nature of the message being presented. Primarily, this occurs through the use of icons that represent whether a message is in agreement or disagreement with the preceding message. It would be interesting to design an environment that mapped more classifications of conversational acts onto a threaded discussion (Cox, Carr, & Hall, 2004; Hara, Bonk, & Angeli, 2000), but this simple extra metadata provides a layer of structure to the threads that improves its fit to the needs of those participating in the conversation.

Another very common document-centred approach to discussion is found in blogs, where discussion grows around the initial blog posting. This has been used educationally, in a number of settings (Dron, 2003), and has benefits as a means of allowing learners to generate their own structure for dialogue (Downes, 2004).

An alternative technique is to enable real-time collaborative browsing of Web sites. The Quek™ system (http://www.q42.net/quek/) is a superb example of this approach. Although it is not intended to be used in an educational environment, it does much to reduce the loneliness of browsing the Web and enables transient dialogues to shape themselves around the site being visited.

The main problem with generating dialogue through structure is the level of constraint that it imposes. Once the initial document has been posted, it is typically (though not necessarily) ossified. Discussion is forever constrained to the subject of the document and cannot easily adapt to changing needs and conditions. Although there is no technical reason why this should be so, the document provides the meaning and context of the discussion. Changing a document that has formed the basis of a discussion may make the existing discussion irrelevant to the current document.

Structure Through Dialogue

Examples of the generation of structure as a direct result of dialogue are slightly harder to find than those that pin dialogue to a structure, but they do exist in at least rudimentary forms. For example, a wiki represents, in some respects, a kind of ossified dialogue, along with a structure that has been generated through that process. Another way of looking at it might be that it is both instructivist (through the content it presents) and constructivist (through the process that leads there).

Each decision to modify a wiki is clearly that of an individual, but the overall shape of the wiki is controlled by no one individual or group. Its form is emergent. There is even an emergent pattern of behaviour, which occurs through one user copying or being influenced by another or others.

Scale makes a significant difference here. A massive wiki of the sort exemplified by Wikipedia is so distributed that no single individual or small group could hope to understand it or control it, with links permeating the entire system that have their own emergent structure. However, it is perfectly feasible to use a wiki in a more constrained way: to attempt to curb the increasingly chaotic structure and content, even Wikipedia has now moved to a model that incorporates a certain amount of editorial management, providing (at least for some pages) a balance of top-down and bottom-up control.

Collectively Generated Structure

A system that truly generates structure through dialogue would have a form that could not be accurately predicted by any of its participants, but which would emerge from their collective behaviour. This is exactly what was observed earlier as being a characteristic of social software. The informal learning environments of social software communities can provide both constraint and freedom, allowing people to actively create or to passively receive, as well as to negotiate control. In more formal education, systems of this nature currently exist, albeit in a rudimentary form (Chapter XIV). The potential benefits of such systems are manifold, but in particular:

- **They are inherently learner-centred:** They allow structure to evolve over a period of time to fit the needs of the group of learners using them.

- **They are true learning ecologies:** Where the interactions of individual agents within the systems cause changes to the whole system, just as natural ecosystems constantly not only adapt to the constraints of the slower changing environment, but also develop a dynamic equilibrium internal to the whole system.

- **They are potentially cost-effective:** From an economic perspective, a system that, in effect, assembles itself, is likely to be more cost-effective than one that requires a design team and all its associated resources. However, this must be tempered by the possibility that they may be less efficient than more conventional systems.

- Through the provision of both choice and constraint, at one and the same time, they cater to diverse learning needs, offering support when it is needed and freedom when it is not.

A particularly interesting characteristic of such systems is that they blur the distinction between extrinsic and intrinsic constraints, as well as context and content. By reifying the process and using it to generate structure, intrinsic constraints become extrinsic, shaping the context of learning by altering the content. If the teacher is seen as the primary vehicle of constraint in a traditional educational context, then a system such as this can be seen as taking on the role of a teacher, in at least this respect. Furthermore, the promise of social software is that it can allow the smaller, faster moving behaviours of individual learners to influence and create the slower, structural elements of the system. In some ways, this may be seen as a reversal of the natural flow of constraint—a process of feedback that creates a new order, adapting ever more closely to the needs of its creators.

Conclusion

This chapter has dwelt upon the relationships between social software, deferred systems, transactional distance, transactional control and models of e-learning, in an attempt to clarify something about the unique nature of networked, computer-based learning environments. Most particularly, it has been established that there is a potential class of interaction between the many and the individual that has hitherto been largely ignored by the e-learning community. When this is combined with transactional control, transactional distance and some self-organising models in the next chapter, the theoretical foundations will have been laid for patterns of design to inform the creation of new and potentially revolutionary forms of learning environment. Such systems might go far beyond the realms of possibility that are embodied in the current gencration of learning management systems.

The chapter ended with a discussion of two distinct ways in which it might be possible to set about building this new class of educational software, either by generating dialogue through structure, or by creating structure through dialogue. While the former approach might have its uses, it is suggested that the latter form might offer the greatest rewards in an educational context, providing order for free and enabling learners to choose to choose without the high overheads associated with traditional e-learning, effectively allowing both high and low transactional control, and consequently both high and low transactional distance within exactly the same virtual environment.

Systems that generate structure through dialogue will, perhaps by their nature, be self-organising. The structure will not be predictable at the start because it will emerge from the many interactions of the learners and teachers within the system. Self-organisation and emergence are characteristics of many natural systems and, with this in mind, the next chapter describes some of the underpinning principles of how self-organising systems develop and hence, how environments that allow self-organisation to occur might be constructed.

References

Allen, C. (2004). *Tracing the evolution of social software.* Retrieved December 29, 2005, from http://www.lifewithalacrity.com/2004/10/tracing_the_evo.html

Anderson, T. (2006a). *Social software applications in formal online education.* Paper presented at the 6th IEEE International Conference on Advanced Learning Technologies, Kerkrade, The Netherlands.

Anderson, T. (2006b). Teaching a distance education course using educational social software. Retrieved January 7, 2006, from http://terrya.edublogs. org/2006/01/02/teaching-a-distance-education-course-using-educational-social-software/

Barker, P. (2005). *A role for weblogs in electronic course delivery.* Paper presented at the Ed-Media 2005, Montreal, Canada.

Boyd, D. (2004). *Friendster and publicly articulated social networking.* Paper presented at the Conference on Human Factors and Computing Systems (CHI 2004), Vienna.

Buckingham-Shum, S., Motta, E., & Domingue, J. (1999). *Modelling and visualizing perspectives in Internet digital libraries.* Paper presented at the Third

Annual Conference on Research and Advanced Technology for Digital Libraries, Paris.

Bush, V. (1950). As we may think. *Atlantic Monthly, 176*(1), 101-108.

Churchill, W. (1943). *HC Deb 28 October 1943 c403*. Retrieved from.

Coates, T. (2002). On the augmentation of human social networking abilities. Retrieved December 29, 2005, from http://www.plasticbag.org/archives/2002/12/on_the_augmentation_of_human_social_networking_abilities.shtml

Cox, G., Carr, T., & Hall, M. (2004). Evaluating the use of synchronous communication in two blended courses. *Journal of Computer Assisted Learning, 20*(3), 183-193.

Downes, S. (2004). Educational blogging. *Educause Review, 39*(5), 14-26.

Dron, J. (2003). *The blog and the borg: A collective approach to e-learning.* Paper presented at the E-Learn 2003, Phoenix, AZ.

Dron, J. (2006). *Social software and the emergence of control* Paper presented at the ICALT 2006, Kerkrade, Netherlands.

Dron, J., Mitchell, R., Boyne, C., & Siviter, P. (2000). *CoFIND: Steps towards a self-organising learning environment.* Paper presented at the WebNet 2000, San Antonio, TX.

Garrison, D. R., & Anderson, T. (2003). *E-learning in the 21ˢᵗ century: A framework for research and practice.* London: RoutledgeFalmer.

Godwin-Jones, R. (2003). Blogs and wikis: Environments for online collaboration. *Language Learning & Technology, 7*(2), 12-16.

Hara, N., Bonk, C. J., & Angeli, C. (2000). Content analysis of online discussion in an applied educational psychology. *Instructional Science, 28*(2), 115-152.

Kelly, K. (1998). *New rules for the new economy.* New York: Penguin Group.

Klamma, R., Chatti, M. A., Duval, E., Fiedler, S., Hummel, H., Hvannberg, T., et al. (2006). *Social software for professional learning: Examples and research issues.* Paper presented at the 6th IEEE International Conference on Advanced Learning Technologies, Kerkrade, The Netherlands.

Laurillard, D. (1993). *Rethinking university teaching: A framework for the effective use of educational technology.* London: Routledge.

Lin, W.-J., Liu, Y.-L., Kakusho, K., Yueh, H.-P., & Murakami, M. (2006). *Blog as a tool to develop e-learning experience in an international distance course.* Paper presented at the 6th IEEE International Conference on Advanced Learning Technologies, Kerkrade, The Netherlands.

Mathes, A. (2004). Folksonomies: Cooperative classification and communication through shared metadata. Retrieved January 8, 2005, from http://www.adam-mathes.com/academic/computer-mediated-communication/folksonomies.html

Mejias, U. A. (2005a). A nomad's guide to learning and social software [electronic version]. *The knowledge tree*. Retrieved January 7, 2006.

Mejias, U. A. (2005b). *Teaching social software with social software: A report.* Retrieved December 31, 2005, from http://ideant.typepad.com/ideant/2005/12/teaching_social.html

Moore, M. G. (1997). Theory of transactional distance. In D. Keegan (Ed.), *Theoretical principles of distance education* (pp. 22-38): Routledge.

Moore, M. G., & Kearsley, G. (1996). *Distance education: A systems view*. Belmont: Wadsworth.

Patel, N. (2003). Deferred system's design: Countering the primacy of reflective IS development with action-based information systems. In N. Patel (Ed.), *Adaptive evolutionary information systems* (pp. 1-29). Hershey, PA: Idea Group Publishing.

Ravid, G., & Rafaeli, S. (2004). Asynchronous discussion groups as small world and scale free networks. *First Monday, 9*(9).

Shirky, C. (2003). A group is its own worst enemy. Retrieved August 1, 2006, from http://www.shirky.com/writings/group_enemy.html

Shirky, C. (2004). *Folksonomy*. Retrieved January 9, 2005, from http://www.corante.com/many/archives/2004/08/25/folksonomy.php

Weller, M., Pegler, C., & Mason, R. (2005). Use of innovative technologies on an e-learning course. *Internet and Higher Education, 8*(2005), 61-71.

Wertheimer, M. (1938). Gestalt theory. In I. D. E. (Ed.), *Source book of Gestalt psychology*. New York: Harcourt, Brace & Co.

Williams, J. B., & Jacobs, J. (2004). Exploring the use of blogs as learning spaces in the higher education sector. *Australasian Journal of Educational Technology, 20*(2), 232-247.

Chapter XIII

Design Principles
for Social Software
in E-Learning

Evolution is to allegory as statues are to birds. It is a convenient platform upon which to deposit badly digested ideas. (Jones, 1999)

Introduction

E-learning environments, in which structure arises from dialogue, exhibit emergent behaviour. If this behaviour is to benefit learners, then it is important for system designers to understand what kinds of features such systems require and, more importantly, how they develop different behaviours, forms, and structures. This chapter presents eight basic principles that may be employed to ensure that the environment may develop through the actions of its users to become sustainable and self-organised.

Principle 1: Design for Change

Low Road and High Road Designs

As Stewart Brand has observed for buildings, *low road* freedom or *high road* flexibility gives a much more powerful and efficient way to survive than *no road* design (Brand, 1997, p. 52). Low road, architecturally dull houses which people live in, may easily grow and adapt over time, gaining extensions, new facades, being gutted then rebuilt from within, thus surviving changes in use and adapting to new uses in an almost organic way. Larger, more monumental high road buildings adapt differently, but still undergo change over many years. On the other hand, elegantly designed buildings, which perfectly fit their purpose, are in a much more precarious position once that purpose has gone. These are what Brand calls "magazine architecture." *No road* designs may be beautiful, but are immutable and ultimately disposable.

It is significant that the common approach to software construction that follows a waterfall process of analysis, design, development, implementation, and evaluation is, more often than not, concerned with the creation of no road designs. Software that is built for a single purpose is the computer equivalent of magazine architecture, elegant, fit for purpose, but when that purpose changes, ultimately disposable. A social system must develop and grow with its community.

Frameworks, Mashups, and APIs

To build software that allows flexible and diverse uses, it must allow some form of adaptation and, ideally, self-organisation to occur after the system has initially been constructed. Good, modular design, ideally using object-oriented principles, is a basic requirement, but is not enough to provide great flexibility. One approach that has already been observed in the ELF framework (JISC, 2004) and the OKI architecture (Eduworks Corporation, 2002), is to build systems out of interchangeable and extensible components.

Content, too, should conform to standards. Minimally, simple but dumb standards such as HTML or XML should be used, and the hiding of content in uninteroperable databases should be avoided. If possible, more meaningful standards such as SCORM, the IEEE-LOM, and other popular learning technology standards that may be found at www.imsproject.org should be used.

It should be possible to exchange information about users, including log-in information, perhaps using standards such as Shibboleth (shibboleth.internet2.edu).

Systems should be as open as possible, allowing others to make use of their services, data, users and facilities.

If at all possible, systems should be released as open source, allowing others to modify and extend their functionality as needs and contexts change.

Mashups, comprised of a combination of Web services, RSS feeds, and other techniques that enable systems to be built out of other systems are widely used in the social software community and offer simple, low-threshold approaches to re-purposing content and behaviour, as well as the promise of interoperability with systems beyond those designed specifically for learning. In an educational context, Stephen Downes's (2004) EduRSS may offer some benefits here, adding pedagogically useful metadata to the RSS standard, without breaking compatibility.

A Spandrel in the Works

Systems themselves should be flexible. Much of what governs the adaptation of biological species occurs as a side-effect of other adaptations, which, in their original context, are of little consequence, but as the environment changes or a species becomes isolated turn out to have the greatest significance. Gould (1978, 1995) calls such adaptations "exaptions," using an argument that hinges on the notion of *spandrels*. Spandrels are non-adaptive side consequences and architectural by-products of what happens when a dome is placed on top of a number of arches. They are the spaces that are left (Figure 13.1).

These spaces are not irrelevant:

Under the spandrel principle, you can have a structure that is fit, that works well, that is apt, but was not built by natural selection for its current utility. It may not have been built by natural selection at all. The spandrels are architectural by-products. They were not built by natural selection, but they are used in a wonderful way—to

Figure 13.1. Spandrels

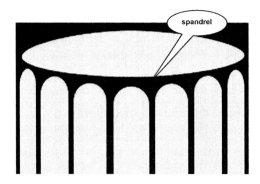

house the evangelists. But you can't say they were adapted to house evangelists; they weren't. (Gould & Lewontin, 1979)

If organisms were perfectly adapted to a co-evolved environment, then a major disturbance to that environment, such as the extinction of the dinosaurs, would have an equal effect on other species, such as mammals, like Brand's notion of magazine architecture. Exaptions are latent capabilities, able to become adaptations, if the conditions arise.

In the context of software design, many of the systems employed in the service of e-learning were not built for that purpose. E-mail remains enormously popular, for example, because it is ubiquitous, simple, directed, and flexible. When designing learning environments, over-engineering may, at times, be a good thing, providing affordances that may not be anticipated. At other times, it makes more sense to aim for something that is of more general use that may be repurposed in ways that can only dimly be anticipated.

Principle 2: Use Stigmergy

The biologist Grasse coined the word "stigmergy" in the 1950s (from the Greek *stigma* or "sign" and *ergon* or "work") to describe the behaviour of termites when building their complex nests or mounds (Grassé, 1959). Left to their own devices, termites wander aimlessly picking up balls of mud held together with pheromone-laced saliva and dropping them. However, they are more inclined to drop these balls of mud where there is already an odour of pheromones. The stronger the odour, the more inclined they are to drop mud there. This means that clusters of mud soon start to form. Because the pheromones disperse, the odour is stronger at the top of each clump than at the base, and so the clumps of mud grow slowly into columns. As the columns grow, they begin to attract each other, resulting in mud being dropped preferentially on the side facing the nearest column. This, in turn, leads to the development of arches. The arches get filled, following the same simple rule, leading eventually to cathedral-like structures that might appear to a casual observer to have been purposefully designed, but are actually the result of the simple process of leaving signs in the environment that do work.

Stigmergy as a Widespread Phenomenon

The principle of stigmergy leads to the formation of ant trails. Ants wander aimlessly until they find food, which they then bring back to the nest, leaving a trail of pheromones. Other ants are inclined to follow pheromone trails, so are led to the food, again leaving their own trails on the way back to the nest. As a consequence, as more ants return to the nest the trail gets stronger, attracting still more ants. Eventually, the food runs out and the trail disperses. A significant feature of this process is that it will inevitably lead to the most efficient route being chosen. For example, where two twigs are placed across a stream separating the nest and the food source, the larger, more navigable of these will be preferentially used as the trail of pheromones will be stronger and an optimal usage pattern will develop (Bonabeau, Dorigo, & Theraulaz, 1999, pp. 31-36). Stigmergic behaviours underpin other types of ant behaviour, including nest tidying, where the untidiness of a nest acts directly as a sign that it should be tidied.

Stigmergy in Human Systems

Stigmergy may be seen in a wide range of human interactions. For instance, money markets are complex systems that achieve a level of organisation, not through the planning of an individual, but through the combined effects of buying and selling, which in turn influences other buyers and sellers. In this case, the sign left in the environment is money. Bank runs, where the fact that some are withdrawing their money means that others are inclined to follow, represent an example of this process that has run out of control.

Buskers (street entertainers) have long understood this principle and will "seed" a hat left on the street with small change, knowing that this will act as a sign to passers-by to drop more money in. Similarly, they know that the most effective way to attract a crowd is for a crowd to be there in the first place. People are attracted to form a crowd by the presence of other people.

Footpaths in forests or on open ground form in a stigmergic way, as people are inclined to follow an already beaten path more readily than one that is not (Ball, 2004, p. 168).

Gladwell (2001) draws attention to the effects of reducing graffiti in New York subways as a means of reducing crime, observing that it follows the "broken window" effect, whereby the presence of broken windows communicates both a lack of caring, on the part of the community, and a signal to wrong-doers that crime is not such a bad thing. He writes: "The impetus to engage in a certain kind of behaviour is not coming from a certain kind of person but from a feature of the environment" (p. 142). Gladwell suggests that one of the main causes of a sudden fall in crime rates in New York was the methodical removal of graffiti from the subways, along with a number of other relatively small factors that acted as signals that criminal behaviour was unacceptable. Signs left in the environment were causal factors in the sustenance of a criminal culture and their removal was one of the reasons for its relative demise. As with many complex systems (including, perhaps, the termite mound), this was unlikely to be the whole story, and Levitt and Dubner (2005, pp. 128-129) argue persuasively that other factors almost certainly played a role.

Two Forms of Stigmergy

Two distinct forms of stigmergy are identifiable:

1.   **Sign-based:** in this form of stigmergy, the signs left in the environment are distinct from the forms that arise. This is the case in, for instance, the formation of termite mounds and ant trails or the role of money in stock markets.

2.   **Sematectonic:** in this form of stigmergy, the signs left in the environment *are* the forms that they give rise to. This is the case in, for instance, the formation of crowds around a street entertainer or the nest tidying behaviour of ants, who will tidy the nest only if it is untidy.

Structure through Dialogue

Stigmergy is the mechanism that underlies a number of computer systems that employ social navigation, which is to say those which make use of the behaviour of others to guide and influence users of the system (Kurhila, Miettinen, Nokelainen, & Tirri, 2002). Social navigation uses information gleaned from user behaviour, which is then fed back through the interface to influence the behaviour of others. If it works in real-time, it is sometimes described as *aware-ware*, or it can capture the history of usage, an approach variously known as *history-rich* or *wear-ware*. Some authors describe these variations as *direct* and *indirect* (Wexelblat & Maes, 1999). Social navigation is an inherently stigmergic process. Direct social navigation is equivalent to sematectonic stigmergy, while indirect social navigation tends to be sign-based.

For example, the changing font sizes of tags in del.icio.us, technorati.com, and many others are directly related to the number of times the tags have been used, and in turn, affect the likelihood of them being selected again. They are thus an example of sign-based stigmergy. People are drawn to chat rooms in which there is a lot of activity, and repelled by those that are empty. This is an example of sematectonic stigmergy. Even Google exhibits this behaviour: people tend to select items from the first page or two of results, even though better options may exist in later pages. As a result, it is more likely that these items will be referred to, increasing their page rank (Gregorio, 2003). A number of purpose-built e-learning environments have been created that employ social navigation and similar stigmergic processes, some of which will be looked at in the next chapter.

The self-organising behaviour achieved through both forms of stigmergy has one very important feature from the perspective of the generation of learning environments: structure is formed through "dialogue." In this sense, the dialogue is often very simple, a single set of signs which usually work solely through their intensity, not through a varied meaning. Nonetheless, it supports Bakhtin's definition of the word (Morris, 1994).

It is not always clear whether there is the intention to communicate with some other in stigmergic communication: when people gather around a street entertainer, they are seldom intentionally signalling their interest to others, although that is the effect that is achieved. It is something that just happens, almost as a by-product of another process. However, it acts in many ways resembling more conventional verbal dialogue, including that:

- it provides a bridge between individuals, creating an awareness of the "other";

- it acts as a motivator to action and influences behaviour; and

- there is a clear message, a recipient and a medium, even if the message itself is not necessarily intentional or directed.

Stigmergy may provide the means for learners to select the level of control they need, whether as creators of structure or those that are guided by it.

Stigmergy is Often Unavoidable

When there is a gathering of users in e-learning environments, some element of social navigation is virtually inevitable. The number of messages or depth of threads in an asynchronous discussion forum may attract or repel users. As Preece (2000) claims: "Too few people, and there will not be sufficient discussion to retain people's interest and draw them back; too many participants, and the community may become chaotic, and people will start to leave" (p. 171).

Populous chat rooms tend to attract users; empty rooms repel. The use of hit counters, comments, and annotations provide tangible and affective indicators of the presence of others, quite apart from any other semantic information they may contain. This influences navigation for better or worse. A fully populated wiki is usually more attractive than one that is empty; popular rooms in a MOO encourage further visitors to join.

To some extent, all learning environments that involve a means of identifying people or their actions may be seen as developing a kind of structure through the simple fact that they reify the behaviour of their users. However, this structure is fuzzy and a side-effect of the process, the effects of which may not be predicted or wanted by the systems' designers. When designing social online learning environments, it is essential to be aware of the potential ways that stigmergy may operate, whether the effect is wanted or not.

Principle 3: Survival of the Fittest

Stigmergic processes alone are not usually enough to build a self-organising system. Without some form of negative feedback, they can spiral out of control, leading to undesirable effects like bank runs and other positive feedback cascades, or examples of the Matthew Principle, where the rich get richer and the poor get poorer.

Natural stigmergic systems are limited in various ways, such as the gradual fading of stigmergic pheromones or an ant's nest becoming tidy. Human systems may be influenced by more complex phenomena outside the stigmergic system, such as the busker feeling hungry and going home, the money running out at the bank, and so on. If stigmergic systems are to be built that do not run out of control then it is vital that they are either self-limiting or can otherwise be constrained in their effects. At the same time, it is generally desirable, in keeping with principle one, to encourage variation and change for the better. Stigmergic systems tend to exhibit a single kind of behaviour and a single signal that creates it. An educational system should be able to adapt and cater to a variety of changing needs. Perhaps the most effective method, that may be drawn from nature, of both achieving variety and limiting out-of-control positive feedback in a self-organising system, is the process of evolution.

The Principles of Evolution

The principle of evolution can be expressed very simply: if there is reproduction with variation together with competition between the items which reproduce, then those items which are fittest will survive whilst those that are not will die out. The consequences of the theory are immense and profound, playing a large (if not the largest) role in generating the massively diverse order found in nature as well as some of the patterns of history, as well as the spread of ideas and beliefs.

Lamarckian Evolution Works Better

Darwinian evolution relies on random variations in parents being passed down to offspring. This is not necessarily the most effective mechanism for adaptation.

Lamarck's earlier concept of acquired inheritance, whereby changes in the phenotype acquired during an organism's lifetime are passed on to the offspring, may work better. This has been demonstrated in computer simulation by Ackley and Littman. As Kelly (1994) reports, "Lamarckian evolution produces smarter answers because it is a smarter type of search" (p. 393).

Lamarckian evolution appears to be at least one of the mechanisms underlying cultural and technological evolution, and therefore perhaps e-learning (Price, 1997). If systems are to be designed that self-organise through evolutionary processes, there is nothing to prevent them being Lamarckian in nature. In traditional education, for instance, good practice in teaching may be mimicked and successful organisational structures will be duplicated. Given that many interconnected systems of this nature will develop, competition will arise. There are finite ways any individual can teach, and any mode which is selected will have succeeded at the expense of other plausible alternatives. The significant factor is not the means of inheritance, but the competition between the offspring.

There are other mechanisms that might allow evolution to occur that are not a result of random mutation. For instance, Margulis (1998, p. 36) developed a notion of symbiotic evolution that allows for the "infections" of a parent (notably beneficial infections which led to mitochondria and chloroplasts, for instance) to be passed on to the offspring, thus improving the offspring's chances of survival. Although infections are seldom considered to be a good thing in computer systems, the embedding of one subsystem within another (for instance, e-mail in an LMS) might be considered to be broadly equivalent.

The important point about evolution is not that it is the result of genetic variation; merely that, it is a result of a selection process. Nor does that selection process have to be "natural." For example, Dawkins (1986) developed computer programs to generate "biomorphs," simple line drawings which were selected simply by deciding which the experimenter preferred.

When designing an emergent e-learning environment, it is useful if the patterns and structures that emerge may be duplicated and modified. Among the most elegant examples of this is Ning™, which allows whole systems and components of systems to be inherited from old ones. At a smaller scale, good approaches in blogs and wikis can inspire others to apply similar principles. Useful, but general, tags in tagging systems can be refined. Feeds from one RSS-enabled system can be incorporated and transformed in others. At a larger scale, design approaches from one system may be incorporated into another; the ubiquitous tag cloud presents an obvious example.

Survival of the Fittest

The "fittest" in any given system is that which survives in the system. In an educational system, success does not imply that the factors affecting selection of a given mode will correspond to improved learning outcomes. Such choices may be affected by organisation, administrative, physical, social, aesthetic, historical, and many other constraints. It does mean that death is the greatest teacher, and weaker or simply unluckier parts of the system fail to survive. Their weakness is only in relation to the system and, in natural systems, chance and historical accident (e.g., meteors and earthquakes) play a large defining role. A mutation has to be more successful than its competition within a given system. If it is not, however slight the disadvantage, it will not thrive. Even with a slight advantage, the chances of novel forms succeeding are slender. More often than not, the previously established system will correct any changes within it. What is required is a mechanism to allow speciation to not only occur, but to result in change to the system itself. Parcellation holds part of the key to this.

Principle 4: Parcellate

Speciation, Parcellation, and Scale

The title of Darwin's "The Origin of Species" emphasises the importance of speciation. Any system that is able to adapt must allow change to occur and allow change to be reproduced and embedded, if successful.

For Darwin, speciation occurs as a natural consequence of descent with modification and competition, hence leading to the survival of the fittest. This relies on the fact that the evolutionary landscape is not flat and featureless. Contingent occurrences, such as continental drift and the isolation of land-masses caused by rising water levels, lead to different environments and consequently different adaptations, leading to the formation of distinct species.

Parcellation is central to the evolution of species. As Gould (1978) says:

New species arise in very small *populations that become isolated from their parental group at the* periphery *of the ancestral range. Speciation in these small isolates is* very rapid *by evolutionary standards....*

Major evolutionary change may occur in these small, isolated populations. Favorable genetic variation can quickly spread through them. Moreover, natural selection tends to be intense in geographically marginal areas where the species barely maintains a foothold. In large central populations, on the other hand, favorable conditions spread very slowly, and most change is steadfastly resisted by the well-adapted population. Small changes occur to meet the requirements of slowly altering climates, but major genetic reorganizations almost always take place in small, peripherally isolated populations that form new species. (p. 61)

Calvin (1997) similarly puts parcellation at the heart of the evolution of species. The point is expanded upon by Jones (1999), and Darwin himself devotes the whole of chapter 12 of *The Origin of Species* to analysing the geographical distribution of species in terms of the formation of niches caused by geological features (Darwin, 1872). The logic is compelling and highly significant to the design of self-organising learning environments. Once again, scale matters. Without the formation of niches and clustering effects, there is little opportunity for speciation and hence for new structures to form. If monolithic systems are developed, then there is little chance for useful mutations to develop. This helps to explain some of the weaknesses of centralised learning management systems identified in Chapter XI.

Price (1995) relates this to an educational context, identifying the need for parcellation in an institutional learning environment, claiming that a large number of authorities suggest that "innovation and learning happens most easily in isolated populations." It is interesting that once again scale is an issue, just as it has been throughout, when looking at issues of choice. If the larger scale structure were dominant, it would be more likely to stifle the development of innovation. By parcellating the environment, smaller scale structures can develop relatively autonomously, allowing opportunities for diversity.

Large-Scale Integration and Connection

The corollary of the need for parcellation is the need for large-scale integration, minimally to maintain diversity and variability. This, in turn, is influenced by the amount of space available: "the larger the island, the greater the number of species" (Gould, 1995, pp. 116-117, p. 124). The search for maximum variability leads to a dilemma, where there is a need to encourage evolution (hence a need for small and isolated populations), but also to encourage variation (hence a need for large populations and the large areas they require). In natural evolution, this combination of scales is achieved over time by such events as the dropping of ocean levels or a collision of continents, but must be engineered as part of the structure of a designed system. Without connections, systems will not self-organise. On the other hand, the fact that the entire Web is seldom more than a click away means that it may, from a naïve perspective, be more of a problem to disconnect than to reconnect. This is less of a problem than it seems: structure influences behaviour so, if direct connections are provided, then it is more likely that they will be followed than those that take more effort to reach, even if that effort is only very slight.

Parcellation and Social Software

It is no coincidence that many of the most successful forms of social software involve some form of tagging. Tags provide ecological niches where diverse elements can thrive. Wikis offer a natural form of parcellation as each page or group of linked pages operates by its own rules. Social networking sites rely upon a relatively closed circle of friends, where the degree of separation is not too great: a friend of a friend may be as far as it goes, or a specific school year group.

Scale is, as ever, a significant factor. Shirky (2003) puts it well: "You have to find a way to spare the group from scale." Coenen (2006) makes the interesting observation that larger social groupings are less constraining, making them less effective as a means of building social ties. Failure to recognise this may be a factor that is leading to some of the larger social software sites cracking under their own weight as popular tags encompass ecosystems that are monstrously huge. While selection pressure tends to push out the least successful, the most successful become almost plague-like in their success. When this happens, it is common for further differentiation to occur in new and related tags, and for new, but related, technologies to step in to fill the gap. Clusty (clusty.com) is a good example of this—a social search engine that actively parcellates the evolutionary landscape.

Parcellation in E-Learning Environment Design

The lesson for the design of systems, which will evolve effectively, is to encourage parcellation, but to allow the occasional collision of ecosystems or the spreading of their areas. This lesson should be heeded by those who wish to centralise the control of education. Without islands of separate development, those variations which may prove useful when the environment changes (as it inevitably will), will not be in place and there is a potential for a catastrophic breakdown, as seen in the demise of the dinosaurs. The weaknesses in the centralised LMS signal such a failure.

In the smaller scale universe of educational transactions, any learning environment must be capable of supporting and nurturing diversity, to allow successful changes to be reproduced and achieve stability, to allow the useful to succeed in the evolutionary contest. The integrated LMS can provide this to some extent, by packaging courses and modules in separate spaces, inside which, a variety of different micro-environments (discussion forums, chat rooms, publication mechanisms, and so on) may develop in different ways. Unfortunately, although different tutors may use these spaces differently, the top-down design embedded in their structure can limit the benefits of parcellation. On mountains, creatures like mountain goats will thrive. Oceans are poor environments for mountain goats, but great for fish. The constraints of the environment limit the range of possible options that may be chosen within it. There has to be sufficient flexibility of form to allow new forms and structures to evolve. Used with care, hierarchies can help to guide the kind of system that evolves and assists in parcellation, but it is always important to be mindful of the effects of scale: the large influence the small, the slow influence the fast.

Principle 5: Consider the Entire System

Virtual learning environments are not isolated spaces. The educational process is a system of interacting parts, minimally the teacher and learner, but also consisting of a wide range of other factors, including the content, the physical setting, the chronological space, the social setting, cultural expectations, and much more. Together, they form what is perhaps best described as a learning ecology (Seely, Brown, & Duguid, 2000). Every part of the ecology has an effect on the learning experience.

The systemic nature of all educational experience has been noted by many, and several have observed that it is a complex system. Pace Marshall (1995), for instance, describes schools thus: "As complex learning systems, schools are far more organic and dynamic than linear. We, therefore, must design them to function less like clocks, and more like kaleidoscopes."

Pines (1998) suggests that "universities may be viewed as a collection of interacting communities each of which functions as a complex adaptive system." It is instructive to note the many levels of self-organisation that Pines identifies. An educational system is not just a single entity, but a collection of systems, which themselves are collections of systems. He cites interactions between disciplines within faculties and between faculty and students as clear examples, although he notes that the latter interaction has an unfortunate tendency to be one-way. This is unsurprising given the previous observations about hierarchies of scale: the large influence the small more than vice versa.

Moore (1993) observes that distance learning represents a departure from the "craft" approach to teaching and should more correctly be thought of as a system: "A distance education system should be thought of as a network of knowledge sources, processors, managers, communication media, and learners."

The interdependency of each part of the system means that making a change to one part means making a change to the whole:

For example, the exact nature of the design, the communications technology used for delivery, and the interaction depend on the sources of knowledge, the student needs, and the learning environment in the particular course. Selection of a particular delivery technology or combination of technologies should be determined by the content to be taught, who is to be taught and where the learning will take place. Design of the instructional media depends on the content, the delivery technology, the kind of interaction desired, and the learning environment. All these will be influenced by policy and management. Furthermore, changes in one component of a distance education system have immediate effects on all of the other components. (ibid.)

This accords with Cox's (1997) view, that "what actually governs complex systems is rarely the industrial age's notion of design at all. Rather, they evolve, shaped by an interaction in which system and environment minutely adjust to each other as biological organisms evolve within ecologies."

Laurillard's (1993) conversational framework is also systemic in nature, and is explicit about the effects that each actor in the system has on each other:

Given ... the integrative nature of the learning process, the inseparability of knowledge and action, and of process and outcome, there is no logical ordering of parts of the process, as each part is constituted in its relation to the other parts. (p. 50)

Like any natural ecosystem, systems in education exist at every scale, interacting with others and profoundly affecting their behaviour.

For the designer of learning environments, it is vitally important to consider the context of use and the wider system of which it is a part. No networked computer system is entirely closed and, most of the time, other tools, environments, and indeed the entire Web are just a mouse click away. More significantly, most people using such environments will be doing so within a very specific context. In an institutional environment, it is likely that learning will be highly constrained by course structures, lesson plans, assessments, and the will of teachers, as discussed in chapter five. In the workplace, the demands of the job will strongly influence how learners will engage with a system. Just-in-time learning implies a strong motivation to achieve a specific goal. The more self-organising the environment, the more it will shape itself to the contexts in which it is used.

Effective e-learning environments should not be viewed as somehow isolated from the world and their context of use, but should be seen as richly interconnected subsystems of much larger wholes. In particular, it is useful to be aware that systemic behaviour may arise in unexpected and sometimes counter-intuitive ways, where small changes can have large effects, and big changes may have little, if any, impact. Again, it is important to build systems which are flexible and evolvable, so that systemic weaknesses can be overcome. Where necessary, not just the physical form of the system, but the rules that govern its behaviour should be capable of evolving. An ideal system would do this by itself, pulling itself up by its own bootstraps without the intercession of what Dennett (1995) calls "skyhooks," external agencies external to the system itself.

Principle 6: Build From the Bottom Up, Design From the Top Down

One of the most distinctive characteristics of social software is that it leads to an emergent structure. By definition, this structure must arise from the bottom up. Any structure imposed from the top down will impose its own dynamic on the emergent structure, imposing the will of the designer rather than enabling control by the learners.

On the other hand, a totally unconstrained system is impossible. Building a computer system implies making choices, thereby reducing or removing other choices. There are few, if any, absolutely flexible systems. Even were the users given the ability to manipulate the binary code to produce anything they wished, the designers of the hardware would still impose constraint. Even if the users could design the hardware, physics and economics would impose constraints.

There is a broad spectrum of potential control that might be given to users of a system. On the whole, this should not be too great: in exactly the same way that too much choice is harmful to learners, too much flexibility, in the potential forms that software might take, would be more constraining than liberating. Those who want as little constraint as possible should probably learn to program and write the routines themselves.

Top down decisions must be made—decisions that will dictate the range of structures that might emerge. The designer of a social software environment should play a role more akin to a city planner than an architect, more akin to an architect than an engineer. The essence of the role is to create spaces that are alive with possibility and potential. This is not a science, but an imaginative engagement.

If not a city planner, then the social software designer is like a party planner, pulling together the place, the context, the objects and (of course) the people who will make the party a success. Top down thinking is necessary—the shape of the room, its location, the food and drink available, all result from the planner's decisions and all play a role in the success or failure of the party, but there, the planner's role ends. When the guests are assembled, the party commences.

The act of building software is the act of making decisions and applying constraints on those who use it. The kind of flexibility that is required is not absolute, but should be sufficient that the designer of the system should be unable to predict the precise form that it will take when it is used.

Hierarchies of Control

Because needs and contexts will vary and systems should flexibly adapt to different potential users and uses, it is generally wise for the system designer to delegate some control over how the system operates to one, more, or all users of the system. Most systems will provide greater or lesser control to administrators. Many systems provide differing levels of control to different roles: teachers, power users, teaching assistants, and so on. In the context of emergence, this is a potentially risky strategy. A hierarchy of control implies increasing levels of constraint the further down the hierarchy it goes. The issue of scale is again significant here: the larger and slower disproportionately influence the smaller and faster. Although some sort of administrator role is unavoidable, it is more in keeping with the principles espoused here that administrative control is more flatly distributed. For example, users may be granted rights to control certain aspects such as locking, user creation, group management, and so on, rather than being given an absolute role, and local responsibility should always be devolved as much as possible to the users themselves.

Pedagogic Flexibility

Part of the top-down design should involve consideration of potential pedagogies. It would usually be too presumptuous to embed a single specific pedagogy: all learners are different, and different pedagogies assume different degrees and scales of learner and teacher control, apart from anything else. However, structure influences behaviour, and different design decisions at the top level will inevitably lead to different affordances for different pedagogies: no system, even one that evolves, is completely pedagogically neutral (Friesen, 2004). Therefore, it is sensible to have some idea in mind at the start as to the range of pedagogical approaches that a system may support. As always, this should never assume a fixed stance, but should be designed to adapt to a variety of potential uses and, where possible, allow different pedagogies to emerge through use.

Principle 7: Build for Trust

Safety in an e-learning environment is among the most important factors in building an effective learning community (Bonk, 2002). Safety is based on trust, whether it be trust of the teacher, trust of other members of the community, trust in the tools, or trust in the environment. The word "trust" applies to a wide range of interactions between agents, both human and otherwise. Perhaps the most widely accepted definition is that of Gambretta, translated by Castelfranchi and Falcone (1998) thus: "Trust is the subjective probability by which an individual, A, expects that another individual, B, performs a given action on which its welfare depends."

As the teacher retreats into the background and learners become the creators of their own learning environments, trust becomes a significant issue. There are many reasons why this is a particular issue when dealing with social software. In particular:

- Social software is potentially highly susceptible to intentional attack, whether through modification of content, spurious tagging, spamming of comments, and track backs, or any one of many more objectionable practices;

- Often, social software reveals aspects about its users that they may not feel comfortable sharing with everyone;

- Without a recognised source of authority, veracity is hard to ascertain.

- As Shirky (2003) says, to build social software systems, "you need barriers to participation."

Access Control

Some forms of social software are less susceptible than others. For example, it is one of the guiding principles of wiki design that it is harder to deface a page than it is to undo the defacement. The constant succession of eyes means that any offensive, inaccurate, or otherwise unwanted changes will be removed or altered. This process is often referred to as soft security (Cunningham, 2006). However, in a diverse world that includes bad people as well as good, and that also contains programmers with the skill to automate attacks, this is not always enough. It is important to observe that the largest wiki of all, Wikipedia®, has found this process to be imperfect for some pages, and is now policed by a team of editors who control a small but significant set of pages.

Other systems, such as Elgg™ (elgg.net), a social software environment designed specifically for education, take an alternative tack, providing fine-grained access control that may be controlled by a system administrator and/or an individual user. People may reveal what they want to reveal, and allow what they want to allow.

Administrators can lock as much as they wish to lock, and grant access according to a fine-grained security policy. Less sophisticated, but still more controllable than an open wiki, the Dwellings system (dwellings.cofind.net) allows the creators of resources to decide whether or not others may change them. This method distributes control from the bottom up: in effect, every user is an administrator of his or her own local space. The system is a little inflexible though, inasmuch as it allows resources to be locked, but not hidden. Some systems work the other way around and enable the user to ignore specified users, hiding those who are a nuisance or who are boring. Slashdot™ (Slashdot.net) provides a particularly elegant means of identifying others as "friend, neutral," or "foe," thus enhancing positive social ties as well as de-emphasising those that are negative.

These examples all exhibit an important trait: the user has some control over the balance between private/protected and public space. Similar principles apply to systems such as Flickr and del.icio.us, as well as most blogging environments, where access can be limited or denied to specified resources.

Identifying and authorising users has more benefits than just keeping bad people out. Most notably, it makes it possible to identify the creators of content, and establishes awareness of social presence. The presence of others can be a valuable means of encouraging feelings of comfort within an online system (Rourke, Anderson, Garrison, & Archer, 2001).

Technological Weaknesses

Technology must be trustworthy: if not, this can be a highly constraining factor in a learning activity. Inability to interact with software or hardware can seriously affect the learner's sense of safety and security. Therefore, it is important to ensure that learners are able to use the technology, that the technology works, and is as usable as possible (Simpson, 2002). Things that might help to reduce trust may include lack of system reliability, perceived insecurity, lack of usability, inaccessibility, or inadequate levels of control. Trust in a system may be based on other factors beyond the immediate environment, such as its interaction with firewalls, its perceived susceptibility to attack, beliefs about the operating system it runs on, faith in its system administrators, doubts over the level of funding, its cost, and so on—perhaps even its market share or perceptions of the company that produces it. While some of these aspects may be out of the control of the system designer, for those wishing to implement such systems these are important considerations.

Visibility

Another potential contributor to trust is the capability of the system to support reciprocity, manage reputation, and sustain group stability (Coenen, 2006). Trust within groups is a social process, and must be visibly so. Shirky (2003) claims, "You have to design a way for there to be members in good standing. Have to design some way in which good works get recognized."

Whatever approach is taken to improving trust, it is important that the mechanisms are made visible. Users will be far less likely to have faith in a system that obscures its workings than one that does not. Equally, trust is likely to be increased if users are known, especially if this is combined with mechanisms such as ratings, testimonials, contact-sharing tools, or similarity indices that help to identify trustworthy people.

Principle 8: Design for Sociability

Social software stands or falls on its community of users. If the foregoing principles are adhered to, there is a good chance that the more people make use of the system, the more effective it will become.

Building a system for sociability is notoriously difficult, when compared with designing one for simpler sorts of usability. In particular, while it is possible to use processes and theories that relate to how people socialise in the design process (Barab, MaKinster, Moore, Cunningham, & The ILF Design Team, 2001), it is hard to test the efficacy of a system that only becomes functional when occupied by indefinitely many users. It is possible to base designs on pre-existing successful patterns, to model performance, to attempt simulations, and to use varied personas to identify individual motivation, but the nature of a deferred system that relies on its users to give it shape means that it has to be implemented before it can be properly tested. This adds special emphasis to Principle one—the need to design with change in mind—and goes hand-in-hand with the need for trust.

Conclusion

Even if the recommendations are not all followed to the letter, the eight principles presented in this chapter should be considered when building any sustainable social software environment in which control is intended to be emergent. It is possible to view any use of software as an educational environment in terms of:

- **Adaptability:** the extent to which the software can be adapted, changed and integrated;

- **Stigmergy:** the ways in which structure emerges from dialogue;

- **Evolvability:** the extent to which emergent patterns of use and emergent structures are duplicated and amplified or diminished in competition with each other;

- **Parcellation:** the ways in which the environment is able to be segmented and its parts differentiated;

- **Context:** the environment's place in the context of other systems;

- **Constraint:** the level of control exerted by the system designer and/or administrators of the system;

- **Trust:** the features the environment provides to ensure reliability, safety, and security;

- **Sociability:** the features the environment provides to facilitate social interaction and a sense of the presence of others.

Meta-Principles: Connectivity and Scale

A defining characteristic, or meta-principle, that emerges from all of this is the connected nature of the various parts of a complex system, and the fact that order emerges from a myriad of small and local interactions. There is a strong interdependency between most of the principles, and changes in one will typically affect others. For example, trust is intimately related to sociability and may be strongly affected by context, parcellation, and stigmergy. Constraint may arise from context, and affect trust.

Another meta-principle is that of multiple scales: scale is particularly significant when considering adaptability, stigmergy, evolvability, parcellation, context, and constraint. The scale at which a system is viewed is always significant, so any application of the principles should include an awareness of the scale or scales at which they are applied, and the possible interactions between the larger and the smaller scale subsystems.

Out of a considered awareness of such principles will emerge a system that is both governed by the behaviour of its parts, and which also governs that behaviour. This is natural behaviour for social software. To create a system wherein structure is derived from its own behaviour provides the means to create learning environments with a design principle more akin to gardening than to engineering—systems that grow and form by themselves. The next chapter will present a range of learning environments that begin to move in that direction, examining the ways in which they adhere to the eight principles.

References

Ball, P. (2004). *Critical mass: How one thing leads to another*. London: Heinemann.

Barab, S., MaKinster, J. G., Moore, J., Cunningham, D., & The ILF Design Team. (2001). Designing and building an online community: The struggle to support sociability in the Inquiry Learning Forum. *Educational Technology Research and Development, 49*(4), 71-96.

Bonabeau, E., Dorigo, M., & Theraulaz, G. (1999). *Swarm intelligence: From natural to artificial systems*. New York: Oxford University Press.

Bonk, C. J. (2002). Frameworks for research, design, benchmarks, training, and pedagogy in Web-based distance education. In M. G. Moore & W. G. Anderson (Eds.), *Handbook of distance education* (pp. 331-348). NJ: Lawrence Erlbaum Associates.

Brand, S. (1997). *How buildings learn*. London: Phoenix Illustrated.

Calvin, W. H. (1997). The six essentials? Minimal requirements for the Darwinian bootstrapping of quality. *Journal of Memetics, 1*.

Castelfranchi, C., & Falcone, R. (1998). *Principles of trust for MAS: Cognitive anatomy, social importance, and quantification*. Paper presented at the 3rd International Conference on Multi Agent Systems.

Coenen, T. (2006). *Structural aspects of online social networking systems and their influence on knowledge sharing*. Paper presented at the IADIS International Conference on Web Based Communities, San Sebastian, Spain.

Cox, B. (1997). Evolving a distributed learning community. In Berge and Collins (Ed.), *The online classroom in K12*: Hampton Press.

Cunningham, W. (2006). Why wiki works. Retrieved July 19, 2006, from http://c2.com/cgi/wiki?WhyWikiWorks

Darwin, C. (1872). *The origin of species* (6th ed.).

Dawkins, R. (1986). *The blind watchmaker*. London: Longman.

Dennett, D. (1995). *Darwin's dangerous idea*. Harmondsworth: Penguin.

Downes, S. (2004). Edu RSS. Retrieved July 28, 2006, from http://www.downes. ca/xml/edu_rss.htm

Eduworks Corporation. (2002). *What is the open knowledge initiative(TM)?* Massachusetts Institute of Technology.

Friesen, N. (2004). Three objections to learning objects. In R. McGreal (Ed.), *Online education using learning objects* (pp. 59-70). London: Routledge.

Gladwell, M. (2001). *The tipping point: How little things can make a big difference.* London: Abacus.

Gould, S. J. (1978). *Ever since Darwin- reflections in natural history*: Burnett.

Gould, S. J. (1995). The pattern of life's history. In John Brockman (Ed.), *The third culture: Beyond the scientific revolution.*

Gould, S. J., & Lewontin, R. C. (1979). The spandrels of San Marco and the panglossian paradigm: A critique of the adaptationist paradigm. *Proceedings of the Royal Society of London, Series B, 205*(1161) (pp. 581-598).

Grassé, P. P. (1959). La reconstruction du nid et les coordinations inter-individuelles chez Bellicoitermes natalensis et Cubitermes sp. La theorie de la stigmergie: Essai d'interpretation des termites constructeurs. *Insect Societies, 6,* 41-83.

Gregorio, J. (2003). Stigmergy and the World Wide Web. Retrieved December 13, 2003, from http://bitworking.org/news/Stigmergy/

JISC. (2004). *The e-learning framework (ELF): Summary.* Joint Information Systems Committee.

Jones, S. (1999). *Almost like a whale.* London: Doubleday.

Kelly, K. (1994). *Out of control: The new biology of machines.* London: Addison Wesley.

Kurhila, J., Miettinen, M., Nokelainen, P., & Tirri, H. (2002). *Use of social navigation features in collaborative e-learning.* Paper presented at the E-Learn 2002, Montreal, Canada.

Laurillard, D. (1993). *Rethinking university teaching: A framework for the effective use of educational technology.* London: Routledge.

Levitt, S. D., & Dubner, S. J. (2005). *Freakonomics: A rogue economist explores the hidden side of everything.* London: Allen Lane.

Margulis, L. (1998). *The symbiotic planet: A new look at evolution.* London: Orion.

Moore, M. G. (1993). Is teaching like flying? A total systems view of distance education. *The American Journal of Distance Education, 7*(1).

Morris, P. (Ed.). (1994). *The Bakhtin reader.* London: Edward Arnold.

Pace Marshall, S. (1995). Chaos, complexity and flocking behaviour: Metaphors for learning. *Wingspread Journal, Summer 1996.*

Pines, D. (1998). *Designing a university for the new millenium: A Santa Fe perspective.* Paper presented at the Fred Emery Conference of Sabanaci University, Istanbul, Turkey.

Preece, J. (2000). *Online communities: Designing usability, supporting sociability.* Chichester, UK: Wiley.

Price, I. (1995). Organisation memetics: Organisational learning as a selection process. *Management Learning, (26),* 299-318.

Price, I. (1997). *Punctuated strategic equilibrium and some strategic leadership. Challenges for university 2000.* Paper presented at the Second International Conference on the Dynamics of Strategy, Surrey, UK.

Rourke, L., Anderson, T., Garrison, D. R., & Archer, W. (2001). Assessing social presence in asynchronous text-based computer conferencing. *Journal of Distance Education, 14*(2).

Seely Brown, J., & Duguid, P. (2000). *The social life of information.* Boston, MA: Harvard Business School Press.

Shirky, C. (2003). A group is its own worst enemy. Retrieved August 1, 2006, from http://www.shirky.com/writings/group_enemy.html

Simpson, O. (2002). *Supporting students in online, open and distance learning* (2nd ed.). London: Kogan Page.

Wcxelblat, A., & Maes, P. (1999, May 2-15). *Footprints: History-rich tools for information foraging.* Paper presented at the CHI '99 conference on Human factors in computing systems, Pittsburgh, PA.

Chapter XIV

Social Software in E-Learning:

Beyond Blogs and Wikis

The Borg is the ultimate user. They're unlike any threat your Federation has ever faced.

Q to the U.S.S. Enterprise-D crew (Startrek.com, 2006)

Introduction

This chapter describes a number of e-learning environments, including two that are written by the author, that employ principles of the sort found in Chapter XIII. None of these are perfect: although most are used by real groups of learners, they are research environments, more tools to think with than production systems. Some of their flaws present wicked problems that must be solved before they can be genuinely useful, but all point towards interesting futures.

The learning environments presented here are all forms of social software. All exhibit some characteristics that are designed to allow structure to develop through the interactions of learners with the systems and each other. As a result, they have the potential to allow different learners to exercise both greater and lesser transactional control within the same system and at the same time.

The chapter begins with some overviews of example environments, situating them in the context of the design principles presented in the previous chapter. The examples are not chosen arbitrarily, but many others might have been chosen instead: this is a growing genre. Two of the author's own environments are then presented, in more detail, to give examples of ways that the principles may apply in practice, demonstrating strengths and weaknesses that are further explored in the following chapter.

Examples of Self-Organising Learning Environments in the Context of the Eight Principles

Educo

The Educo system uses social navigation to influence the behaviour of its users (Kurhila, Miettinen, Nokelainen, & Tirri, 2002). It combines a collaborative document navigation system with annotation and discussion tools, providing a document-centric environment shaped by dialogue. Users are represented as dots clustering around iconic representations of documents. The more dots there are, the more users are gathering around specific documents, a process which in turn attracts further users. Other signs provide indicators at a slower scale of the relative popularity of documents over time. Educo influences, but does not determine, behaviour. At any point, users are able to choose an unconventional or unpopular path through the docu-verse, but should they feel insecure or uncertain (as would be typical of a new or non-autonomous learner), there are clear routes that they might take through the material, using cues such as overall popularity, current visitors, and annotations. This combination of choice and constraint is potentially very powerful. The user may ride the crest of a wave, following other learners in real-time. The wave does not leave a trail that can be followed, nor is it possible to know which way the group may head from one moment to the next. There is no view of the future, only the present and the past.

Educo and the Eight Principles

• **Adaptability**: Educo can integrate with the Web at large, using a potentially open corpus of resources, and it incorporates traditional discussion systems. However, it is not open to other systems and uses no integration technologies beyond the basic protocols of the Web. It is not open source, so the ability of others to make changes is very limited.

- **Stigmergy:** Educo is highly stigmergic, making use of both sematectonic and sign-based stigmergy to influence and guide learners.

- **Evolvability:** Educo encourages survival of the fittest: documents stand or fall based on how much they are used. There are no explicit mechanisms for inheritance.

- **Parcellation:** the document-centricity of the system leads to natural parcellation of the environment, but this only occurs at a single scale, and documents might be more accurately viewed as species in a single ecosystem than separate ecological niches. However, there are two temporal scales: the slower-changing rating of overall popularity and the current popularity shown by the number of visitors.

- **Context:** Educo is not intended for use as a stand-alone system and occupies a supporting role in institutional learning, hence constraining behaviour and ensuring that it develops as an educational ecosystem.

- **Constraint:** the structure generated through stigmergy is emergent, and there are few constraints on the kinds of document or potential uses to which the system may be put.

- **Trust:** Educo makes use of logins. The heavy emphasis on the presence of others and the succession of eyes that this entails, along with its use of more conventional discussion tools, makes this a safe and nurturing environment.

- **Sociability:** the diversity of communication tools and emphasis on the presence of others makes this a highly sociable environment.

OurWeb

The same team that created Educo have also produced a number of others, the latest of which is OurWeb, a tool for collaborative knowledge building that draws heavily on the previous system (Miettinen, Kurhila, Nokelainen, & Tirri, 2005). OurWeb is a document-centred system, which combines different forms of annotation and associated discussion forums, and a wiki. This places it firmly in the area of systems that generate dialogue through structure and vice versa. However, it also uses explicit and stigmergic "footprints" to indicate areas of activity, which are personalised in the sense that they will only show up if the user has not previously visited a particular document. It captures levels of activity, measured as "reading time," which provide implicit data about levels of interest as well as amount of access. The authors of the system pay special attention to the way that learners are supported in negotiating the domain of study through use of the system. It has only been used on a small course for a small group of students. It would be interesting to observe what might happen were it to be used for a larger group, but it seems likely that it might become overwhelmed by a mass of footprints and contradictory information gleaned from the activities of multiple users with multiple intents.

OurWeb and the Eight Principles

- **Adaptability**: Unlike its forebear, OurWeb makes extensive use of other components, most notably the wiki. Its use of a wiki enables a great deal of structural change that is in the hands of its users. Like Educo, it can integrate with the Web at large, using a potentially open corpus of resources. It is not open source, so the ability of others to make changes is very limited.

- **Stigmergy**: Through its use of footprints and other cues based on learner activity, OurWeb is highly stigmergic, making use of both sematectonic and sign-based stigmergy to influence and guide learners.

- **Evolvability**: Due to the use of a wiki, evolutionary pressures apply to the content itself as well as the structures defined by annotations and social navigation cues. Each change to a page may be seen as a different (mutated) generation.

- **Parcellation**: The document-centricity of the system leads to some parcellation of the environment. The use of annotations operates at a different scale than that of the page itself, as do the stigmergic footprints. This leads to parcellation at a micro-scale.

- **Context**: OurWeb is not intended for use as a stand-alone system and occupies a supporting role in institutional learning, hence constraining behaviour and ensuring that it develops as an educational ecosystem.

- **Constraint**: The structure generated through stigmergy creates an emergent structure, as does the use of a wiki. The system designers have paid some attention to navigation through the system, exercising a certain amount of control.

- **Trust**: OurWeb makes use of logins. Others are mainly visible through their annotations and stigmergic signs that they have been in the environment. Because annotations are ascribed to individuals, the trust mechanisms are quite visible.

- **Sociability**: Annotations and wiki pages can act as effective tools for mediated dialogue.

ChatCircles

ChatCircles is a real-time chat system written in Java™ that represents users as circles on a background space (Donath, Karahalios, & Viegas, 1999). The more recently and actively a user has been chatting, the larger the circle appears. To hear what one user is saying, it is necessary to move one's own circle closer. The combination of activity indicators and the inevitable clustering as people move their circles within hearing range of active speakers, results in a structure, determined by the positioning of individuals within the working space. Users are able to choose where to go and who to speak to, but if they wish to relinquish this right, then there are clear indicators of where it would be most profitable to go.

ChatCircles is a more intuitive chatting space than a traditional linear, text-based, asynchronous interaction because it provides some forms of non-verbal communication, which help to give more hints to its users about each others' behaviour and intentions. The extra richness that this provides is exhibited as structure, but the creation of that structure is distributed. This structure arises simply as a result of using the system and of being actively involved in dialogue. ChatCircles also provides the means to view historical data on interactions.

ChatCircles and the Eight Principles

- **Adaptability:** ChatCircles is a very self-contained environment that neither gives nor receives from any other.

- **Stigmergy:** ChatCircles is an extremely stigmergic environment, largely employing sematectonic stigmergy. However, it also offers various views of the system to provide historical information that are more sign-based.

- **Evolvability:** Evolution in ChatCircles is rapid and continuous. Conversations live or die according to the level of participation and number of participants. There appear to be no reproductive mechanisms.

- **Parcellation:** Parcellation occurs naturally, partly due to clustering and partly because each chat exists in its own virtual space. However, these spaces are not connected, so the benefits of connections between areas are not realised. The ability to view historical data offers parcellation at different temporal scales.

- **Context:** ChatCircles is very open and can be used in almost any context; its form evolves to the needs of the context in which it is used. It is not a complete learning environment and will only become one when used in a learning context.

- **Constraint:** Again, because of its open structure, ChatCircles takes an aggressively bottom-up approach. The constraints supplied by designers and administrators are minimal, with most of the structure evolving through the interactions of its users.

- **Trust**: A log-in is required, though largely as a means of identification rather than a serious attempt at authentication. The presence of others may be a reassuring factor and the operation of the system is completely visible.

- **Sociability**: The essence of ChatCircles is sociability—it is its raison d'etre.

The Knowledge Garden

The Knowledge Garden is a visual representation of knowledge as a garden, composed of flowers that move when touched (Crossley, Davies, McGrath, & Rejman-Greene, 1999). It incorporates a VRML interface to the Jasper shared information store—a system that stores and indexes documents. In the Knowledge Garden, clusters of associated URLs are visualised as flowers growing. Leaves that are little used wither on the stem and eventually fall off. The colour of flowers codes for document status (updated, unchanged, dead) and, when selected, the flower stems wave for a while like real flowers that have been touched. A visitor seeking interesting information is thus drawn by colour and movement created by other users of the system. Each user has an avatar, the position of which records users' perceived availability based on mouse clicks, keyboard presses, and the last time their e-mails were read. Users can prune the stems that are not wanted and even take cuttings to grow in their own private gardens. An interactive space is created where the environment is formed out of the active participation of its users, a place where knowledge can be shared independently of physical space and formal organisational groupings. Despite its gardening metaphor, the Knowledge Garden is more akin to a jungle, evolving as an ecosystem without the explicit attention of a single gardener. Sadly, it appears that it is no longer being actively developed, nor has it been released to the community.

The Knowledge Garden and the Eight Principles

- **Adaptability:** The Knowledge Garden is a layered system which draws on other components through the use of agents. This design approach is well-suited to adaptation and change. Because it is an early system, it does not adhere to common modern standards, but it does make effective use of the Web; it integrates with e-mail and its design could easily be adapted to use more recent methods. Regrettably, this cannot be done, as it is not open source.

- **Stigmergy:** The Knowledge Garden employs primarily sign-based stigmergy to capture navigation paths at more than one scale.

- **Evolvability:** The use of withering, cuttings, and pruning makes the Knowledge Garden a highly evolvable system, incorporating both natural selection and descent with modification.

- **Parcellation:** The system is naturally parcellated, with clusters forming around specific subject areas.

- **Context:** The system may be used in a wide range of contexts and is not limited to a specific domain. However, its main application is clearly to support a specific community and it is uncertain as to how well it would scale beyond a specified area of interest.

- **Constraint:** The Knowledge Garden relies heavily on bottom-up processes, although the underlying Jasper system employs more formal techniques for indexing and classifying data.

- **Trust:** This is a system for known users in a relatively closed community, so trust arises more from the context than from the system itself.

- **Sociability:** Support for sociability is embedded in this system, which considers knowledge as a feature of people and communities, rather than simple codified information.

The Knowledge Sea

The Knowledge Sea began as a system using AI techniques to provide recommendations to its users of where to go next (Brusilovsky & Rizzo, 2002). The system presents a two-dimensional map to educational resources, each cell of which is used to group together related resources. Nearby cells are considered to be fairly well related, while those further off are considered less so. The system is organised using neural net technologies to help identify similarities between documents. As well as proximity as a guide to relevance, the original Knowledge Sea used colour to indicate "depth" of resources to be found in a particular cell, ranging from light blue (1-4 resources) to dark blue (more than 10 resources). In addition to this, it used red dots to indicate the presence of further resources, other than those created by the tutor for the learning activity in question. The first Knowledge Sea did not make use of the behaviours of its users in the manner observed in systems discussed previously. Instead, it is more of a system to enhance the abilities of teachers to present resources in a learner-centred manner. Structure was generated not through dialogue between its users, but between the teacher and the computer. However, like the other systems presented here, the resulting navigation features provided a combination of choice and constraint to the learner, without significant intentional structuring on the part of the teacher.

In its latest iteration, the Knowledge Sea incorporates two distinct stigmergic mechanisms, which explicitly aim to influence each learner based on the activities of others. On the one hand, there is an implicit recommendation made each time a learner visits a resource, which deepens the colour of the cell in which it resides. On the other, explicit comments are elicited from the learners about the resources using a comment engine known as AnnotatED, which places comments into different categories, which depend on the purpose of the note to recommend, comment on, or post a query about the resource (Brusilovsky, Chavan, & Farzan, 2004). This explicitly pedagogic metadata helps to shape the system to achieve educational ends. By combining content-based, implicit, and explicit cues, Knowledge Sea II is designed with learning in mind.

The Knowledge Sea and the Eight Principles

- **Adaptability:** Though engineered effectively in a manner that allows the developers to make rapid changes, the Knowledge Sea is not yet open to other systems, either by incorporation or through exposing its services. However, its purpose is primarily to integrate other resources on the Web. It is not open source.

- **Stigmergy:** The use of social navigation pervades the latest iteration of the Knowledge Sea, through depth indicators and other cues such as the red dots, using sign-based stigmergy.

- **Evolvability:** The various navigation cues provided by the Knowledge Sea are intended to provide indications to users of their relative usefulness. Those that are more successful are the evolutionary winners. However, there is little sign of reproduction with variation.

- **Parcellation:** There is strong use of parcellation, including the categorisation techniques, and in the use of stigmergic indicators such as red dots, which provide rich metadata about the value of different areas. The different categories of annotation also parcellate the landscape further.

- **Context:** The Knowledge Sea is an educational system, designed to be used in a traditional, educational context. As such, its users are more controlled by the external context than the internal dynamics of the system itself.

- **Constraint:** In addition to bottom-up stigmergic techniques, the Knowledge Sea uses many top-down design decisions, especially in the use of AI to help categorise resources and in the explicit metatdata used to categorise annotations. This is a system built for a purpose that makes pragmatic design choices to fit that purpose.

- **Trust:** The Knowledge Sea makes use of logins primarily as identifiers, rather than for authorisation. Trust is distributed, and works on the assumption that the group will make useful decisions, rather than individuals.

- **Sociability:** Because it is intended to be used within a closed community, the system has little need for strong social features, although ascribable annotations help to form community bonds.

Comtella

Comtella is a bookmark-sharing system, aimed at educational uses, whereby classes of students can collectively generate useful lists of resources (Vassileva, 2004). It encourages collaborative categorisation of resources, using topics and groups of topics. Unusually, this is not a Web-based system, but instead, relies upon a client application downloaded to the desktop. The benefits this brings are richer and more varied interactivity, including the ability to download original documents for caching and the operation of a peer-to-peer, server-less network, based on Gnutella. The interface emphasises those documents that are considered more useful, using a simple rating gauge as well as annotations. The system rewards users who are more active by bumping up their relative status. Comtella also matches users' preferences to improve recommendations: it decreases a relationship weighting between users when they disagree in their ratings of resources, which, from the other's perspective, in turn affects the apparent weightings of resources each has rated. Comtella thereby gains some of the benefits of automated collaborative filters and adaptive hypermedia.

Comtella and the Eight Principles

- **Adaptability:** Comtella's use of its own extensions to the Gnutella peer-to-peer protocol makes it potentially interoperable with other systems using the same approach. It has spawned peer applications that use the same protocols, notably Comtella Discussions, a forum system employing a combination of social navigation and peer recommendation (Webster & Vassileva, 2006).
- **Stigmergy:** The use of social navigation in Comtella is extensive and pervasive.
- **Evolvability:** Because of its use of social navigation, competition is an inherent feature of the system, especially when combined with status indicators. However, there appear to be few explicit mechanisms for replication with variation.
- **Parcellation:** Comtella seems weak with respect to parcellation. Vassileva (2004) reports on problems with saturation once all relevant documents have been retrieved, and there appears to be little variation in the structure that emerges.

- **Context:** Comtella has mainly been used in an institutional context, but there is no reason, in principle, that this should remain so, apart from the aforementioned problems with limited parcellation. The system is open and may easily be repurposed for many potential learning activities. Having said that, it is interesting that Vassileva reports on a need for tutor intervention to get things started. In common with most others presented here, this is not a system that is able to pull itself up by its own bootstraps, relying on other contextual elements to bring about learning.

- **Constraint:** Comtella is a very open system, with a structure that is formed from local interactions. The designer plays a relatively limited role in this, although the limited approach to ratings (essentially on a good-to-bad scale) means that it cannot develop much richness in the kinds of recommendations it provides.

- **Trust:** Logins are required, but mainly for identification and it is not only possible, but encouraged, that learners may assume multiple identities. The peer-to-peer protocols used open up further issues with trust as peers might potentially be unreliable or untrustworthy.

- **Sociability**: The fact that this is not only a community of people but also of machines helps to amplify the community aspects of Comtella. When allied with Comtella Discussions, it might become a particularly sociable environment.

Two Examples in Greater Detail

The examples provided so far begin to show the promise of social software for education. Each has its strengths and weaknesses. The remainder of this chapter concerns two of the author's own systems: CoFIND and Dwellings. Both have been designed with self-organising principles in mind from the start, but they take different approaches to design. CoFIND is primarily a collaborative book marking system, while Dwellings is intended as a more complete environment for learning. Both systems are full of flaws: both are works in progress and are not ready for the mainstream. These are tools for exploring ideas and approaches to software development that have fed the research leading to the eight principles: they are not finished examples of the state of the art.

Copyright © 2007, Idea Group Inc. Copying or distributing in print or electronic forms without written permission of Idea Group Inc. is prohibited.

CoFIND

Under sporadic development since 1998, CoFIND (collaborative filter in N dimensions) is a social book marking system—a collaborative directory of Web sites which allows learners to add, categorise, and rate learning resources that they have found and wish to share (Dron, Mitchell, & Boyne, 2003).

As well as being able to add resources (Web site URLs and so on), CoFIND allows learners to create *topics* and *topic groups*, which behave much like the tags in other social software such as del.icio.us or Flickr, allowing users to categorise resources in a flexible and largely unrestrictive manner. Topics exist in a shallow hierarchy below topic groups, which thus parcellate and provide the larger, slower moving environment in which topics evolve.

Qualities

CoFIND's most distinctive feature is its use of tags known as *qualities*: user-created pedagogical metadata that allow learners to say more about a resource than whether it is simply good or bad. Examples might include "*good for beginners,*" "*detailed,*" "*useful,*" and so on. Qualities are entered by users of the system and thus allow current needs to be reified and become available to the whole learning community that uses it. These are somewhat like disembodied user models, actively invented by the users themselves rather than the system designers. This is significant, as it recognises the primary characteristic of learning—it involves change. A system building a model of its learners based on past behaviour is necessarily going to be looking at a historical snapshot that does not match the learner's current state. Qualities allow learners to choose what kind of learning needs they have when they need to choose them, without committing them to that kind of need in the future.

Evolving Metadata

Once a quality has been entered into CoFIND, it may be re-used by anyone wishing to rate any resource. To prevent rarely used qualities clogging up the system, evolutionary mechanisms cause little-used qualities to dwindle and eventually die, while those that are more frequently used rise to the top of the selectable list, reinforcing success. Although all surviving qualities are available to be used for ratings for all topics, the order in which they are displayed and the font used varies according to topic. Within a given context, more frequently used qualities are displayed more prominently. When new qualities are added, it is possible to explicitly allow them to inherit the ratings of a previous quality. For example, if a user were to add a quality called "simple," it could inherit the ratings that had previously been used with "good for beginners," giving it a head start in the competition. Evolutionary pressure ensures that inappropriate inheritance (for instance, if "simple" were to inherit ratings from "complex") is swiftly punished, as an inappropriate choice would fail to return useful resources. A novelty weighting is given to each new resource that is proportional to overall use of the system. This is necessary as it decays each time the system is used: a single weighting would disproportionately disadvantage new resources in a very active system.

Not only qualities but topics, groupings of topics, and the resources themselves, are in a constant evolutionary struggle. They compete for list position and prominence, which is the key (but not the only) stigmergic sign that encourages learners to select certain paths to resources and not others. Each combination of topic group, the topics it contains, and the qualities used to rate resources forms an ecological niche, connected to others, but parcellated from the rest. Like the larger scale, slower moving metadata or topics, topic groups and qualities, within each ecological niche, resources battle for survival and success.

Other Cues

CoFIND contains a wide range of subtle and less subtle stigmergic cues to influence learners in different ways. For example, differently-sized bullet points indicate the number of resources that may be available within a topic (the assumption being that more is better), small graphics indicate topics that have been recently visited (indicating what is of most current interest to the learning community), and "new" signs show new topics and resources (on the assumption that novelty is a significant factor when revisiting the learning environment).

A Collectively Generated Structure

CoFIND self-organizes at a range of temporal, conceptual, and spatial scales, each affecting the other, leading to small, clustered ecosystems around subject areas and learner needs, where rated resources that have been perceived to be useful to learners may be found. It achieves dynamic stability without degenerating into chaos or stagnation. Stigmergy forms the environment, while evolutionary processes sculpt it, placing topic against topic, quality against quality, and resource against resource, creating small, parcellated ecosystems formed around subject areas and student needs, connected through bridges of shared resources and metadata. Thus, CoFIND both generates and mirrors a "group mind." One student has reflected that "I am reminded … of the Borg (Star Trek), a race who are a "collective" and share one consciousness." It is hard to avoid making a pun about the resulting learning experience being a process of assimilation, but the notion of a collective consciousness captures the essence of the system well.

CoFIND as a Learning Environment

CoFIND is a self-organising environment that reflects the needs of its users. If those needs are to learn, then it becomes a learning environment. If not, it becomes something else. This seemingly trivial observation is central to understanding how a useful structure can arise in such a system.

One of the ways that CoFIND may be used is to act as a framework for what Mayes and Fowler (1999) describe as "tertiary courseware," allowing learners to benefit from what other learners have already discovered. Another use is as a mechanism for assessment that is formative both for the assessor and the assessed. Dron et al. (2002) discuss two distinct uses of CoFIND to allow students to evaluate each other's coursework, leading to two completely different sets of qualities. In one assignment, where the students' work was of use in later assessments, the qualities that emerged were recognisably pedagogically valuable: "useful," "comprehensive," "simple," "good for beginners," and "good overview." By contrast, in a later assignment, which was more summative in nature with little perceived value beyond the exercise itself, the most popular qualities were: "invokes that holiday feeling," "good," "a valiant attempt," "floats like a brick," with "good for beginners" and "simple," tying for fifth place. Even these last two qualities meant something different to those who used them than in the initial assignment, describing the sites themselves rather than their value to learners. The latter assignment was dropped after this, partly as a result of this study. The following year a repeat of the first assignment led to the qualities "simple," "good layout, subject made easy to understand," "good overview," "good for beginners," and "beautiful." Although some doubt might be expressed about the pedagogical utility of "beautiful" even this may have some value for some learners. A similar pattern can be seen in qualities used to rate third party HTML tutorials, a matter of some concern to the students, where the most popular qualities used are "good layout, subject made easy to understand," "good overview," "useful," "good for beginners," and "interesting read, simple and clean layout."

The evidence suggests strongly that the system adapts to whatever needs or concerns that the learning community expresses, with stigmergic signs reinforcing slight tendencies, while Darwinian selection kills off tendencies that are of less utility to the group. This is still the subject of continuing research, however. In an early iteration of CoFIND, a student exploited the social navigation algorithm to draw attention to his own site, which was not of particularly high quality or interest to the group as a whole. As might be expected, the system did indeed encourage many others in the group to visit the site. When they found it to be less useful than anticipated, they no longer visited it and it was swamped by others in the evolutionary niche in which it resided (Dron, Mitchell, & Boyne, 2003). Although the system has developed since then, and it has become harder to exploit CoFIND in this way, students using CoFIND on taught courses still find ways to get around it. For example, one student recently categorised his own site under virtually every topic in the system, no matter how inappropriate to its content, ensuring that visitors to any of its ecosystems would see it and, perhaps, visit it, rate it, and boost its popularity. This is very similar to a successful attack perpetrated on del.icio.us at around the same time (Shirky, 2005). CoFIND's algorithm applies a very small weighting each time a site is visited that is independent of its context. Although the site was not very successful in any one topic, the small incremental weighting the site gained through being visited in many different topics led to it being disproportionately successful in the topic to which it was best suited, where it attracted positive ratings. This led to the expected feedback loop so that it became still more successful. However, even here, other sites that were probably worthier eventually usurped its pole position and, although it never became unpopular, it was out-competed by several other sites.

The Cold Start Problem

Despite its use of inheritance, CoFIND is badly afflicted by the cold start problem that affects most collaborative filters that rely on explicit ratings (Harney, 2000). This is massively magnified through CoFIND's use of qualities. The cold-start problem is a vicious circle that occurs where a system relies on recommendations to return good results, but in its early days, there are few recommendations, therefore it does not return good results. Because of this, few people are inclined to use it, and so few ratings are given. Where there is only a single dimension of value, it takes some time for a sufficient body of ratings to accrue before the collaborative filter can start producing useful results. Each further dimension adds to the problem by spreading ratings more widely, diluting the ratings pool. Unfortunately, CoFIND is, by design, intended to support a relatively small and focused group of learners so its circle is particularly vicious. It takes a long time for a small group of learners to build up a sufficiently large number of ratings, so CoFIND is of limited use in its early development. When learners first visit the system, it will not return many interesting results so they are less inclined to visit again. Solutions have included "seeding" the system with a range of useful rated resources and providing extrinsic motivation such as exhortations from the tutor to use it and/or the provision/deduction of marks for using/failing to use it. Each of these methods is unsatisfactory, providing skyhooks rather than allowing the system to pull itself up by its own bootstraps.

CoFIND and the Eight Principles

- **Adaptability:** CoFIND can both import and export RSS feeds, allowing it to be used as or with a larger system. It has an open authentication approach that allows different protocols to be plugged in, although, by default, it offers a simple, free-to-sign-up system.

- **Stigmergy:** CoFIND makes extensive use of sign-based stigmergy, including varying font sizes, list position, and icons used for both data and metadata.

- **Evolvability:** CoFIND is built to evolve. As well as its heavy use of natural selection, it incorporates an explicit inheritance mechanism.

- **Parcellation:** CoFIND actively parcellates its landscape with topics, topic groups, and qualities, maintaining some narrow channels between them through shared metadata so that successful variations can spread.

- **Context:** CoFIND's main use so far has been to support institutional learning, but it is a self-organising system that will adapt to a wide range of uses. In theory, its parcellation and evolutionary mechanisms should enable it to scale well, although it has only been used with a few hundred users so far. However, its cold-start problem means that it needs a lot of nurturing in its early development. CoFIND alone is not a complete learning environment, so will be contained by (as well as contain) others.

- **Constraint:** CoFIND's design allows for largely bottom-up growth, including data and metadata and the structures that consequently form. However, the shallow hierarchy of topics and topic groups is, to some extent, a constraint designed to keep ecosystems manageable.

- **Trust:** CoFIND needs to identify individuals, but whether strong authentication is used or not depends upon the underlying authentication system. CoFIND's main mechanism for trust is based on a belief in the wisdom of the crowd. Lacking a user model, many of its inner workings are exposed. However, it is difficult for users to fine tune how it emphasises and de-emphasises metadata and resources, which is due to be addressed in its next iteration, where the learner will be able to decide the importance of different metrics used, including explicit ratings, implicit ratings, novelty, and personal ratings. Its usability is poor, as most effort has been put into its adaptive mechanisms, but the system is under active development to improve its interface.

- **Sociability:** There is relatively little support for sociability in this system. In fact, all data and metadata are intentionally made anonymous. An earlier version of the system included a discussion forum spliced on, but this has since been removed, as CoFIND is intended only as a component of a larger system, not a complete environment.

Dwellings

Dwellings is an explicitly stigmergic environment that draws on some of the lessons learned from CoFIND, combined with principles based on Jane Jacobs's "The Death and Life of Great American Cities" (Jacobs, 1961). Jacobs analyzed the ways that self-organization in cities can arise out of simple dynamic processes and structures. In particular, she saw diversity as a central driver of success and safety in city areas. CoFIND seeks to bring a wide range of resources together in a system based on natural ecological processes. However, unlike jungles, human environments are filled with intelligent agents. Although the underlying processes of stigmergy are not affected by the relative intelligence of the agents, to completely ignore this factor means that potentially rich interactions are not as well exploited as they might be. As cities are at least partially self-organising human constructs, it was a logical progression to look at ways of constructing learning environments that in some ways mirror their dynamics.

A further motivation for the construction of Dwellings was the observation that Web 1.0 Web sites were mostly lonely spaces, with interaction limited to small, well-defined areas. Even now, it is often hard to tell whether one is the sole visitor to a Web site or one of millions. Given the importance of learning communities to enable learning (Laurillard, 1993; Vygotsky, 1978; Wenger, 1998), this seemed an unnecessary restriction.

Building a City that Thrives

Jacobs (1961) gives central importance to sidewalks in contributing to the dynamics of the city. For Jacobs, the key lies in movement and the "succession of eyes" that sidewalk culture promotes. She identifies four key factors that lead to thriving city districts:

1.   a mixture of primary uses;
2.   short blocks;
3.   a mixture of old and new buildings; and
4.   a dense concentration of people.

From these precepts, the design of Dwellings draws on the following principles:

1.   In a city, a mixture of primary uses is necessary to provide diverse reasons to be there in the first place. High concentrations of single-use buildings lead to times of the day when the streets are deserted with limited traffic between them. People come, transact their business, then leave. Similarly, a virtual learning space should not be limited to a single purpose. Such an environment should contain much that would be irrelevant for many users, but offering reasons for constant traffic and serendipitous encounters.
2.   In a city, where blocks are too long, they set up impenetrable borders that separate one street from another. In the context of a virtual learning environment,

links are to be encouraged throughout, allowing maximal choice of learning paths. There are issues here that do not arise in physical cities. A totally connected hypertext would have no discernible structure at all. Therefore, the focus should be on sufficient, but not excessive, linking.

3. Jacobs demands a mixture of old and new buildings due to their relative costs, leading inevitably to diverse uses. For e-learning Web sites, this equates to low-road and high-road designs of learning resources, mixing the expensive and complex with the simple and low-threshold. Diverse design values can facilitate the satisfaction of diverse needs.

4. A dense concentration of people contributes to safety, interaction, and serendipitous encounters. In an e-learning environment, there should be opportunities for encounters with others at every opportunity.

Dwellings is not unlike a MOO, apart from its explicit city metaphor, and its use of self-organising stigmergic processes. In use, Dwellings is most easily imagined as a kind of collaborative Web browser within a Web browser, allowing its users to see each other and to interact while visiting Web sites, visualized as buildings on a virtual sidewalk. Users can create buildings and streets at will, as well as leave graffiti on those buildings and provide links (intersections) to other streets (Figure 14.1). If they wish, the creators of streets or buildings may choose to lock them, preventing others from making changes. Locking does not affect the ability of others to add graffiti, nor does it have any effect on other stigmergic cues, such as footprints or building prominence.

The environment is explicitly stigmergic in a number of ways:

•   Entry into the system is through a list of links, shown in order of the most-visited but also indicating the number of current visitors. Users are thus able to choose at the outset between most popular and most populated.

Figure 14.1. Dwellings

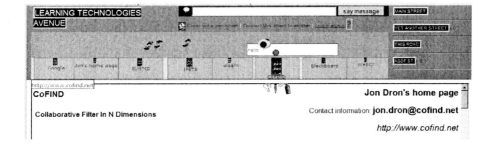

- Users themselves are represented as icons on the sidewalk. Borrowing from ChatCircles (Donath, Karahalios, & Viegas, 1999), it is only possible to "hear" what other users are saying by moving closer to them. Like ChatCircles, an indicator of who is currently talking (a speech balloon) is provided so that users are attracted to spaces where discussion is taking place. This, in turn, leads to clusters of users, which thereby act as sematectonic stigmergic cues, drawing more users towards them in real time.

- Users leave footprints where they have been, which fade over a few minutes to grey, then disappear altogether, after a few more minutes. Thus, it is easy to see buildings of recent interest, and users are attracted through sign-based stigmergy to buildings with many footprints nearby.

- Buildings grow and shrink according to use over time, providing a different scale of stigmergic cue, indicating overall popularity within a given street. Again, through sematectonic stigmergy, users are drawn to larger buildings, which in turn makes the buildings larger.

- Links to adjacent streets are shown in order of popularity, encouraging users to visit those that are considered interesting. Furthermore, there is an indication of how many users are currently visiting each street, again drawing users to those that are of current interest.

- Buildings attract graffiti. Those which are of most interest attract most graffiti, which can come to act as a simple asynchronous discussion tool, very much like the discussions that grow through annotations to weblogs. Buildings with a lot of graffiti are potentially more attractive than those without, applying sematectonic stigmergy.

The range of scales is intentional, based on the principles described in chapter five. The resulting structure has greater richness and complexity than might be found were there a more uni-dimensional scale. Similarly, the geographical isolation of streets makes them each a micro-ecosystem, connected only to those nearby.

The system has been through a number of iterations, each of which has become progressively more abstract in its representation of streets, dwellings, and users. The purpose of the environment is not to duplicate reality; many existing VR systems, such as ActiveWorlds™ and Second Life™, do this already. Rather, its purpose is to represent those features that are most valuable in a city and translate them into a more universal Web setting. It has been found that if too much reality intrudes, it encourages users to think of it as an impoverished mirror of reality rather than the self-organising, dialogue-structured environment that it is intended to be. It is likely that, in future iterations, even words like "street," "building," and "graffiti" will be dropped as they simply serve to confuse users as to the purpose of the environment. The central point of the system is to support a community of users to collaboratively create and discover Web sites, and to organise those sites in a continuously adapting structure that evolves to fit the needs of those users.

Observations of Dwellings

In an early trial of the system, a group of eight postgraduate students (largely the same group described previously in the context of synchronous and asynchronous discussion) was allowed free reign to do as they wished, with no explicit requirement to treat it as a means to enable learning (Dron, 2003a).

Students spent most of their time chatting to others on the streets, displaying less interest in the buildings than in each other. To an extent, this resulted from the constraints of the exercise, which was carried out over a single ninety-minute session, so there was little opportunity to explore further or to attempt to achieve any specific learning objective. However, it also indicates the greater significance of the faster moving parts of the environment, which is what might be predicted as the system is predicated on the significance of local interactions.

The Importance of the Presence of Others

When asked what it was that attracted them to particular streets, most respondents placed primary importance in the presence of others, with only one citing the name of the street as the key motivator. Similarly, most students commented on the demotivating effect of empty streets. Opinion was more divided on reasons for visiting specific buildings, where the name was mentioned as frequently as the number of people nearby. However, the evidence of the server logs gives a different picture. There was a large amount of clustering around a limited subset of pages, with no obvious pattern linking clusters to the students' interests in those pages. An exception to this was one of the students' own pages, that she spent a significant amount of time promoting to the others through the chat system. The most popular street was the first on the list, which retained its popularity throughout the session as a central meeting place, eventually providing a route from almost everywhere to almost everywhere. The stigmergic signs that made it prominent in the first place also encouraged users to link their own streets to it and it became a conduit to other places.

Control through Creation

A feature that greatly appealed to the students was the ability to create their own environments and to encourage others to visit them. This was an early version of Dwellings, which lacked a locking mechanism. The system had been set up to allow anyone to edit any object (streets, buildings, links between streets, and so forth) turf-wars broke out between students who modified each other's buildings. This led to strong feelings of protectiveness among the students, who spent time defending their own patches of ground against others. Often, when somebody built on a street that a student considered to be their own, the owner would erase or modify the building to suit his or her own purposes.

As a result of the observation of these conflicts, the next iteration of Dwellings introduced locking. A similar exercise conducted with this new functionality revealed an interesting characteristic: students were far more cooperative, working together to build interesting streets. Most interestingly, although all students were aware of the ability to lock streets and buildings and most experimented with the functionality, no one actually used the locking mechanism. The mere knowledge that locking could occur was enough to encourage feelings of trust and safety (Dron, 2005).

Another related behaviour that occurred in both systems was that, having created their own streets, students linked them to as many other streets as possible, on the (correct) assumption that this would encourage visitors to those streets to visit them. These unforeseen side effects of the design of the environment suggested a powerful means of overcoming the cold-start problem that has plagued CoFIND throughout its development. Whereas CoFIND represents a single collaborative environment, which actually submerges the individual in the collective mind, Dwellings reintroduces the individual to the scenario, encouraging and valorising self-interest. There is a clear indication that students wish to exert control over the environment, influencing the choices of others, if at all possible.

Dwellings and the Eight Principles

- **Adaptability:** Because it acts as a container for other sites, Dwellings is good at integrating different systems. However, it does not (yet) enable perfect interoperability where different login credentials need to be supplied. It does not conform to any particular interoperability standards. It is released as open source.

- **Stigmergy:** Dwellings makes very extensive use of both sematectonic and sign-based stigmergy, including the use of footprints, variations in building prominence, the presence of others, and ordering of street signs.

- **Evolvability**: Through its use of stigmergy, Dwellings facilitates survival of the fittest. Replication with variation depends on its users: inspiration from others is a major advantage of any social software system (Dron, 2003b).

- **Parcellation:** Dwellings is, by design, highly parcellated, with each street forming a separate ecosystem, with greater or lesser connectivity with the wider system, depending on how users choose to create them. It also parcellates through stigmergic cues that operate at a range of different temporal scales.

- **Context:** Dwellings is a very open system, which can evolve in almost limitless ways. For this reason, to be a learning environment requires it to be used in a learning context.

- **Constraint:** Although the city metaphor provides limits on the kind of things that can be done there, Dwellings is generated almost entirely from the bottom-up, with structural subsystems of stigmergic cues operating at a range of scales. Having said that, those who get there first are able to lock streets and buildings, providing more of a top-down structure, albeit one that defers the design decision to users rather than administrators or the creator of the software.

- **Trust:** One of the main motivations behind Dwellings is to enable trust, through a succession of eyes. The ability to lock dwellings and streets is a further means of offering security. Logins are used for identification rather than authorisation, but the system is designed with sufficient flexibility to incorporate more rigorous authentication, if necessary.

- **Sociability:** Dwellings is built for sociability, with both real-time and asynchronous interactions, as well as many cues that indicate presence, including in the recent past, the further past, and the present.

Conclusion

This chapter has explored a number of examples of systems, employing the eight principles described in the previous chapter. All, in some way, generate structure through the interactions (more or less dialogic) of users. Some patterns recur, notably the need for parcellation, the emergent behaviour of the group, an evolutionary approach that means the fitter (whatever that may mean in a given context) gain preferential emphasis, the application of stigmergic principles (both sign-based and sematectonic), and some form of communication between the inhabitants.

Though most are produced with some pedagogic intent, this is embedded in relatively few. It is notable that Dwellings, Comtella, ChatCircles and OurWeb, for instance, become learning environments if, and only if, they are used that way, but are otherwise fairly generic deferred systems, capable of being used in other ways. These and other issues are discussed in the next chapter, which is an investigation of the barriers to success in self-organising learning environments.

References

Brusilovsky, P., Chavan, G., & Farzan, R. (2004). *Social adaptive navigation support for open corpus electronic textbooks.* Paper presented at the AH 2004, Eindhoven.

Brusilovsky, P., & Rizzo, R. (2002). Map-based horizontal navigation in educational hypertext. *Journal of Digital Information, 3*(1).

Crossley, M., Davies, J., McGrath, A., & Rejman-Greene, M. (1999). The knowledge garden. *BT Technology Journal, 17*(1).

Donath, J., Karahalios, K., & Viegas, F. (1999). Visualizing conversation. *Journal of Computer Mediated Communication, 4*(4).

Dron, J. (2003a). *Sidewalks on the information superhighway.* Paper presented at the E-Learn 2003, Phoenix, AZ.

Dron, J. (2003b). *The blog and the borg: A collective approach to e-learning.* Paper presented at the E-Learn 2003, Phoenix, AZ.

Dron, J. (2005). *A succession of eyes: Building an e-learning city.* Paper presented at the E-Learn 2005, Vancouver, Canada.

Dron, J., Mitchell, R., & Boyne, C. W. (2002). *Evaluating assessment using n-dimensional filtering.* Paper presented at the E-Learn 2002, Montreal, Canada.

Dron, J., Mitchell, R., & Boyne, C. W. (2003). Evolving learning in the stuff swamp. In N. Patel (Ed.), *Adaptive evolutionary information systems* (pp. 211 - 228). Hershey, PA: Idea Group.

Harney, J. (2000). IT self-help. *Knowledge Management.*

Jacobs, J. (1961). *The death and life of great American cities.* London: Pimlico.

Kurhila, J., Miettinen, M., Nokelainen, P., & Tirri, H. (2002). *Use of social navigation features in collaborative e-learning.* Paper presented at the E-Learn 2002, Montreal, Canada.

Laurillard, D. (1993). *Rethinking university teaching: A framework for the effective use of educational technology.* London: Routledge.

Mayes, J. T., & Fowler, C. J. H. (1999). Learning technology and usability: A framework for understanding courseware. *Interacting with Computers, 11*, 485-497.

Miettinen, M., Kurhila, J., Nokelainen, P., & Tirri, H. (2005). *OurWeb: Transparent groupware for online communities.* Paper presented at the Web Based Communities 2005, Algarve, Portugal.

Shirky, C. (2005). Tags run amok! Retrieved August 1st, 2006, from http://many.corante.com/archives/2005/02/01/tags_run_amok.php

Startrek.com. (2006). The borg: Video documentary. Retrieved July27th, 2006, from http://www.startrek.com/startrek/view/features/documentaries/article/5299. html

Vassileva, J. (2004). *Harnessing P2P power in the classroom.* Paper presented at the ITS 2004, Maceio, Brazil.

Vygotsky, L. S. (1978). *Mind in society.* London: Harvard University Press.

Webster, A., & Vassileva, J. (2006). *Visualizing personal relations in online communities.* Paper presented at the AH 2006, Dublin, Ireland.

Wenger, E. (1998). *Communities of practice: Learning, meaning and identity.* New York: Cambridge University Press.

Chapter XV

Problems with Social Software for E-Learning

Natural selection, the blind, unconscious, automatic process which Darwin discovered, and which we now know is the explanation for the existence and apparently purposeful form of all life, has no purpose in mind. It has no mind and no mind's eye. It does not plan for the future. It has no vision, no foresight, no sight at all. If it can be said to play the role of watchmaker in nature, it is the blind *watchmaker.* (Dawkins, 1986)

Introduction

While many have made use of social software within a traditional course structure, and many social software sites might be seen as educational (or at least of value to learners), the potential benefits of self-organisation in social software are yet to be achieved.

This chapter is concerned with identifying the main outstanding research questions and potential pitfalls for those seeking to develop software that is based on the self-organising principles outlined in the previous chapters. Although the example systems described in Chapter XIV begin to show how choice and constraint can co-exist in an e-learning environment, there are several big issues that need to be addressed before they can achieve their promise.

Sequence

The fundamental meaning of "structure" for Moore (1983, 1996) seems to imply that it provides (perhaps among other things) the sequencing of a learning trajectory. Sequencing is a fundamental aspect of the teacher role in education. If a learner is relinquishing control, it is over the choices that determine his or her learning trajectory. The view of the role of a teacher as a purveyor of sequence is echoed by many. Collins et al.'s (1989) theory of cognitive apprenticeship makes great use of the concept of "scaffolding" as a means of abstracting problems and providing a stepped approach to a problem. Elaboration theory is almost entirely based on the structuring and sequencing of learning, based on conceptual, procedural, or theoretical grounds (Wilson & Cole, 1992). Gagné (1985) requires that the teacher identifies objectives and guides learning. Two of Bruner's (1966) four stipulations for a theory of instruction are: it should specify ways a body of instruction should be structured for easy assimilation by the learner and specify the most effective sequences to present materials to be learned. Even Malcolm Knowles (1975), whose theory of andragogy requires explicitly self-directed enquiry with teachers, fellow students and materials available but not imposed, suggests that the teacher is there to manage the process, guide the interactions, and design sequential activities (Carlson, 1989). Similarly, Saba (1999) identifies teacher roles as including "informing the learner of the objectives required by the course" and "developing study plans for achieving objectives agreed upon between the learner and instructor in the learning contract."

Unfortunately, an effective and coherent sequence is very hard to generate as an emergent feature of a learning environment, although various options have been proposed and tried.

Surfing the Emergent Wave

Although several of the systems described in the previous chapter carve out a kind of sequence through the combined behaviours of their users, effectively allowing them to surf an emergent wave, it is far from clear that the sequence is optimal, useful, or even whether it makes sense, pedagogically or semantically. In most of the systems described, it is more a question of being dragged along with the crowd, riding a wave, rather than there being a visible path with a history and (above all) a future. The trajectory of the masses is neither predetermined nor predictable. Any narrative that emerges can only be observed in retrospect and is at one step removed from the experience of following the trajectory with a goal in mind.

A teacher, who is able to understand the overall narrative and to fit the steps along the way into that framework, determines sequence in a traditional learning environment. A stigmergic or self-organising system that attempts to do the same thing is hampered by the fact that it is concerned with small, local interactions and (by definition) does not take a top-down view.

Using Learning Outcomes and Prerequisites

It would be perfectly feasible, within a constrained system, to identify and match learning objectives and prerequisites for each learning object, thereby fitting them together in a meaningful and orderly sequence. Such an approach is suggested by Masthoff (2002). However, the amount of effort involved in doing so is likely to far exceed the potential utility for learners that it would entail and would act as a brake on the growth of the system. It suffers not only from all the cost-associated weaknesses of the scatter-gun approach of Engines for Education (Schank, 2004), but also, a large overhead in supplying sufficiently effective and meaningful metadata in the form of learning objectives and prerequisites. Worse still, learning outcomes are fuzzy, context-related, and dubious constructs, at best and, at worst, absolutely meaningless. Learning outcomes attempt to convert "knowing how" into "knowing that," are only meaningful in the light of background-knowledge and experience, and fail to capture the unexpected and, (perhaps) most important, learning that may occur serendipitously or consequentially (Hussey & Smith, 2002). They may be useful in certain constrained settings, but are not a universal panacea.

Combining Paths

Another alternative available for constrained groups of learning resources (or closed corpi) is that users' paths may simply be combined (Bollen & Heylighen, 1998). A similar approach is suggested by Tattersall et al. (2004; 2005). If a number of people exploring the same set of material have taken different paths, it would be a simple enough matter to identify those paths that are most popular by selecting, for each choice along the way, that which is most popular. Although this might provide future learners with a map of the area that may be refined through future iterations, it suffers from the same problems that the surf-riding approach of current systems: the blind may be leading the blind and there is no guarantee that there will be any meaningful narrative to the paths. In fact, a combinatorial approach probably militates against it, unless there is a strong tendency for most people to follow exactly the same path. To an extent, this is an issue of scale. For example, Tattersall et al.'s (2005) approach relies on distinct chunks that are described as activity nodes (vaguely akin to individual segments of a learning trajectory) which are, somewhat, self-contained and used in a constrained setting. By limiting the range of potential paths and keeping the possibilities tightly constrained, it is possible that such a method might work. Indeed, it bears a certain resemblance to what might happen in a traditional institutional setting, where learners give each other advice on good modules. However, it is unlikely to work effectively in a large or open corpus, especially at a finer scale and/or where learners' needs are significantly divergent.

Using Ontologies

Karampiperis and Sampson (2004) make use of existing ontologies, mapped to learning objects, to carve out a path. As learning objects according with the IEEE-LOM will have associated metadata, then an ontology that contains the appropriate terms (and which itself may have been generated by bottom-up processes) might be used to associate different learning objects into a meaningful sequence. Although such approaches may possibly work within a rigorously controlled closed corpus, it is unlikely that they would be much help when dealing with an open corpus such as the Internet, especially given the relative rarity of suitably marked-up learning objects in the first place. Even if sufficient objects were available, the content of learning objects may overlap or even be contradictory, may approach the subject at different levels of detail, may use different vocabularies, might vary stylistically, may use different approaches to navigation, make different assumptions about learners and, even if all these issues were dealt with, would almost inevitably fail to create a coherent and meaningful narrative. Even if it did, the narrative path would accord with the structure of the ontology, which may significantly differ from the most optimal learning path for learners. The structure of knowledge does not necessarily bear any resemblance to the best way of learning that knowledge.

An Emergent Path?

It would be more in keeping with the principles of self-organisation presented here to consider only local information. In such a scenario, it would be sufficient to know that a resource should be looked at before or after another, from an individual learner's perspective. Combining a variety of such perspectives might lead to an emergent path, through a set of resources. To an extent, each of the systems described earlier applies this principle, inasmuch as the current needs of a specific group of learners are always likely to predominate at any given moment. As a result, the group as a whole determines its own trajectory, captured and reified at the moment that is significant to all. As well as the aforementioned issues of coherent narratives, there are two weaknesses to this approach

1. It assumes a congruence of needs, whereas the reality of any group of learners is that some progress at a different rate to others and, even where rates of development are similar, different learners have different needs.

2. Learners are inevitably imprisoned within Vygotsky's zones of proximal development (Vygotsky, 1978). A human teacher can view a subject from further back to see the place of a particular piece of knowledge within a larger whole. Learners who are limited to what they already know and glimmers of what they do not know are, of necessity, unable to see the whole plot (or they would be knowers, not learners).

The seeming intractability of this problem is somewhat lessened by the fact that learners are seldom just interacting with local information like termites or ants. Firstly, they have different starting points. If the paths from these points overlap, then those closer to the end of the path may assist those near the beginning. Secondly, a self-organising system needs to be fed with new information, and there are many ways that this can be discovered. Many learning resources, such as text books and Web sites, provide a full picture of a given subject of study, and most provide some kind of structure, often pedagogically informed. Unlike termites, people do not work in a vacuum of limited local knowledge and self-organised learning environments are not their only means of interacting with the world. Not only that, learners are, hopefully by nature, imaginatively engaged with the subject of study, and are able to make leaps from one idea to the next, as they actively construct their knowledge. If such systems are considered in a context in which choices are made between different sets of viable, pre-existing options (which may be controlled by teachers), then it is possible to imagine a balance of learner and teacher choice that might be liberating for both. As ever, transactional control is dependent on the scale at which it is viewed, and there is no reason why, in principle, an emergent sequence might be composed of larger chunks while resources at a finer scale might offer more constraint. However, because of the variety of potential pedagogical approaches, as well as potentially overlapping or contradictory subject matter, it is hard to see how the end result of assembling disparate resources would be particularly efficient from a learner perspective and, without substantial support of a more traditional kind (whether via a flesh and blood teacher or an artificial intelligence), may make little sense at all. The collaborative generation of sequence remains among the most pressing research concerns in the area of self-organising learning environments.

The Impoverished Dialogue
of Stigmergy

Although Bakhtin's definition of "dialogue" (Morris, 1994) is sufficiently broad to admit stigmergic interactions, stigmergy provides the palest of shadows of a genuine conversation. While Bakhtin and the odd semiotician might accept that it is dialogue, it is far removed from the kind of thing found even in the impoverished third-order monologue identified by Buber (1947b):

There is genuine dialogue—no matter whether spoken or silent—where each of the participants really has in mind the other or others in their present and particular being and turns to them with the intention of establishing a living mutual relation between himself and them. There is technical dialogue, which is prompted solely by the need of objective understanding. And there is monologue disguised as dialogue, in which two or men, meeting in space, speak each with himself in strangely tortuous and circuitous ways and yet imagine they have escaped the torment of being thrown back on their own resources

Although stigmergic systems imply a notion of "social translucence" (IBM_Social_Computing_Group, 2003), where cues leave hints and shadows of the presence of others and communication is indirect, such systems do not (so far) make it easy to have "in mind the other or others in their present and particular being." Indeed, it is an integral part of the nature of such systems that they rarely focus on an individual, but instead, emphasise group behaviours, reflecting them back to the learners. Such dialogue that exists tends to be impersonal and, to some extent, a by-product of other processes, behaviours, and intentions.

The Significance of Silence

One of Buber's (1947a) more profound insights is that silence plays a key role in establishing bonds and relationships between individuals: "For a conversation no sound is necessary, not even a gesture. Speech can renounce all the media of sense, and it is still speech" (p. 3). Many electronic forms of discourse are susceptible to criticism based on this aspect of Buber's philosophy. For example, it is very hard to experience Buber's idea of communion through stillness or silence in a discussion forum. Silence in a discussion forum is measured only in the absence of others, not in their presence, and is perhaps its default behaviour.

Presence

Although browsing through back-postings can give a sense of the presence of the ghosts of others, the lack of physical presence is a loss not substituted by other means. This is, by far, the most common comment of learners reflecting on various uses of communication technology in a postgraduate course that the author teaches on the subject. These are some representative comments from the learners:

"Yet, how to show disagreement and our expression online. The facial expression is missing in this kind of interaction."

"I would like to mension that virtual communication cannot displace face to face communication and real life's social relations."

"One difficulty I am now facing is my sense of isolation."

"When i consider italian language and the importance that body language has in our culture, so many thoughts can be expressed with just one body sign. How can we reduce this gap of electronic communication?"

In a system where communication is less direct, the psychological gap between learners may be too hard to bridge through stigmergic mechanisms alone.

Richness of Dialogue

Many of the uses that language is put to in a verbal conversation are not duplicated in stigmergic dialogue. For instance, even the simple variant on Exchange Structure Analysis, used by Cox et al. (2004) to analyse online synchronous conversations, makes use of the following roles: *challenge, justify, clarify, feedback, inform, inquire, reason,* of which only *feedback* and *inform* could be unequivocally said to exist in stigmergic communication. Similarly, Hara et al.'s (2000) analysis of an asynchronous discussion uses *elementary clarification, in-depth clarification, inferencing, judgement,* and *application of strategies,* with a context consisting of explicit interaction, implicit interaction, and independent statement, suggesting a rich variety of uses for dialogue that go far beyond stigmergic dialogue and the cues currently offered by social navigation. Other forms of content analysis use more complex models still. Many of these forms and roles are a significant part of the negotiation of control that occurs in a conventional dialogue.

Loveless Dialogue

In environments such as CoFIND, Dwellings, or the Knowledge Sea, communication is mediated in part by metadata and in part by the resources themselves, which are, thus, a vehicle for a kind of Freirian co-intentionality that partially transcends, but cannot replace, language. Freire's (1970) formulation gives the dialogue between teacher and learner a central role in developing a rich, negotiated understanding. Stigmergic dialogue gives no special place to the teacher and all learners are co-intentional with each other. Unfortunately, their communication is abstracted, lacking human connection or what Vandenberg (2002) poetically describes as "pedagogic love."

Alternative Sources of Communication: Filling the Gaps

On the bright side, the impoverished dialogue of stigmergy is not necessarily a major problem for learners, assuming that the stigmergic system is not the only means of communication. Moreover, if stigmergic principles are used to augment rather than supplant those other means of communication (for example, through the use of presence indicators in Dwellings or energy rankings in Comtella Discussions), then it may help to reduce such feelings of isolation to a significant degree. Stigmergy may supplement, but it does not and should not replace. As ever, it is important to remember that no learning activity takes place in an isolated context and it is important to consider the overall learning ecology. These are systems that help guide learners through resources and spaces that have been designed by people with clear intentions and intelligence.

There is much research still needed to discover and explore ways that stigmergic dialogue can support the ranges of intention and use that underpin traditional dialogue. Indicators or agreement, disagreement, and so on, that enrich the D3E environment (Buckingham-Shum, Motta, & Domingue, 1999), may act as foundations for one potential approach, as may use of simple emoticons found in many forums, chat, and IM environments. Such differentiators may act in different ways, like the wide range of pheromones secreted by some ants, providing different signals for different purposes. A central research area for stigmergy in e-learning is in the provision of rich structures that meaningfully reflect the nature of learner engagement.

Stigmergy and Creativity

Not only is it a weak form of dialogue, stigmergy alone cannot lead to novelty and creativity. Termites will never be in a position to build mock Tudor cottages, no matter how much they evolve—at least not through stigmergic processes. Traditional verbal dialogue is a highly creative process, which allows individuals to explore each other's conceptions and spark new and original ideas. Again, stigmergic systems may be found wanting, but they are not alone in the e-learning ecosystem. The central purpose of stigmergic dialogue in the systems discussed so far is to structure resources, dialogues, interactions, and so on that are already complex and potentially creative objects, acts, and activities.

Complexity through Evolution

Although stigmergy cannot support creativity, nature does provide an example of a simple process that does lead ineluctably to greater complexity, in the form of evolution, whereby the combination of chance, reproduction, variation, and competition results inevitably in a speciated ecosystem of ever increasing complexity and order.

Most social software and all environments that apply social navigation are to some extent evolutionary in nature, suggesting that a well-constructed environment that uses such principles may well evolve to ever greater peaks of fitness. Although this will simply be through the selection process and has little to do with the content of what is being selected, there may be feedback loops that encourage or motivate the purveyors of the resources to attempt to improve them, again leading to further evolution. It is, of course, necessary that the success or failure of the resources within the system be fed back to their creators, in order for this to occur. Again, social software assumes the presence of intelligent beings engaging in social activities, augmenting connections, and structuring the spaces in which they occur, but not replacing them.

Can Systems for Learning Evolve?

Evolutionary principles are embedded in many of the systems described here, most notably in CoFIND, but any system that emphasises more useful resources will necessarily do so at the expense of those that are less so. Even allowing for the formation of niches, whereby different resources are considered useful in different contexts for different learners, there are sure to be losers in the evolutionary struggle.

For truly successful evolution to occur, the rules of change themselves must be subject to the same principles of evolution that they control (Kelly, 1994). This is problematic in an educational environment, where what is required is something that is useful now, not that will evolve into something useful later. This is a problem that has been addressed by evolutionary theorists, who, for example, describe the gradual evolution of the eye as a series of stages each of which provided something advantageous to the organism (Jones, 1999). Unfortunately, this does not map neatly to educational environments, as there are already hordes of carefully designed and effective approaches to teaching and learning that would out-compete any slowly evolving system, at least in the early stages. This is an ecosystem, involving learners who inhabit a world filled with learning opportunities. As with collaborative filters, the cold start problem would prevent learners from ever using a system that was less effective than a pre-existing solution. Evolution demands the survival of the fittest, so where something is already very fit for its purpose, there is no reason that anyone would wish to use something less fit. The evolution of radically different structures, than those envisaged by designers, therefore, still seems a long way off.

The Written Word as Stigmergic Sign

It may be considered that the written word actually represents the highly evolved form of stigmergy. Written words are, after all, signs left in the environment that influence behaviour, and are perhaps, a perfect example of sign-based stigmergy. They even have a ready-made syntax and great richness of expression. Although there may be an element of truth in this and it is certainly true that *some* words in *some* contexts can behave this way (the qualities in CoFIND are a prime example of this), there are some significant differences. In particular, the fact that words can serve many different purposes makes them less clearly signals in their own right. Both natural and human instances of stigmergy provide unequivocal and largely unambiguous messages. Although, whether or not they are followed is more of a statistical phenomenon than a necessary effect: ants do not interpret the presence of ant-trail pheromones as an invitation to clean the nest and investors do not interpret the fact that many people are investing in a particular share as meaning it is time for dinner. More significantly, words are usually created by some individual or group of individuals, with a shared purpose, with the specific intention of causing some effect. It is not usually the case that more of the same words will cause more of the desired effect (there are exceptions, but that is just the point about ambiguity), and even where they do, it is not the words themselves that are performing the signalling but the quantity of them.

Are Crowds Wise?

Surowiecki's (2004) book, *The Wisdom of Crowds*, is a compelling investigation of ways that the collective intelligence of a group can often exceed that of its individual members. Surowiecki cites a wide range of examples, such as guessing the number of sweets in a jar, identifying the location of a lost submarine, and predicting market prices, where the average of a number of individual estimates is more accurate than those of any individual. However, such intelligent behaviour has a limited range of applications and comes with a strong proviso that it only works effectively where each individual making up the collective is an autonomous agent, little affected by the behaviour of others. In all the systems described in the previous chapter, it is central to their operation that the environment is changed by the behaviour of the individuals, thereby breaking that cardinal rule. The problem that Surowiecki identifies is that, where people follow the lead of others, the intelligence of the group is only as great as that of the first contributors, which is unlikely to be optimal. An experiment performed by the author has demonstrated that this principle is a little more complex than Surowiecki suggests, as people are diverse and often intentionally fickle in their responses, but it is certainly true that the statistical behaviour of the group as a whole conforms with his predictions (Dron, 2006). As educational social software systems actually go out of their way to amplify preferences, this is a serious charge.

Introducing Delay

There are several possible answers to this problem. One would be to accept it at face value and to introduce a delay into the system that limits the effects of stigmergy until sufficient signs are available. Much of the work behind CoFIND has been involved in doing exactly that, tuning it so that the rate of change is slow and staggered, but related to the levels of activity within the individual parts of the system. However, this approach would be counter-productive in systems which make use of real-time interaction and would amplify the cold start problem significantly: not only would the number of ratings prove insufficient, before a certain time, there would be none at all.

Using Evolution to Cull Useless Recommendations

The use of evolutionary processes provides another means of stunting the growth of bad ideas, as demonstrated in the CoFIND system. However, even CoFIND is somewhat susceptible to intentional attack. For systems without explicit culling, the effect is more exaggerated. For example, "Google bombing," where a large number of people intentionally gather their resources to influence Google's results by linking to a particular site, is sufficiently common to merit its own entry in Wikipedia (http://en.wikipedia.org/wiki/Google_bomb). At the time of writing, a search for "miserable failure" will point to George W. Bush's biography, while a search for "liar" leads to a biography of Tony Blair. The lesson to be learned is that people are usually going to be smarter than computer systems that are capturing emergent patterns of use, at least for the foreseeable future.

Embracing the Effect

Another approach is to positively embrace the effect and to let it run its course. For example, although people are drawn to other people in the Dwellings system, once they are on a particular street, they tend to enter a building frenzy, creating and destroying a lot of sites in quick succession, eventually leading to streets of higher utility. This works partly because of the distancing effects of mediated online working: in this case it is actually a virtue that the forms of interaction are impoverished when compared with those that are face to face. Just as online discussion environments tend to diminish the prominence of the teacher, so they limit the ability of dominant individuals to influence others, albeit only slightly. In the Dwellings system, those who are creating buildings are doing so largely independent of others, although they may be influenced in the kind of content that buildings may contain by those that have gone previously. As is the case with CoFIND, evolutionary pressures make it far more likely that an effective group aggregate will be achieved, rather than a simple follow-the-leader design.

The Matthew Principle

There is a fine line between the self-organisation of a stigmergic system and the out-of-control positive feedback loop of the Matthew principle. This effect greatly enhances the importance of early contributors, who may or may not be the most qualified to contribute. However, in an e-learning environment, this eventuality may be forestalled by the diversity of users and responses to social navigation or stigmergic stimuli. The author has performed experiments that show users tend to follow a diverse range of strategies when presented with visual stimuli and, although there are often strong tendencies displayed to, say, follow links presented in larger fonts at the top of a list and so on, there is always a significant number of users who will behave differently, especially when competing visual cues are combined (Dron, 2005, 2006). This diversity helps to limit the potentially disastrous effects of allowing the blind to lead the blind.

Various aspects of system design can also be used to limit the pernicious effects of the Matthew principle. For example, parcellation limits the spread of poor choices to particular ecological niches and, although the fact that evolutionary principles operate at a range of scales means that whole niches can lose the evolutionary struggle as a result, the effects may not spread to the entire system.

Pedagogical Concerns

Truly self-organising environments will only self-organise to become learning environments if the intention of their users is to learn. However, it is also important that their structure has the potential to lead to pedagogically useful results. While evolution will inevitably lead to greater complexity and a better fit to the environment, its application to education does not necessarily imply that the most fit will be the most educationally useful. Educational systems are complex and the people that use them and are a part of them have complex and diverse motivations to do so. CoFIND's qualities are one answer to the problem, inasmuch as they are (when used as intended) pedagogical metadata describing the value of resources in a learning context. However, there are many views of what might be pedagogically useful, but these views are frequently conflicting. CoFIND and the Knowledge Sea, for instance, implicitly assume that a guided resource-based approach can be effective. Few, if any, make any attempt to embed recognised learning cycles or instructional design principles. Indeed, to some extent it might be seen as an unnecessary top-down constraint to do so. On the other hand, self-organisation may be applied at any scale and does not have to permeate every scale. It is possible to envisage systems that provide a means to select pedagogical designs in an emergent fashion, and some work on patterns and frameworks is moving into this area (Dalsgaard, 2005; Tattersall et al., 2005), but this remains an area where further research is needed.

Conclusion

The use of social software and other tools that embed self-organisation in education is in its infancy and researchers have, so far, only begun to scratch the surface of their potential. It may be that the problems discussed in this chapter are insuperable and such software will be sidelined to a peripheral role in recommending stuff or improving user interactions—another component in the hybrid environments enabled by technologies and standards such as ELF. If this were the only outcome of this radical variant on traditional approaches to e-learning, then it would not be a bad one. However, it would be better to see such ideas infiltrating the entire learning environment, augmenting discussions, shaping static media, defining and adapting assessments, and seeping in to all the rich paraphernalia that support e-learning. The arguments in favour of such systems seem persuasive and it would be a lost opportunity to not embed self-organising processes in much educational software.

This is a brave new world that has only begun to be explored. In the final chapter, the various threads that have been discovered so far will be drawn together and an attempt will be made to extrapolate from them, to speculate on some possible futures for e-learning.

References

Bollen, J., & Heylighen, F. (1998). A system to restructure hypertext networks into valid user models. *The New Review of Multimedia and Hypermedia, 4,* 189-213.

Bruner, J. S. (1966). *Toward a theory of instruction.* Cambridge, MA: The Belknap Press of Harvard University Press.

Buber, M. (1947a). *Between man and man.* London: Routledge.

Buber, M. (1947b). *Tales of the Hasidim: Early master* (O. Marx, Trans.). New York: Schocken.

Buckingham-Shum, S., Motta, E., & Domingue, J. (1999). *Modelling and visualizing perspectives in Internet digital libraries.* Paper presented at the Third Annual Conference on Research and Advanced Technology for Digital Libraries, Paris.

Carlson, R. (1989). Malcolm Knowles: Apostle of andragogy. *Vitae Scholasticae, 8*(1).

Collins, A., Brown, J. S., & Newman, S. E. (1989). *Cognitive apprenticeship: Teaching the craft of reading, writing, and mathematics* (Technical Report No. 403). Cambridge, MA: ERIC.

Cox, G., Carr, T., & Hall, M. (2004). Evaluating the use of synchronous communication in two blended courses. *Journal of Computer Assisted Learning, 20*(3), 183-193.

Dalsgaard, C. (2005). *Learning frameworks as an alternative to repositories.* Paper presented at the ICL 2005, Villach, Austria.

Dawkins, R. (1986). *The blind watchmaker.* London: Longman.

Dron, J. (2005). *Discovering the complex effects of navigation cues in an e-learning environment.* Paper presented at the E-Learn 2005, Vancouver, Canada.

Dron, J. (2006). *On the stupidity of mobs.* Paper presented at the WBC 2006, San Sebastian.

Freire, P. (1970). *Pedagogy of the oppressed* (M. B. Ramos, Trans.). New York: Continuum.

Gagné, R. (1985). *The conditions of learning* (4th ed.). New York: Holt, Rhinehart & Winston.

Hara, N., Bonk, C. J., & Angeli, C. (2000). Content analysis of online discussion in an applied educational psychology. *Instructional Science, 28*(2), 115-152.

Hussey, T., & Smith, P. (2002). The trouble with learning outcomes. *Active Learning in Higher Education, 3*(3), 220-233.

IBM_Social_Computing_Group. (2003). Social Computing Group FAQ. Retrieved April 28, 2003, from http://www.research.ibm.com/SocialComputing/SCG-FAQs.htm#WhatIsSocialTranslucence

Jones, S. (1999). *Almost like a whale.* London: Doubleday.

Karampiperis, P., & Sampson, D. (2004). *Adaptive instructional planning using ontologies.* Paper presented at the ICALT 2004, Joensuu, Finland.

Kelly, K. (1994). *Out of control: The new biology of machines.* London: Addison Wesley.

Knowles, M. (1975). *Self-directed learning.* Chicago: Follett Publishing Company.

Masthoff, J. (2002). *Towards an authoring coach for adaptive Web-based instruction.* Paper presented at the Second International Conference on Adaptive Hypermedia and Adaptive Web-based Systems, Berlin, Germany.

Moore, M. G. (1983). On a theory of independent study. In D. Sewart, D. Keegan, & B. Holmberg (Eds.), *Distance education: International perspectives* (pp. 68-94). London; Canberra: Croom Helm.

Moore, M. G., & Kearsley, G. (1996). *Distance education: A systems view.* Belmont: Wadsworth.

Morris, P. (Ed.). (1994). *The Bakhtin reader.* London: Edward Arnold.

Saba, F. (1999). Architecture of dynamic distance instructional and learning systems. *Distance Education.* Retrieved August 19, 2001, from http://www.distance-educator.com/der/architecture.html

Schank, R. (2004). *Engines for education.* Retrieved September 22, 2004, from http://www.engines4ed.org/hyperbook/index.html

Surowiecki, J. (2004). *The wisdom of crowds.* London: Little, Brown.

Tattersall, C., Berg, B. v. d., Es, R. v., Janssen, J., Manderveld, J., & Koper, R. (2004). *Swarm-based adaptation: Wayfinding support for lifelong learners.*

Paper presented at the Adaptive Hypermedia and Adaptive Web-Based Systems: Third International Conference, Eindhoven, The Netherlands.

Tattersall, C., Manderveld, J., van den Berg, B., van Es, R., Janssen, J., & Koper, R. (2005). Self organising wayfinding support for lifelong learners. *Education and Information Technologies, 10*(1-2), 111-123.

Vandenberg, D. (2002). The transcendental phases of learning. *Educational Philosophy and Theory, 34*(3), 321-344.

Vygotsky, L. S. (1978). *Mind in society.* London: Harvard University Press.

Wilson, B., & Cole, P. (1992). A critical review of elaboration theory. *Educational Technology Research and Development, 40*(3), 63-79.

Chapter XVI

Potential Futures
of E-Learning

For what is the Heart, but a Spring; and the Nerves, but so many Strings; and the Joyntes but so many Wheeles, giving motion to the whole Body.... Art goes yet further, imitating that Rationall and most excellent worke of Nature, Man. For by Art is created that great LEVIATHAN called a COMMON-WEALTH or STATE (in latine CIVITAS) which is but an Artificiall Man. (Hobbes, 1973)

Introduction

This chapter begins with a brief overview of the argument that underpins this book. The bulk of the chapter is then concerned with the future, both far away and near at hand. It makes few definite predictions, but does give examples of possible paths for e-learning over the next few years, bearing in mind the potential benefits that have been explored through the past few chapters, and the potential dangers that stand in the way of success.

The Argument of This Book in 10 Stages

In brief, the argument that underpins this book can be summarised as follows:

1. A person's learning trajectory may be seen as an ongoing series of activities that are intended to enable learning to occur.

2. Transactional distance, a measurement of the relative degrees of structure and dialogue in a learning transaction, may be mapped to a single dimension of transactional control, albeit with some loss of descriptive power.

3. Dialogue may be seen as negotiated control, while structure may be seen as teacher control. It is impossible to have both at once because no one can be both in control and out of control at once in the same context.

4. Transactional control is concerned with who makes decisions about the activities undertaken to enable learning, and who decides upon changes in a learning trajectory. Control is a compound of many factors, both extrinsic and intrinsic to the activity, is typically distributed among participants in the activity, and may be considered at a wide range of hierarchical scales.

5. The ideal for any learner is to be able to choose whether to take control or to relinquish it, at every scale and every step along a learning trajectory. Many traditional institutional approaches to teaching militate against this, although dialogue (especially one-to-one) is effective if conducted openly and on equal terms.

6. Environments influence behaviour.

7. Social software, in which the group is a first-class object within the system, offers the potential for the learner's choices to strongly affect the environment and the environment to strongly affect the learner's choices.

8. In some senses, social software allows learners to engage in a form of dialogue as well as to benefit from the resulting structure, thereby providing both high and low transactional distance, not at the same time, but under the continuous control of the learners.

9. Because transactional distance maps to transactional control, such software applied in an educational context may allow learners either to choose their own learning trajectories or to have those choices made for them.

10. In such an environment, the self-organising feedback loop derived from the collective intelligence of its inhabitants offers the potential for a qualitatively different and (probably) better learning experience.

The examples of software that have been provided here do not yet do this theory justice and illustrate stabs in the right direction, rather than fully-formed self-organising learning environments. There is a long way to go before the promise is fulfilled.

The current generation of social software, especially in incarnations such as Elgg™ that are built for learning, offers many of the facilities that the next generation will employ, allowing structure to emerge out of dialogue. The challenge for now is to ensure that this structure is helpful to learners. At the moment, the best means available is to take advantage of the effects of scale and to integrate such environments into existing institutional or organisational settings. Like several others, the author's institution is currently integrating Elgg with its existing LMS, so that it can be treated as a part of the same environment. The result is less of a mash-up than a graft, with the seams clearly visible, but it is a good start. The solution is not perfect, partly because of the clash of top-down and bottom-up approaches, and partly due to the confusion that can arise out of duplicated functionality (Anderson, 2006). However, if learners are given careful guidance and the opportunity to explore, this kind of blending can offer a gentle route into self-directed learning.

The Future of E-Learning

It is a dangerous and foolhardy thing to attempt to predict the future of such a young and volatile discipline as e-learning, but there are some themes that appear to be developing, and potential routes that may be followed. The Edinburgh Scenarios are an attempt to map out the possible scope of these routes. They are the results of an

Figure 16.1. The Edinburgh Scenarios (Adapted from Cross, 2004)

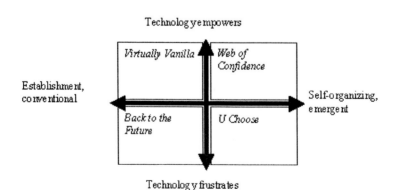

attempt by an assortment of prominent e-learning gurus and interested bystanders to provide a framework for understanding the possible futures of e-learning over the coming few years (Cross, 2004). As a result of questions started by the Scottish Enterprise and Global Business Network, two critical uncertainties emerged: the sources of power, influence and new ideas, and the role of technology in society. From this, the matrix shown in Figure 16.1 was drawn, to indicate the possible ways that technology and education might coincide.

Of the possibilities presented in the Edinburgh Scenarios, few bode well for the emergence of systems of the sort that have been advocated here. In either of the two scenarios where technology frustrates (perhaps stifled by issues of trust or disillusionment caused by the dehumanising aspects of such systems), the future of e-learning is bleak and its role is peripheral. Of the remaining two, in the *virtually vanilla* scenario, power and control is embodied in established players, such as Universities and large corporations. Such a scenario describes an industrial model of e-learning that Otto Peters once identified and valorised (Peters, 1994), which might charitably be seen as commoditising learning. In such an environment, collaborative processes that do not involve significant value for money are unlikely to succeed. This would be a disastrous result, establishing a focus on the easily measurable aspects of learning and creating a culture of managerialism in which the learner is nothing more than a customer and the wares are accreditation.

Of all the potential futures, only the *web of confidence* offers the potential to exploit the full power of an e-learning ecology. In this scenario, technology empowers learners to control their own learning by whatever means are appropriate; power is distributed and flexibility becomes the crucial factor in enabling lifelong learning. The systems described in the foregoing chapters are very much focused on these areas, but only begin to scratch the surface of the possibilities that this entails.

For all of the potential areas of concern, the pictures of the future that are drawn in the Edinburgh Scenarios are not uniformly depressing and each possible future has some benefits to some learners and some purveyors of learning. The *U-choose* scenario would be of great benefit to many learners denied access to traditional forms of education, the *virtually vanilla* scenario would perhaps provide a better education than its unaugmented equivalent, and even *back to the future* would allow traditional teachers to exercise their skills without having to learn new ones.

What Does "Better" Mean?

The *web of confidence* is by far the most optimistic and empowering of the possibilities suggested by the Edinburgh Scenarios, and it would be encouraging to think that emergent learning environments will play a significant role in bringing this scenario about. As always, scale matters and it is far from certain that this will occur. The learning environments described in chapter 14 are tiny ecosystems within much larger environments and are subject to many pressures that mean their utility and effectiveness is only one driver for success. The classic examples of "better" technologies being surpassed by those that are "inferior," such as the Qwerty keyboard versus the Dvorak keyboard, Betamax versus VHS, or the Apple Mac versus the PC, serve as ample warnings that being "best" (according to the experts) does not imply being a winner. In reality, each of these examples is far from unequivocal and there is a good case to be made that in each instance the "better" technology succeeded or, at the very least, the fittest, suiting the widest and most predominant range of needs (Cohen & Stewart, 1994, pp. 322-323). Self-organising processes are not only blind but also deaf to the opinions of experts.

Even if the *web of confidence* scenario plays out as hoped for, the viability of such systems could be affected by issues as diverse as the demands of learners who have learned dependence through schooling, the pressures of commercial players defending software patents, government policies, or teachers defending their traditional status. What is "better" in an evolutionary environment is what succeeds and survives. A better learning experience is only one of many competing factors that contribute to the dynamics of an educational environment. Perhaps the methods of building and using e-learning environments that have been recommend here may make a small contribution to the widespread systemic change that might lead to the *web of confidence*, but perhaps they will be overwhelmed by others, shown to be inadequate or simply not noticed.

The Future of E-Learning Environments

If it is assumed (as those working in e-learning must assume) that the future will reside somewhere in the upper two quadrants of the Edinburgh Scenarios, it will be vital to prevent the *virtually vanilla* option becoming the predominant form. Although it has its place in some settings and may benefit some learners, it is not the answer. Slow-moving, large-scale, monolithic, learning environments (including the entire surrounding ecology of learning, not just the virtual space) that embody a rigid hierarchy will inevitably exert their control on the faster moving, smaller scale components. While some steps may be taken to shoehorn a learner-centred approach into such industrialised education, it is an uphill struggle and most will give up and roll downhill again.

The Same, Only More So

It is certain that the current technologies employed in learning environments—content provision, asynchronous communication, synchronous communication, assessment, and so on—will not go away, although they will undoubtedly grow in sophistication and, hopefully, ease of use. Learning technologies will spread from the Web and e-mail into other mass-user technologies such as mobile phones and digital and interactive television. The podcast, which provides audio learning in an accessible and distributable format that far exceeds the reach of early tape-based approaches, will continue its move into the mainstream.

A central driver to this diversification will be component-driven, service-oriented, and perhaps, agent-driven interoperability. Whether or not institutions remain slaves to the Blackboardosaurus, an ever increasing diversity of needs and available technologies will require designs that allow different instances to be constructed which use a subset of these, and that interoperate to a greater extent.

Micro Habitats and Personal Learning Environments

In the current generation of learning management systems, it is the norm to provide a personal view of the environment to the student, showing only the courses on which the student is registered and, perhaps, other tools such as e-mail. While there are often options for customising this view, the current generation of tools are still firmly set in a framework defined by administrators, teachers, and software developers. It is not unlikely that a personal virtuality that consists of a myriad of connected and communicating micro-habitats will become the norm. Virtual communication and knowledge exchange spaces will be tied together, loosely or tightly, into personal learning environments (PLEs). Many of the micro-habitats, of which a PLE is composed, will be some form of social software. They may be mashed together into complex, almost city-like structures that suit the users' needs, whether as teachers or as learners.

It is already possible to see this kind of thing happening in the social software community, if not to any great extent in educational software. Sometimes this mashing up may be entirely free-form, as individuals habitually and almost unconsciously switch between IM, RSS aggregators, Web sites, search engines, e-mail, and other technologies, treating the whole of cyberspace as one environment, navigating it as they might navigate a city. The author's desktop, for example, is filled not only with a perpetually open Web browser, e-mail, and RSS reader, but also reference tools (dictionaries, encyclopaedias, currency converters, HTML/CSS references, and so on), news feeds, instant messengers, IP telephony, search tools, Internet radio systems, weather reports, and a host of other more or less connected systems.

Sometimes this may be facilitated through a single environment: sites such as MySpace® are built around a personal profile space; RSS aggregators provide a custom view of the social software space. Many of the social software systems on Ning™ take data from other places and knit them together to create something new.

Many applications exist that combine RSS feeds and services provided by social software. For example, the Daily Mashup (http://dailymashup.com/) combines Flickr™, del.icio.us™, and Yahoo™ news. FlickrMap (http://www.flickrmap.com/) allows the user to put Flash™-based maps of the world on his or her site using geographical data associated with pictures uploaded to Flickr in order to show photographs of a given area. FlickrGraph (http://www.marumushi.com/apps/flickrgraph/) graphically displays social networks of Flickr contributors. This sort of application is not limited to small, federated systems. It is even possible to install a Blackboard® Building Block, which displays selected RSS feeds as well as lists of learning objects from MERLOT, or to incorporate a small chunk of JavaScript, which uses another site to display them (http://jade.mcli.dist.maricopa.edu/feed/).

Virtuality

The kinds of virtual worlds that already exist, mainly in online games, will provide an ever more immersive and "realistic" experience. While there are dangers that such environments may become mere simulacra of reality and provide a comfortable space in which to reinforce the control-based traditional models of learning and teaching, there is a more hopeful scenario. The opportunities for these spaces to be enhanced and augmented, to break the rules of physical spaces, to be created as an emergent feature of their use, much as can be seen in today's primitive social software, are immense. Combining media-rich gathering spaces for humans, with ever more sophisticated AI and an indefinitely malleable environment, may provide alternatives for learners that are truly mind-bending. However, the central rule of letting learners choose to choose, of providing sign posts and not fence posts (in this case, possibly literally), will still apply as strongly as ever. As with any social software, the dangers of inappropriate structures being developed should not be under-emphasised. That said, the fact that conversation and stigmergic cues are naturally embedded give reasons to hope that this kind of environment offers great opportunities for development.

Augmented Reality, Ambient and Locative Software

There is a good chance that the borders between the virtual world and the real will become more blurred. Locative software that is aware of where people are will present them with appropriate and relevant information. Reality will be augmented with devices that offload cognitive functions such as remembering people's names and details of their lives, or linking facts, performing arithmetic, and even making some judgements on machines, changing the nature of the kind of learning needed. No longer will people need to absorb vast quantities of information, but instead, may concentrate on what they do with that information, transforming learning needs and consequently education. Computers, already embedded in many of the devices that are integral to social existence, will become increasingly interlinked, allowing everything from televisions to shirts and, perhaps, even human bodies themselves to become part of the federated learning environment that will seep into every part of everyone's lives—a pervasive, ubiquitous and ambient presence. To a significant extent, this process has begun: there are now more mobile phones in the United Kingdom than people (Thomson, 2005), digital television (with its interactive facilities) is considerably more popular than analogue (OFCOM, 2005), and most households own a computer (OFCOM, 2006). Most of the population carry computer chips embedded in cards in wallets and purses, and before long they will be in many of the items in stores, in the form of RFID tags. It is possible (though unusual) to purchase Internet-connected refrigerators, toasters, and chopping boards. This is only the beginning. Environments equipped with ambient intelligence are already available that adjust lighting, heating, air conditioning, and so on, according to who is there and how many. Smart rooms equipped with sensors, cameras, and microphones can identify patterns of behaviour and respond accordingly. Clothing has been created that communicates the heartbeat of one to another, linking people in ways that have hitherto been impossible. In educational terms, such adaptive and adaptable technologies are changing the way that computers are thought of: not just as tools, not just as media, not just as environments, but as an integral component of every environment, shaping not just virtuality, but reality as well. This trend is enhanced by Santa Claus machines, devices that "print" in three dimensions. It is already possible to buy devices off the shelf that enable complex three dimensional designs to be reproduced as physical objects with almost as great ease as a page is printed from a word processor or drawing program. Soon, this ease of construction may even extend to whole buildings (http://www.contourcrafting.org/). The educational possibilities for such tools seem endless. In terms of control, however, the issues will be complex. To what extent will these ambient devices enhance our own control? Who will decide on the objects that we use to learn? Will real sign posts and fence posts be created? As the future veers in sight, learners and teachers need to maintain a grasp of what and who is in control and sure that this is in accordance with their learning needs.

Artificial Intelligence

Artificial intelligence (AI) may offer many solutions to the problems of learning, not as stand-alone technologies, but embedded within the fabric of many different systems. If a machine has sufficient intelligence, then it is as reasonable to delegate control to an intelligent machine as it is to delegate control to a teacher. Indeed, if the machine is sufficiently intelligent to engage in a meaningful dialogue, then this could provide an effective means of negotiating control. However, for the foreseeable future, a machine is unlikely to have sufficient domain knowledge, let alone understanding of learner needs or conversational ability, to be of more than academic interest. If, as some (Koper, 2004; Stojanovic, Staab, & Studer, 2001) suggest, the Semantic Web gathers sufficient momentum, domain knowledge may become less of an issue, but an intelligent Web is still some way off.

AI techniques are already embedded in various systems used in education. For example, latent semantic analysis technologies may be used quite effectively to assess free-text essays and answers to questions (Hunt & Whittington, 1999; Williams & Dreher, 2005), offering control to learners needing to know how successful they have been. Intelligent agents may be used to adapt content or to offer advice, though the much-disliked Microsoft™ paper clip serves as a reminder of the dangers of such technologies and there are still issues of trust to resolve (Korba et al., 2005).

The use of AI techniques to augment social software offers a promising synergy. For example, Sloep et al. (2006) use latent semantic analysis to identify problems and to provide an outline answer to questions posed on a wiki, which may then be modified by experts and/or peers to provide a fuller solution. A different approach to the use of AI is taken by Koper (2004), who proposes the use of Semantic Web technologies to describe learning designs, thereby assisting in their retrieval and re-use in a number of learning contexts. This is a significant extension of the more conventional, finer grained approach that looks at uses of the Semantic Web to assemble appropriately tagged learning objects (Stojanovic, Staab, & Studer, 2001), or of using knowledge ontologies to structure learning (Karampiperis & Sampson, 2004). Koper's approach relates to activities at a larger scale, suggesting patterns of pedagogy rather than abstract structures of knowledge. Especially were it to be combined with a means of representing different aspects of pedagogical processes (Sicilia & Lytras, 2005), this is a potentially elegant way to combine top-down design with some learner control. It enables a significant amount of learner direction, albeit at a fairly large scale, within a framework defined by a subject expert or teacher, and enables the decisions of many to influence an individual's path without the chaos of a completely unstructured system. Koper (2004) describes the effect thus:

There are no central control actors; the control is expected to emerge under favourable conditions (local feedback, pattern detection) and in a democratic way. This is another way of saying that a person can take all the other roles in a learning network.

The goals of this research are closely aligned with those of this book, although the use of an imposed structure seems to be an unnecessary skyhook. An ideal system would self-organise at every scale.

Imagining a Scenario or Two

The following scenarios are not intended to be anything more than a game, playing with a few ideas about the near future. In no way should they be considered as serious predictions, but they are helpful in describing some of the potential benefits of the approaches that have been espoused in this last section of the book, and perhaps some of the systemic effects they might help to engender.

Scenario 1. Just in Time Learning of a Simple Skill

This Year or Next

I wish to learn something simple—perhaps how to boil an egg. In the past, I might have looked it up in a cookery book or browsed the Web using Google. Nowadays, I ask the Semantic Web to tell me the answer. It tells me straight away, perhaps using implicit or explicit ratings to identify trustworthy and reliable sources. No need for emergence here, just decent metadata and some well-designed resources properly linked and associated at a semantic level through RDF. Based on the instructions that I receive, I boil an egg.

I know that I can boil an egg because I do so; it tastes good and I do not suffer from any adverse side-effects such as burns, broken kitchen implements, or food poisoning.

In a Few Years Time

Why should I need to learn this stuff? I feel hungry. A tattoo on my arm or perhaps my wristwatch checks what I need for a nutritionally balanced meal, I state my preference, and it is served, perfectly cooked. The refrigerator has already ordered the eggs to replace the ones it has used, based on previous patterns of consumption in my household.

Scenario 2. A More Complex Skill Requiring Much Study and Practice

This Year or Next

I wish to learn an intellectual skill, perhaps how to write computer programs. In the past, I might have looked for evening classes. If I were lucky, I might find myself in a small class that allowed me to ask questions of an experienced teacher. If not, I might have put off the process for life. I might have browsed the books in my local library or book shop, or trawled through a wide range of tutorials available on the Web. In time, I might have learned to program this way, especially if the tutorial or book that I chose suited my style of learning and gave me just the level of autonomy that I required.

If I were an especially autonomous learner whose ZPD were close enough to my goal already, or if I were just particularly determined to succeed, then perhaps I would have pulled out a manual and bashed at it until I began to understand the problem.

In an emergent future, I enter the learning environment and express my learning needs: I want to learn to program in Java™ (an archaic language that is still quite widely used despite the many modern alternatives that have superseded it).

My learning environment already knows quite a lot about me—my past, what I have studied, at what level, the learning objects I have accessed, the communities that I have been a part of. It also knows about others who have expressed similar learning needs, and it knows about how they have dealt with the learning resources that are available: which were popular, which worked best, which were evaluated most highly according to the criteria that I have implicitly or explicitly expressed. It is able to assemble this information because it is a part of a system of systems, all following recognised standards for interoperability and communicating intelligently with each other. From this information, it assembles a route for me with many choices, although it has highlighted those that it thinks are sensible, based on a unique ecology that is an amalgam of its knowledge about me, its knowledge of others like me, relevant learning objects, learning communities, and learning services. It has also highlighted, to a greater or lesser extent, what it believes to be less appropriate, but still sensible choices. As I go through, it brings me into contact with others who might help me, either because of their expertise or teaching skills, or because they are in a similar state as me and might help me to understand my needs and theirs through a process of dialogue. Perhaps it identifies those who are nearby that I could talk with face to face.

As I become more proficient (a fact of which the system is profoundly aware), the ecology around me changes, adapting to my changing needs, presenting me with all manner of assistance with my learning needs. The computer's awareness of my needs is not only determined by the traditional objective tests that still haunt the system, but also by analysing the implicit or explicit opinions of others (some experts, some not) and the kinds of path that I am taking, which it compares constantly with those of others. In a kind of reversal of the evolutionary struggle, only the things which help me to learn survive. Throughout the process, I am continuously aware of others and often in dialogue with them, clarifying problems and resolving issues. Often I am the one that is helping, and in so doing, I help myself through a process of teachback (Pask, 1976), perhaps through sharing stories (Jonassen & Hernandez-Serrano, 2002). Sometimes I stray from the path that the computer suggests for me and I find serendipitous gems, learning resources, people, approaches, and so on that help me to learn. Somehow, and miraculously, these discoveries are woven into the fabric of the environment for me and for others to return to.

I know that I have learned to program in Java because I can write programs in Java of the sort that I wish to write. Perhaps others think they are fine too.

In a Few Years Time

Java has gone the way of all things, but the new way of building systems still requires skills in problem solving and problem stating. In some ways, it has become more complex, as applications built nowadays have to interact with many others in many places, across many platforms, which include a Web not just of virtual objects, but of things and people. Luckily, the standards are well defined and if we want to know where to find a server, what a service does, and why we should care, we just ask an agent that will find it on our behalf.

I do not need to learn a programming language, but somehow I need to take my existing knowledge of how to manipulate virtual reality and extend it sufficiently to solve my current problem, which is to take everything that anyone has ever said about e-learning and identify consistencies and inconsistencies between theories, with a view to generating an adaptive e-book on the subject. Of course, what I am authoring is not something that I expect my readers to read from start to finish. I expect it to adapt to each reader's needs, based on its knowledge of the reader and its understanding of how it has been used by other readers. It will be my means of communicating my thoughts, in a manner that will be most useful to whoever reads it, at a level they find meaningful and related to aspects of their lives that make it relevant and helpful. Therefore, it will be a standard software construction task.

Understanding how to construct systems that adapt to others' needs is a complex task which, not only requires me to know about software construction, but also the ways that people learn, how to make use of adaptive technologies, which services are available to help me complete my task, and so on. Perhaps I even need assistance with literary style. Some of these needs may be satisfied by existing social software, which helps me to identify the paths that others have taken when attempting similar things in the past. Some of these needs are more complex and will change as I attempt the task and encounter problems. Social software helps to alert me when I need assistance, suggesting potential ways that I can find help including people, services, and even places.

I know that I have succeeded because I have accomplished my task successfully and feel confident that I could attempt a similar project again.

Scenario 3. A Way of Being

This Year or Next

I wish to become a doctor. There is only one way to achieve this: to be accredited by my country's medical association. This process is long and arduous, involving a set of hurdles that include academic learning and evidence of successful practice in a guided, scaffolded hospital environment. In the academic phase of my learning, I have found some things easy and some things hard. I have found out about the easy things by exploring resources on the Internet, following guided exercises and assessments that, due to trust relationships between systems at different locations exchanging information using RDF, have given me accreditation for successful achievements. The harder things, and those that I have found difficult to achieve through the Internet alone, have required me to attend a teaching hospital, where I have picked up practical tricks of the trade and received accreditation for them in the conventional way.

How do I know that I have succeeded? At each stage along the way, there are different measures of success. While "attending" my validating institution, I have repeatedly attempted a set of multiple choice questions, because those are what I find most appropriate to my needs. After some years, I managed to get them all right. Some of the other people who are learning with me have taken different routes, including portfolios based on practice that show evidence of their knowledge and skills, and others who have engaged with more skilled colleagues who have questioned them and probed their understanding in an assortment of ways.

In a Few Years Time

I wish to become a doctor. In the past, I might have struggled to achieve a set of qualifications that would allow me to enroll in a course at a medical school, gone through a competitive process to get a place, then studied for many years, interspersed with periods of apprenticeship and guided practice, until finally, the powers that be granted me a licence to practice. If I were a good doctor, I might continue learning throughout my career. If not, I might hope that nobody notices that I am killing patients and am unaware of the latest treatments.

In an emergent future, there are no hurdles to jump through before I start learning, or rather, the hurdles are continual and small. I am presented with tasks and resources that are appropriate to my needs at every point throughout the process. The system puts me in contact with people who will help me and will be able to judge whether I am really suitable for this role (it might have done this sooner, if I had expressed the need for this). Virtual reality systems allow me to practice in a safe environment.

At some point, the system becomes aware that I know and understand enough to be recommended to join the medical profession as an intern, an apprentice working under the guidance of other doctors. The system knows that I am able, not only because I have completed a few objective tests, but also as a result of the opinions of others and my role in the community as a perceived expert. Perhaps I have made use of a number of simulators (open source tools which are available to one and all because money that used to be channelled into teaching doctors is now available to assist their creation), which have fed back their knowledge of my skills or lack of them into the system, following open standards. Throughout the process, the system is constantly recommending what I should do next, but it never insists on this and always offers me choices about how and when I should approach the next learning task or activity. I never feel afraid or alone because I am constantly surrounded by a supportive electronic community, which includes not only experts and teachers, but also others who are at a similar learning stage to my own. Each of these people brings his or her own unique knowledge and understanding to the community, encouraging creativity, variety, and diversity of thinking. Even as I begin to work as a doctor, augmented reality devices and tools offer me as much (or as little) assistance as I need in making diagnoses, providing treatments, and consulting with colleagues. These tools communicate and interact with technologies embedded in the clothing or tattooed into the skin of the patients I treat, proactively offering advice and warnings of problems I might otherwise have missed.

I know that I have become a doctor because I am accepted into the community of doctors as an equal and am allowed to treat patients. Because the electronic environment has become such an integrated part of my life, I continue to be involved, sharing my knowledge and learning from others for the rest of my career.

What Becomes of the Teacher?

The role of the teacher (as a person, rather than a role) in any future scenario, based on the principles of social software and all that it entails, becomes diffuse, but by no means vanishes. There will be a continuing need for subject expertise, effective guidance, pedagogically sound source materials, meaningful feedback, and support. For the foreseeable future, the self-repairing educational system will maintain itself against radical change. Centrally controlled schools will continue to churn out centrally-controlled learners—dependent addicts of the information-transfer model of teaching. Even in the distant future, there will be a sufficient diversity of needs that will ensure that this kind of teaching will have a place and, at some scale, it will always be needed.

Perhaps the virtually vanilla scenario will triumph, as the large and slow parts of a system usually do. However, as the e-learning tools become more sophisticated, more capable of supporting a collectively generated system of support and guidance, this may slowly mutate. Driven by the need for relevant, on-the-job, just-in-time learning and perhaps the odd government initiative, an increasing number of learners will seek non-traditional routes to lifelong learning. The teacher in this environment will find it hard to maintain the automated, industrialised, managerially driven producer model of education that continues to pervade higher education institutions. Gradually and perhaps almost imperceptibly, the smaller, faster moving parts of the system will change the larger, slower moving leviathan of the educational machine.

Are These Scenarios Plausible?

The technologies and standards to drive such scenarios are available today and those familiar with the state of the art may actually find them rather quaint and passé. However, it may take quite a long time for the bureaucratic infrastructure that supports them to catch up. This is particularly true where accreditation is required. The Bologna Declaration on the European Space for Higher Education (European Commission, 2000) provides a framework for converging higher education institutions around Europe which, after several years, is beginning to come together. This allows credit achieved in one institution to be transferred to another. However, it works at a relatively high level of granularity and it would not (and probably should not) be possible to apply it at the level of lessons or even chunks of lessons, tying learning to a traditional institutional structure.

The promise of emergent, social, educational systems sounds much like those proposed by the AI community for many years and indeed they have much in common and perhaps make use of techniques developed by AI researchers. However, what is distinctive about them is that the real intelligence resides, not in the machines but, in the people who use them. The intelligence that such systems do possess is dedicated to combining and using the intelligence of real people.

Ubiquity and Economics

It may be perceived that significant brakes on progress may be economic and, to an extent, social. PC ownership is far from ubiquitous, even in the developed world, and Internet access perhaps less so. Even in the United Kingdom, one of the most networked nations, only 66% of households own a PC (OFCOM, 2006). However, the growth of digital television services that incorporate Internet access as well as the increasing ubiquity of mobile phones mean that figures may fail to give a reliable estimate of those who are able to benefit from online education. Whatever the actual figures may be the fact that there is substantial and continuing growth is uncontested. The author visited Delhi two years in succession and, on both occasions, he visited the same Internet café, one of thousands that had sprung up in the city. In the first year, a group of patrons shared an extremely unreliable and manually dialled modem connection. The café was open to the street and the odd roaming cow occasionally joined the patrons while they surfed and checked their e-mail. The following year, the same café had acquired glazing and a fast (if still unreliable) DSL connection. The same pattern repeats the world over. The point at which it becomes cheaper and more efficient to learn using technologies in the more developed nations is reached quite soon, but in developing nations, where labour is cheaper than machines, this may take a little longer. Initiatives such as OLPC (http://laptop.org/) aim to make computers available to a far wider audience, while others believe that the solution may be found in the far more widely available mobile phone. Such initiatives are constantly lowering the barriers to a ubiquitously networked future.

Where Next? Closer Up

A learning environment that effectively combines choice and constraint, as well as seamlessly solving the problems of sequencing, pedagogy, communication depth and so on is probably a little way off, but there are already many e-learning environments that make use of social navigation, neural networks, AI, and collaborative mechanisms such as collaborative filtering. Unfortunately, very few of them are designed as serious production environments with the interoperability, stability, and scalability that is necessary to compete with the large learning management systems that dominate the e-learning landscape. Fortunately, this is in the process of changing. The open architecture of OKI promises a fair level of interoperability between components of different systems, while the ELF Project offers even greater potential; especially so as the ELF and OKI communities are actively working on interoperability between the two standards. Combined with increasing interoperability at the level of the information presented via increasingly convergent standards such as SCORM, IMS, and IEEE-LOM, it will soon be possible to incorporate more exotic tools into traditional learning management systems without having to let go of the comfortable and familiar tools of the corporate favourites. Standards designed for learning environments are by no means the only important players here. Increasingly, the move towards PLEs encompasses mash-up technologies such as RSS and Web services to integrate a wide range of information sources, social groups, and diverse systems. It is perhaps too early to identify the eventual winners, but it seems likely that the general direction is one of interoperability and choice. However, this is largely dependent upon the extent to which the monoliths have pervaded educational systems. Once a system has become embedded, it is very difficult to break out of it without major upset and disruption. In this respect, developing nations and latecomers to such technologies may have an advantage over those who dived in early.

It is not unreasonable to remain optimistic. Even should the monoliths prevail, it is certain that they will be forced to interoperate and engage with other, more open systems, if only to absorb them. Although the top-down structure of the traditional LMS is inevitably constraining, the effects of the small and fast-moving will, as in most natural and artificial systems, eventually influence the large and slow. Already, the concept of the PLE is beginning to invade the space of the traditional LMS. If all goes well, the stage is set for a gentle but pervasive revolution in e-learning, finally allowing it to achieve what the visionaries have been claiming for it for many years.

Conclusion

E-learning is still very much in its infancy. As the Edinburgh Scenarios suggest, it may yet die stillborn or, worse, continue its path of development towards being a tyrannical means of control. There is good reason to feel hopeful about the future, however. When employing the principles underpinning social software, e-learning presents some unique benefits, in terms of control that might play a part in the transformation of education.

E-learning is part of a far wider complex system, which serves many other purposes apart from helping learners to learn. Like any complex system, perhaps a small change will send it tumbling into a completely different state or, alternatively, perhaps different forces will self-organise around it and accommodate even quite large changes, leaving it much as it was before.

The view presented here, of educational systems as a rich interplay of choice and constraint, provides clear indications of how existing and emerging tools may be used to guide the learner and offers a strong agenda for future developments. One of e-learning's greatest potential contributions to education lies in its unique ability to resolve the dilemma of choice and constraint, of letting learners choose the degree of control they exercise over their learning trajectories. The new generation of environments offer new ways of communicating that are qualitative different from those that have come before, where communication changes the world, not by its effects, but by its reification—by its very existence. As always, structure influences behaviour. At last, it is the turn of the underdog: from now on, perhaps more than ever before, behaviour will also influence structure.

References

Anderson, T. (2006). *Social software applications in formal online education.* Paper presented at the 6th IEEE International Conference on Advanced Learning Technologies, Kerkrade, The Netherlands.

Cohen, J., & Stewart, I. (1994). *The collapse of chaos.* Harmondsworth: Penguin.

Cross, J. (2004). The Edinburgh scenarios. Retrieved August 9, 2004, from http://www.internettime.com/lcmt/archives/001121.html

European Commission. (2000). *The Bologna declaration: an explanation.* Retrieved. from http://europa.eu.int/comm/education/policies/educ/bologna/bologna.pdf.

Hobbes, T. (1973). *Leviathan.* London: Dent.

Hunt, H., & Whittington, D. (1999). *Approaches to the computerized assessment of free text responses.* Paper presented at the Computer Assisted Assessment Conference, Loughborough.

Jonassen, D. H., & Hernandez-Serrano, J. (2002). Case-based reasoning and instructional design: Using stories to support problem solving. *Educational Technology Research and Development, 50*(2), 65-77.

Karampiperis, P., & Sampson, D. (2004). *Adaptive instructional planning using ontologies.* Paper presented at the ICALT 2004, Joensuu, Finland.

Koper, R. (2004). Use of the semantic Web to solve some basic problems in education. *Journal of Interactive Media in Education, 2004*(6), 1-23.

Korba, L., Yee, G., Xu, Y., Song, R., Patrick, A. S., & El-Khatib, K. (2005). Privacy and trust in agent-supported distributed learning. In F. O. Lin (Ed.), *Designing distributed learning environments with intelligent software agents* (pp. 67-114). Hershey, PA: Information Science Publishing.

OFCOM. (2005). *Digital television update - 2005 Q1.* London: Office of Communications

OFCOM. (2006). *The communications market: Nations and regions.* London: Office of Communications.

Pask, G. (1976). *Conversation theory- applications in education and epistemology:* Elsevier.

Peters, O. (1994). *Otto Peters on distance education: The industrialization of teaching and learning.* London: Routledge.

Sicilia, M.-A., & Lytras, M. D. (2005). On the representation of change according to different ontologies of learning. *International Journal of Learning and Change, 1*(1), 66-79.

Sloep, P. B., van Rosmalen, P., Kester, L., Brouns, F., & Koper, R. (2006). *In search of an adequate yet affordable tutor in online learning networks.* Paper presented at the Sixth International Conference on Advanced Learning Technologies, Kerkrade, The Netherlands.

Stojanovic, L., Staab, S., & Studer, R. (2001). *E-learning based on the semantic Web.* Paper presented at the WebNet 2001, Orlando, Florida.

Thomson, I. (2005). UK now has more mobiles than people. *IT Week.*

Williams, R., & Dreher, H. (2005). *Formative assessment visual feedback in computer graded essays.* Paper presented at the Informing Science and Information Technology Education 2005, Flagstaff, Arizona.

Glossary

AI: Artificial intelligence: A wide variety of computational methods that resemble thought processes in living organisms.

AJAX: Asynchronous JavaScript and XML: The main technological approach underlying Web 2, enabling Web applications to perform and behave like more traditional desktop applications.

Asynchronous discussion: Discussion that occurs discontinuously over a (typically) prolonged period

Aware-ware: Software that provides an indication of the presence of others, often used to provide a form of social navigation.

Behaviourism: A way of viewing education and learning as a set of stimuli and measurable responses, exhibiting the desired behaviour. A popular and effective approach to some forms of training, but much maligned as a form of education in higher learning.

Blog (or Weblog): Online journal or diary. Usually provides some means of annotation or comment. Often uses a system known as Trackbacks, a kind of two-way link between a posting on one blog and a posting on another. Typically may be subscribed to and or combined with other blog postings using an RSS reader or aggregator.

Blogosphere: The space inhabited by the blogging community, a universe of sites which are parcellated, yet linked together by small isthmuses of connections.

Blogroll: List of links in one blog to others that are linked or related.

CMS: Course management system: An LMS with a focus on institutional higher learning.

Collaborative filter: Also known as a recommender system. A piece of software that makes use of the opinions of others to recommend resources. Automated collaborative filters are a sub-variety that match similar patterns of preference in different users to achieve a closer match to needs.

Complicity: Complex behaviour arising from simple rules (e.g., the weather or the formation of traffic jams).

Constructivism: A group of theories that are based on the principle that knowledge is not simply transferred but actively constructed and thus depends upon previous knowledge, context, intention, and so on. Social constructivism suggests that this is an inherently social process and is best accomplished in dialogue with others.

ELF: E-learning framework: A service-based framework based on the widely Web services technologies, allowing the construction of very rich and varied LMS systems using multiple technologies.

Evolution: The process of natural selection, whereby reproduction with variation combined with competition for a limited resource, results in ever increasing complexity and suitability to the environment.

Exaption: In evolutionary terms, a side effect of other changes that may become an adaptation if the conditions are suitable.

Flash: A proprietary format owned by Macromedia for displaying interactive multimedia content on a Web page.

Google bombing: An example of how social software can be manipulated. Involves intentional clubbing together of many sites to push a particular site to the top of a Google search, using a given search term. Often used for political ends.

History-rich: A form of social navigation that reveals the history of the browsing of others (usually through some form of annotation).

IEEE-LOM: A standard for learning objects.

IM: Instant messenger, a class of application that remains resident on your computer at all times, so that you can instantly contact and be contacted by others. Normally text-based, but some provide audio and video chat as well.

IMS: Used to stand for instructional metadata standard but now just stands for IMS.

Instructivism: A (frequently pejorative) term used to describe approaches to teaching that are teacher-led and deal with knowledge transmission rather than knowledge construction

IRC: Internet relay chat, a real-time text communication protocol that involves visiting an IRC server to meet and interact with others.

IRC: Internet relay chat, a venerable protocol used for asynchronous text chat over the Internet.

Java™: A programming language owned and created by Sun that allows programs to be run on many different computer platforms, including Windows®, Macintosh®, and Linux® operating systems, as well as mobile phones and servers. Object-oriented, complex but powerful.

LMS: Learning management system: A VLE that includes management functionality.

Mashup: A term derived from the music industry, used here to describe intentional combinations of two or more Internet-based systems using technologies such as Web services and RSS. A common feature of Web 2.0 applications.

MLE: Managed learning environment: The UK's preferred name for an LMS.

MOO: MUD – object-oriented: A more sophisticated form of MUD that allows participants to create the text-based environment themselves, including objects that may possess (sometimes) very rich behaviours, making them perhaps the most sophisticated integrated learning environments available today. Widely used in education before the advent of the Web; they are highly evolved systems. Nowadays, often used with a Web interface to make them a little friendlier, they are nonetheless complex environments, which usually take some time to learn to use.

MUD: Multi-user dungeon: A form of text-based virtual reality originally designed for mainframe computers in the early 1970s, typically enabling both synchronous and asynchronous communication, and employing a spatial metaphor for moving around the environment.

OKI: Open Knowledge Initiative: A project started by MIT that defines a standard LMS architecture, allowing disparate LMS systems and their components to work together. Mainly Java-based, but can be used with PHP as a result of the Harmoni project.

Parcellation: A central feature of evolutionary and other self-organising systems— separation of one part of an environment from its surroundings.

PLE: Personal learning environment: Typically an amalgam or mashup of tools and applications.

Podcast: Audio, usually provided using MP3 technology, presented via an RSS feed.

RDF: Resource description framework: The XML-based standard underpinning the Semantic Web.

RLO: Reusable learning object

RSS: Variously can stand for really simple syndication, RDF site summary or rich site summary. A means of exchanging lists of information widely used by numerous forms of social software, including blogs and CoFIND.

SCORM: Shareable content object reuse model: A standard primarily used to enable content to be transferred between one LMS and another.

Semantic Web: An initiative intended to describe resources in a manner that allows machines to make intelligent decisions about how they relate to each other and how they may be used.

Sematectonic: A form of stigmergy in which the sign and the change to the environment are the same thing.

Simplexity: Simple behaviour resulting from complex interactions (e.g., the regular rhythm of the heartbeat).

Social navigation: Making use of the behaviour of others within a networked environment to influence the behaviour of others, through changes in the interface. Inherently stigmergic (see Stigmergy).

Social software: Software that treats the group as a first class object within the system.

Stigmergy: A process of communication through signs left in the environment. In sematectonic stigmergy, the signs and changes to the environment are the same thing, while in sign-based stigmergy the signs left in the environment are separate from the behaviour they engender.

Synchronous discussion: Discussion that occurs in real-time (or thereabouts).

Threaded discussion forum: A discussion where messages are posted to a central server and displayed according to replies and responses.

Transactional control: The control exercised or capable of being exercised by an individual in a learning transaction at the point at which a learning trajectory changes direction.

Transactional distance: Michael G. Moore's theory that sees distance in an educational transaction as a pedagogic, not a physical phenomenon. Concerns three dimensions that may be used to describe any educational transaction: dialogue and structure (control and sequencing by the teacher) which are inversely related, and learner autonomy, which is not.

VLE: Virtual learning environment: An environment intended to support learning, typically combining tools for communication, presentation, assessment, and so on.

VoIP: Voice over IP: Use of the Internet to provide telephony.

VR: Virtual reality: An attempt to represent a user within a three dimensional environment that mimics reality.

Wear-ware: Software that changes simply as a result of being used. Often used in social navigation.

Web 2.0: A popular term which means little, but is generally used to describe the richly interactive environments enabled by approaches such as AJAX.

Web services: An assortment of XML-based standards that allow compliant applications to exchange messages and to interoperate.

WebMeeting: A real-time interaction with others through Web-based systems that typically provide video, audio, slide presentation, text chat, real-time polling and other classroom- or meeting-like features.

Wiki (Wiki Wiki Web) **Web:** Pages that anyone and everyone can edit freely, quickly and easily (from "Wiki Wiki," Hawaiian for "quickly").

XML: Extensible Markup Language, a very flexible language for defining other languages, used for very many other standards such as Web services, RDF, IEEE-LOM, and RSS.

ZPD: Zone of proximal development: Vygotskian concept, loosely speaking the current scope for learning something new beyond which it gets too confusing or difficult.

About the Author

Jon Dron is a principal lecturer at the University of Brighton, UK, where he teaches in the School of Computing, Mathematical & Information Sciences. His subject areas include learning technologies, Web mastery, network management, and communication technologies. Dron's doctorate was on self-organisation in network-based learning environments, and he continues to build and research systems in this area. He has published over 40 peer-reviewed articles on this and other aspects of e-learning, as well as many invited papers and presentations. His first degree was in philosophy and, after spending several years as a professional musical entertainer, he gained a Master of Science in information systems. In 1997, following some time as a technology manager, he settled on a career in academia. Dron is a national teaching fellow of the Higher Education Academy, UK.

Index

I

independence 31
independent learner 164
instant messaging (IM) 200–201, 233
institutional learning 84, 235
instructor 23
integrated tools 208–227
interaction 238
  group-content 238
  group-group 239
  group interaction 104
  learner-group 240
  teacher-group 240
Internet 121, 129, 139, 146
  relay chat (IRC) 189
intrinsic 60
  constraint 61
  control 101
ITS 154

J

joint control 99
judgement 100

K

Knowledge
  Garden 276
  Sea 277
knowledge 45, 124

L

learner 19, 23, 80
  -control 77–78
  -led presentation 99
  autonomous 125, 164
    learner 120, 123
  control 139
  dependent 164
  independent 164
  needs 121
  self-direction 46
  semi-dependent 125
learning 57, 65, 78, 122
  activities 2
  distance learning 19

e-learning 7
  ecology 8, 164
  institutional 235
    learning 84
  management system (LMS) 165, 209–210, 222
  outcome 296
  resource-based 140–160
  self-directed learning 29, 43, 46
  style 128
  traditional institutional learning 97–118
  trajectory 2, 78, 84, 97, 120
lecture 104
  traditional lecture 112
linear
  chat system 199
  media 123
linearity 191
list-serv 233
locative 316

M

machine intelligence 236
magazine architecture 249
mashups 234, 249
Matthew principle 147, 305
media 122, 204
  linear 123
moderator 163
MOO 190
Moodle 211
Moore 18
Moore, Michael G. 45
MySpace 234

N

navigation 127
negotiated control 104
NetMeeting 204
network 233
Ning 234

O

OKI 249
online
  discussion 162

Single Journal Articles and Case Studies
Are Now Right at Your Fingertips!

Purchase any single journal article or teaching case for only $25.00!

Idea Group Publishing offers an extensive collection of research articles and teaching cases in both print and electronic formats. You will find over 1300 journal articles and more than 300 case studies on-line at **www.idea-group.com/articles**. Individual journal articles and cases are available for only $25 each. A new feature of our website now allows you to search journal articles and case studies by category. To take advantage of this new feature, simply use the above link to search within these available categories.

We have provided free access to the table of contents for each journal. Once you locate the specific article needed, you can purchase it through our easy and secure site.

For more information, contact cust@idea-group.com or 717-533-8845 ext.10

Databases, Data Mining & Data Warehousing

Distance Learning & Education

E-Commerce and E-Government

E-Government

Healthcare Information Systems

Human Side and Society Issues in IT

Information Technology Education

IT Business Value, Support and Solutions

IT Engineering, Modeling & Evaluation

Knowledge Management

Mobile Commerce and Telecommunications

Multimedia Networking

Virtual Organizations and Communities

Web Technologies and Applications

 Idea Group Inc.   www.idea-group.com